POST-WAR PUBLIC HOUSING AND WELL-BEING

This collection illustrates the evolving role of housing as a symbol of modernity, a tool for economic recovery and a response to societal transitions. It argues that understanding earlier efforts to integrate well-being in the twentieth century can provide valuable insights for contemporary actors in the built environment who are working to address these issues today. As such, it explores and shines light on this lesser-known history, drawing on case studies, it focuses on the intersection of public housing, well-being and social change in the aftermath of the Second World War. With case studies from the UK, US, Singapore, Japan, Germany, China and Spain, this volume provides insights into how these countries have shaped the values, designs and institutions of their dwellings. By incorporating diverse cultural contexts, it contributes to a nuanced understanding of housing dynamics and well-being. Through a multidisciplinary lens, this volume encourages a re-evaluation of living conditions and fundamental values, emphasising the dynamic interplay between humans, their social environment and diverse living environments.

This book is essential for scholars, researchers, professionals, students, policymakers and practitioners in cultural history, architecture, planning, urban studies, sociology, education and public policy.

Izumi Kuroishi is a Professor at Fukushima Gakuin University and is the chair of Japan Lifeology Academy.

POST-WAR PUBLIC HOUSING AND WELL-BEING

Modernity, Economic Recovery, and Social Change

Edited by Izumi Kuroishi

Routledge
Taylor & Francis Group
NEW YORK AND LONDON

Designed cover images: Milena Villalba (top left), Apple Maps (top right), Katharina Borsi (bottom left), and Izumi Kuroishi (bottom right).

First published 2026
by Routledge
605 Third Avenue, New York, NY 10158

and by Routledge
4 Park Square, Milton Park, Abingdon, Oxon, OX14 4RN

Routledge is an imprint of the Taylor & Francis Group, an informa business

Library of Congress Cataloging-in-Publication Data
Names: Kuroishi, Izumi (College teacher) editor
Title: Post-war public housing and well-being : modernity, economic recovery, and social change / edited by Izumi Kuroishi.
Description: New York, NY : Routledge, 2025. | Includes bibliographical references and index.
Identifiers: LCCN 2025004630 (print) | LCCN 2025004631 (ebook) | ISBN 9781032865300 hardback | ISBN 9781032865294 paperback | ISBN 9781003527930 ebook
Subjects: LCSH: Public housing--History--20th century
Classification: LCC HD7288.77 .P67 2025 (print) | LCC HD7288.77 (ebook) | DDC 363.585--dc23/eng/20250618
LC record available at https://lccn.loc.gov/2025004630
LC ebook record available at https://lccn.loc.gov/2025004631

ISBN: 9781032865300 (hbk)
ISBN: 9781032865294 (pbk)
ISBN: 9781003527930 (ebk)

DOI: 10.4324/9781003527930

Typeset in Sabon
by KnowledgeWorks Global Ltd.

CONTENTS

LIST OF CONTRIBUTORS

Katharina Borsi is an Associate Professor at the University of Nottingham. Her research focuses on the history and theory of housing and urbanism. Her publications include *The Berlin Tenement and the City* (2025) and *Housing and the City* (2022).

John Boughton is an Honorary Senior Research Fellow at the School of Architecture of the University of Liverpool. He is the author of *Municipal Dreams: The Rise and Fall of Council Housing* (2018) and *A History of Council Housing in 100 Estates* (2022) and has published in the *Historian* and *Labor History*.

Lilian Chee is an Associate Professor of Architectural Design and Visual Cultures at the Department of Architecture in the National University of Singapore, where she serves as Assistant Dean at the College of Design and Engineering. Her work includes *Architecture and Affect* (2023), *Art in Public Space* (2022) and *Remote Practices* (2022)

Benjamin Gianni is an Associate Professor in the Azrieli School of Architecture & Urbanism at Carleton University where he leads the Urbanism program. He is the Vice President of the International Council on Canadian, Chinese, and African Sustainable Urbanism (ICCCASU).

Rafael Gómez-Moriana, based in Barcelona (Spain), is an Adjunct Associate Professor at the University of Calgary and the Director of the School of Architecture, Planning and Landscape's Barcelona term-abroad programme.

Carola Hein is a Professor of History of Architecture and Urban Planning at Delft University of Technology and a Professor at Leiden and Erasmus University and the Director of the Leiden-Delft-Erasmus Port City Futures Centre. Her recent (co-)edited books include *Port City Atlas* (2023), *Oil Spaces (2021)*, *Urbanisation of the Sea (2020)* and *Adaptive Strategies for Water Heritage* (2020)

Lim Kun Yi James is a part-time practicing Architectural Associate at Lekker Architects and a graduate Research and Teaching Assistant at the National University of Singapore under the Department of Architecture, and the Department of Communications and New Media. He currently assists A/P Dr Lilian Chee.

Mitsuo Kinoshita is a Professor in Japanese history at Faculty of Letters, Nara University, Japan. His publications include 'Sanctions, Targetism, and Village Autonomy: Poor Relief in Early Modern Rural Japan,' in *Public Goods Provision in the Early Modern Economy: Comparative Perspectives from Japan, China, and Europe*, edited by Masayuki Tanimoto and R. Bin Wong (2019).

Izumi Kuroishi is a Professor in Fukushima Gakuin University and is the chair of Japan Lifeology Academy. She contributes to *Interiors in the Era of Covid-19: Interior Design between the Public and Private Realms (2023), Design and Modernity in Asia: National Identity and Transnational Exchange 1945-1990* (2022), *The Routledge Companion to Architectural Drawings and Models (2022)* and edited *Constructing the Colonized Land: Entwined Perspectives of East Asia around WWII (2014)*

Nodoka Nagayama is a Professor in German history at Faculty of Economics, Aoyama Gakuin University, Japan. Her publications include 'Economic Integration of Expelled Persons and Refugees from East Germany and Housing Construction in West Germany in the 1950s,' in Aoyama Keizai Ronsyu (2024).

Montserrat Pareja-Eastaway, PhD in Applied Economics, is the Co-director of the Barcelona Housing Chair and a Professor of the Department of Economics at the University of Barcelona. She is a specialist on housing markets and policies in Europe and has contributed to numerous projects and publications and was recently selected as the ENHR Chair.

Barbara Penner is a Professor at the Bartlett School of Architecture, UCL. She is the author of *Bathroom* (2013) and co-editor of *Extinct: A Compendium of Obsolete Objects* (2021) and *Gender Space Architecture* (2000). In 2020, she contributed a foreword to the University of Minnesota's Press reissue of Catherine Bauer's *Modern Housing*.

ACKNOWLEDGEMENTS

The people and institutions who have contributed to the research and writing of this book are too numerous to detail, but I would like to thank some in particular.

This research project and its publication have been generously supported by Kajima Research Foundation. I greatly appreciate the members of Kajima Research Foundation and all of the contributing authors expanding scholarship into new areas in housing studies. There are many scholars' supports for our project, including Toshio Otsuki, Tetsumi Horikosi and Miyuki Ota, who kindly offered their knowledge in our primal stage. I also appreciate Routledge editors' encouragement and my editor Melissa Fisher's wonderful support to complete this project.

I acknowledge, one of the contributors, Barbara Penner and Federica Gofti's friendship, and my husband Masafumi Kuroishi's continuous encouragement in the last three years.

Finally, I must thank my past teachers, Marco Frascari and Joseph Rykwert, my past father, mother and my sister, for holding a light of hope to complete this project.

INTRODUCTION

Izumi Kuroishi

The concept of well-being has gained increasing attention in the twenty-first century, as economic prosperity alone has proven insufficient to achieve true happiness. Indeed, in the wake of global crises, we are witnessing a comprehensive reassessment of societal values throughout the world. In particular, the COVID-19 pandemic has spawned a growing body of work that demonstrates the importance of various aspects of how housing shapes physical and mental well-being, including housing quality, building design and the importance of biophilia.[1]

Twentieth-century social norms, particularly those centred on modernisation and post-war economic growth, still influence housing policies and architectural practices. Despite efforts to shift focus, change remains difficult. However, architects and other professionals have long tried to incorporate 'well-being' into housing policies by addressing social issues and proposing alternative approaches.

This book argues that understanding earlier efforts to integrate well-being in the twentieth century can provide valuable insights for contemporary actors in the built environment who are working to address these issues today. As such, it explores and shines light on this lesser-known history. Drawing on case studies it focuses on the intersection of public housing, well-being and social change in the aftermath of World War II. It shows that housing is not merely a tool for providing shelter, but a critical space where broader debates about and actions towards human dignity, social equity and the meaning of life have long taken place. By examining the historical, cultural and political contexts of public housing in the US, UK, Germany, Spain, Japan, Singapore and China, it highlights the multiple – and often conflicting – values that have influenced the pursuit of well-being in post-war public housing design. Ideas of well-being evolve over time amongst varied stakeholders and are influenced by multiple national and cultural backgrounds.

The authors in this book take issue with conventional narratives that reduce public housing to a function of political economy. As such they foreground the lived experiences of residents and emphasise the importance of well-being as a complex, multidimensional, historically and constructed concept. Through an interdisciplinary approach, drawing on architectural history, social history, cultural geography and economics, the various

DOI: 10.4324/9781003527930-1

authors trace genealogies of the evolution of well-being discourses and practices within housing policy and architecture. By comparing different national and cultural contexts, they reveal how public housing has and can serve as both a battleground for ideological conflicts and a site for imagining more equitable futures. In doing so, they provide fresh insights into how housing systems historically and today can support or undermine the well-being of individuals and communities. By unearthing this lesser-known past, the book, as a whole, illuminates a history of comprehensive, human-centred approaches to designing the living environment, one that pre-dates but arguably shapes current discussions on well-being in housing and architecture today.

Historical Background and Theoretical Debate on Well-being

Traditionally, well-being has been associated with objective indicators such as income growth and economic functionality, such as employee engagement and fulfilment. In recent decades, however, scholars within a wide range of disciplines including philosophy, psychology, anthropology and geography have expanded the concept and the way it is 'measured.' Much of this growing body of work emphasises the more qualitative dimensions of well-being and has deeply shaped discussions regarding people's quality of life and human rights. However, scholarly research in this area has not fully considered how ideas, values and practices surrounding well-being influenced housing and architectural practices, particularly when it comes to the post-World War II period (1945–1970). On the other hand, there was a lack of consideration of how the quality of housing affects residents' happiness and the importance of their taking an active role in shaping their living environment.

Philosopher Amartya Sen's 'capability' approach (1992), for example, challenges conventional welfare models which emphasise material wealth. His framework takes into account the freedom individuals have to live their lives. Although he does not explicitly use the term 'well-being,' Sen explains that freedom should depend on who people can become and what they are able to do. Quality of life should be analysed in terms of the core concepts of 'functionings.' Functionings are states of being and doing; 'capabilities' refer to the set of valuable functionings that a person has effective access to. Thus effective environmental and living conditions shape individuals' experiences of 'the Good life.' Notably, scholarly work on social obstacles to community buildings in underdeveloped areas focuses on questions regarding quality of life.

Psychological theories have also contributed to an evolving understanding of well-being. Daniel Kahneman, for example, examines well-being through the lens of hedonic theory, focusing on the balance of pleasure and pain in people's lives.[2] Martin Seligman, in his work on positive psychology, emphasises human flourishing and highlights subjective factors such as relationships, meaning and engagement.[3] Both Kahneman and Seligman recognise the complexity of well-being, acknowledging that it depends on both objective conditions and subjective experiences. They proposed the significance of the psychological, hedonistic and sustainable elements of well-being, beside the economic and medical well-being to form a comprehensive notion of well-being. Philosopher Guy Fletcher offers a more integrative view, analysing different theories of well-being, such as hedonism, desire fulfilment and objective list theories.[4] He advocates for a hybrid theory that accounts for ethical concerns and political contexts, illustrating the complexity of well-being and its multifaceted, evolving nature.

Contemporary Frameworks for Housing and Well-being

In the early twenty-first century, nations also began to increasingly focus on developing the social infrastructure to improve people's lives, enhance the natural environment and achieve better work-life balance.[5] Specifically alongside economic goals, countries developed quality-of-life indicators to guide policymaking, aimed at reducing inequality and protecting the environment. For example, the OECD's launch of the Better Life Index (BLI) in 2011, which measures well-being across 11 dimensions –including housing, employment, health and subjective well-being – reflects this shift. Several countries, including Canada, Germany, France and Japan, have since adopted similar measures.

During this period of time, scholars also continued to develop ideas of well-being. In their 2012 edited book *Well-being and Place*, medical anthropologists and human geographers Sarah Atkinson, Sara Fuller and Joe Painter, for example, introduce psychological and physiological dimensions into the discourse of well-being; they emphasise that well-being processes emerge in specific places, especially in housing and spatial planning contexts.[6] Their work highlights the role of subjective well-being and emotional attachments to places, underscoring the importance of local participation in planning to understand well-being from a community perspective. They emphasise encouraging and respecting resident's engagement with respect to working on environmental sustainability and local enhancement. Their ideas and methods have been utilised as a practical guide to community well-being.

The aftermath of the COVID-19 pandemic has further highlighted the connection between well-being and social systems, prompting governments to rethink well-being indicators in light of new challenges. In Japan, for example, the Cabinet Office's 2022 'Survey Report on Satisfaction and Quality of Life' points to the enjoyment of life, financial security and work-life balance as central to life satisfaction. These considerations of 'well-being' are emerging at a time when people with different values must coexist and adapt to rapidly changing social conditions. Much contemporary academic work seeks to overcome the dichotomy of subjective/objective approaches.[7] It seeks to capture the complex relationship between human life, place and social value, what emerges from work, particularly in the areas of housing, is that it is essential to examine how people continuously engage with and struggle for better housing.[8] These approaches thus provide the scaffolding for a new academic framework for contemporary and historical housing studies, one where human dignity and dwelling spaces are viewed from the occupants' perspectives.

Architecture and urban planning, in this sense, should prioritise creating liveable and socially cohesive environments for people across time and place. Sometime ago philosopher Martin Heidegger emphasised this connection, insisting on the need to unify living, thinking and building, while pointing out the importance of understanding the meaning of dwelling in people's lives. His perspective is timely for today's housing concerns. In 1954, he wrote:

> What is the state of dwelling in our precarious age? …However hard and bitter, however disabling and threatening, the lack of housing remains, the real plight of housing is not merely the lack of housing. The real emergency of housing is, in fact, older than the world wars and their destruction, older also than the growth of the earth's population and the condition of industrial workers. The real emergency of dwelling is that mortals

> must always seek anew the essence of dwelling, must always learn to dwell. What if the homelessness of man is that he does not even think of the true need of dwelling as a need? But as soon as man thinks of his homelessness, it is no longer a misery. Rightly considered and well kept in mind, it is the only summons that calls mortals to their abode. But how else can mortals respond to this summons but by attempting on their part, on their own, to bring dwelling to the fullness of its essence? This they accomplish by building out of dwelling and thinking for the sake of dwelling.[9]

Recently Jonas Holst examines how architect Jørn Utzon inherited and transformed Heidegger's concept of well-being. Holst argues that Utzon opposed the modernist and postmodernist obsession with abstraction, maintaining instead a focus on the inhabitant's relationship with material reality. According to Holst, for Heidegger, 'building is a way for the inhabitant to create a space in which he or she can retreat in order to be less exposed, to obtain a point of reference for orientation, and to live well.'[10]

Heidegger understood the challenges faced by post-war Germany in terms of rebuilding people's identity and social orders. He argued that housing needed to be reconceptualised to serve the well-being of people's everyday life. Yet not all of his ideas materialised. Indeed, as social and political systems rapidly evolved, the relationship between housing and well-being changed dramatically, not only in Germany but globally. In general, the ideas of human well-being were not fully realised within public housing. The chapters in this book suggest that architects and others throughout the last century did, nevertheless, attempt to create more habitable dwellings; and that there are lessons to be learned from their endeavours that apply to today's renewed focus on well-being in the built environment.

The Historical Significance of Public Housing

Public housing has historically served as a critical tool for government intervention in the provision of affordable housing, reflecting broader social and political values. From its origins in the late nineteenth century as a philanthropic model, it became a symbol of modernity and social progress, playing a central role in post-war reconstruction and urbanisation efforts. Public housing was not merely a shelter solution but a means to promote productivity, national unity and social stability. During World War II, public housing served governments as a mechanism to ensure the availability of labour and promote productivity, often with nationalist ideologies underlying these efforts. After the war, alongside new technologies, public housing became a tool for economic recovery, industrialisation and urbanisation. In this study, we focused on how public housing spaces have transformed as a representation of life values and human rights in each society.

By the 1970s, however, economic globalisation, along with the rise of neoliberalism policies, based on the theories of Milton Friedman, Friedrich August von Hayek and others, led to a shift towards privatisation, even in welfare states. Despite this trend, public housing remained a site of resistance, where individuals and communities shaped their own housing experiences. The COVID-19 pandemic exposed increasingly stark inequalities in housing access, as wealthier individuals moved to safer living environments while others faced housing insecurity. Many individuals lost jobs, incomes and even their places to live. They suffered health and mental problems due to the insufficient space of their house, and they were isolated from community and social services of care. Their recent experiences expose the ever-growing need for affordable public housing and practices that focus on the physical, emotional and financial well-being of those housed. For example, the post-war government system of public housing in Japan was class based: homeowners, middle-class tenants and low-income people who were supported by local councils. This division led to poor quality council housing and financial pressure on the middle class.[11] The uncritical continuation of a pre-war social epistemology based on this kind of administrative principle has created an invisible but deeply rooted problem.

Focus of This Study

This book focuses on seven key countries (case studies) – Japan, Germany, Spain, the US, the UK, China and Singapore – chosen for their political-economic systems, distinctive approaches to public housing and the valuable lessons their experiences offer.

The US and the UK represent strong 'democratic' and 'civic' traditions based on their capitalist systems and as leading cases of public housing from the pre-war period. In both countries, especially after the war, there were struggles between different social classes and ethnic groups over their conditions of well-being and civic dignity in housing due to contradictions with the capitalist systems.

In Germany, after the traumatic wartime political situation, the country established a federal system of government in 1949. With the US's Marshall Plan fund and a sustained pre-war cooperative housing system, the aim was to achieve social balance. As a result, housing was recognised as a public good and distanced from capitalist notions of ownership. However, the legendary housing estates represented a more complex coexistence of socialist and democratic ideals of well-being through the everyday lives of residents.

Spain has also undergone significant political transformations: a Civil War (1936–1939) following a Republican period, 40 years of Francoist dictatorship (1939–1975) with varying degrees of capitalist market integration, and the establishment of democracy in 1978 with the adoption of the current Constitution. Throughout this process, strong family and personal networks compensated for the weakness of the welfare state, playing a crucial role in Spanish society's well-being. During the dictatorship, cultural and regional identities across the Autonomous Communities were suppressed in favour of a homogeneous Spanish national identity, a policy that would later face challenges in the democratic era.

China maintained a strong communist government in the post-war period, but it gradually combined with a capitalist economic system creating huge market for housing. The unification of communist and capitalist ideals, rather than citizenship or democracy, created a specific sense of well-being in housing focusing on a balance between the communist government's totalitarian control and individual's satisfactions to form 'moderately prosperous' or 'basically well-off' society. (ref. Chapter 8).

Another Asian country, Singapore, gained its political independence in 1965 becoming a capitalist republican government. However, under Lee Kuan Yew's authoritarian, efficiency-oriented control of internal security and speech, the country experienced rapid economic growth. This process put enormous psychological pressure on the people. Institutional regulations and architectural ideals were interactively appropriated to accommodate with residents' everyday life (ref. Chapter 11).

In Japan, the emperor's sovereignty and tyrannical government gave way to popular sovereignty, democracy and capitalism after the war, but conservative and paternalistic institutionalism was maintained for political reasons. As a result, ideas of the public sphere, human rights and subjective identity remained unresolved under the pressure of economic recovery. In a sense, public housing was used to educate people to conform to institutional ideals of lifestyle. However, with the growth of capitalism and people's desire for diversity in housing, it lost its norms of social security and infrastructure.

These countries represent different political ideologies, economic, socio-cultural and geographical conditions, providing a rich comparative analysis of how housing systems continuously respond to the integrated issues of well-being, and how architects, institutional officers, private sectors and residents responded to appropriate to them.[12] Drawing on 'historical case studies,' this book explores how stakeholders' responses and appropriations in the different countries' and contexts intersected with evolving notions of well-being. By drawing on diverse national contexts, each chapter illustrates the ways in which housing has shaped and reflected broader debates about human dignity, social equity and community life.

This book also specifically examines how public housing design, space, technologies and lived experiences have intersected to shape the practice of well-being. By examining these seven countries as case studies, it draws attention to the different ways national, political, socio-cultural, geographical and economic conditions shaped people's inquiries for and realisation of their well-being. What emerges is not only diversity and change, but also a 'convivial' response, akin to that theorised by philosopher Ivan Illich in his *Tools for Conviviality*, where people design and choose to optimise their own living spaces to survive changing environments and disasters.[13] People in different cultural contexts have developed conceptions of well-being that have led to changes in ideas about housing and the recognition of what is essential for people's overall meaning of life.

Composition of This Study

The chapters collectively argue that public housing is more than a response to material needs. It is a space where social ethos, urban issues and accessibilities, ideological and personal affluence and new dimensions of environmental and psychological complexities converge. The thematic focus on well-being allows the book to highlight both the successes and challenges of public housing in fostering social cohesion and individual fulfilment. Each chapter examines how different countries approached the design and implementation of public housing, revealing the cultural, political and economic factors that influenced their success or failure in supporting human well-being.

Highlighting issues of social ethos and well-being, for the US, Barbara Penner, in Chapter 1, explores Catherine Bauer's contributions to modern American housing, which marked a shift from quantitative measures of housing need to a focus on social and psychological dimensions of living. Penner's analysis illustrates how Bauer's advocacy for considering the well-being of residents laid the foundation for a deeper understanding of housing's role in shaping people's lives. In Chapter 2, John Boughton discusses post-war British housing, showing how public health and well-being concerns initially framed public housing projects but later evolved to encompass social engagement and community fulfilment. In Chapter 3, Izumi Kuroishi explores how Japanese architects like Sakae Komada, Wajiro Kon, Kiyoshi Ikebe and Kiyonori Kikutake redefined the concept of *Seikatsu* (life) to emphasise the integration of social, psychological and physical well-being in housing design. This nuanced trajectory and historical shift reveal how public housing served as a critical arena for contesting the meaning of everyday life.

Turning to a focus on well-being in urban space and accessibility, Katherine Borsi, in Chapter 4, examines the case of Berlin, she examines the housing estates of East and West Berlin, Märkisches Viertel and Marzahn, which serve as a valuable example of the relationship between urban planning, housing design and well-being. She illustrates how these flagship projects embodied modernist ambitions but also framed social interactions and community building, contributing to well-being within contrasting political regimes in Germany. With respect to Spain, in Chapter 5, Montserrat Pareja-Eastaway analyses how the Franco regime's emphasis on home ownership left low-income families vulnerable during economic downturns, such as the 2008 financial crisis and the COVID-19 pandemic. This chapter highlights the importance of resident involvement in housing design and explores innovative approaches, like Barcelona's La Borda cooperative, which aimed to improve quality of life through collective housing solutions. In Chapter 6, Carola Hein returns us to the study of Japan and examines Nishiyama Uzo's humanist approach to post-war urban planning in Japan. Inspired by figures like Ebenezer Howard and Le Corbusier, Nishiyama advocated small, community-centred units, promoting well-being through human-scale design. His ideas integrated traditional Japanese structures with modern planning concepts, shaping housing policies that emphasised social cohesion and everyday livability.

The next chapters focus on well-being and ideological and personal affluence. In Chapter 7, Nodoka Nagayama analyses the post-war German context, revealing how the evolving notion of well-being influenced housing policies and consumption patterns. In Germany, well-being often extended beyond material comforts to encompass activities that encouraged social interaction and relaxation outside the home. Rapidly modernising economies like China also provide compelling example of how public housing policies have evolved to manage urbanisation and promote well-being. In Chapter 8, Benjamin Gianni compares post-war housing policies in China and the US, highlighting the cultural, political and economic contexts that shaped housing production. In Chapter 9, Mitsuo Kinoshita traces the long-term trajectory of housing security in Japan. By examining how historical attitudes towards housing, rooted in self-reliance and market-based solutions, continue to shape contemporary housing policy, this chapter underscores how deeply embedded socio-economic systems influence the broader pursuit of well-being.

The final chapters in the book explore new dimensions of environmental and psychological issues of well-being in the twenty-first century. In Chapter 10, Rafael Gómez-Moriana discusses the growing emphasis on sustainability in the twenty-first century, which expands the concept of well-being to include ecological responsibility. He explores how the Balearic Housing Institute in Spain has integrated low-carbon, bioclimatic designs into public housing, reflecting the recognition that housing must not only support individual well-being but also contribute to environmental sustainability. In Chapter 11, Lilian Chee and Lim Kun Yi James examine Singapore's aging-in-place initiatives, focusing on aspects of well-being in the context of elder care and dementia. Their analysis reveals how Singapore's housing arrangements are challenged by increased pressures in balancing physical and emotional needs of an ageing population. The chapter examines the impetus to radically mobilise the potential of public housing in the wake of such demands.

Through these chapters, this book demonstrates how public housing has evolved diversely into a site where the complex interplay between social ideals, political structures and individual well-being takes place. By focusing on the material, political and cultural dimensions of housing, this book offers a comprehensive understanding of how public housing systems can either enhance or undermine the well-being of individuals and communities across different regions.

Acknowledgement

This research project and its publication have been generously supported by Kajima Research Foundation. I greatly appreciate Prof. Kamata, who had encouraged me to challenge this project, all of the contributing authors and their efforts to expand scholarship into new areas in housing studies. I also appreciate Routledge editors' patient and productive suggestions to realise this project. Lastly, I acknowledge my editor Melissa Fisher's wonderful support, my old Frascari schoolmate Federica Gofti's friendship, and my husband Masafumi Kuroishi's continuous encouragement in the last three years.

Notes

1 Zhu, Yushu and Holden, Meg. *Housing and Psychosocial Well-being during the COVID-19 Pandemic* – PMC, https://pmc.ncbi.nlm.nih.gov/articles/PMC10033258/
2 Kahneman, Daniel. 2003. Well-Being: Foundation of Hedonic Psychology.
3 Seligman, Martin E.P. 2011. *Flourish: A Visionary New Understanding of Happiness and Well-being*, Free Press.
4 Fletcher, Guy. 2017. *The Routledge Handbook of Philosophy of Well-Being*, Routledge.
5 Guy, *The Routledge Handbook of Philosophy of Well-Being.*
6 Atkinson, Sarah, Fuller, Sara, and Painter, Joe eds., 2012.*Well-being and Place, Routledge.*
7 Gilroy, Rose. 2012. "Well-being and the Neighborhood: Promoting Choice and Independence for all Ages," *Well-being and Place*: 73–88.
Gibson M., Thomson H., Kearns A., and Petticrew M. 2011. "Understanding the Psychosocial Impacts of Housing Type: Qualitative Evidence from a Housing and Regeneration Intervention," *Housing Studies* 26(4): 555–73
Coolen H., Meesters J. 2012. "Editorial Special Issue: House, Home and Dwelling," *Journal of Housing and the Built Environment* 27(1): 1–10.
There has been many research going on about the community mutual aid activities in the damaged area housing after the Great Tohoku Earthquake analysing the local people's integrated relationship between the individual and the communal ways of life to sustain their quality of life. See *Community Responses to Disasters in the Pacific Rim: Place making in Displacement,* edited by Shu-Mei Huang and Elizabeth Maly, Routledge, 2023. The author contributed'Making a Community Around a Table: Reconstruction of Mutual Help System by Tea Parties(Ocha-kai) and Lunch Parties After the Great Eastern Japan Earthquake' to this book, pp190–206.
8 Clapham, D. 2011. "The Embodied Use of the Material Home: An Affordance Approach," *Housing, Theory and Society* 28(4): 360–76.
Japanese Academy of Lifeology, Current situation and outlook for Covid-19: Proposals from the Study of Lifeology, edited by Izumi Kuroishi and Special committee of the Nippon Lifeolog Academy, Kokusai bunkensha, 2022.
9 Heidegger, Martin, "Building Dwelling Thinking," *Martin Heidegger Basic Writings from Being and Time (1927) to The Task of Thinking (1964) revised and expanded edition, edited, with general introduction and introductions to each selection*, by David Farrell Krell, Harper San Francisco, 1993, pp 363. (presented originally in a lecture in 1951 and published in 1954),

10 Holst, Jonas. "Rethinking Dwelling and Building," *ZARCH* 2:52-61(2014)
11 Hirayama, Yosuke. 2020. *Karizumai to Sengo Nihon*, Seido sha.
Homma, Yoshihito. 2004. *Sengo Jutaku seisaku no kensho*, Shinzansha Publication.
12 To explain the international divisions of housing welfare systems according to each countries' political ideologies, Gøsta Esping-Andersen proposes three types of welfare capitalism – socialist, conservative corporatist and liberal. This examination led to the discussions of affordability, accessibility and housing right. Since the 1960s, Jim Kemeny suggested dividing European housing policy into unitary and dualist models based on the balance between private for-profit and public non-profit rental markets. Also, Mark Stephens emphasises greater diversity and dynamism in political conditions, focusing on how individuals' subjective experiences contribute to changes in housing policy. International comparative research on housing has been based primarily on objective aspects, such as the number and size of housing units and how these figures vary in relation to economic, political, and institutional systems. However, more recent studies, such as those by Kathleen Scanlon and others in 2014, also consider cultural and geographical factors. Comparative studies of housing in architectural planning, such as those taken up by the work of Christine Whitehead, explore how public, private, and co-operative institutions and ideologies relate to the physical planning and production of housing and community space in different countries.
13 Illich, Ivan. 2001. *Tools for Conviviality*, Marion Boyar.

References

Atkinson, Sarah, Sara Fuller, and Joe Painter eds. 2012. *Well-being and Place, Routledge.*
Esping-Andersen, Gosta. 2001. "*The Three Worlds of Welfare Capitalism: Theory and Dynamics of Comparative Welfare States.*" *Minerva Welfare Library* 47: 26–27.
Fletcher, Guy. 2017. *The Routledge Handbook of Philosophy of Well-Being*, Routledge.
Heidegger, Martin. 1993. "Building Dwelling Thinking," *Martin Heidegger Basic Writings from Being and Time (1927) to The Task of Thinking (1964) Revised and Expanded Edition, Edited, With General Introduction and Introductions to Each Selection*, by David Farrell Krell, Harper San Francisco, 363. (Presented originally in a lecture in 1951 and published in 1954)
Hirayama, Yosuke. 2020. *Karizumai to Sengo Nihon*, Seido sha.
Homma, Yoshihito. 2004. *Sengo Jutaku seisaku no kensho*. Shinzansha Publication.
Huang, Shu-Mei, and Elizabeth Maly eds., 2023. *Community Responses to Disasters in the Pacific Rim: Place Making in Displacement*, Routledge.
Illich, Ivan. 2001. *Tools for Conviviality*, Marion Boyar.
Japan Cabinet Office. 2022. "Survey Report on Satisfaction and Quality of Life."

SECTION I

Well-Being and Social Ethos

1

'HOW DO PEOPLE WANT TO LIVE?'

Catherine Bauer and Social Questions in Modern American Housing

Barbara Penner

How Do People Want to Live?

For any housing architect today, this is a vital question. It also seems a straightforward one – until one attempts to answer it. There is the problem of evidence: what is the best method to determine, in a meaningful way and at a meaningful scale, people's needs in relation to housing? How do we define need or needs in the first place? To what extent do we also take people's preferences and wants into account? And, of course – and trickiest of all – their desires? How should people's physical, economic and cultural differences be accommodated? Should questions reflect known living situations or should they be used to open up new ways of living, perhaps even those which haven't yet been imagined?

The question of how housing needs have been evaluated through the twentieth century is rarely discussed explicitly. And yet, the assumption that housing needs had to be assessed and precisely responded to emerged as one of *the* distinguishing features of the programmes of modern housing and architecture. Indeed, they served to justify one of the grandest claims of modern architects: that they were operating in a new scientific or sociological mode, which would improve human lives across society (Gropius 1956a). And this idea – that housing needs can be identified and satisfactorily met through design – is still alive and well today in exercises like public consultations and post-occupancy studies.

This chapter aims to provide a historical account of the varying means by which housing needs have been evaluated and influenced design in the modern period. As this field is vast, the chapter follows one figure who serves as a guide to key shifts: Catherine Bauer. For three decades between the 1930s and the 1960s, Bauer was a leading American 'houser,' a campaigner for good-quality public housing and planned communities. She was also a powerful advocate for social scientific research throughout her career, arguing that understanding housing needs was essential for any 'rational democratic country' (Bauer 1953, 371–73, 389). Through her commentary, we see how America began to move away from quantitative to qualitative definitions of dwellings, from the 'basic' to the 'liveable,' the mechanistic to the socio-psychological, and the universal

DOI: 10.4324/9781003527930-3

to the particular. In sum, by considering the housing surveys that Bauer most admired through the decades, we begin to understand how 'human need' was reconceptualised as 'human needs.'

Housing Need: Property Surveys and Censuses

As a disclaimer: the decision to focus on American housing means that this history looks at least superficially different to that of European or other modernist housing histories. This is because America is a very specific case study: thanks to the country's individualism and commitment to property rights and free markets, municipal housing of the kind that characterised European countries was widely regarded for most of the nineteenth and early twentieth centuries as untenable, except in times of war (Rodgers 1998, 160–208). But spurred on by the tremendous want and inequality created by the Great Depression of 1929, public housing would be introduced as part of the extraordinary package of programmes developed by President Franklin D. Roosevelt to counteract it, known collectively as 'The New Deal.'

In intervening in housing, Roosevelt was responding to the determined campaigns of groups such as the Regional Planning Association of America (RPAA), whose leading figures included philosopher Lewis Mumford, architects Henry Wright and Clarence Stein, economist Edith Elmer Wood and Catherine Bauer. The RPAA pushed the American government to implement a European-style housing programme in order to provide high-quality affordable dwellings for workers. Bauer made the case most forcefully in her 1934 jeremiad, *Modern Housing* (Bauer [1934] 2020). She examined the period between 1919 and 1932 when European governments built 4.5 million units of workers' housing rehousing approximately 16% of its population, and asked how the 'miracle' could be replicated in the United States (Bauer [1934] 2020, 124, 126–27). In all cases, she emphasised, governments had removed housing from the free market and taken control of it themselves, imposing strict construction standards and rent controls which ensured communities were viable long-term.

Under pressure to act, the American federal government entered the public housing arena in 1933 as an emergency measure to stimulate construction, setting up a Housing Division as part of the Public Works Administration. It then entered the housing field permanently with the passing of the United States Housing Act of 1937, co-authored by Bauer, now working as a union organiser and lobbyist (Radford 1996). But the moment the government committed itself to intervening directly in housing, it had a major problem on its hands. In order to build a national housing programme, it needed reliable and fast ways of assessing housing need in order to conduct the kind of comprehensive planning that was common in the countries which the RPAA and Bauer championed as models (Dehaene 2007). Extensive data was needed in order to work out where new housing was required, what kind of housing should be provided, at what standard, and at what cost.

Considering existing sources of information, American housing authorities found a dearth of useable data to guide them. This is not to say there were no exposés of poor housing: since the late nineteenth century, there had been an explosion of social surveys by sociologists and charity or citizens groups, the best known of which was Jane Addams and Florence Kelley's famed *Hull-House Maps and Papers* (1895). Often written by female moral reformers with the aim of slum improvement, many of these works, however, had what would be dismissively characterised as a 'charity smell' (quoted in Penner 2020, xxiv); that is, they were seen to be the work of amateurs and to lack the scientific neutrality that bodies like the newly formed United States Housing Authority (USHA) needed to assess projects and authorise expenditure. So, the USHA turned to different tools: property surveys, inventories and estimates.

One of the most widely used of these tools was Real Property Surveys developed and deployed by the Works Progress Administration and the USHA. To give one example of how comprehensive they were: by 1941, San Francisco's newly formed housing authority was able to release a study of the city's housing drawn from its Real Property Survey. The authority stated that over a two-year period, 'every one of the 222,715 dwelling units in the city and county of San Francisco was catalogued and evaluated' (Taper 1941, 3). The survey provided a breakdown of many factors: population, type of structure, exterior material, condition, age of building, owner occupancy, dwelling units (type and location), facilities (electricity, heating, etc.), duration of occupancy and rooms. It also described the people living in these dwellings, noting their race, and specified whether or not they had children.

The ability to zero in on the areas which had the highest concentrations of supposedly substandard housing was crucial because to qualify for federal government assistance,

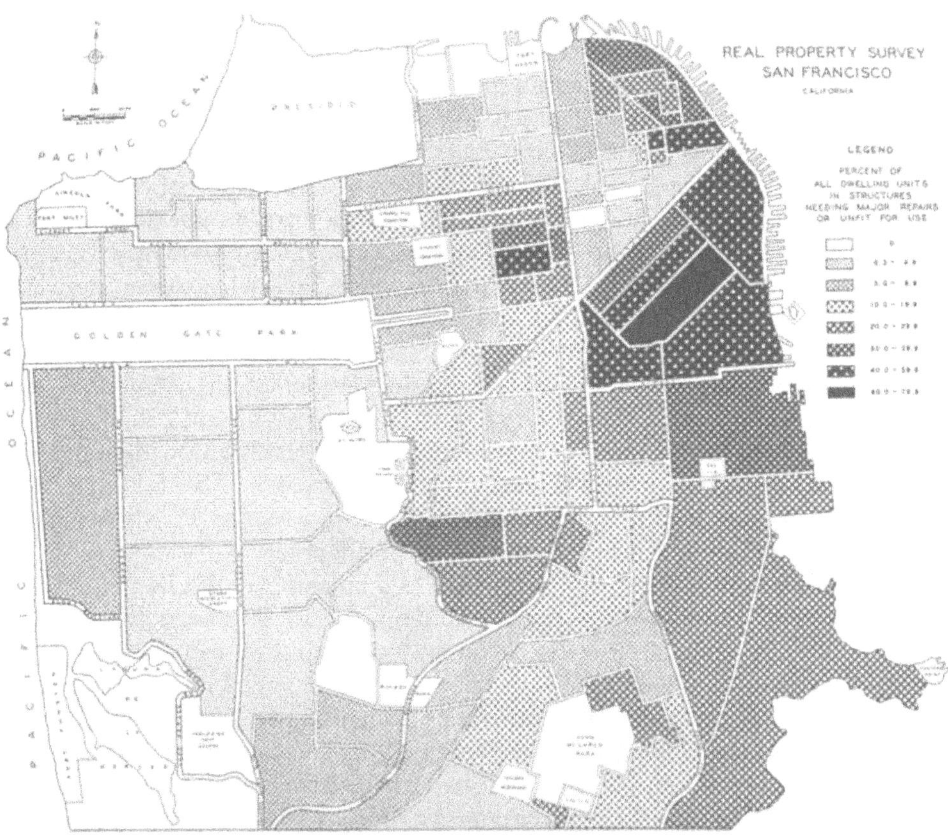

FIGURE 1.1 San Francisco Real Property Survey Condition of residential structures.

Source: Taper (1941, 22).

local housing authorities had to propose to clear slums – whole neighbourhoods – before building new units in their place ('equivalent elimination'). Surveys were the main tool by which to identify areas for clearance. Real Property Surveys operated at a local level, however, and did little to describe the American housing situation overall or to predict housing need in future. To address this, another tool was introduced: the nationwide Census of Housing, launched in 1940. The Census of Housing replaced the scrappier information collected by earlier censuses. It published more extensive statistics on the size and quality of the housing supply and estimated the future number of people and families across America, projecting housing requirements decades ahead.[1]

All of these surveys and inventories were quantitative, filled with statistics, data and numbers. They assessed housing need at a meta scale and were crude as instruments; for instance, a 'substandard house' according to the 1940 Census was an urban dwelling that did not have a private bath and an indoor flush toilet. While such indices could help assess a house's level of repair and sanitation, the focus on floors, roofs, foundations and plumbing inevitably led to a highly mechanistic understanding of what made a house functional or 'liveable.' As one contemporary observer noted, housing was reduced to 'naked shelter' (Jeanes 1933, 61). Location, room sizes, light and air were not considered, let alone qualitative factors such as convenience, neighbourhood or communal relationships.

Catherine Bauer accepted the necessity of statistical exercises as housing could not, by definition, be *modern* without a systematic, planned approach. As time passed, however, she grew increasingly frustrated by the housing world's fixation with counting bathtubs. Her disillusion on this score was probably inevitable. Bauer, along with her RPAA colleagues, had always been very inspired by the visionary Scottish town planner, Patrick Geddes, and his expansive concept of the 'civic survey,' which prioritised organic interactions between people and their environments. In *Modern Housing*, Bauer quoted Mumford's Geddesian assertion that 'The modern house is a biological institution,' which had to meet physiological *and* social needs (Bauer [1934] 2020, 141). 'Biological standards' went way beyond the usual functionalist demands for cross-ventilation, sanitation, or fireproofing; they also included qualities such as quiet, attractive views, facilities for outdoor recreation, easy access to schools, shops and work, and choice for tenants (Bauer [1934] 2020, 141–47).

Bauer noted these factors were not captured by existing surveys. To understand housing conditions 'biologically,' a more qualitative engagement was needed. And, in the early 1930s, Bauer saw the emergence of an alternative: surveys that directly engaged the tenants of proposed housing, which moved away from approaching 'housing need' as an abstract problem to prioritising 'housing needs' as a human one. Who was to commission these surveys? Architects themselves. Their motivation to do so was that the project of modern housing required them to take on far more than they had done in the past. Instead of operating on a piecemeal basis, modern architects were now to design entire neighbourhoods – housing, plus nurseries, shops, laundries, play spaces, workshops and gardens – complete communities. With the brief's greater complexity came a greater need to understand what provisions would most materially and emotionally benefit tenants. In short, the aim of surveys shifted from the reform tradition of detecting substandard housing to investigating positively how healthy homes might be created that would enhance well-being. As one proponent of this new approach declared, 'Housing projects must be more than mere sanitarily constructed and equipped dwellings. They must be sources of community happiness' (Stonorov 1937, quoted in Sandeen 1985, 667).

Housing Needs: Full-Fashioned Hosiery Workers

As it happened, in her new role as executive secretary to the Labor Housing Conference Secretary, Bauer would be a direct witness to one 'pioneering' example of a tenant survey (Riemer 1951, 147).[2] In 1933, the architects Kastner & Stonorov commissioned a survey of 1,385 families, mostly members of the American Federation of Full-Fashioned Hosiery Workers Union in Philadelphia. Conducted with the aid of Bryn Mawr's College's Department of Social Economy and Social Research, the survey aimed to guide the design of the Carl Mackley Houses, initiated by the union and supported by PWA loans, making it 'the first expression of the public housing movement under the New Deal' (see Radford, Chapter 5; Sandeen 1985, 645–67). The architects Alfred Kastner and Oskar Stonorov, both émigrés, brought firsthand knowledge of Europe's housing 'miracle' to the project. The Mackley Houses thus consciously bridged international experiments in housing and planning and fledging American efforts.

Conscious of blazing a trail for others to follow, Kastner & Stonorov were very deliberate in their approach. In today's terms, we might say they were modelling good practice for those that would follow. It is telling that they did not only undertake a tenant survey but also published it, opening with an inspirational quote from Franklin D. Roosevelt and a text explaining their rationale and methods. They made the ground-breaking assertion that every architect 'should have before him a study of the actual group that is to be housed rather than plan for an indeterminate group whose requirements and economic status can only be assumed' (Jeanes 1933, 1).[3] Their starting point was a questionnaire, one of the most common tools in the surveying kit. Additionally, however, surveyors got to know their 'actual group' by visiting the homes of hosiery workers who would be eligible for the Mackley Houses (Jeanes 1933, 69). They spoke with families for between ten minutes and an hour, to find out everything from their current housing conditions – what were they lacking? – to the economic difficulties they faced and how their living costs might be lightened.

The results were carefully reported and presented in charts inspired by the Vienna Circle sociologist Otto Neurath, another great champion of scientific rationality as a tool for social enlightenment. Much of the report's first section was devoted to exploring the specific problems facing hosiery workers in Philadelphia, especially the high costs of home ownership and the inability of existing houses to accommodate changing life cycles. These were known problems which had had motivated the Union to build rental housing to begin with. More impactful in terms of the eventual plan was the finding that 71% of families wanted a swimming pool, far more than tennis courts as the architects assumed. A pool became the centrepiece of the Mackley Houses' design and soon after would feature on the cover of the Museum of Modern Art's exhibition catalogue *Architecture in Government Housing* (1936), selected by Bauer as a symbol of the new housing movement's aspirations.

The report's other stand-out element was the six-page 'Architect's Discussion' at the end, where the architects responded to the survey's findings. After deciding the survey proved there was 'need' for a housing development, they moved on to the question of location and design. They argued that, given the call for flexibility and land costs, this need would be most appropriately met by European-style modern housing – multi-family superblocks with communal facilities available on a rental

SCHEDULE USED IN SURVEY

Name of Union Member________ Occupation________
Address________ Dist.________ Rel. of Interviewed________
Number of People in House

Over 50	17 - 49	Under 17

Number of Members of Full Fashioned Hosiery Union in House________
Number Added to Household in Last Year________ Number Temporary________
Times Moved in Last Year________ Ever Owned Home________
Reasons for Moving________
Cost of Home________ Year Purchased________ Year Built________
Remodelling Costs________ Taxes Yearly________
1st Mortgage________ Yearly Interest: 1st M.________ 2nd M.________ Total________
2nd Mortgage________ B & L : Years Paid________ Years to be Paid________
Months in Arrears________ Total Monthly Payments________
Cost of Repairs in Last 2 Years________
Monthly Rent________ Including Gas________ Refrigeration________
Water________ Household Service________
Rental Changes in: Heat________ Electricity________
1930________ 1931________ 1932________ Telephone________ Furniture________
Months in Arrears________
Costs: Telephone (per average month)________ Coal (Tons per Winter)________
Electricity " ________ Water________
Gas " ________
Amount Borrowed in Last Year________
List All Potential Wage Earners in House (not boarders):

Person	Occupation	Organised / Unorganized	Actual Weekly Wage	No. Days Working per Week
1.				
2.				
3.				
4.				
5.				

Income from Garage________
Transportation:

Person	Means	Times per Week	Person	Means	Times per Week
1.			5.		
2.			6.		
3.			7.		
4.			8.		

Amount of Garage Space Needed________ Monthly Rent________ Future Plans________
Nearest Park________ Times Used per Month________
Recreation Facilities Desired by Family:
Tennis Courts________ Playground________ Handball________ Basketball________
Swimming Pool________ Baseball________ Soccer________ Others________
Type of House: Row____ Detached____ Semi-Detached____ Duplex____ Apt.____ Other____
Number of Rooms in House
Living Room____ Bedrooms____ Kitchenette____ Bath____ Porch____ Garage____
Dining Room____ Kitchen____ Closets____ Shed____ Attic____ Others____
Conveniences: Lighting: Gas________ Electricity________ Other________
Laundry : Stationary Tubs________ Washing Machine________
Refrigeration: Ice________ Mechanical________ None________
Cooking : Gas____ Coal____ Wood____ Electricity____
Improvement of Front Yard________ Back Yard________
Condition of House Structurally________ Good________ Fair____ Poor____
Would you Like Having your Home on One Floor?________
Interest in Project________
(Code: M - Male, F - Female, Circle around Married Pair, x Union Member)

FIGURE 1.2 Kastner and Stonorov questionnaire.

Source: Jeanes (1933, 69).

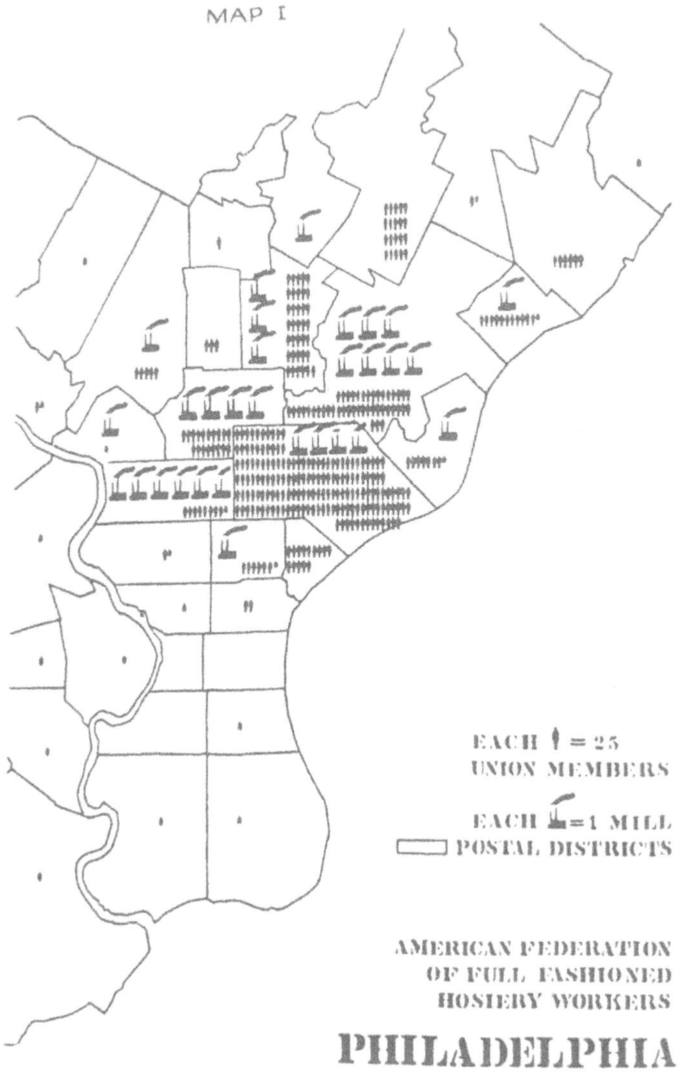

FIGURE 1.3 'Map 1.' Distribution of 9,000 union members and mills in Philadelphia.

Source: Jeanes (1933, 8).

basis – a self-fulfilling conclusion that has led some historians to regard Kastner and Stonorov's survey sceptically (Pommer 1978, 239). It is undeniable that the architects' preference for European-style communal living made their design choices seem a foregone conclusion. But, rather than regarding this as disingenuousness on the architects' part, we can equally see it as a symptom of the challenge they faced in these early experiments in modern living, as they sought to cover 'New Deal theory' with the 'flesh of [...] reality' (Bauer 1957, 140).

If asked directly, few – if any – interviewees would ever state a preference for modern models of housing because they had no experience of them. Rather, they were

FIGURE 1.4 Carl Mackley Housing, Philadelphia. Designed by Kastner and Stonorov, executed under the direction of W. Pope Barney.

Source: Cover of exhibition catalogue Architecture in Government Housing, New York, The Museum of Modern Art (MoMA), June 8–July 13, 1936. The MoMA Library, catalogue no. 300061901. Digital image, MoMA, New York/Scala, Florence.

most familiar with speculative housing options, in this case, the vertical rowhouse type, which the union actively wished to counter at the Mackley. The best Kastner & Stonorov could hope to find was that future tenants weren't *against* multi-family housing, which the surveyors did establish ('In general workers did not oppose apartments; contrary to general belief they seemed *open to conviction*' [italics mine]; Jeanes 1933, 61). Here the survey had another role to play. Through dialogue and personal contact with tenants, surveyors could 'win them over to the community idea,' laying the ground for more cooperative ways of living and stimulating further demand for it (Jeanes 1933, 60–61). This more operative view of the survey's role was in line with Patrick Geddes's 'civic survey' as a tool for community engagement and education (Dehaene 2007, 39).

This almost propagandistic approach to the survey seems to fly in the face of any scientific ideal of neutrality. And this perceived tendency to act in the name of people's 'happiness' without heeding their specific desires helps account for the cynicism that often greets user surveys or public consultation exercises today. Yet there is no reason to doubt Stonorov's sincerity when he said his goal was to produce 'places where people Love to Live' (Stonorov 1937, quoted in Sandeen 1985, 667). Merely invoking 'love' in the context of housing raises it above 'naked shelter' and, in including amenities like the swimming pool, we see the architects consulted tenant preferences where they could. But modern housing was caught up in a paradox: it was an experiment which aimed to change the expectations of those surveyed. In other words, architects could not neutrally ask tenants about wants because they always aimed to make them want different and possibly unanticipated things.

As the federal government's public housing programme accelerated, then, tenant surveys came to perform another vital function for architects. They provided a crucial means by which early design projects could be assessed in order to inform future standards and designs. Assuming that expectations evolved as housing improved, they tried to detect the gaps between what had been built and what should be built, always with an eye to stimulating greater 'love' for modern housing. This more expansive remit meant that, as well as functional needs, surveyors were to evaluate tenants' 'satisfaction' to discover features that worked and shortcomings that needed addressing in so far as possible. Bauer wholeheartedly approved of this shift in emphasis, declaring, 'ultimate satisfaction of consumers and citizens is the only real test of success in housing' (Bauer 1952a, 11). As examples, she often admiringly cited two studies carried out in the 1940s by another one of her friends and allies, New York-based architect Elisabeth Coit.

The Tenants' Viewpoint

Elisabeth Coit was an architect who, like many of the other figures mentioned in this paper, toured European modern housing in person in the 1930s and was committed to seeing an equivalent affordable programme established in America. And, like Bauer and Stonorov, Coit did much to make this ambition a reality, particularly in two professional roles: first as a war-time technical researcher for the Federal Public Housing Authority; and second as a Principal Project Planner for the New York City Housing Authority from 1948. But she was never an uncritical adopter of European modernism, denouncing design features that prioritised aesthetics over function. To give one example, Coit criticised balconies in German housing for being too small, serving mainly as an 'architectonic grace note' (Coit 1935, quoted in Fletcher 2021) rather than as a usable space for tenants, in a way that prefigured many postwar criticisms of technological symbolism.

In 1937, Coit won the American Institute of Architects' Langley Fellowship for housing research. For the next two years, she undertook an ambitious tour of 120 housing projects in America built by co-operatives, limited-dividend companies, philanthropies, life insurance companies and defence agencies, as well as the first USHA developments built after the 1937 Housing Act (Fletcher 2021). She consulted reports with the purpose of 'always checking the planning theory against the actual living habits and desires of the occupants' (Coit 1942, 71), making clear that her focus was working-class rather than middle-class Americans, whose views dominated most existing literature on housing preferences (Coit 1941, 11). She reported on the results of her survey of housing projects in two publications, *The Octagon*, the official journal of the American Institute of Architects, and, more concisely and graphically, in *Architectural Record*.

The latter précis, 'Housing from the Tenant's Viewpoint' (1942), opened with the statement, 'What rooms were designed for and what they are actually used for are frequently quite different things. Thus does the nicest theory fall before the fact' (Coit 1942, 72). Coit then summarised points of difference between 'theory and fact,' drawing on the views of residents, housing managers and others. In keeping with her promise to collate and compare rather than criticise, her tone was non-judgemental; her suggested interventions, pragmatic. For instance, she noted that, in most low-cost housing, the kitchen was over-congested, whereas bedrooms were under-utilised. Coit proposed simple planning changes, such as a larger kitchen and different circulation paths, to use space more efficiently while providing greater flexibility for residents. She also defended 30-inch height window sills, generous balconies and closets – especially closets – which cost-cutting housing authorities often dispensed with but, she noted, were 'vociferously' demanded by tenants (Coit 1942,

Yet Coit also weighed in on larger issues which cast a threatening shadow over the long-term security of America's modern housing programme, especially its increasingly mean minimum standards. Under constant political pressure to reduce expenditure and to avoid competing with private developers, the USHA drastically reduced the minimum space standards for housing, in spite of evidence that showed that apartments with smaller net room sizes were difficult to rent even during the Depression years. Coit obliquely drew attention to the dangers of this strategy: in reducing sizes, the USHA was making its offerings unattractive to renters and playing into the hands of its opponents. (How could one argue for a need for public housing if the units that existed were vacant?) Coit pointed to examples and studies which argued for larger room areas. She observed their advantages in terms of liveability and future-proofing and stressed they would be better able to resist obsolescence (Coit 1942, 75, 81–82).

Above all, by foregrounding the tenants' viewpoint at every turn, Coit reminded architects and planners of the point that also emerged at the Mackley: unless residents believed modern housing was delivering an improved quality of family life, it would never be accepted in America. For this reason, Coit never dismissed tenants' wishes as irrational, even when they flew in the face of what experts said they should want. In contrast to the technocratic tone that filled most housing reports, she avoided 'othering' residents, presenting their demands and desires sympathetically, from the father who craves solitude to his teenage daughter longing for some 'low cost version of the Hollywood boudoir' (Coit 1942, 72), but who will settle for a quiet place to study. Presciently, she warned architects against paternalism, stressing that tenants wished for 'a feeling of freedom, of independence, and of opportunity for self-expression' (Coit 1942, 73). Flying in the face of moralistic attempts to influence behaviour, she even argued that, for tired workers at the day's end, a beer garden would be more appreciated than adult education classes.

Coit's tenant-centred approach was matched in the deliberate way she presented her survey findings. She frequently quoted tenants, bringing their voices directly into her reports. In her next publication, the even more substantive *Public Housing Design: A Review of Experience in Low-Rent Housing* (1946) for the Federal Public Housing Authority, photographs of residents were pointedly included alongside Coit's expert technical guidance and architectural representations (Public Housing Design 1946). The candid photos of tenants illustrating their preferred ways of living made a striking contrast to the usual professional photographs of buildings devoid of people. 'Sitting areas increase the livability of apartment projects,' read one typical caption. 'Mothers like to watch their

FIGURE 1.5 The kitchen – general headquarters for many home activities.
Source: Public Housing Design (1946).

young children at play,' read another. Coit illustrated a wide range of users of all ages and ethnic backgrounds: mothers, babies, children and older women featured especially often, both inside and outside, child-minding, doing laundry, cooking, gardening, playing and socialising.

One did not need to read the analysis which accompanied these images to get Coit's message: that the activities and preferences illustrated were not incidental to the success of projects but were fundamental to it. Musing on how minimum standards, applied arbitrarily, would fail to meet needs, Coit stressed: 'Here is where intimate and sympathetic understanding of the families to be housed is vital to the success of the project, where actual need must be recognized and where the value of true and justifiable amenity must be appreciated' (Public Housing Design 1946, 96). While she offered a survey of what was known of tenant experiences so far, she also suggested there should be no set formula for how to approach housing in future; rather, she identified challenges for the designer and a process for thinking them through, always bearing in mind local conditions and potential tenants.

Social Questions in Housing

Coit was not alone in shifting focus towards preferences and wants in the immediate postwar period. As well as Coit's work, Bauer cited other efforts she felt were particularly promising in terms of suggesting design improvements and encouraging experimentation. Strikingly, given that she was usually the first to criticise amateur housing reformers, she was a fan of the Women's City Club of New York's 1948 survey of 458 families, *Better Housing for the Family*. Focusing on four built public housing projects in New York City, this study spoke of the 'many valuable lessons' that could be learned from the 'trial-and-error stage of [early] public housing' (Friedman 1948, 2) and applied to future projects. It also worked from the premise that specific, usually overlooked or even silenced groups,

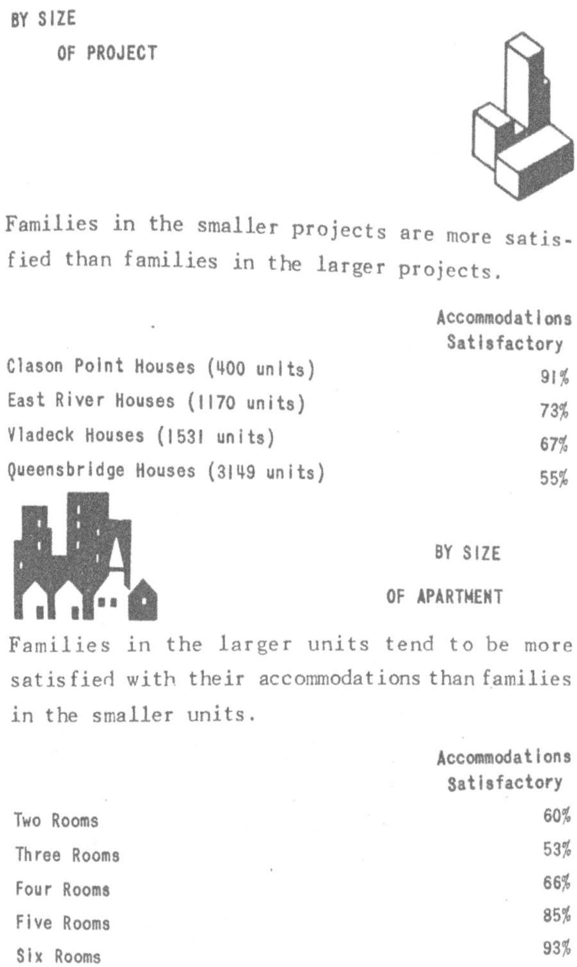

BY SIZE OF PROJECT

Families in the smaller projects are more satisfied than families in the larger projects.

	Accommodations Satisfactory
Clason Point Houses (400 units)	91%
East River Houses (1170 units)	73%
Vladeck Houses (1531 units)	67%
Queensbridge Houses (3149 units)	55%

BY SIZE OF APARTMENT

Families in the larger units tend to be more satisfied with their accommodations than families in the smaller units.

	Accommodations Satisfactory
Two Rooms	60%
Three Rooms	53%
Four Rooms	66%
Five Rooms	85%
Six Rooms	93%

FIGURE 1.6 Women's City Club of NYC – 'Do your present accommodations meet most of your needs?'

Source: Friedman (1948, 17).

had much to offer to design, in this case, the 'housewife' and 'her actual experience in day-to-day living ...' (Friedman 1948, 2).

To be clear: Bauer never felt that surveys of 'actual experience' would replace property surveys or censuses, but rather would act as a check on overly rigid and formulaic approaches to housing policy and design. 'Statistics will still be vitally important,' she clarified in 1947, 'but only as suggestions, not be to be turned into exact formulae' (Bauer 1947). From the beginning, Bauer was wary of the tendency of modern housing to become overly machinic and fixed in its approach, stressing, as did Coit and the Women's City Club, that needs were fundamentally dynamic and emergent. And tenant surveys affirmed a feedback loop did exist: preferences changed as people were exposed to new types of housing. As *Better Housing for the Family* put it: 'advances [in public housing] have in turn raised her [the housewife's] values, have widened her horizons, and have stimulated her to look ahead to further improvements in her living conditions ...' (Friedman 1948, 50).

In Coit's and the Women's City Club's work, such observations and sentiments translated into concrete suggestions for improvements at the smallest scale (interior details such as towel racks and outdoor clothes lines) all the way up to the communal scale (amenities such as meeting rooms and nurseries). But this did not go far enough for Bauer, who at this point felt people's options in terms of housing types were too constrained by precedent and existing models, including modern ones. In a teasing 1949 exchange with Bauer on her wish for greater experimentation and variety, Coit proposed:

> How about giving a bunch of simple, ordinary families an unpartitioned space (let's say the bath is enclosed, with plumbing lines for kitchen fixtures on one side of it) and a collection of boltable partitions to find out what families want in space relations? ... Maybe monk's cells for bedrooms, with a common dressing and clothes storage space, and a super living-dining-cooking space would come out, or no bedrooms at all, but a sleeping porch with cubicles, a chichi parlor and a commons, how do I know?
>
> *(Coit 1949)*

Despite the joking tone, Coit's limited range of options reinforces the sense she is still essentially cycling through known variations. By contrast, Bauer was after something more radical – 'entirely *new* kinds of home, neighbourhood and civic arrangement' (Bauer 1952a, 11). These were to respond to how people wanted to live, while also escaping the limits of what they knew. 'What we really need to know therefore,' Bauer stated, 'is what people would want if they understood the full range of possibility on the one hand, and all the practical limitations on the other' (Bauer 1952a, 11).

Bauer detailed her position in the very long essay, 'Social Questions in Housing & Town Planning.' This was first published in January 1951 in the *Journal of Social Issues*, which was the outcome of a collaboration between planners, architects and social scientists, and Columbia, MIT, and Harvard Universities, now cited as a significant milestone in the rise of 'environmental design.'[4] In her article, Bauer painstakingly attempted to synthesise her long-held ideas about how housing research could be used to direct future housing policy and development. As she admitted, she was better at asking key questions than at explaining how they might be explored. But she was at least sure who could work out the how: social scientists whose empirically derived insights into social questions would support more ambitious interventions into the built environment.

Bauer's position on the benefits of social scientific research was shaped by her encounter with sociologist Leon Festinger's landmark publication *Social Pressures in Informal Groups: A Study of Human Factors in Housing* (Festinger et al. [1950] 1963), whose implications electrified her. As a member of Research Center for Group Dynamics at MIT, Festinger began with the premise that group membership was one of the most important factors in people's satisfaction with their social lives (Festinger 1951, 154). In public housing, however, group membership was not voluntary (i.e. people did not control where or beside whom they lived), and was thus deeply shaped by architects' spatial arrangements. This finding was based on Festinger's empirical study of MIT housing, Westgate and Westgate West, built for married veteran students and their families, which proved that proximity – the distance between houses and the direction they faced – powerfully affected whether or not friendships developed. In turn, the ease with which people made friends was the greatest factor in determining their satisfaction with their housing; this was even more important to them than their homes' physical state (Festinger 1951, 159).

We can see why Bauer and others were excited by Festinger's study. While tenant surveys provided knowledge of local conditions, and Coit's had helped establish physical standards that could guide designs, Festinger was promising to illuminate questions of dwelling at a social and civic scale – 'the whole pattern of civic life' (Bauer 1951a, 6). Yet he did so while continuing to provide architects with the kind of practical micro-detail that they could use to improve a design's social cohesiveness, for example, layouts that promoted group communication (courtyards) and features that decreased social isolation (stairwells and mailboxes). This precision was important because, with some notable exceptions such as Kastner and Stonorov, most architects complained existing user studies were so vague or unrealistic that they were impossible to use.

We discussed one common problem already in relation to the Hosiery Workers study: when asked how they wanted to live, people tended to default to what they knew, reproducing known options that did not break out of the status quo. But equally, when people did give full rein to their desires, the result could be a 'Christmas list' of items that architects could not hope to deliver (Riemer 1951, 146). Lurking behind such criticisms and resistance, however, was another, more existential anxiety: that, in responding to users' preferences, architects' independence and authority would be eroded. In 'Architect – Servant or Leader?' (the name says it all), Walter Gropius warned against 'docilely' attending to Gallup Polls – a by-word for popular opinion in his writing – or even heeding an individual client's views, arguing, 'We have to lead him [i.e. the client] into a conception which *we* must form to fit *his* needs' (Gropius 1956b, 96–97; Reimer 1951, 146).

Festinger offered a way out of the impasse. In social scientific research, the confusing morass of subjective feedback on housing was checked against more objective methods. Festinger's team, for instance, used the same direct techniques commonly deployed in tenant surveys (questionnaires and interviews) but counterbalanced them with participant observation and sociometry (the study of interpersonal relations). The legitimacy of Festinger's conclusions was further enhanced by the 'scienticity' of his presentation, such as the use of 'sociograms' and matrices to support the finding that courtyards improved

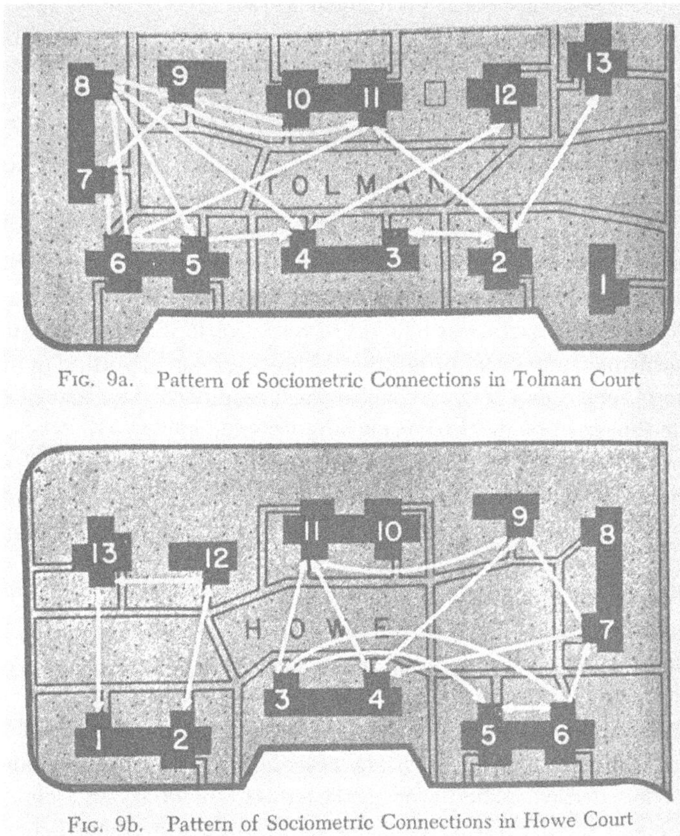

FIGURE 1.7 Patterns of sociometric connections at Westgate Housing, Cambridge, Massachusetts.

Source: Festinger et al. ([1950] 1963, 134).

social communication. These lent visual credence to the claim there could be a 'science of housing,' led by experts (now definitely including architects), which transcended the bewildering noise of client preference and wants. Architects could take preferences and behaviours without ceding their own authority. Indeed, adding social questions to their remit only enhanced their status.

For all of these reasons, it is not surprising to find that a number of influential architects, particularly those in academe, welcomed social scientists into the fold. As Avigail Sachs observes, 'For many architects ... this basic link [introduced by Festinger] between social behavior and housing patterns heralded the future of environmental design' (Sachs 2018, 81). This would have a major effect on postwar architectural education, as it became commonplace to have sociologists and psychologists embedded in design teams and schools between the 1950s and the 1970s. And they were productive, introducing topics from human sensing to social organisation, and opening up conversations around topics such as perception, personal space, territoriality, cultural patterns and communication. In time, however, this development would bring difficult new dilemmas of its own.

Coda

A full examination of these difficulties lies beyond the remit of this chapter, not least because Bauer, our guide, died prematurely in 1964, before they became totally apparent. But Bauer knew that a backlash was underway, linked to the growing crisis in public housing that she and her allies, informed in part by tenant surveys, had foreseen. Coit's research, for instance, led her to caution that the government's mean minimum space standards and cost-cutting made their units far less appealing; in the postwar period, the continuing pressure on costs and standards meant public housing mainly came to serve those with no choice about where to live, mostly poor, minoritised groups (Bauer 1957, 219). Meanwhile, Bauer's particular bête noire was that, in the name of renewal, housing authorities had further intensified programs of slum clearance, putting up massive blocks of extremely high-density housing on cleared sites, despite the fact that user surveys consistently revealed these to be disliked, especially by families.

In a published rebuke to Minoru Yamasaki, one of the architects of Pruitt-Igoe in St. Louis, the project that came to symbolise public housing's failure, Bauer called the turn to high-rises 'indefensible retrogression,' warning, 'opportunism today can be a boomerang tomorrow' (Bauer 1952b, 227; Bristol 1991). She was swiftly proven right as factors from poverty to lack of opportunity coalesced and many public housing projects became sites of crime and violence. One result of this rapid downward spiral was that, instead of asking 'how do people want to live?,' social scientists and architects got caught up in asking, 'how do people *not* want to live?.' Much postwar research focused on diagnosing the environmental causes of stress, such as overcrowding, and the pathologies that supposedly resulted – mental illnesses, delinquency and racial conflict. By contrast, Bauer's championing of social science had never been premised on what one sociologist described as 'the constraints of the organism' (Gutman 1972, xiii); rather, she was attracted by the promise of such collaborations to increase housing quality and tenants' sense of belonging and satisfaction – what we now refer to as 'well-being.'

Possibly even more damaging to the appeal of public housing, the remedies then proposed by many environmental design studies smacked of determinism, coercion, or worse. (Bauer admitted that her own fear about the 'sociocratic' tendencies of social scientists sharpened after reading Aldous Huxley's *Brave New World*; Bauer 1951b). Evidently, the central dilemma remained: how could findings about human behaviour be reliably yet ethically translated into equitable housing 'solutions' that promoted flexibility and freedom for users? Understanding the complexity of environmental factors did not automatically produce a programme of action. While recognising that housing studies had become much better at showing the human costs of housing deprivation nationally, architectural critic Ada Louise Huxtable scathingly observed, 'These reports rarely, if ever, give answers to anything. Each, in its own way, simply states the problem' (Huxtable [1973] 1976, 28). The growing sense of study fatigue and statis was likely a factor in the outpouring of enthusiasm for Jane Jacobs; while a proponent of the close-grained observation of people and places, she dismissed as absurd any attempt to turn this into science (Jacobs [1961] 1992, 440).

Despite such challenges, Bauer would never alter her view that, through systematic engagement with users, housing and community planning would create greater well-being on a social and civic level and that real love for public housing would be the result. The question 'How do people want to live?' remained fundamental, generative and

FIGURE 1.8 Student drawing of home in EHV [Easter Hill Village, 2523 Hinkley Ave], #4/4.

Source: Kathy Bass (second-grade student), 1966. Box 6, Clare Cooper Marcus Collection, Environmental Design Archives. Environmental Design Archives Exhibitions, accessed September 10, 2024, https://exhibits.ced.berkeley.edu/items/show/3231.

affirmative for her and, crucially, for those she influenced. Months before she died, Bauer was sent a report by a Berkeley Master's student, Clare Cooper (soon Cooper Marcus), on Easter Hill Village in Richmond, California, a low-income housing project designed by architects Donald L. Hardison and Vernon De Mars ten years before (Cooper Marcus 1975; see also Sachs 2018, 97–98). Cooper evaluated the architects' design according to residents' perceptions of it, notably consulting children's perspectives. While she uncovered many gaps between the architects' intentions and the residents' priorities, her end goal was to create concrete guidelines that could bridge her findings and future moderate-income housing designs. With her guidelines, Cooper took a significant step towards developing the principle and method of post-occupancy evaluation, which today regarded as one of the best means of bringing user-based housing research to bear on the ongoing experiment that is housing.

Notes

1 Before the 1940 Census of Housing was fully tabulated, however, the country declared war and the situation rapidly changed, which again shows some of the weaknesses and vulnerabilities of a long-term predictive approach.

2 Though employed by the Labor Housing Conference, Bauer shared Kastner & Stonorov's architectural offices in Philadelphia, hence knew this survey well (Radford 1996, 182).
3 The survey itself was conducted by engineer William W. Jeanes, a wealthy Quaker who had helped finance the project, and who went on to become became manager of The Carl Mackley Houses (Jeanes 1933, 1).
4 This special issue emerged from a symposium held in Cambridge in 1949. Participants included many of the great and the good in their respective worlds, from Robert Merton to Kevin Lynch to William Wurster (Bauer's husband). Mumford and Coit, among others, contributed comments by letter (Bauer 1952a). On the rise of environmental design in America, see Sachs (2018), esp. Chapter 3.

Bibliography

Bauer, Catherine. 1947. Letter from Catherine Bauer to Anatole Solow (June 3, 1947), Catherine Bauer Wurster Papers, BANC MSS 74/163, the Bancroft Library, University of California, Berkeley, Professional Papers: Organizations, carton 1, folder 11.
Bauer, Catherine. 1951a. "Social Questions in Housing and Community Planning." *Journal of Social Issues* 7 (1–2): 1–34.
Bauer, Catherine. 1951b. Letter from Catherine Bauer to Burnham Kelly (April 30, 1951), Catherine Bauer Wurster Papers, Professional Papers: Correspondence, Box 20, folder 18.
Bauer, Catherine. 1952a. *Social Questions in Housing and Town Planning*. London: University of London Press, Ltd.
Bauer, Catherine. 1952b. "Low Buildings? Catherine Bauer Questions Mr. Yamasaki's Arguments." *Journal of Housing* 9 (7): 227, 232, 246.
Bauer, Catherine. 1953. "The Home Builders Take a 'New Look' at Slums—and Raise Some Questions." *The Journal of Housing* 10 (10): 371–73, 389.
Bauer, Catherine. 1957. "The Dreary Deadlock of Public Housing." *Architectural Forum* 106 (5): 140–42, 219, 221.
Bauer, Catherine. (1934) 2020. *Modern Housing*. Minneapolis, MN: University of Minnesota Press.
Bristol, Katherine G. 1991. "The Pruitt-Igoe Myth." *Journal of Architectural Education* 44 (3): 163–71.
Coit, Elizabeth. 1941. "Notes on the Design and Construction of the Dwelling Units for the Lower-Income Family – Part I." *The Octagon* 13 (10): 10–30.
Coit, Elizabeth. 1942. "Housing from the Tenant's Viewpoint." *Architectural Record* 91 (4): 71–84.
Coit, Elisabeth. 1949. Letter from Elisabeth Coit to Catherine Bauer (May 2, 1949), Catherine Bauer Wurster Papers, Professional Papers: Correspondence, Box 15, folder 14.
Cooper Marcus, Clare. 1975. *Easter Hill Village: Some Social Implications of Design*. New York: Free Press.
Dehaene, Michiel. 2007. "Surveying and Comprehensive Planning: The 'Co-Ordination of Knowledge' in the Wartime Plans of Patrick Abercrombie and Max Lock." In *Man-Made Future: Planning, Education and Design in Mid-Twentieth Century Britain*, edited by Iain Boyd Whyte, 38–59. Abingdon: Routledge.
Festinger, Leon. 1951. "Architecture and Group Membership." *Journal of Social Issues* 7 (1–2): 152–63.
Festinger, Leon, Stanley Schachter, and Kurt Back. (1950) 1963. *Social Pressures in Informal Groups: A Study of Human Factors in Housing*. Stanford, CA: Stanford University Press.
Fletcher, Jessica. n.d. "Elisabeth Coit." *Pioneering Woman of American Architecture*. https://pioneeringwomen.bwaf.org/elisabeth-coit/, accessed 12 September 2024.
Fletcher, Jessica. 2021. "Where Tenants and Tenets Don't Agree: Elisabeth Coit and the Planning Practices of the New York City Housing Authority (1934–51)." *Buildings & Landscapes: Journal of the Vernacular Architecture Forum* 28 (2): 71–95.
Friedman, Beatrice S. 1948. *Better Housing for the Family*. New York: Women's City Club of New York, Inc.
Gropius, Walter. 1956a. "Sociological Premises for the Minimum Dwelling of Urban Industrial Populations." In *Scope of Total Architecture*, 105–16. London: George Allen & Unwin Ltd.

Gropius, Walter. 1956b. "Architect – Servant or Leader?" In *Scope of Total Architecture*, 96–97. London: George Allen & Unwin Ltd.
Gutman, Robert. 1972. "Preface." In *People and Buildings*, edited by Robert Gutman, xi–xv. New York: Basic Books, Inc.
Huxtable, Ada Louise. (1973) 1976. "Measuring the Dream." *The New York Times*, 23 December 1973. In *Kicked a Building Lately?*, 28. New York: Quadrangle/The New York Times Book Co.
Jacobs, Jane. (1961) 1992. *The Death and Life of Great American Cities*. New York: Vintage Books.
Jeanes, W. W. 1933. *Housing of Families of the American Federation of Full-Fashioned Hosiery Workers (Local Nos. 1 and 39, Philadelphia, June-July 1932)*. n.p.: Kastner & Stonorov.
Penner, Barbara. 2020. "Foreword." In *Modern Housing*, edited by Catherine Bauer, vii–xliv. Minneapolis, MN: University of Minnesota Press.
Pommer, Richard. 1978. "The Architecture of Urban Housing in the United States During the Early 1930s." *Journal of the Society of Architectural Historians* 7: 235–64.
Public Housing Design. 1946. *Public Housing Design: A Review of Experience in Low-Rent Housing*. Washington, D.C.: National Housing Agency/Federal Public Housing Authority.
Radford, Gail. 1996. *Modern Housing for America: Policy Struggles in the New Deal Era*. Chicago: The University of Chicago Press.
Riemer, Svend. 1951. "Architecture for Family Living." *Journal of Social Issues* 7 (1–2): 140–51.
Rodgers, Daniel T. 1998. *Atlantic Crossings: Social Politics in a Progressive Age*. Cambridge, MA: Harvard University Press.
Sachs, Avigail. 2018. *Environmental Design: Architecture, Politics and Science in Postwar America*. Charlottesville, VA: University of Virginia Press.
Sandeen, Eric J. 1985. "The Design of Public Housing in the New Deal: Oskar Stonorov and the Carl Mackley Houses." *American Quarterly* 37 (5): 645–67.
Taper, Bernard. 1941. *San Francisco's Housing: A Digest of the Real Property Survey*. Vol. 3 of the *Real Property Survey of San Francisco Works Project No. 665-08-3-173*.

2

IDEAS OF HEALTH AND WELL-BEING AS UNDERSTOOD AND APPLIED IN THE DESIGN AND PLANNING OF POST-WAR BRITISH PUBLIC HOUSING

John Boughton

Introduction

The link between physical health and housing may seem both obvious and long-established. The notion of well-being is a more recent and, in some respects, looser concept but one that more explicitly integrates psychological health, even perhaps an idea of happiness or contentment.[1] In this essay, I trace how evolving notions of health and well-being shaped the agenda of housing reform in Great Britain. I begin in the late nineteenth century since core principles established at that time persisted into the interwar period and beyond. The rapid growth of public housing in the 1920s and 1930s and the impact of the Second World War provide the context for post-war housing reform and new planning ideals promoting personal and social well-being that will be my principal focus.

The Origins and Motivations of the First Public Housing

In Britain, into the 1980s and in contrast to most other states, the predominant form of public housing was that built by local authorities, that is council housing (as it was called) built under national legislation and with the direct financial support of central government. The 1890 Housing of the Working Classes Act provided its founding basis.

The case for state intervention had become widely accepted by the turn of the century. Britain's early industrialisation was accompanied by a huge rise in population – from around 10.5 million in 1800 to 37 million in 1900 – and breakneck urbanisation; over 80% of the population lived in settlements of over 2,500 population by 1900. The squalor of urban working-class habitation (not necessarily worse than that in rural areas but more concentrated and visible) alarmed governing Victorian elites. While sincere humanitarian concern existed, fear was perhaps the more powerful motivating force for action – fear of the slum-dwellers' alleged immorality and criminality; fear of disease, then little understood, that might breach social divisions; fear of the unfitness of this new urban working-class. Sociological studies emerged to complement and amplify an alarmist popular literature exposing slumdom and its denizens: the work of Charles Booth and

DOI: 10.4324/9781003527930-4

FIGURE 2.1 Model housing, 1844, Streatham Street, central London: designed by Henry Roberts for the Society for Improving the Condition of the Labouring Classes.

Source: Photograph by John Boughton.

Seebohm Rowntree demonstrated that around one-third of the British population were living below the poverty line.[2] Medical Officers of Health employed by councils provided local details of appalling conditions. The growth of labour and socialist organisations in the later decades of the century coinciding with the extension of the franchise to some working-class men in 1867 and 1884 added pressure from below for action. Ultimately, however, it was the notions of 'respectability' and 'fitness' that shaped the governing classes' political response to housing squalor in this pre-democratic age.

The quest for working-class 'respectability' (one shared by better-off working-class activists) was evidenced in the 'Model Dwellings' promoted by Five Percent Philanthropy from the 1840s. Around 30 model dwelling companies had been established by the turn of the century; private housing companies run with charitable purposes that sought middle-class investment but limited contributors to a maximum 5% return on investment. These model dwellings themselves (often so-called 'block dwellings' in the five-storey, balcony-access, tenement form that would later be widely adopted in inner-city public housing) offered basic but solidly built and sanitary accommodation. As significant, however, as their physical form was the close supervision of tenant behaviour imposed that demanded sober lifestyles and the regular payment of generally higher rents. Such regulation and cost excluded many of the working class in greatest need.

'Fitness' meant good health but increasingly, as social Darwinist and eugenicist ideas of racial fitness took hold, the ability to compete economically and militarily against rival nations. The news that 8,000 of 11,000 Manchester volunteers were found unfit for service during the Boer War (1899–1902) gave added urgency to this quest for 'National Efficiency.' In this period, a concern for well-being (the term itself is anachronistic) is best understood as essentially a ruling-class preoccupation with societal order and national strength.

The need to improve working-class living conditions had therefore acquired political salience and impetus. Public health reforms culminated in 1875 in legislation imposing strict rules on newbuild regulating street widths, water supply and sewerage, window sizes, and so on. Some 2.5 million of these so-called 'bye-law houses' – the terraced housing still common across inner-city Britain – were built before the First World War. At the same time, the powers of local authorities to demolish housing unfit for human habitation were extended. Such powers were sparingly exercised, partly as a result of council conservatism but, more significantly, because limited means existed to replace cleared housing. Speculative builders, whose profits lay in middle-class suburbia, were uninterested in building decent working-class housing. Philanthropic efforts lacked the scale and financial strength to step into the breach. Central government turned to a machinery of representative local government (county councils were established in 1898, district councils in 1894) created to meet such challenges.

Much early public housing comprised multi-storey tenement blocks; many progressive thinkers thought such housing merely replicated the bleak inhumanity of contemporary industrial capitalism. The art critic and philosopher John Ruskin, much revered in the nascent British labour movement, invested in the smaller-scale and more picturesque schemes favoured by housing reformer Octavia Hill and judged his preference for one school of architecture over another 'on a comparison of their influences on the life of the workman.'[3] The artist and socialist William Morris was more pungent, declaring Five Percent Philanthropy a 'miserable palliation of the evil,' merely housing workers 'as careful masters house their machines.'[4]

The preference of liberal reformers was the cottage with garden front and back, and their ideal – as articulated by Ebenezer Howard – was the Garden City, a new town that combined the urban attractions of the city in terms of employment and infrastructure with the natural qualities of the countryside.[5] Though Letchworth, the world's first Garden City, was founded in 1903, Howard's schema could not practicably be applied more widely. Instead, a much scaled-down and far more limited version was adopted in the form of the so-called Garden Suburb, cottage homes (often in quasi-vernacular Arts and Crafts style) set in leafy surrounds.

A number of co-partnership societies, combining characteristics of the tenant co-operative and limited dividend company, were founded before the First World War to promote such schemes but they catered principally to the better-off working class and lower middle class. Increasingly, progressive municipalities built garden suburbs (or cottage estates) on a larger scale, particularly after the 1909 Housing and Town Planning Act allowed them to escape the well-meaning rigidities of bye-law housing. Nevertheless, the tension between the cottage home ideal and the pressures towards denser, multi-storey

FIGURE 2.2 Rushby Mead, 1911, Letchworth Garden City: workmen's cottages built for the Letchworth Cottages and Buildings Limited and taken over by the Howard Cottage Society Limited.

Source: Photograph by John Boughton.

accommodation remained a powerful one within public housing throughout its lifetime. This tension, unresolved to the present, contains various strands. One is in the simple, apparently common-sensical, notion that a house and garden offer a healthier environment, particularly for children, than an above-ground flat. But it also reflects an absence – the lack in England (Scotland is different) of a tradition of middle-class tenement living such as found in the cities of mainland Europe. Lacking this social cachet, the assumption of an ingrained English antipathy towards multi-storey housing became commonplace. While a few architects and planners emerged to propose a positive case for the social and communal benefits of multi-storey living, in general, it was defended pragmatically and therefore with an inevitable sense that it represented something second-best.

The Impact of the First World War and Public Housing in the Interwar Years

The sacrifice and upheaval of the First World War brought housing reform to the forefront of political debate as a genuinely democratic state emerged in its aftermath.[6] Prime Minister Lloyd George promised 500,000 new homes that would 'make Britain a fit country for heroes to live in.'[7] This was a pledge that recognised the continuing toll of

FIGURE 2.3 The Footpath, Dover House Estate, Wandsworth: a cottage estate built by the London County Council under the 1919 Housing Act.

Source: Photograph by John Boughton.

the nation's poor housing conditions (exacerbated by wartime neglect) but reflected as powerfully the political need to reward soldiery and citizenry for wartime sacrifice and a fear, exaggerated by revolutions in Russia and Germany, of working-class unrest. The initial promise, contained within the report of the wartime Tudor Walters Committee established to advise on post-war housing reconstruction, was for two-storey parlour homes 'of cottage appearance' with front and back gardens at a density of no more than twelve an acre.[8] In practice, the Report largely rejected the picturesque detailing that might have provided a what might today be recognised as of 'cottage appearance' in favour of a plainer, more cost-effective, neo-Georgian style that would become ubiquitous in succeeding decades.

Christopher Addison was appointed the first Minister of Health and Housing (a significant combination of departmental responsibilities that remained in place until 1951) and oversaw the passage of the 1919 Housing Act. The Act required local authorities to build where a compulsory housing survey had proven need and offered generous central government financial support to do so. In the event, only 176,000 council houses were built under its terms before public spending cuts curtailed the programme. Critically, however, the Committee had determined that post-war public housing should be superior to that built before the war, reasoning both that the contemporary housing crisis affected

FIGURE 2.4 The London County Council's Becontree Estate, east London, photographed circa 1930.

Source: Public domain.

all classes, not just the poorer working class, and that working-class expectations themselves were rising. As a result, the standards it set in terms of space and quality remained a benchmark until after the Second World War.

Whilst public housing standards were to fall in the short-term, subsequent legislation boosted council housebuilding until, by 1939, some 1.1 million council homes had been built compared to the 24,000 built before 1914. These were for the most part the same mix of cottage homes and tenements, largely the former, that had featured earlier. And, as was the case earlier, they initially catered for the better-off working class in regular employment who could pay council housing's higher rents. However, in 1930 and 1933, new legislation targeted the rehousing of slum dwellers, in greatest need yet typically excluded from earlier schemes. Two years later, overcrowding (to be surveyed in each local authority area) was added to the criteria of unfit housing.

In general, the health benefits of decent sanitary housing were held to speak for themselves but by the later 1930s, a new generation of sociologists and planners were sometimes critical of what might be called the psychosocial effects of the large new peripheral estates emerging and specifically their lack of social infrastructure and community. Ruth Durant (later better known as Ruth Glass) described the Watling Estate in outer London as 'not much more than a huge hotel without a roof' due to the numbers commuting to work and the transience of its population. Durant found that around one in ten households were leaving the estate annually, mostly to return to their earlier, inner-city haunts, closer to family, friends and established employment.[9] Similar figures were reported in comparable estates.

Nationally, a New Estates Community Committee (comprising members from the National Council of Social Service, the British Association of Residential Settlements and the Educational Settlements Association) had been formed in 1929. It helped establish a community centre on the Watling Estate built in 1933. This largely middle-class activism might to some seem to represent little more than the improving agenda that had marked philanthropic housing in the nineteenth century but, with its focus on community, it presaged one of the major concerns of post-war planning. This was a largely unremarked shift but one that reflected the increased provision of services directly addressing physical health and the improving health standards of the general population. These changes permitted a greater concern with the less tangible, more sociological, aspects of well-being.

Planning and the Second World War

The Second World War itself strengthened the demand for planning in a number of ways. Firstly, it created an unprecedented machinery of state that could be mobilised by a peacetime government with the will to use it. Secondly, it reignited calls for peacetime reform. The demand for a better and fairer Britain was a reiteration of the expectation that sacrifice should be rewarded but one amplified by the perceived betrayal of promises made after the First World War.

Much work was done in this regard by the wartime Coalition government which established blueprints for a comprehensive system of social security in the 1942 Beveridge Report, a National Health Service in a 1944 White Paper, and a commitment to full employment in the same year. Though Beveridge famously identified 'Squalor' as one of his five giants to be slayed in the post-war world, his Report focused solely on 'the problem of rent' to be addressed, he suggested, by a flat-rate national housing allowance for those in need.[10] However, broader issues of housing reform received greater and more sustained attention from other contemporary bodies. The 1940 Report of the Barlow Commission on the Distribution of the Industrial Population (motivated by severe unemployment in areas of traditional industry in the north of England, south Wales and central Scotland and the congestion of some metropolitan districts) anticipated the programme of New Towns launched in 1946. The 1942 Burt Committee on House Construction investigated industrialised methods of housebuilding as a means to meet post-war demand.[11]

Most relevantly to our theme, the 1944 Dudley Committee report on the 'Design of Dwellings' made a series of recommendations to improve the quality of council housing and council estates.[12] These focused primarily on improved space standards – which, in fact, closely resembled those proposed in the earlier Tudor Walters Report – but also included such self-consciously 'modern' features as gas and electric cookers replacing coal-fired ranges, larger kitchens replacing the sculleries of older designs and through lounges in place of the front parlours now thought stuffy and old-fashioned. (The Committee's criticism of the monotonous form of interwar council estates was more fully addressed in a 1948 Report from the Central Housing Advisory Committee on 'The Appearance of Housing Estates.'[13]) It is noteworthy that for all its good intentions and positive ideals, planning remained a very largely top-down and paternalistic exercise. Elected central and local government provided some form of democratic representation but ideas of direct consultation with those affected, let alone their popular participation, were exceedingly rare. Quantitatively, a 1944 White Paper envisaged the construction of 750,000 new homes to make good those destroyed or damaged by wartime bombing and a further 500,000 to replace existing slums.

At the same time, several hundred local councils across the country commissioned plans for post-war reconstruction.[14] Sir Patrick Abercrombie, Professor of Town Planning at the University of London, was the doyen of the field, authoring (with local partners) in 1943 both *The County of London Plan* and *A Plan for Plymouth*. Abercrombie's detailed and comprehensive prescriptions were intended to rectify what he and his fellow planners identified as the principal defects of many of Britain's larger cities – the 'haphazard mixing of industry and housing,' the obsolescence and monotony of much of that housing, the paucity of green open space, and traffic congestion.[15]

His and similar proposals of a practical cast would be adopted in varying degrees in the post-war era but it is also worth capturing some of the more visionary hopes that informed his thinking and perhaps the spirit of the age more widely. Abercrombie suggested, for example, that 'with the return of "community" will come the spirit of companionship unknown to the youth of yesterday who vainly sought it in the car or the cinema.' His criticism of an emergent consumerism was matched (in the gendered language of the day) by a belief that the plan:

> must give the craftsman, musician and painter with undiscovered talent a chance to show himself ... a plan which allows for a higher standard of living well within our grasp, with its call for space and beauty rather than for mere economy.[16]

Abercrombie's vision – of a creative, socially engaged citizenry nurtured by an affluent but high-minded society – seems to transcend the narrower focus on physical health that previously prevailed and it is interesting to note a significant spike in the use of the term 'well-being' in British books published at this time.[17]

This would prove fleeting, however, as prosaic post-war constraints and practicalities dampened such utopian ideals. Nevertheless, the principle that a better, more rationally ordered and more socially just country should emerge from the sacrifice and destruction of war remained powerful in Britain. The country had suffered severely in the war but less heavily than the occupied or vanquished states of Europe. Crucially, it had emerged victorious in a progressive cause. The slogan of the Labour Party that won a landslide victory in the post-war general election resonated powerfully: 'Now Win the Peace.'

Key Concepts in the Planning and Design of Post-war Public Housing

The 'neighbourhood unit' was one key motif of post-war planning. The concept was imported from America and first meaningfully applied in a British context in Barry Parker's design of Manchester City Council's huge Wythenshawe Estate in the 1930s. But Abercrombie emerged as its foremost champion and a detailed description featured as an appendix to the Dudley Report. The 'neighbourhood unit' was envisaged as a community of around 6,000–10,000 people (based on the catchment area of the local elementary

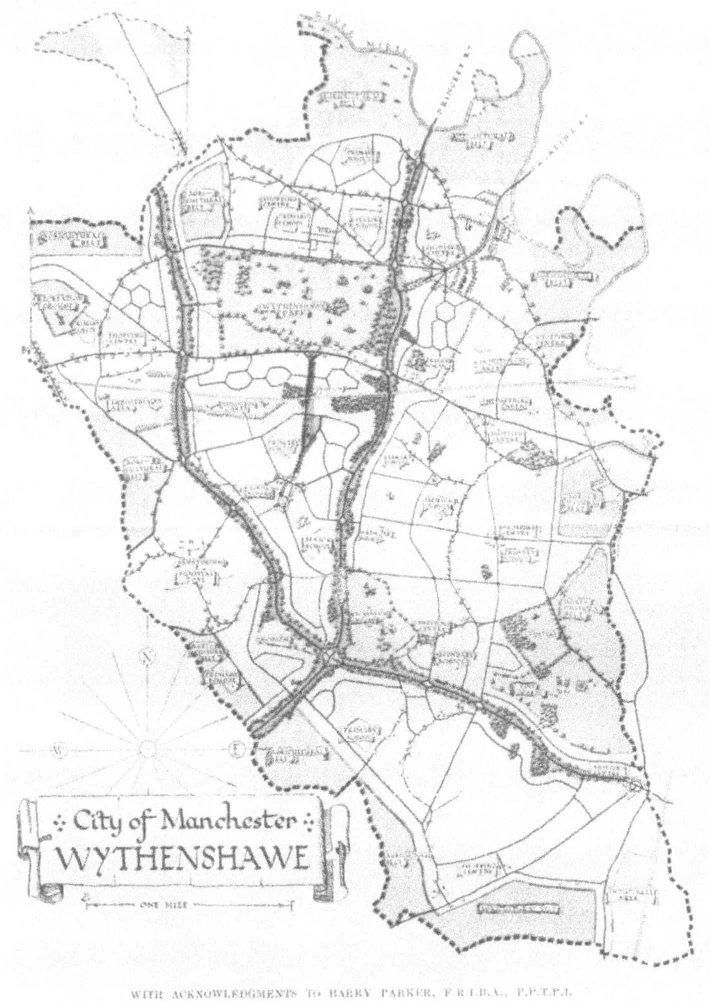

FIGURE 2.5 Barry Parker's plan for the Wythenshawe Estate, Manchester.

school) with its own shops, community buildings and amenity spaces. The facilities provided and neighbourliness promoted were intended to correct what many perceived as the sterility and lack of community of interwar council estates.

The Lansbury Estate in east London, the venue of the 1951 Festival of Britain's Live Architecture Exhibition, was to be its exemplar, containing not only a mix of housing and expected services but also the London County Council's first purpose-built old people's home and the country's first pedestrianised shopping precinct. (The Festival of Britain itself, described as a 'corporate reaffirmation of faith in the nation's future,' was intended to mark this modern, forward-looking Britain.[18]) The Stowlawn Estate in Bilston, the West Midlands, was a more aberrant example. The local council had employed Oscar Neurath, an émigré Austrian polymath, as a consultant in 1944 in the hope he might 'make Bilston happy.' Neurath had worked with the Social Democratic administration

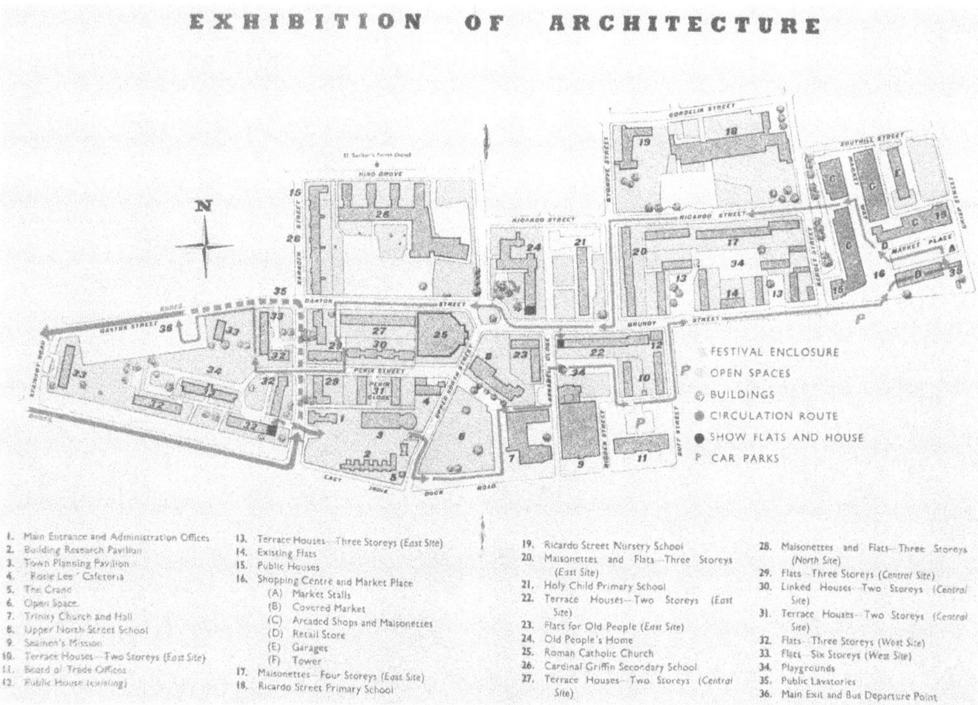

FIGURE 2.6 Site Map of the 1951 Festival of Britain Live Architecture Exhibition.

Source: Photograph by RIBApix.

of Red Vienna on housing matters and fled the city after the fascist coup in 1934. Unusually, he urged full consultation with residents in creating the mixed community and generous provision of shared facilities that he believed would promote social cohesion and contentment. He died in 1945 but the estate plans proposed by Sir Charles Reilly (emeritus Professor of Architecture of the University of Liverpool) – based, in his words, on 'the English Village Green and the small squares of the country town, where children can play and neighbours see one another and retain the friendliness of the little streets and slums' – were intended to further his project.[19] In the event, an estate emerged, shorn for reasons of economy, of the children's nurseries, laundries and cafeterias that Reilly (and Neurath) envisaged as promoting communal living; the greens remained as simple open space though subsequently most have been lost to infill housing.

For the most part, the neighbourhood unit ideal died a gentler death. Promised community infrastructure was almost invariably delivered more slowly than housing and more modestly than promised, reflecting both the understandable priority given to new homes as such and a financial regime that subsidised housing rather than communal facilities. More importantly, however, an increasingly affluent and mobile working class increasingly practised forms of sociability – or conversely willingly adopted more home-bound and domesticated life-styles – that rarely conformed to the drawing board visions of planners and sociologists, particularly those rooted in romanticised versions of the allegedly close-knit slum community described in Peter Willmott and Michael Young's

FIGURE 2.7 Somerford Grove, Hackney, showing flats, family housing and the community hall.

Source: Photograph by John Boughton.

influential post-war study as a 'sociable squash of people and houses, workshops and lorries.'[20]

A second key element of post-war public housing planning, presaged in the Dudley Report and re-emphasised in the Ministry of Health's 1949 *Housing Manual*, was 'mixed development.' Interwar council housing had provided overwhelmingly two- and three-bedroom family homes; mixed development aimed to cater for previously neglected groups by supplying homes appropriate to a range of people and households in different life stages. The supposition was also that the more mixed community that would emerge was a healthier and more sustainable one. (The concept had the additional and not insignificant benefit to planners and architects of allowing a more interesting range of building forms and types to be built than found in the very uniform interwar cottage estates.)

Somerford Grove, designed by one of Britain's foremost planners and architects Sir Frederick Gibberd for the Metropolitan Borough of Hackney in London in 1951, represented the ideal – a tight mix, set in largely-traffic-free surrounds, of three- and four-storey blocks of two- and three-bedroom flats, two-storey blocks of one-bedroom flats and bedsits, two-storey terraced family housing, and a terrace of single-storey bungalows for elderly residents. In general, the concept – a common sense one, given how many on council housing waiting lists did not require a family home – was applied with less finesse, particularly in the phase of large-scale slum clearance and redevelopment that took off from the later 1950s. At this point, mixed development was implemented far more randomly, typically on the larger estates of the day via a simple mix of high-rise and low-rise with no obvious coherence. There remained exceptions in architect-designed schemes, notably that of Dawson's Heights, a Borough of Southwark estate in south London completed in 1972, where its young architect Kate Macintosh created a deliberately intimate mix of flats for all ages. As she argued, channelling a little of Willmott and Young, 'if large blocks were to be accepted and loved, as a new way of living, they must try to replicate the best characteristics of the terraced street; that families of different sizes and age groups should intermingle, as their needs and strengths would be diverse and complementary.'[21]

A third concept, mentioned in both the 1944 Dudley Report and 1949 *Housing Manual* but amplified in the latter's 1953 revision, was the Radburn system, a form of planning that separated traffic and people. It originated in Radburn, New Jersey, that Clarence Stein – influenced in turn by the British Garden City movement – had devised in 1928 as a 'town for the motor age' in which vehicles were confined to service roads to the rear of housing approached by pedestrian footways and set amidst green open space. As traffic grew exponentially (1.8 million motor vehicles were registered in the UK in 1942; some 10.2 million by 1962), there were clear safety arguments for the idea but these were

FIGURE 2.8 The Queen's Park South Estate, Wrexham.

Source: Photograph by John Boughton.

augmented and complemented by what A.W. Cleeve Barr called in his influential 1958 book, *Public Authority Housing*, 'the social value of landscaping, the direct daily contact of people with grass, trees and gardens.'[22] (Cleeve Barr became chief architect to the Ministry of Housing and Local Government the following year.)

The Queen's Park South Estate, dubbed the 'Wrexham Experiment,' in north Wales was an early model. When completed in the late 1950s, it comprised around 1,500 homes in its nine sections. The housing was traditional two-storey terraced housing very much of its time but the scheme's advocates talked of its 'remarkable feeling of spaciousness' and the seemingly obvious benefits of a 'separation of pedestrian ways and traffic ways giving greater safety and convenience to all, but especially to children.'[23] Some similar estates were built in pure form across the country; a modified Radburn in which most but not all houses faced green open space and service roads were limited was more common.

In fact, the vogue for Radburn-style planning was relatively short-lived. Critics complained about the illegibility of the estates, arguing that it was hard to locate homes not deployed along conventional streetlines and that the estates' footpaths and open-plan layouts created a lack of privacy. Other criticisms related to the vulnerability of rear service roads and detached garaging to anti-social behaviour. It's an example of how the conventional wisdom of one age regarding the seemingly obvious health and well-being benefits of one form of planning can be rapidly overturned by that which succeeds. This might reflect the fact that planners, like generals, are in a sense always fighting the last war; in other words, often formulating ideas and plans soon superseded by changing circumstance. In hostile commentary, it was held to reflect the recalcitrance of grassroots lives to top-down social engineering.

Nevertheless, the benefits of healthier housing remained central to the public housing programmes of the post-war period, nowhere more so than in the proposals to relieve inner-city overpopulation, the decongestion announced in wartime planning. The London County Council built 13 so-called out-of-county estates in, or rather around, London; 45,000 homes in all by 1965. These were the often-decried peripheral estates but, for all the sometimes justified criticisms of their isolation and lack of facilities, their health benefits seemed incontrovertible. Margot Jefferys' study of the South Oxhey Estate in Hertfordshire showed that, of applicants taken from the Council's waiting list, well over half had been rehoused on health grounds and a third due to overcrowding. And yet by the mid-fifties, the estate's children (forming 40% of its overall population), who had been shorter than the London average in the 1940s, were 'rather taller and heavier than the London children had been in 1949.' Most residents praised the estate's fresh air, open spaces and cleanliness; 'housewives with young children, especially those with infants of pre-school age, expressed positive views on the estate rather more frequently than others.'[24] In Harlow New Town in 1964, the infant mortality rate stood at 5.5 per 1000 compared to the national average of 12.3 and for those under four weeks at 6.0 compared to 14.2.[25] At its most basic, this new public housing saved lives and probably created a few too; Harlow earned the nickname 'Pram Town' for its fertility.

The New Town programme inaugurated in 1946 represents the acme of those aspirations to build a healthier Britain – environmentally and sociologically – that fired the post-war imagination. In the first wave, eleven were created in England (eight around London), two in Scotland and one in Wales. They were built by Development Corporations – unelected bodies appointed centrally comprising technical experts and politicians – on

FIGURE 2.9 Late-1950s suburban-style housing in Gossops Green, Crawley New Town.

Source: Photograph by The Voice of Hassocks.

greenfield sites (save existing small settlements) in layouts that incorporated the key planning ideas of the day such as the neighbourhood units, mixed development and separation of people and traffic previously discussed alongside comprehensive zoning regulations that separated districts by function. By 1970, when the entire programme including its later iterations was wound up, the 32 New Towns established boasted a population of well over two million.

The bulk of New Town housing was built by the Development Corporations themselves. To take a single example, 81% of Crawley's 13,596 homes in 1962 were owned by Crawley Development Corporation, mostly – as was typical – in the form of suburban low-rise. Unusually, therefore, a large proportion of the town's middle-class population lived in public housing. This gave plausibility to the hope of the post-war Labour government that Britain should become a society less marked by differentials of class and income. Lewis Silkin, Minister of Town and Country Planning, introduced the 1946 New Towns Act with a paean to the classless communities he believed might emerge:

> No doubt they may enjoy common recreational facilities and take part in amateur theatricals or each play their part in a health centre or a community centre. But when they leave to go home, I do not want the better-off people to go to the right, and the less well-off to go to the left. I want them to ask each other 'are you going my way?'.[26]

It's a poignant statement that also incorporates the common view of housing reformers (as witnessed in the earlier quotation from Abercrombie) that improved conditions might also 'improve' their residents by encouraging more rational recreation and increased community participation.

Silkin's egalitarian hopes echoed those of Aneurin Bevan, Labour's Minister of Health and Housing. Bevan believed council housing should serve 'general needs,' a cross-section of the population. When he spoke for Labour's 1949 Housing Act, Bevan famously invoked that 'lovely feature of English and Welsh villages, where the doctor, the grocer, the butcher and farm labourer all lived in the same street' and what he called 'the living tapestry of a mixed community.'[27] The legislation was the first to remove the stipulation that council housing be designated as housing for the working class. Practically, Bevan's commitment to attractive and high-quality public housing was demonstrated by more generous space standards (by 1949, the average new three-bed council home occupied 98 square metres; a 37 per cent increase on similar housing of the 1930s) and the insistence that a five-person household should benefit from two inside toilets.

These standards were watered down by the Conservative governments in power from 1951 to 1964 but the commitment to large-scale public housebuilding was maintained; the largest number of council houses built in a single year – some 229,000 – was built in 1953. But the Conservative politicians differed in their attitude towards public housing. For them, owner occupation was the gold standard; council houses were seen to cater to those who could manage or aspire to no better. Hence, the 1954 Housing Act restricted central government grant support to council housing built as part of slum clearance redevelopment programmes and housing for elderly people. In this way, council housing maintained its traditional role as housing for the less well-off (even as working-class living standards rose in this period), increasingly so as owner occupation spread down the social order.

Mass Public Housing in the 1960s

However, this mid-50s' shift also reflected an objective change of circumstance. The emergency housing programme of post-war repair and reconstruction was largely complete and attention returned once more to slum clearance. In a period of increased prosperity, the goal to eradicate slum housing completely was one broadly shared by both major parties and found expression in the housebuilding targets (encompassing housing of all tenures) they set: in 1963, the Conservatives pledged to build 350,000 new homes a year; Labour initially countered with a promise of 400,000 that rose to 500,000 at the time of the 1966 general election. Whilst these figures were not fulfilled, the pace and scale of demolition and redevelopment nevertheless proved problematic and increasingly controversial as new public housing, particularly in its more modernist and multi-storey manifestations, came to be seen by some as harming public health and individual well-being rather than promoting it.

While low-rise council estates were criticised by some for their monotony and a few architectural critics condemned the New Towns for their extensive suburbia ('prairie planning' in the words of one), it was a growing surge of multi-storey housing that received wider censure.[28] Retrospectively, the upsurge of high-rise was seen by its fiercest critics as a symbol of planning hubris and political arrogance but there were sound, seemingly inescapable, reasons for the shift towards multi-storey public housing that occurred from mid-century. Firstly, there was the growing opposition to suburban sprawl.

FIGURE 2.10 An illustration, by Gordon Cullen, from chapter 1, New Ways of Living, of the Parker Morris Report (1961)

The green belt policies preserving open space on metropolitan fringes designed to curb it created what was called contemporarily a 'land trap' – a lack of available land on which to build. That shortage was exacerbated by the high cost of inner-city land and zoning restrictions that further restricted the space available for newbuild. The necessity of high-rise construction was compelling, both recognised and boosted by a new subsidy regime set by central government in 1956 that provided higher grants for taller buildings. The visual prominence of the point blocks and slab blocks that emerged in the country's larger cities exaggerates their overall significance; at peak in 1966, high-rise schemes of five storeys or more accounted for just a quarter of council housebuilding. Nevertheless, negative perceptions of modernist high-rise, as well as genuine problems that arose, created a powerful backlash that would see the trend towards multi-storey housing reversed after 1968.

In the early 1960s however, optimism around the progressive nature and positive benefits of public housing remained high and its contribution to improved health and well-being assumed. Though there is no specific reference to improved health and none to the still rarely used term 'well-being,' this is best seen in the report published by the Ministry of Housing and Local Government's Central Housing Advisory Committee in 1961, *Homes for Today and Tomorrow* (better known as the Parker Morris report after its author). The report began by noting the 'New Patterns of Living' apparent since the publication of its predecessor, the 1944 Dudley Report: 'in material terms people are better off than ever before ... all these changes are beginning to mean an easier, more varied and more enjoyable home life.' The Report went on, in disarmingly simple fashion, to summarise its conclusions: 'the major changes required can be summed up in two words – space and heating.' This in essence meant improved space standards and new central heating systems that allowed a range of family members to make best use of all available rooms.[29] The apparently narrow focus is misleading, however. New council housing was already assumed to provide secure, sanitary and well-equipped accommodation; the requirement now was to fit it to more affluent lifestyles and changing generational needs. Parker Morris standards were adopted voluntarily by the new London boroughs formed in 1965 and applied by central government mandate to all new public housing in the New Towns in 1967 and council housing generally in 1969. The then Labour Minister of Housing Anthony Greenwood hoped that private developers would emulate these new quality benchmarks.

The general assumption prevailed in Britain that higher-rise flats were unsuitable for families with younger children but this was a principle increasingly overruled in the rush to rehouse in the 1960s. The concern of some planners and academic sociologists that new council schemes weakened forms of community they believed prevalent in traditional neighbourhoods or otherwise desirable was expressed even more powerfully in the case of high-rise developments. 'Deck-access' housing emerged in the 1950s as one apparent solution. Balcony-access tenements – essentially a more modestly executed form of deck access – had been common since the later nineteenth century but now these access galleries, enhanced in size and function, were envisaged in the language of the day as 'streets in the sky.' Park Hill in Sheffield, built between 1957 and 1961, was its foremost model. Based on a close study of community life in the slums it replaced and enjoying the services of a resident sociologist, the estate comprised a series of interlinked 4- to 13-storey slab blocks, its 969 homes connected by three-metre-wide decks and supplied with a genuinely impressive range of community facilities.

FIGURE 2.11 Park Hill, Sheffield, Photographed 2021.

Source: Photograph by Jim Osley.

Park Hill's initial success encouraged its emulation. The North Peckham Estate, for example, completed by the London Borough of Southwark in 1972 comprised 1,444 homes in 65 five-storey blocks, all joined by second-floor walkways that allowed residents, in the celebratory account of the local council, to 'walk freely along this two and half miles of deck away from the dirt, noise and danger of London traffic.'[30] Later, both estates fell on hard times and their walkways came to be viewed less as means of sociability and more as conduits of antisocial behaviour and criminality – 'rat runs' in the language of the day. (The North Peckham Estate was demolished in the 1990s.)

The work of Oscar Newman in the US and latterly Alice Coleman in the UK explained this fall from grace readily as a result of the schemes' lack of Defensible Space. Coleman's 16 elements of 'design disadvantage' – including multiple storeys, common entrances, shared walkways and decks, and the consequent blurred boundaries between public and private space – were essentially a description of the principal features of modernist public housing.[31] It should, however, be pointed out that the gravest threat to residents' well-being in these and similar estates – in fact, in public housing of all forms at this time – lay in their deteriorating economic circumstances, specifically the mass unemployment that was a consequence of British industrial decline from the later 1970s.

Back in the 1960s, modernism – if understood in simple terms as the use of modern design, materials and techniques to build at scale – held sway, particularly in high-rise construction. The use of industrialised methods or system building (the manufacture of prefabricated components and their onsite assembly) became central to the housing drive and government policy, specifically in the requirement that a certain proportion – 25% in 1963, rising to 40% when Labour took office in 1964 – of local authority housing be built using such methods. The size and facilities of the flats that resulted were almost invariably far superior to any their tenants, most moving from slum housing and overcrowded accommodation, had known before but the political emphasis – at both national and local level – was on quantity at least as much as quality.

Off-the-peg contracts bought wholesale from the few major contractors that could deliver such schemes became the norm; in 1966, at the peak of the system building boom, 55% of new council housing starts came in such package deals. In this respect, the concern for residents' health and well-being was restricted to a straightforward belief that their new homes were superior – more sanitary and better equipped – than those they had known before. It's telling that the phrase 'mod cons' takes off in the 1960s; an informal contraction denoting the modern conveniences such as washing machines and fridges now increasingly found in working-class homes. In this respect, the new homes were better than their predecessors and generally initially liked by their new residents. But industrialised methods were too often poorly and hurriedly applied and problems of damp and condensation commonly emerged. The partial collapse of Ronan Point, a 22-storey tower block built for the London Borough of Newham, in May 1968 suggested wider structural issues. Mercifully, since the minor gas explosion that occasioned the collapse occurred in the early morning and the block was new and under-occupied, just four people died but the assumption that the mass public housing of the period inevitably benefited its residents was severely shaken.

Of course, multi-storey housing had long had its critics, particularly in Britain which lacked an established tradition of urban middle-class tenement living and where early housing reformers had argued so passionately for the cottage dwelling. Such sentiments revived in the later 1960s and had acquired media currency by the 1970s as design flaws and social problems emerged on some recently built estates. In 1968, the academic sociologist Pearl Jephcott conducting fieldwork in Glasgow's Red Road Flats (a scheme of six 31-storey point blocks and two 27-storey slab blocks) criticised their lack of community facilities and the early 'signs of social problems since the lifts were proving most inadequate,' a situation exacerbated (as was true of most public housing of this time) by the 'high proportion of child-users.'[32] Her influential study *Homes in High Flats* (subtitled 'Some of the human problems involved in multi-storey housing') was published in 1971.

The 1970s: Public Housing on a Smaller Scale

The collapse of Ronan Point didn't end high-rise construction or the use of industrialised methods – too many building contracts were already in the pipeline; system-built schemes were made safer – but it did provide a powerful symbolic marker of a changing public and political mood. A 1966 study of Deeplish, a so-called 'twilight area' of decayed terraced housing in Rochdale, for the Ministry of Housing and Local Government concluded the area could be revitalised through individual housing improvement grants and a new government strategy of 'environmental improvement.' A 1968 White Paper *Old Houses into New Homes* and the 1969 Housing Act that followed established General Improvement Areas and Housing Action Areas to replace the 'redevelopment areas' which had previously licensed wholesale clearance. Crucially, it had become clear that the unit costs of high-rise construction were significantly more than those for lower-rise housing whilst high-rise blocks failed (due to the open space required to prevent overlooking and overshadowing) to provide higher density housing. The special high-rise subsidy had been abolished in 1967. Central government's preference for rehabilitation (rather than demolition) of older properties and low-rise development was now clear.

It reflected growing public disenchantment with modernist mass public housing that was fuelled by increasingly negative, and sometimes sensationalist, media coverage of its alleged deficiencies. To take a single example of this changing narrative, an early resident of Balfron Tower – a 26-storey brutalist tower block in east London designed by Ernő Goldfinger for the London County Council – stated of her new flat that she 'wouldn't change it for Buckingham Palace.' According to Ursula Blackwell, Goldfinger's wife (the couple lived briefly in the tower after its opening in 1968), 'I have heard many people who live low down say they would like a flat higher up. I have heard no tenant who lives high up say they would like a flat lower down … they all said the flats were lovely.'[33] And yet 10 years later, one 59-year-old resident told a local reporter that he felt like 'a battery chicken in a box'; a young mother complained of being 'cooped up in the flat all day' with her two pre-school children.[34] High-rise blocks came to be seen as a cause of social isolation. When their lifts failed (as was far too frequently the case in these earlier years), this was literally the case. To many, high-rise blocks in particular had come to seem deleterious to health and well-being.

Others had become critical of the paternalist and top-down process by which redevelopment took place. Newcastle City Council, in the north-east of England, had been among the councils most determined to rebuild; in 1963 it planned to demolish and replace 25% of the city's entire housing stock within 20 years. And yet in 1968, as

FIGURE 2.12 Housing in the Byker Estate, Newcastle.
Source: Photograph by John Boughton.

criticisms grew of its sweeping plans and their mixed results, the Council appointed Ralph Erskine to design a new estate that would replace the Byker area's dense terraced housing. Erskine had an established reputation for people-centred design; he sought for Byker 'a complete and integrated environment for living in the widest possible sense,' one that would maintain 'as far as possible, valued traditions and characteristics of the neighbourhood itself' and would emerge with consideration of 'the wishes of the people of all ages and many tastes.'[35] Consultation did occur and eventually an attractive and very colourful estate emerged, famous for its tall perimeter block (the Byker Wall, built to shelter the estate from winds and traffic noise) but more notable for the richly landscaped, low-rise, high-density housing in its lee.

Byker as a model of participatory planning and estate design was in practice to remain highly unusual but a vogue for low-rise, high-density public housing took off in the 1970s seen by many as a deliberate corrective to the overweening ambition and missteps of the previous decade. In Camden, a new, relatively wealthy and politically progressive London borough formed in 1965, Borough Architect Sidney Cook firstly rejected system building – 'I'll use standardised plans if you can find me a standardised site,' he said – and then recruited a talented team of younger architects to implement his vision.[36] Foremost among them was Neave Brown. Brown thought that in 'discarding the street for the tower and the slab, we threw away a whole pattern of life with a quite inadequate understanding of its complexity and value.' Brown's goal, however, was not merely to recapture some of the 'traditional social and physical form and virtues of the city' but

FIGURE 2.13 Cressingham Gardens, Lambeth; one of the estates overseen by Borough Architect Ted Hollamby.

Source: Photograph by John Boughton.

'to try and improve on them.'[37] Brown and his colleagues designing estates across the borough created not a pastiche of the old terraces nor a simulacrum of suburbia but a radically new form of housing – stepped section blocks in what became Camden's starkly modernist signature style of white-painted rendered concrete and dark-stained joinery.

Across the Thames in Lambeth, Ted Hollamby, the Borough's Chief Architect, was developing an ostensibly more villagey, brick-built form of low-rise, high-density housing but one based on a similar critique of sixties' missteps. 'People,' Hollamby argued, 'do not desperately desire to be housed in large estates, no matter how imaginative the design and convenient the dwellings.' But, he continued rhetorically, 'do they really like the monotonous, equally vast and characterless suburb?'. What they wanted, he thought, was 'fairly small-scale and visually comprehensible environments,' what might be described (though he doesn't use the phrase) as urban villages. To this end, he advocated an architecture that was 'anti-monumental, anti-stylistic, and fit for ordinary people.'[38] Small touches – front doors that faced each other, kitchen windows overlooking walkways, generous planting throughout – promoted neighbourliness and contact with nature.

It's surprising perhaps that notions of health and well-being do not feature explicitly in this discourse but they should, I suggest, be taken as implied. The principally quantitative approach to public housebuilding in the 1960s was superseded, in the most innovative and thoughtful of new schemes, by qualitative methods claimed by advocates to be built on a more human scale that fostered belonging and neighbourly interaction. To some degree, this shift represented the financial realities of a more constrained economic environment and reduced public spending. It reflects also what might be seen as the success of the volume building of the preceding era; so many houses had been built that a degree of tenant choice exposed less popular estates, some soon to be designated 'failing.' But it remains, above all, a conscious attempt to build on a smaller, more intimate scale than found in the larger and occasionally anomic schemes of the 1960s.

The Decline of Public Housing

From the mid-1970s, council housing faced a perfect storm. Progressive legislation guaranteeing those in 'priority need' council homes (typically households with children and/or those with special health needs) met, from 1979, a New Right Conservative government intent on reducing council housing by, firstly, selling off existing stock to sitting tenants and, secondly, limiting newbuild. This led to what has been called the 'residualisation' of council housing. To some degree, it came practically to be seen (and was positively advocated as such by some on the right) as housing of last resort – a safety-net for the poorest and most disadvantaged of society. At the same time, unemployment rose to record highs as Britain's traditional heavy industries declined, contributing to some of the social problems noted earlier that affected council estates most severely (in some youth unemployment reached 50%). In the longer term, working-class owner occupation had risen and was further boosted by the Right to Buy granted to council tenants. Psychologically, council housing came to seem less desirable, second best perhaps, even to those who had been its natural constituency. From the 1980s into the 2010s, the principal emphasis with regards to social housing lay less with building anew and more in the regeneration and occasional demolition of existing stock. This has been a controversial process in which, in many cases, existing multi-storey blocks (some suffering from real or alleged construction flaws) have been demolished – to the opposition of some residents – and their replacement by lower-rise housing of various tenures and a restored, 'traditional' streetscape.

At peak, around 31% of British households lived in council housing; at present, the proportion living in social rented homes is around 17% (divided approximately equally between those renting from local authorities and those renting from housing associations) while 19% live in private rental housing. Owner occupation has fallen from a peak of 71% in 2003 to 65% currently. These figures underlie the current housing crisis in which social rent housing is unavailable to many who need it (around 1.2 million households are on waiting lists; around 105,000 households statutorily entitled to social rent housing are in inadequate and temporary accommodation); many cannot afford to buy; and rents in the insecure private rental sector have become increasingly unaffordable. Local authorities are building on a small scale – around 6000–7000 homes a year (compared to the average of 126,000 homes built annually between 1945 and 1979) – and are generally building well and in sustainable forms that address both the climate crisis and the fuel poverty of their tenants. Nevertheless, while party political emphases differ to some extent, the immediate prospect of a major revival of social housebuilding is uncertain.

Conclusion

The link between decent and affordable housing and health and well-being seems as obvious today as ever. In the nineteenth and earlier twentieth century, it was charted with statistical rigour by Medical Officers of Health and the first social scientists. The visual impact of housing squalor – those dense terraces so removed from more romanticised notions of traditional 'Merrie England' – and its observable impact on its residents were equally compelling to many.[39] These conclusions established, the case for the health benefits of new and improved housing and environments was often implicit rather than explicit in public housebuilding programmes after the Second World War. That improved housing improved physical health was taken for granted so what emerged more powerfully in the discussions around public housing was its impact on the psychological welfare of its residents. The totems of post-war housing reform – aside from the foundational goal of slum clearance – were neighbourliness and community. Community itself was often understood by planners and politicians to mean both increased social participation and improving rational recreation and, among those on the left, reduced class division.

As Britain became more affluent, as new forms of domesticated recreation emerged, and as the more prescriptive post-war planning concepts confronted recalcitrant realities on the ground, the more idealistic, even utopian, hopes of post-war housing reformers receded. From the later 1960s, health concerns, particularly those emphasising psychological wellness, sometimes focused on public housing as a *cause* of ill-health rather than its solution. Well-being as a specific term of art takes off exponentially in the 1980s, its emergence and popularity reflecting the decline of physical health concerns and the eclipse of more communitarian ideals.[40]

At present, as a once marginalised private rental sector grows, social rent housing remains in relative decline, and owner occupation seems unattainable to many, housing campaigners reemphasise basics. The Health Foundation pressure group, for example, calls for housing that is both affordable, stable and secure and well connected to community, work and services.[41] Environmental health practitioners point to the prevalence of specific health hazards in all tenures of housing but most significantly in the weakly regulated private rental sector. Advocates of social housing employ a looser idiom of personal well-being stressing once more how decent, secure and affordable housing provides the foundation of an individual's physical, social and psychological health. Within contemporary academic study of housing, there is significant interest in the assessment of subjective well-being as influenced by housing type, condition and tenure.[42] In this respect, the contemporary language of personal well-being offers both a more holistic and more diffuse approach to housing policy than the more physically and sociologically specific goals of the post-war years.

Notes

1 The online Oxford English Dictionary provides the following definition: With reference to a person or community: the state of being healthy, happy, or prosperous; physical, psychological, or moral welfare. Oxford English Dictionary. ND. https://www.oed.com/search/dictionary/?scope=Entries&q=well-being. Accessed 25 October 2023.

2 Charles Booth published *Life and Labour of the People in London* in a series of editions and volumes between 1889 and 1903. Seebohm Rowntree published *Poverty: a Study of Town Life* (a survey of the northern city of York) in 1901.

3 Ruskin, John. 1894. *Modern Painters, vol. 5*. Boston, MA: Estes and Lauriat, 217.
4 Morris William. 19 July 1884. "The Housing of the Poor", *Justice*, 4–5.
5 Ebenezer Howard published *Tomorrow: A Peaceful Path to Real Reform* in 1898, better known in its 1902 edition as *Garden Cities of To-morrow*.
6 All men, and property-holding women, were granted the vote in 1918. Universal suffrage was achieved in 1928.
7 Speech at Wolverhampton, 23 November 1918. "Mr Lloyd George on his Task", *The Times*, 25 November, 13.
8 Local Government Board. 1918. Report of the Committee to Consider Questions of Building Construction in Connection with the Provision of Dwellings for the Working Classes in England and Wales and Scotland. cd. 9191. London: HMSO.
9 Durant Ruth. 1939. *Watling, A Survey of Life on a New Housing Estate*. London: P.S. King & Son Ltd.
10 Beveridge, William. 1942. Social Insurance and Allied Services, Cmd 6404, London: HMSO, 76–90.
11 Post-War Building Studies No.1. 1944. *House Construction by an Interdepartmental Committee Appointed by the Minister of Health, the Secretary of State for Scotland and the Minister of Works*. London: HMSO
12 Ministry of Health. 1944. *Design of Dwellings: Report of the Design of Dwellings Sub-Committee of the Central Housing Advisory Committee*. London: HMSO.
13 Ministry of Health. 1948. *The Appearance of Housing Estates: Central Housing Advisory Committee, Report of the Sub-Committee on the Means of Improving the Appearance of Local Authority Housing Estates*. London: HMSO.
14 Larkham Peter J. and Lilley Keith D. 2001. *Planning the 'City of Tomorrow': British Reconstruction Planning, 1939–1952: An Annotated Bibliography* https://bcuassets.blob.core.windows.net/docs/CESR_Reconstruction_bibliography_2010.pdf. Accessed 25 October 2023.
15 The broad themes and specific quotation are drawn from Forshaw, J.H. and Abercrombie, Patrick. 1943. *The County of London Plan*. London: Macmillan and Co, 3-5
16 Watson, J Paton and Abercrombie, Patrick. 1943. *A Plan for Plymouth*. Plymouth: Underhill (Plymouth) Ltd, 86.
17 Google Ngram Viewer. ND. https://books.google.com/ngrams/graph?content=well-being&year_start=1800&year_end=2019&corpus=en-GB-2019&smoothing=3. Accessed 18 April 2024.
18 Cox, Ian. 1951. *The South Bank Exhibition: A Guide to the Story it Tells*. London: HMSO.
19 Reilly quoted in the *Birkenhead News*, 12 April 1944.
20 Willmott, Peter and Young, Michael. 2013. *Family and Kinship in East London*. London: Routledge, 98. The book was first published in 1957.
21 Kate Macintosh speaking in *Utopia London*, a 2010 film directed by Tom Cordell.
22 Cleeve Barr, A.W. 1958. *Public Authority Housing*. London: Batsford, 42.
23 Stephenson, Gordon. 1954. "The Wrexham Experiment: the Queen's Park South Estate". *Town Planning Review*, vol. 24, no. 4, 290.
24 Jefferys, Margot. 1964. "Londoners in Hertfordshire: The South Oxhey Estate" in Glass, Ruth et al., *London: Aspects of Change*: London: MacGibbon and Key, 228.
25 "Harlow New Town Death Rate Well Below Average", *The Times*, 25 September 1964, 7.
26 New Towns Bill, HC Deb, 8 May 1946, Hansard, vol. 422, cc. 1072–184, https://api.parliament.uk/historic-hansard/commons/1946/may/08/new-towns-bill. Accessed 25 October 2023.
27 Housing Bill, HC Deb 16 March 1949 vol 462 cc2121-231, https://api.parliament.uk/historic-hansard/commons/1949/mar/16/housing-bill. Accessed 25 October 2023.
28 Cullen, Gordon. 1953. "Prairie Planning in the New Town". *Architectural Review*, vol. 114, no. 679, 34.
29 Ministry of Housing and Local Government. 1961. *Homes for Today and Tomorrow*, London: HMSO, 1–2.
30 "Life at Deck Level", *Southwark Civic News*, July 1968.
31 See Newman, Oscar, 1972. *Defensible Space: Crime Prevention through Urban Design*. London: Macmillan and Coleman, Alice. 1985. *Utopia on Trial: Vision and Reality in Planned Housing*. London: H Shipman
32 Jephcott, Pearl. 1971. *Homes in High Flats*. Edinburgh: Oliver and Boyd, 30.

33 Quoted in Oldham, Ruth. 2012. "Ursula Goldfinger's Balfron Tower Diary and Notes". *C20: The Magazine of the Twentieth Century Society*, 1 September.
34 *East London Advertiser*, 21 July 1978.
35 Malpass, Peter. 1979. "The Other Side of the Wall". *Architect's Journal*, vol 169, no 19, 1979, 963.
36 Cook quoted in Watkinson, Fabian. 2001. *The Most Expensive Council Housing in the World*. London: Twentieth Century Society, 3
37 Quoted in Swenarton, Mark. 2017. *Cook's Camden: The Making of Modern Housing*. London: Lund Humphries, 41.
38 Hollamby speaking on 'The Architect's Approach to Architecture' at RIBA, 24 January 1974, quoted in the *Architects Journal*, vol. 159, no. 6, 1974, 251.
39 The concept of 'Merrie England' (in a deliberately archaicised spelling) was an idealised representation of a more bucolic society, typically placed in an indeterminate historic past. The notion emerged in literary circles as Britain industrialised.
40 The striking increase in the use of the term from around 1980 is seen very clearly in the Google Ngram Viewer search referred to previously.
41 The Heath Foundation, 'How does housing influence health?', 31 October 2017. https://www.health.org.uk/infographic/how-does-housing-influence-our-health?gclid=Cj0KCQjwqP2pBhDMARIsAJQ0CzqIOyXhG1ANK0eo6u1JPA0ccJmeSsD2KEfrfkzNSSw2FgbJxRo8tQsaAsTfEALw_wcB. Accessed 30 October 2023.
42 See, for example, Clapham, D., Foye, C., and Christian, J. 2018. "The concept of subjective well-being in housing research". *Housing, Theory and Society*, 35 (3). 261–280.

Bibliography

Beveridge, William. 1942. *Social Insurance and Allied Services, Cmd 6404*. London: HMSO.
Booth, Charles. 1902. *Life and Labour of the People in London*. London: Macmillan.
Clapham, D., C. Foye, and J Christian. 2018. "The Concept of Subjective Well-Being in Housing Research." *Housing, Theory and Society* 35 (3): 261–80.
Cleeve Barr, A.W. 1958. *Public Authority Housing*. London: Batsford.
Coleman, Alice. 1985. *Utopia on Trial: Vision and Reality in Planned Housing*. London: H Shipman.
Cox, Ian. 1951. *The South Bank Exhibition: A Guide to the Story It Tells*. London: HMSO.
Cullen, Gordon. 1953. "Prairie Planning in the New Towns". *Architectural Review* 114 (679). 33-36.
Durant, Ruth. 1939. *Watling, A Survey of Life on a New Housing Estate*. London: P.S. King & Son Ltd.
Forshaw, John Henry and Patrick Abercrombie. 1943. *The County of London Plan*. London: Macmillan and Co.
Google Ngram Viewer. https://books.google.com/ngrams/. Accessed 18 April 2024.
Jefferys, Margot. 1964. "Londoners in Hertfordshire: The South Oxhey Estate." In *London: Aspects of Change*, edited by Glass Ruth. London: MacGibbon and Key.
Larkham, Peter J, and Keith D Lilley. 2001. *Planning the 'City of Tomorrow': British Reconstruction Planning, 1939–1952: An Annotated Bibliography* https://bcuassets.blob.core.windows.net/docs/CESR_Reconstruction_bibliography_2010.pdf. Accessed 25 October 2023.
Local Government Board. 1918. Report of the Committee to Consider Questions of Building Construction in Connection with the Provision of Dwellings for the Working Classes in England and Wales and Scotland. cd. 9191. London: HMSO [The Tudor Walters Report].
Malpass, Peter. 1979. "The Other Side of the Wall." *Architect's Journal* 169 (19). 963–969.
Ministry of Health. 1944. *Design of Dwellings: Report of the Design of Dwellings Sub-Committee of the Central Housing Advisory Committee*. London: HMSO.
Ministry of Health. 1948. *The Appearance of Housing Estates: Central Housing Advisory Committee, Report of the Sub-Committee on the Means of Improving the Appearance of Local Authority Housing Estates*. London: HMSO.
Ministry of Housing and Local Government. 1961. *Homes for Today and Tomorrow*. London: HMSO. [The Parker Morris Report]
Newman, Oscar. 1972. *Defensible Space: Crime Prevention through Urban Design*. London: Macmillan.

Oxford English Dictionary Online. https://www.oed.com/?tl=true. Accessed 25 October 2023.
Post-War Building Studies No.1. 1944. *House Construction by an Interdepartmental Committee Appointed by the Minister of Health, the Secretary of State for Scotland and the Minister of Works*. London: HMSO.
Rowntree, Seebohm. 1901. *Poverty: A Study of Town Life*. London: Macmillan.
Ruskin, John. 1894. *Modern Painters, vol. 5*. Boston, MA: Estes and Lauriat.
Stephenson, Gordon. 1954. "The Wrexham Experiment: the Queen's Park South Estate." *Town Planning Review* 24 (4). 271–295.
Swenarton, Mark. 2017. *Cook's Camden: The Making of Modern Housing*. London: Lund Humphries.
The Heath Foundation, 'How does housing influence health?', 31 Oct 2017. https://www.health.org.uk/infographic/how-does-housing-influence-our-health?gclid=Cj0KCQjwqP2pBhDMARIsAJQ0CzqIOyXhG1ANK0eo6u1JPA0ccJmeSsD2KEfrfkzNSSw2FgbJxRo8tQsaAsTfEALw_wcB. Accessed 30 October 2023.
Watkinson, Fabian. 2001. *The Most Expensive Council Housing in the World*. London: Twentieth Century Society.
Watson, J Paton, and Patrick Abercrombie. 1943. *A Plan for Plymouth*. Plymouth: Underhill (Plymouth) Ltd.
Willmott, Peter, and Michael Young. 2013. *Family and Kinship in East London*. London: Routledge.

3

THE IDEA OF LIFE (SEIKATSU) AND WELL-BEING IN JAPANESE PRE- AND POST-WAR HOUSING

Izumi Kuroishi

Introduction

The COVID-19 pandemic highlighted the fragility of social systems, political and economic instability and environmental problems that impact people and everyday life. Architects, governments and other actors in countries, including those belonging to the G7, are now in the midst of rethinking the meaning of well-being. The topic, for example, has been the subject of conversations at OECD World Forums on Well-Being.

The term 'well-being' refers to individuals' social, mental and physical wellness and can refer to a number of factors including hygiene, health, economic conditions and social relationships. In the context of the living environment, the focus is largely confined to measuring housing policies, building conditions, technological advances in facilities and infrastructure, affordability, amenity services and environmental comfort. In interior design and housing welfare studies, scholars are developing new approaches to thinking about how the living environment shapes well-being.[1] Psychosociologists are calling attention to the uneven distribution amongst studies focused on well-being in the COVID-19 period.[2] They argue that social, ethical, cultural and security issues are rarely discussed or addressed in relation to their historical transformation in spatial practices. Their work pushes scholars, including this author, to further re-examine the genealogical transition of the idea of well-being in architecture and housing.

This chapter seeks to address the lacunae in the literature on the history of the evolution of well-being in architecture and housing in the case of Japan. In Japan, the democratisation of post-war society and the political influence of the Cold War period was not simply a modern evolution of civil society. It was also a major often contradictory shift in social norms, lifestyles and cultural values from the pre-war period.[3] The image of the residents during this period also changed, with a widening gap between ideas of residents underlying the standard specifications of post-war public housing projects and the rapidly changing lifestyles of the residents. It is critical then understanding the shifting relationship between the ideas of public housing and society, and how the well-being of housing as a human right was positioned as a social and spatial issue. Specifically,

DOI: 10.4324/9781003527930-5

from the war years to the post-war period, public housing programs were mostly handled by government architectural engineers and kept separate from ordinary architects.[4] However, other architects understood the problems of such a government-centred public housing program; but their positions are not fully recognised and discussed in depth in the history of modern Japanese architecture. Recognising how some architects considered the social significance of the living environment as an essential issue for architecture is important. Doing so enables us to re-evaluate the architectural concept of Seikatsu (life), which has been undervalued for a long time. As such, this chapter examines how an awareness of the meaning of living space was positioned in the architectural field, and how lesser-known architects have influenced the concept of well-being in modern public housing.

Literature Review

The study of well-being has advanced through psychological, economic and institutional frameworks worldwide.[5] Nevertheless, in Japan – where social systems shifted from feudal structures to democracy after World War II (WWII) – well-being research has yet to fully explore issues tied to human rights and identity within its unique socio-cultural context. This underscores the need to investigate Japan's specific socio-cultural and historical background in defining well-being in general, and housing in particular. In particular, Japanese housing scholars identify structural factors diminishing well-being in public housing. Yoshihito Honma, for example, links these issues to the divide between construction and welfare policies, a limited awareness of housing rights and a policy emphasis on quantity over quality.[6] Keino Omoto observes that post-war housing policies inadequately addressed housing quality, attributing this to weakened family support systems and ineffective land policies.[7] Yosuke Hirayama adds that isolation, rigid standards and neoliberal policies deepened inequalities and reduced housing quality for disadvantaged groups.[8] These foundational studies contribute to housing policy discussions. However, they are based on a political science of architectural planning, leading to a limited critique of enduring wartime planning approaches, functionalism and psychological effect of the space on dweller's everyday life.

This study aims to address the gaps in the existing literature by analysing the influence of Occupation Forces, shifts in architects' social roles, and the psychological and cultural implications of spatial quality in public housing in Japan. Also, in Japanese architectural and design history, there is little research on the relationship between the ideas and designs of public housing and other architectural designs, home economics, environmental science and construction technologies. As such, this chapter seeks to uncover perspectives lost due to the separation of architectural history, design theory and housing studies. Its aim is to being to transform the history of housing in post-war Japan.

Methodology of This Study

Engaging in research on public housing for the reconstruction of the Great East Japan Earthquake, and studying residential life during the COVID-19 pandemic, made me aware of the ontological significance of refugees' adapting to changes in family and living environment, transforming their own home and freely creating shared spaces with neighbours and places to interact with nature to create their own locus.[9] I wondered if earlier efforts in Japan's architectural history existed which focused on concerns about the role of human rights, agency, and well-being in the construction of post-war housing design discourses and practices. This led me to conduct research in the Wajiro Kon Archive where I discovered the achievements of Wajiro Kon and Sakae Komada, who expanded their work from the study of the Life Improvement Programme to settlement studies, Lifeology, and the reform of people's life consciousness, covering issues such as hygiene, human rights and environmental planning in living spaces to examine the ontological meaning of dwelling.

I also conducted research on the impact of the occupying forces on changes in living spaces and people's awareness of human right during the post-war period of regime change as well as post-war design and cultural exchange through a survey of materials from the National Archive of the USA and Musashi University Archive holding the material of The Craft Guidance Institute (renamed the Industrial Arts Institute (IAI) in 1952). Beyond this, I examined the work of Kiyoshi Ikebe, based on my own experience of living in one of his houses. This led me to research Noboru Kawazoe, Kiyonori Kikutake and the Metabolism Movement, through an interview with Kawazoe. I also engaged in library research at the Architectural Academy to find how the architects were motivated by the critical condition of Japanese people and the architects' understanding of the social meaning of architecture.

Through the research methods outlined above, I realised that there was a significant distance between the concept and application of architecture in post-war Japan and the issues of social living conditions of ordinary people. There was also connection between some of architects discussed above through their shared critical awareness of 'Seikatsu' which pushed them re-examine the realisation of well-being in dwelling from a new angle. I explore their connection in depth later in this chapter.

Historical Background of the Study of 'Seikatsu' and Housing

An emphasis on 'Seikatsu' (life) has long been present in studies of health and home economics of housing since the beginning of the twentieth century, but with a focus on philanthropic thinking based on American Protestantism, such as the Bunka Seikatsu ron (Cultural Life Study) of Kokichi Morimoto in the 1920s, which later developed into the Seikatsu Kaizen Undo (Life Improvement Movement) of housing and Dojunkai projects after the Great Kanto Earthquake in 1923.[10] However, in the course of urban redevelopment and housing improvement projects from the 1930s, especially after the outbreak of the Sino-Japanese War in 1937, the idea of Seikatsu Kagaku (Life Science), proposed by Lieutenant General and medical doctor Chikahiko Koizumi, became the keyword for rationalising and scientifically organising all aspects of people's daily lives to improve their productivity during wartime. During the war, under nationalistic policies focused on controlling people's lifestyle, the study of Seikatsu in the field of economics expanded to include the area of Seikatsu Hi kenkyu (Life Expense Study) by Junzo Nagano in 1939, and in the field of sanitation and health Seikatsu Kozo (Life Structure Study) by Kyo Kagoyama in 1943.[11]

In 1948, the economist Kazuo Okouchi published *Kokumin Seikatu no Riron* (Theory of the People's Life), which examined both the wartime socio-economic system and the historical contradictions of Japanese capitalism from the end of the nineteenth century.[12]

He argued that the most important issue was the balance between production and consumption, and that the household budget in particular should be prioritised in the national economy in order to improve people's living conditions. He criticised the historical contradiction of Japanese economic policy, which requires people to work hard to save money instead of consuming for themselves, causing negative economic cycles, and suggested that the government and public bodies should invest more in supporting better housing, leisure and shopping facilities, housewives' education and community space to realise their good quality of Seikatsu.

The historian, Yoshio Yamamori, suggests that there are historically two lines in the study of Seikatsu: one is the study of individual activities and aspects of Seikatsu in an objective and empirical way, and the other is the study of the essence of Seikatsu, meaning of people's life, and the principle of integrating them. Despite these scholarships, scientific and technological reductionism in academia had gradually avoided the broad and complex aspects of Seikatsu in the war-time and the post-war recovery development.[13] In other words, those who were aware of Seikatsu issues and consciously studied their relevance in the post-war reconstruction tried to realise the unification of the two lines of Seikatsu studies: as not only individual problems, but also the essence of people's lives.

Following WWII, influences from the Soviet Union and China promoted a focus on Seikatsu of under privileged people in the pursuit of independence from American capitalistic colonialism, inspiring left-wing intellectuals. However, American occupation policies during the Cold War spread a model of democratic life as a basic human right for everyone. Amid these dynamics, leading architects who had previously centred on state and economic concerns struggled to connect with this emerging interest in the Seikatsu of the people. However, as an eminent architectural historian and designer Chuta Ito and a leading scholar Hideto Kishida expressed in *Kenchiku to Seikatsu*, they had difficulties presenting alternative approaches beside their personal stories.[14]

Meanwhile, public housing for the general populace was constructed post-war by Nihon Jutaku Kodan and local government engineers. Despite the subsequent economic recovery, the wartime 'administrative principles of housing planning and methodology' remained in place. Criticising architects for their abstract approaches, engineers like Uzo Nishiyama argued they overlooked societal needs.[15] As Kazuhiko Honjo, a prominent figure within the Nihon Jutaku Kodan, observed, the initial focus of public housing initiatives was on the provision of temporary accommodation for population migration to urban areas and the reconstruction of communities devastated by disasters.[16] Beyond a limited integration of the modernism movement's ideas, Japanese public housing projects prioritised reducing floor space and improving economic, functional quality, scale, and amenities over concepts of well-being. Consequently, Seikatsu was framed through health, governance, economics and technology, sidelining a holistic well-being perspective that includes historical, psychological and cultural aspects of daily life.[17]

In this context, disciplines such as hygiene, folklore, sociology and home economics began addressing living spaces as humane environments, marking a shift from militarism to democracy espoused by the Occupation Forces. These changes reflected broader societal transformations and shaped approaches to architecture and well-being. Their ideas about the concept of living, and the influence of occupation, hygiene, folklore and life studies on evolving understandings of well-being, began to shape how (some) architects began to rethink the relationship between housing and well-being

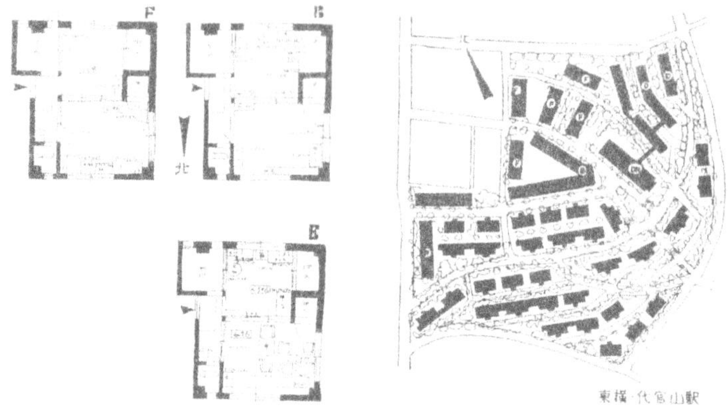

FIGURE 3.1 Dojunkai Daikanyama Apartment House, one model plan and site arrangement.
Source: Nishiyama, Uzo, Sumai Kokongaku, Shokokusha, 1989.

The Post-War Housing Problems and the Occupation Policies

The Post-War Reconstruction Housing Administration in the Early 1945–1950s

Public Housing philosophy and places in Japan during the mid-twentieth century witnessed a shift towards recognising the value of Seikatsu due to a number of factors directly related to WWII including a paucity of housing. The post-war reconstruction housing administration from the mid-1940s to the 1950s was prompted by two key factors: the destruction of cities by air raids during the War and the return of many war veterans to Japan. The resulting housing shortage, estimated at over 4.2 million homes, presented a significant challenge for the government.[18] In the aftermath of the war, the government established the Reconstruction Housing Agency, with the primary objective of facilitating the work of construction engineers from the Jutaku Eidan.[19] The agency promptly initiated the formulation of a reconstruction housing construction plan.

FIGURE 3.2 Dojunkai Daikanyama Apartment House, Interior photo of its kitchen.
Source: Sato, Shigeru, etc. Dojunkai no Apartment to Sono Jidai, Kajima Shuppannkai, 1998.

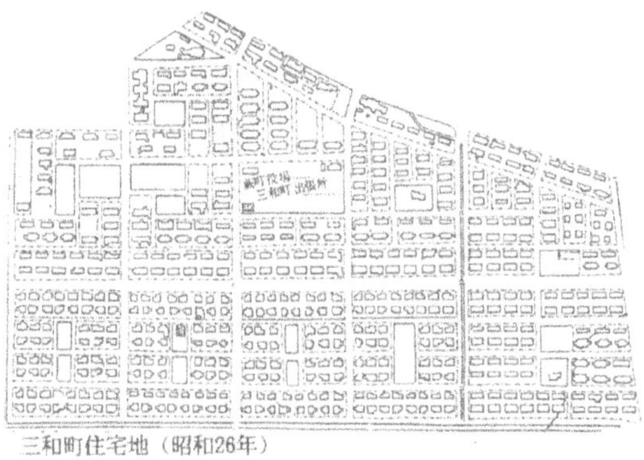

FIGURE 3.3 Jutaku Eidan Mitsuwacho Jutakuchi, site plan 1951.

Source: Arizuka, Reiko. 'Jutaku Eidan Mitsuwa cho Jutakuchi no hensen to kyoju prosesu (Examination of the Transformation of Jutaku Eidan Mitsuwa cho residence and its process of dwelling) 1,' Nihon Kenchikuk gakkai taikai gakujutu kougaishu, 1996.

The initial challenge was to help those affected by the war so that they could survive the winter. It was estimated that approximately 70% of the approximately 20% of the city's housing victims residing in temporary huts and would be unable to survive the winter of 1945. Accordingly, the 'Outline for the Construction of Emergency Temporary Housing in Disaster-Stricken Cities' was established, and the early provision of approximately 300,000 emergency housing units was initiated. With the support of the Occupation Forces, the construction of a minimum scale of emergency winter housing of 6.25 tsubo ($20m^2$) finally commenced.[20]

Meanwhile, the Occupation Forces confiscated materials for the construction of large-scale camps, residential areas and family housing. In response, the Special Construction Division of the War Damage Reconstruction Agency was established in 1946 with the objective of constructing 20,000 family housing units for the Occupation Forces. Given the intensifying scarcity of materials, the Housing Authority introduced even more

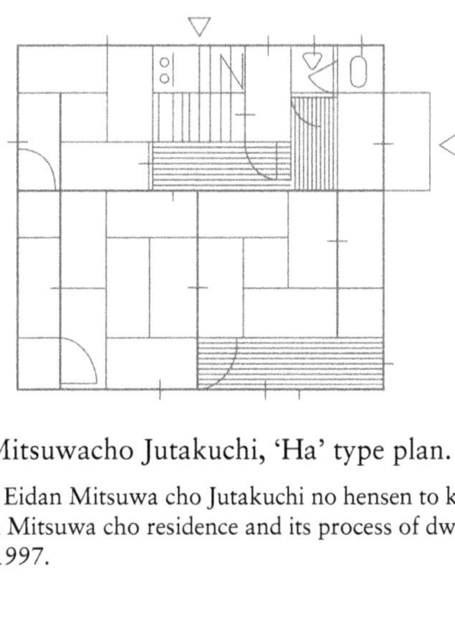

FIGURE 3.4 Jutaku Eidan Mitsuwacho Jutakuchi, 'Ha' type plan.

Source: Arizuka, Reiko. 'Jutaku Eidan Mitsuwa cho Jutakuchi no hensen to kyoju prosesu(Examination of the Transformation of Jutaku Eidan Mitsuwa cho residence and its process of dwelling) 2,' Nihon Kenchikuk gakkai taikai gakujutu kougaishu, 1997.

rigorous 'Reconstruction Housing Standards' than those that had been in force during the war.[21] However, in 1946, the Occupation Forces abruptly terminated the Jutaku Eidan as a socialist organisation. A significant number of the Corporation's construction engineers were compelled to engage in the construction of facilities and housing for the Occupation Forces. Consequently, Japan, which was experiencing a severe shortage of resources, was deprived of a specialist organisation capable of implementing housing reconstruction policies. This resulted in a number of challenges, including a shortage of housing, the improvement of living conditions, the rationalisation of the building trade and production systems and the democratisation of the professional system.[22] The War Damage Reconstruction Agency continued until November 1947, with reconstruction work being carried out with a long-term perspective. This involved the implementation of urban planning for roads, parks, green spaces and other amenities in the disaster areas. However, the Dodge Line, which curtailed the excessive investment in national reconstruction by the Occupation Forces, was issued in 1949. This resulted in urban structure improvement and housing measures being insufficient.

The influence of the Occupation Forces on the Transformation of Japanese Interior design

IAI (Kogei Shidojo (Industrial Arts Institute)) was established by the Ministry of Commerce and Industry with the objective of exchanging information with overseas countries, conducting research into industrial design-related technologies, evaluating the performance of industrial products and engaging in technical research with the aim of improving the design of Japanese industrial products. In its official journal, *Kogei News*, the significance of design as a solution to everyday problems was elucidated in terms of the creative significance of rationality, necessity and joy in life. Concurrently, the introduction of overseas lifestyles and values to Japan was accompanied by discussions on the meaning of regional industry, lifestyles and cultural uniqueness. Conversations were held on physical norms such as furniture and posture, as well as regional economic development. Additionally, IAI designers and engineers endorsed the design of chairs and desks that were introduced to Japan through the lifestyle improvement movement. Furthermore, they conducted a survey of crafts and industrialisation in various regions of Japan and its colonies. They also worked on standardised production and mass production. In 1933, Bruno Taut was invited to provide guidance on the design of standard furniture and housing.[23] In 1940, Charlotte Perriand was invited to Japan, where she articulated the view that design is about 'constantly creating new things through the rich encounter between life and objects.'[24] Additionally, she advocated for the importance of respecting the rationality of regional and historical design and production methods, as well as the principles of form that optimise functionality, aesthetic standards and materials.

Following WWII, from 1946 onwards, the IAI design department, under the guidance of the Occupation Forces, produced 20,000 pieces of furniture, fittings and fixtures for housing in a three-month period, with participation and cooperation across hundreds of factories nationwide.[25] The design department of the Occupation Forces provided comprehensive guidance on technical and design aspects throughout the process. Japanese designers and engineers were instructed in the functionality, durability and cost-effectiveness of integrated systems for the production of mass-market, standardised housing in the US. They were also taught the technology of panel construction and were encouraged to design for consumers who prioritised rationality, functionality, comfort and simplicity in their lifestyles. This led to a greater awareness of the significance of design in enhancing people's lives, with a notable influence on post-war Japanese lifestyles.[26]

Kappei Toyoguchi, the leader of the design team at the IAI, had previously absorbed the ideas of the Bauhaus and CIAM. Upon joining the Industrial Arts Institute, he was introduced to the importance of a comprehensive architectural vision that re-examined the relationship between architecture and craft, functionalist design that fulfilled the practical needs of everyday life, and the development of standardised furniture and products for mass production of high-quality furniture. Before the war, he received guidance from Taut. However, Toyoguchi asserts that the pivotal moment occurred when he was engaged in the actual production of American furniture design, thereby acquiring a tangible and pragmatic comprehension of the interconnection between furniture and lifestyle. He asserted that it was crucial to gain insight into American functionalism, which prioritises human sensitivity, as opposed to European modernism, which is largely theoretical.[27]

Tokujiro Kaneko also posited that the Japanese military exhibited a mechanical and materialistic design ethos, whereas the Americans prioritised human life. The Japanese traditionally regarded furniture as a functional item for work purposes, whereas the Americans placed greater emphasis on its physical comfort as a component of everyday life.[28] Consequently, designers were compelled to re-evaluate the role of furniture in enhancing the comfort and convenience of daily life. They also recognised the importance of incorporating practical design principles to improve the quality of life for the public.

The Introduction of the American Lifestyle by the Occupation Forces

The introduction of the American lifestyle by the Occupation Forces and the subsequent promotion of industrial design had a significant impact on Japanese architects and companies. This is evident in the collection of designs for the dependent family housing for the occupation forces that were published in 1948 by the IAI and the Design Branch. The publication elegantly showcased the architectural design of American residences tailored to the needs of ordinary families. It featured detailed illustrations of the interior furnishings, including kitchen, bathroom and toilet designs, as well as furniture, tableware and window treatments. Furthermore, the publication conveyed the image of a comfortable lifestyle, complete with gardens, schools, hospitals and theatres in the surrounding area. This facilitated comprehension of the American lifestyle among Japanese architects and designers, and it was also introduced to the public as an object of familiar admiration.

In 1947, the *Kogei News* articulated that the objective of the post-war activities of the IAI was twofold: firstly, to expand the sales channels for Japanese design products in the international market; and secondly, to improve the living environment of the Japanese people.[29] The objective of Shinji Koike, the ideological leader of the IAI, was to adapt the concept of industrial design to Japanese culture and lifestyle and to humanise industrial technology. In 1948, Koike held a real-life exhibition of American industrial design in Yokohama with the support of the Occupation Forces. This exhibition displayed American home life in a model room in a three-dimensional, scientific way. In 1949, he

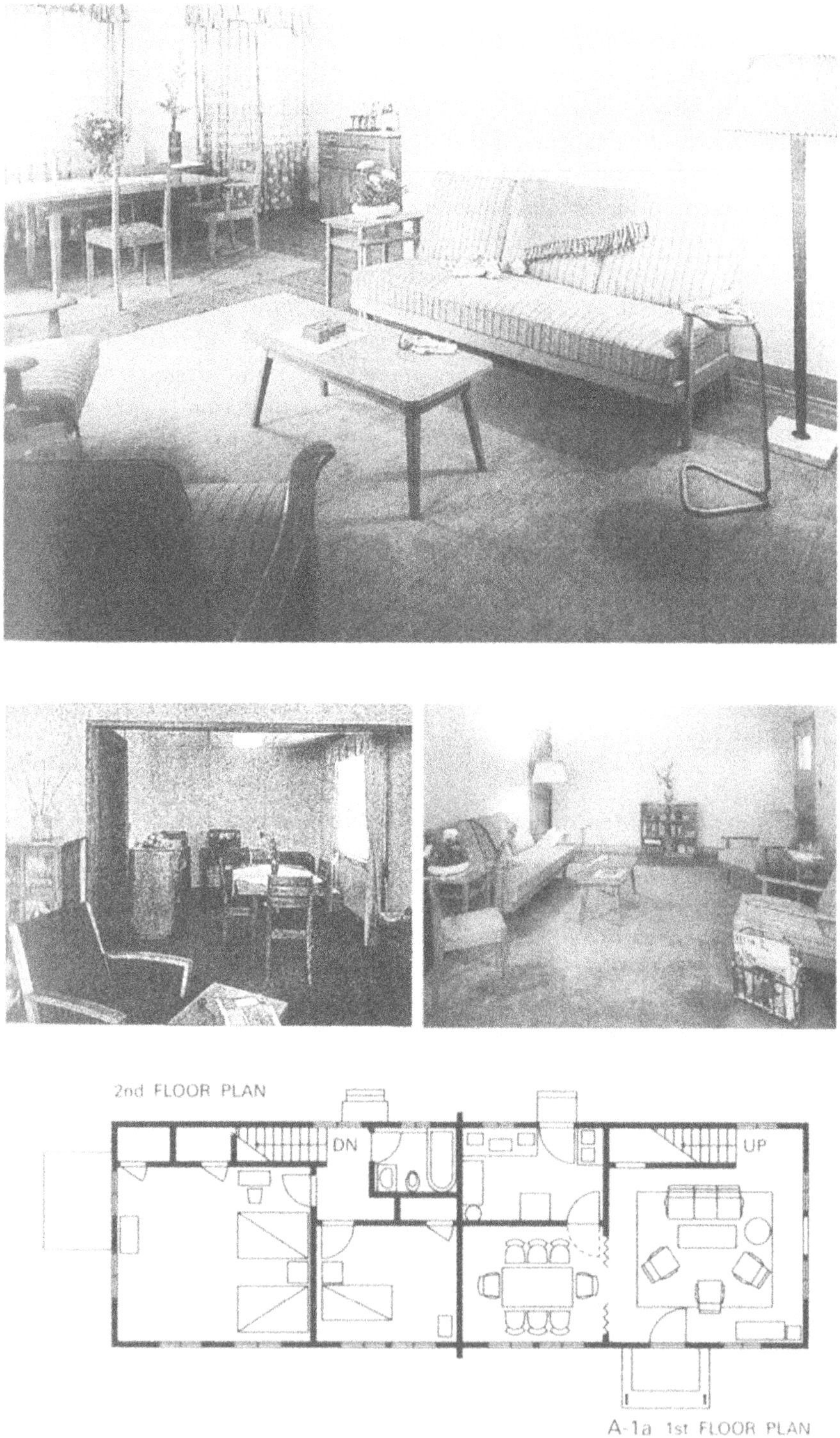

FIGURE 3.5 Interior picture and plan of a dependent house published in the catalogue.

Source: Koizumi, Kazuko, etc. Senryogun Jutaku no Kiroku vol.2, Sumai no Toshokan Kenkyukyoku, 1999.

transformed the notion of craft into the concept of industrial design, which was related to both industry and everyday life. He also explained that it was essential to humanise industrial technology.[30]

The Impact of the Occupation Forces on Post-War Public Housing Projects

Following the completion of post-war housing for the Occupation Forces in various locations by the design branch, the Occupation Forces began releasing housing materials for the construction of Japanese people's reconstruction housing in 1948.[31] The municipal housing constructed using the released materials was of a scale that corresponded to the standards for post-war housing for disaster victims established by the Jutaku Eidan and employed 2 × 4 panels that had been utilised in American wartime housing. In the Toyama Haitsu housing area, the Occupation Forces helped the Tokyo metropolitan office to conduct an experiment to change the refugees' lifestyle by providing cheap beds, organising a support office to teach residents how to arrange furniture and live on wooden floors without tatami mats in a model house. In this area of 1200 households, schools, a police station, a fire station, a food delivery office, a post office, a community centre,

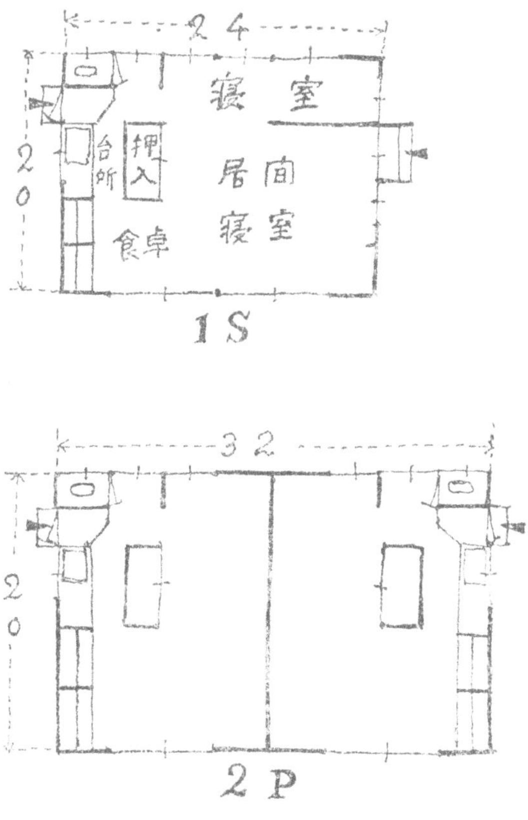

FIGURE 3.6 Toyama Heights House as 'Experimental House for a new Housing Life.'

Source: Kon, Wajiro, Jukyo ron, Kon Wajiro Zenshu, vol.4, Domesu shuppan, 1971.

FIGURE 3.7 Photos of the Toyama Haitsu, one of the Tokyo municipal housings built with the released materials from the Occupation Force. SCAP record, DSCN5693.

a bathhouse, a hospital, a kindergarten and a vocational centre were built to create a new townscape. It was initially planned for the shortage of tatami material but was also intended as an experiment to change Japanese people's lifestyle.[32]

Ken Ichiura and Kameki Tsuchiura, who had participated in the post-war Occupation Forces design branch, had prior experience in designing Western-style Trockenbau prior to the war. Consequently, they were able to combine the construction methods of

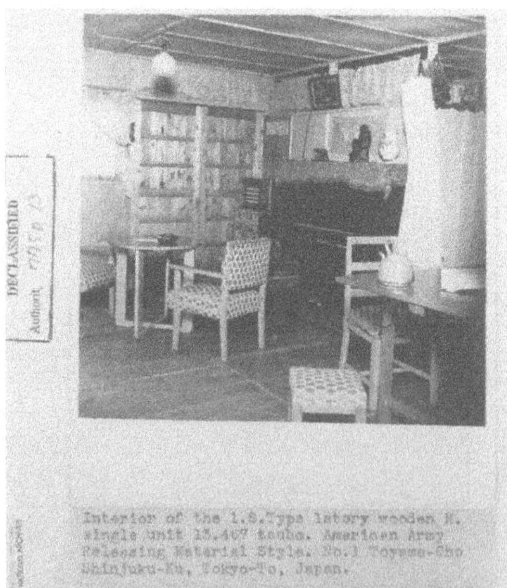

FIGURE 3.8 Photos of the Toyama Haitsu, one of the Tokyo municipal housings built with the released materials from the Occupation Force. SCAP Record, DSCN5698.

American-style prefabricated housing with the skills of Japanese wooden carpenters with minimal difficulty. The construction of the release housing was intended to provide support to businesses facing challenges due to a lack of work opportunities and a significant decline in the number of skilled carpenters and craftsmen. Additionally, it aimed to impart new technical guidance to the Japanese construction industry through the introduction of altered construction methods.[33]

The architects who participated in the design branch played an instrumental role in disseminating American design concepts and techniques in post-war architectural education and the design of commercial, public, residential and urban projects. Ichiura occupied a central position in the research and design of the Jutaku Eidan standard plans prior to the war and played a leading role in the design of the pre- and post-war public housing. The adoption of an American lifestyle that prioritised comfort and enjoyment, as evidenced by the emphasis on dining rooms, kitchens and facilities in small living spaces, and functional planning, which was further emphasized in the post-war period, represented a significant improvement in the quality of the space.

Health Condition of Living as the Fundamental of Well-Being

Researchers led by Kan Sato of the National Institute of Public Health conducted more than 3,000 surveys on the living conditions of people in the remaining houses in Azabu and Ogikubo in 1945. They focused on the conditions of people living in poor housing and living together, the conditions of people in non-war-damaged cities and the transition of housing density. Their surveys provided invaluable insight into the reality of the housing shortage. In particular, the potential health risks associated with the rapid population growth and overcrowding in urban areas following the war were emphasised. The survey results demonstrated the direct impact of poor housing conditions on the transmission of disease and the disruption of daily life and confirmed that the quality of housing is inextricably linked to public health.[34]

The research study also elucidated the criteria for evaluating the living environment, with reference to the World Health Organization's (WHO) 1945 definition of health and the fundamental principles of healthful housing established by the American Public Health Association in 1946. The following criteria were identified as essential for evaluating the quality of the living environment:

1 The prevention of disasters.
2 The satisfaction of human physiological needs and environmental conditions.
3 The satisfaction of psychological needs for living.
4 The maintenance of conditions that prevent the occurrence of disease and infection.
5 The satisfaction of emotional needs; and
6 The satisfaction of living economy.[35]

The focus on these six criteria demonstrated that the quality of housing was not solely a matter of physical safety but was also associated with the general well-being of the residents. Consequently, enhancing housing conditions represents a crucial aspect of improving public health.

In 1947, the Ministry of Construction, which was established by the merger of the Reconstruction Agency for War Victims and the Ministry of Home Affairs, initiated the 'Minimum Housing Standards Research Group' within the Architectural Institute of

Japan between 1947 and 1949.[36] The study group addressed post-war housing issues from a multidisciplinary perspective, encompassing architectural planning, housing policy, building hygiene and epidemiology. It formulated construction standards for public housing, which were designed to enhance the quality of housing in underprivileged districts.[37] These standards subsequently formed the basis for the provision of housing using public funds in Japan's post-war housing policy, thereby facilitating significant improvements in the living environment of residents.

The Gendered Contributions of Female Architects on Individual Well-Being, Empowerment and the Importance of the Domestic Realm

Sakae Komada's Experiment with Living in Takanawa Apartments and media Coverage

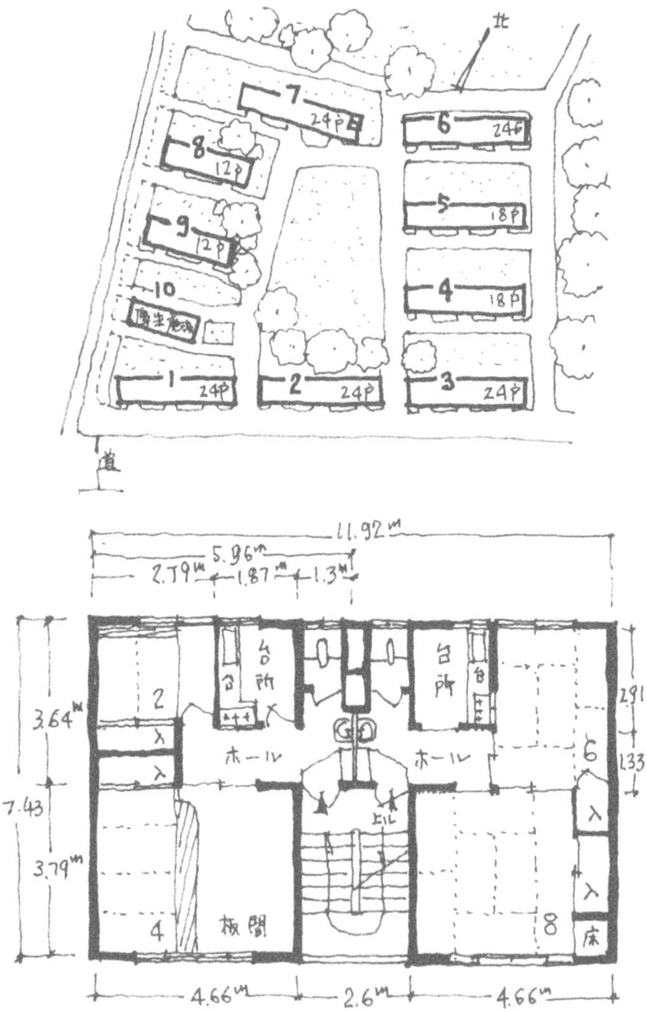

FIGURE 3.9 Takanawa Apartments, site plan and the room type where Komada lived.

Source: Nishiyama, Uzo, Sumai Kokongaku Gendai Nihon Jutakushi, Shokokusha, 1989.

Sakae Komada (1901–1995), a prominent researcher at the National Institute of Public Health, explored links between post-war illnesses and urban housing, alongside studying the daily lives of rural housewives in 1949. Educated in economics and sociology at Mills College between 1928 and 1932, US, and later as a social worker in Japan, Komada has been recognised by scholars like Akiko Nakajima as a pioneering feminist architectural figure advocating for human rights and well-being in post-war housing.[38] Her work emphasised how housing conditions impacted well-being, both physically and mentally. Her participation in a 1948 housing experiment at Takanawa Apartments demonstrated the value of residents' self-driven renovations to suit their needs.[39] Responding to resident requests, she expanded entrances, added washbasins and implemented structural changes that enhanced thermal comfort, showcasing her belief in empowering individuals, particularly women, to actively improve their living spaces. Through magazines and NHK's 'Women's Time' radio series, Komada championed practical independence by sharing strategies for efficient housework, home improvements and the creation of functional, well-lit kitchens, encouraging women to shape their domestic environments as an extension of well-being. Her 'Beautiful Living Handbook' further validated the role of time management and self-sufficiency in achieving a quality daily life.

Meeting Katherine Bauer and the Formation of Sociological Environmental Research

In 1954, Sakae Komada undertook studies at the University of California, Berkeley, where she received support from Katherine Bauer, a distinguished housing policy expert of the period. During this visit, Komada observed the implementation of public housing and welfare policies in the US, thereby deepening her understanding of the impact of the living environment on welfare and health. In particular, she came to understand that welfare and housing in the US were inextricably linked, and that housing was not merely a physical space, but an important factor that directly affected people's well-being.

In 1957, Bauer undertook a visit to Japan, during which she undertook a tour of public housing and housing complexes in Japan, with Komada acting as her guide. She offered a scathing critique of Japan's housing policy, noting that the post-war public housing complexes in Japan provided living environments that were strikingly like those of wartime worker housing. Bauer posited that Japan's public housing projects were devoid of a foundational philosophy aimed at enhancing the quality of life and well-being of residents.[40] Her remarks prompted a re-evaluation of the underlying philosophy of public housing projects in Japan and had a considerable impact on Komada. In response to Bauer's criticisms, Komada furthered her research into the relationship between the living environment and the mental health and well-being of residents, identifying this as an important tool for improving the welfare and quality of life of residents.

From the 1960s onwards, Komada concentrated her research efforts on the living environment of entire cities, developing an approach to understanding it from a sociological perspective. Through a large-scale research project commissioned by the Economic Planning Agency on the topic of 'the living environment and health of urban residents,' Komada conducted a detailed investigation into the relationship between housing and the well-being of residents, including an analysis of the impact of housing on mental health, population issues and the nature of family life.[41] In this survey, she collaborated with experts in a range of fields in eight residential areas. A questionnaire survey was conducted of 2,800 households in seven of the survey areas. The survey investigated three key areas: (1) the relationship between housing and family life, (2) matters related to housing and (3) matters related to health. In addition, in-depth interviews were conducted with one-fifth of the households about two key areas: (1) housing and (2) the residents and their family life. The relationship between the living environment and mental well-being was also examined. The characteristics of this perspective are articulated in the following words from the opening of its Chapter 3:

> We posit that health is not merely the absence of mental illness or disorders. Rather, it must be considered from the vantage point of how individuals live their lives, including how they interact with family, neighbours, and other people with whom they have involuntary contact, and how they cope with the various challenging problems that arise in life.[42]

Komada and her colleagues conducted an interview survey of housewives to investigate the relationship between mental health and the utilisation of domestic space, the emotional perception of the home, and the economic and physical conditions of the house. The findings of the survey indicated that the quality of housing has a notable influence on mental health. It was observed that owning a house or renting a public house is more beneficial for mental health than renting a private house. Additionally, the survey revealed that everyone requires a minimum of 3.5 tatami mats for their living space. Furthermore, the mental health of housewives was identified as a significant factor influencing family life. In other words, the survey demonstrated that the form and quality of housing ownership is directly related to mental and social well-being. It elucidated the impact of the living environment on the mental health, social connections and sense of happiness of residents, emphasising the necessity of a sociological perspective in housing policy. Considering the insights gleaned from Bauer, Komada also adopted a comprehensive approach to housing environment research in Japan, placing greater emphasis on the living conditions and psychological state of residents rather than solely focusing on equipment and sanitation technology.

The research conducted by Komada emphasised the necessity for social housing improvements based on the well-being of residents, as opposed to merely focusing on physical improvements to the housing. This research subsequently served as the foundation for following generations of comprehensive environmental space research, including the development of environmental theory.[43]

Wajiro Kon's Advocacy of Studies of Seikatsu and Dwelling

Background of Wajiro Kon's Study of Seikatsu

Wajiro Kon, a member of the Minimum Housing Standards Research Group, conducted research on rural life and living environments from a folklore and human geography perspective from the 1910s. Specifically, he engaged in urban life surveys

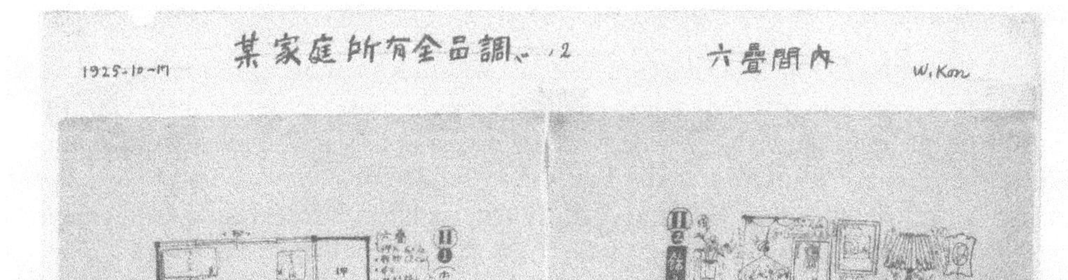

FIGURE 3.10 Wajiro Kon's Newly Married Couple's House Interior analysis in Modernologio.
Source: Kogakuin University, Kon Wajiro Collection.

with detailed sketches of people's fashion and dwelling space after the Kanto Great Earthquake in 1923.[44] His research developed a theory of the origins of housing, paying particular attention to relationship between housing, local customs, production activities and the urban and natural environment in minor daily activities. He posited that the well-being of housing should be considered with an emphasis on the actual conditions and psychological state of the lives of ordinary people.[45] Additionally, Kon asserted that domestic science from the Meiji era had placed an emphasis on economic evolution, civility, efficiency and beautification of family life and needed to be more human-centered.

In 1936, Kon became the chair of Home Science Research and published a series of article in Katei Kagaku (Home Science). He argued that, in the past, we recognised human life with an emphasis on the reproduction of labour power. Now with completely new forms of leisure and entertainment, he suggested that we should consider the connections between rest and work and can anticipate a new form of Seikatsu studies. These ideas foreshadowed some his work that came to fruition during the post-WWII period.[46] In addition, in 1941, he collaborated with the Dojun-kai to present a proposal for improving housing in farming, mountain and fishing villages that emphasised regional characteristics, historical customs and social relationships.[47]

Dwelling Studies

In 1945, immediately following the conclusion of WWII, Kon published *Jūsei-katsu* (Dwelling) for those who had suffered losses and disruptions because of the war. Here, he argued that the people must actively construct their living environment and move away from the wartime period, when it was thought that the so-called noble way of life in our country was to have a mind but no body, and ethics but no life.[48] Furthermore, he highlighted that, in the haste to 'construct' housing in the post-war reconstruction, the fundamental significance of housing as a foundation for life had not been sufficiently contemplated. He thus proposed a re-evaluation of the optimal form of housing, one that aligned with the activities of daily life, including rest, socialisation, work, production and recreation.[49]

Kon highlighted that research into hygiene and living standards during wartime had concentrated on the reproduction of labour, with rationalisation being the sole social policy addressed, and proposed new research into hygiene and living be re-examined from the perspective of overall quality of life, encompassing not only work and production but also leisure and rest. In 'Seikatsu gaku eno Koso'(1951), he further suggested that the study of Seikatsu should be a key area of focus.[50] By analysing the relationship between family, home and house, he proposed to emphasise the idea of Ba(place) as the key to the study of housing, encompassing all these ideas in a realistic way.[51] In particular, he put forth the argument that enhancements to the quality of life in Japanese living spaces were imperative, and he presented the following three perspectives:

1 An examination of the ways in which people move through and use space in their daily Seikatsu.

  Here, Kon identified the 'shift from calculating money to calculating time' as a significant transformation in the post-war era, emphasising the necessity to re-evaluate the optimal allocation of living time and the associated psychological considerations. For instance, he illustrated the daily routines of farmers and highlighted the dearth of respite for housewives, along with the roles and behavioural patterns of family members. He also examined the movement of family members within the domestic environment, highlighting the necessity to alleviate the burden of housework. This analysis not only provided a rationalisation of daily life but also furnished the fundamental data for a review of the social quality of individual daily lives, which had multiple meanings according to the hierarchies between people in the dwelling space.

2 An examination of the correlation between mental and physical health regarding Seikatsu.

  Here, he proposed that the quality of life should be evaluated not merely in terms of function and rationality but also from both mental and physical health. Kon compared the living spaces of manual and mental labourers in Hokkaido and focused on the impact on the occupants' mood and health, which differed depending on the type of work. This analysis indicated that rooms need to enable people to recover from mental and sensory fatigue. For that purpose, rooms with flexible uses are conducive. Furthermore, he demonstrated that housing plans should consider the balance between socialisation, interaction with nature, as well as home management. The study demonstrates how the design of living spaces can facilitate the diverse well-being of residents, extending beyond mere functionality.

3 An examination of the multifaceted functions of living spaces.
Kon examined the concept of the farmhouse as a space that encompasses both production and consumption and demonstrated its versatility in accommodating a range of life events and rituals. He also highlighted the limitations of such living spaces, which were based on a feudalistic view of labour that did not recognise independence or humanity. Here, he emphasised the need to improve the way living spaces are used to contribute to health and well-being. In particular, he emphasised the necessity of considering the living environment not only in terms of work efficiency but also in terms of its capacity to facilitate a change of mood and mental relaxation.

In sum, Kon advanced the argument that housing should not be viewed from the perspective of economic and social policy alone. Instead, he proposed that it should be reevaluated as a 'base of life' that can reduce human relationships and economic burdens in post-war society and improve the overall lives of residents. Furthermore, he emphasised the necessity for architects to consider changes in living habits and human relationships, and to view housing planning as part of a theory of dwelling.[52]

The Practical Application of Based on Seikatsu Study and Communication of Empathy

Kon utilised the findings of his housing studies to support the operation of the lifestyle improvement extension a programme, which was consulted on by Maude Wilson. Wilson had been dispatched to the Ministry of Agriculture and Forestry by the Occupying Forces following the conclusion of WWII. The objective of the lifestyle improvement extension programme was to democratise rural areas and enhance living standards by disseminating fundamental knowledge about life, encompassing nutrition and cooking, household skills, cleaning and child-rearing practices. Additionally, they sought to upgrade the kitchens and toilets in farming villages and alter the conventional wisdom about the role of women. In particular, the members aimed to transform people's lifestyle from only working hard to also enjoying their lives, thinking, dreaming and discussing about their future.

In his treatise, *Ju-seikatsu* Kon posited that housing should not be regarded as a mere physical space, but rather as a locale for a multiplicity of activities, including rest, work, socialisation and entertainment. His philosophy of enhancing the quality of life entailed a cultural and social perspective on the concept of living space. In rural areas, improvements to the living environment might result in a reduction of available space, which could potentially lead to an increase in the burden on women regarding housework and mental stress. To address this potential issue, Kon sought to enhance the quality of life by developing strategies to facilitate the transition from fieldwork to housework and by establishing venues for familial gatherings.

Kon's approach to improving people's lives was also a practical proposal that sought to comprehend the heterogeneous values that exist in the domestic and local community contexts and to pursue collective well-being through empathetic engagement. His proposals for housing and lifestyle improvement placed an emphasis on the importance of

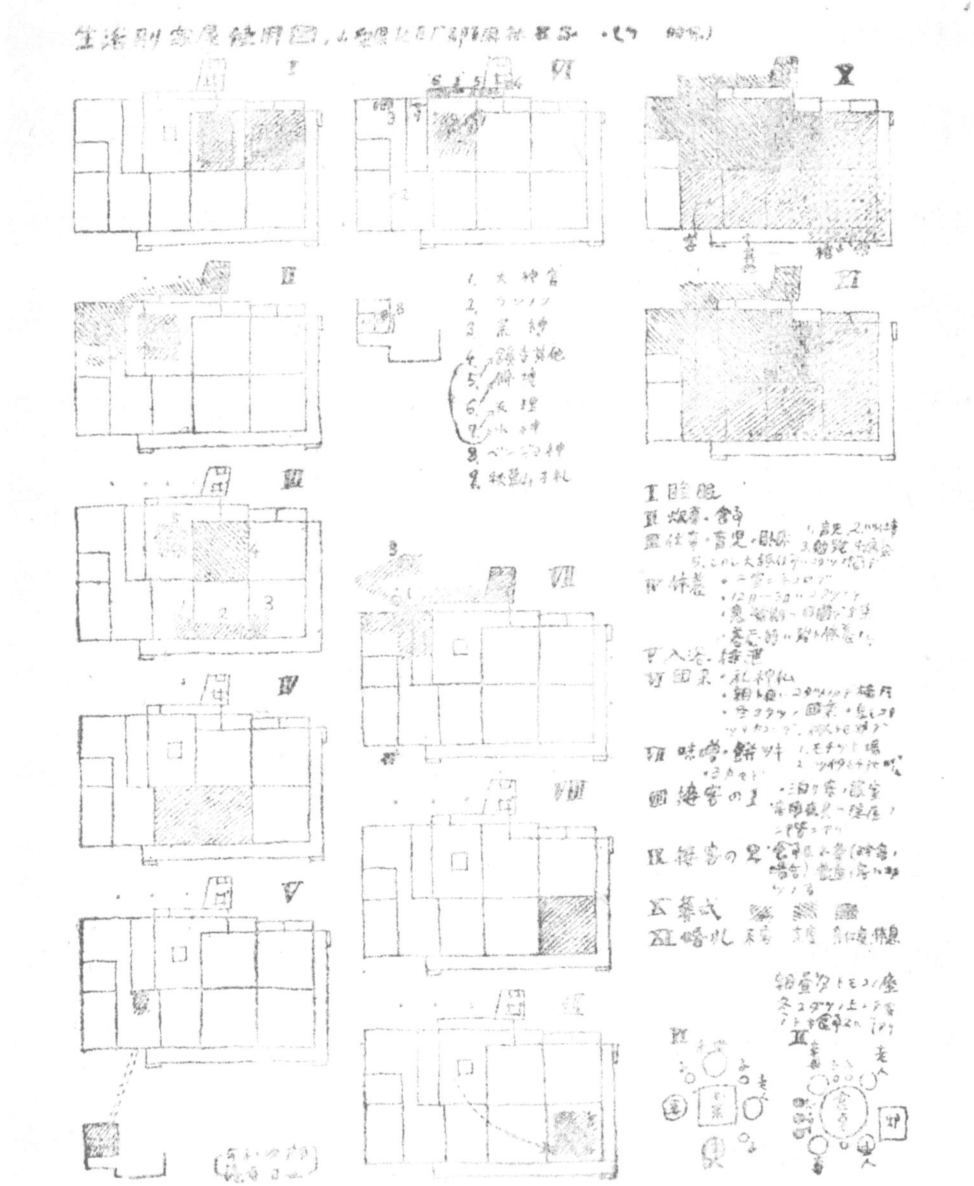

FIGURE 3.11 Diagram of the used space in a house according daily activities.

Source: Kon, Wajiro, Juseikatsu, Kangen sousho, Kangen sha, 1945.

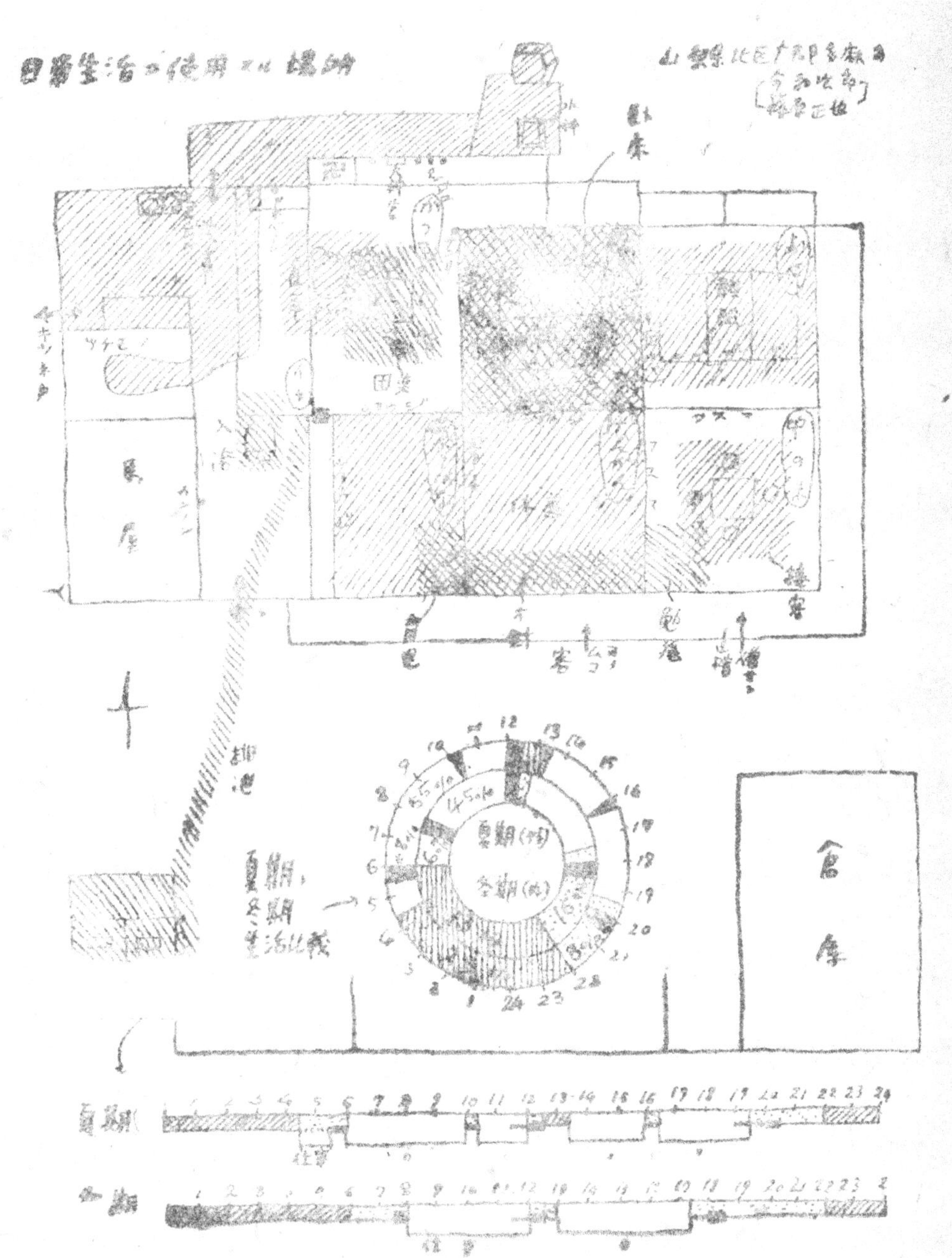

FIGURE 3.12 Places for everyday use and yearly calendar.

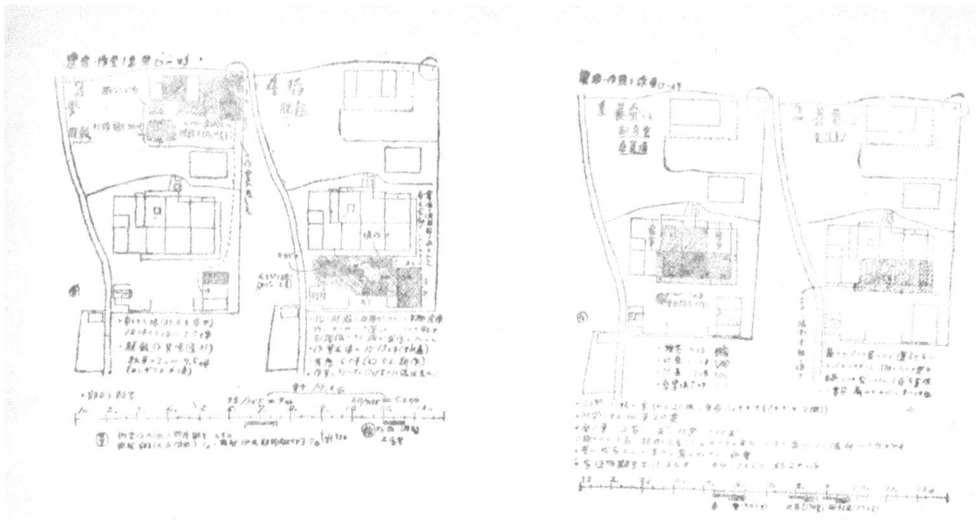

FIGURE 3.13 Locations of the agricultural activities around a house.

both independent and cooperative activities and demonstrated how residents themselves could achieve well-being in the context of changing rural villages and local communities. In 1944, he designed a communal house for five families who had lost their homes in a big fire.[53] While designing the house, he conducted interviews with the families to realise their ideas, trying to preserve the local characteristics of timber construction, along with rationalising the planning of the house and minimising the cost of materials. The five houses are connected by corridors and share a common area with a large bathroom and kitchen. They show the influence of the war-time restriction of freedom of lifestyle by inter-community surveillance, but at the same time, Kon's intention to satisfy both independent and collective ways of living.

In 1972, one year before his death, Kawazoe and eminent scholars of anthropology, sociology, folklore, cultural policy and design gathered to establish Seikatsu Gakkai (Academy of Lifeology) and posted Kon as the first president to succeed and develop his ideas and works by later generation.

The Dilemma of Early Post-War Architects and Their Limited Understanding of Seikatsu

The NAU Architectural Movement inquiring the Role of Architects and Functionalism

The New Architecture Union (NAU), established in 1947, was a post-war organisation that convened architects, engineers and craftsmen from across the country to deliberate on the social function of architecture.[54] In order to avoid any potential conflict with the Occupation Forces, the organisation shared the democratic and pacifist ideals that had been advocated by the CIAM in the 1920s. Its aim was to maintain enthusiasm for post-war architectural reconstruction. In his 1947 publication, *Kenchiku no Hyumanizumu*, Ryuichi Hamaguchi underscored the significance of functionalism for Japanese architects in comprehending international architectural movements and professionalism.[55] He

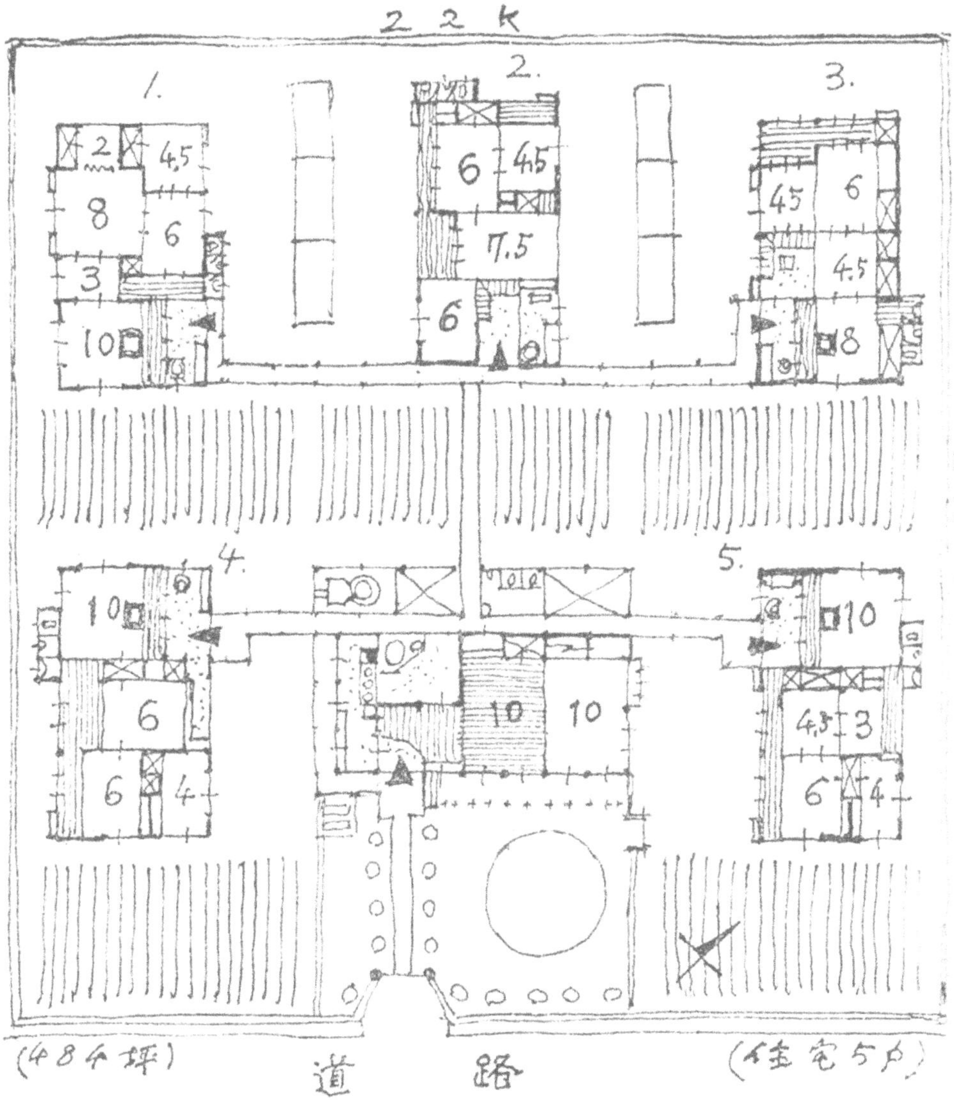

FIGURE 3.14 Kon's plan for the five family's collective housing proposed in 1944.

Source: Kon, Wajiro, Jukyo ron, Kon Wajiro Zenshu, vol.4, Domesu shuppan, 1971.

further emphasised the importance of addressing the themes proposed by CIAM, namely, minimum housing and industrialisation of housing production. He underscored that the design of minimal housing entails the provision of the minimal amount of air, light and space necessary for people to live healthily, thereby exemplifying the concept of 'architecture for people.' Furthermore, he asserted that this was a foundational tenet of modern architecture, grounded in humanism and social production theory, and a pivotal aspect in the reconstruction of Japanese architectural culture.

Conversely, Marxist architects were critical of the CIAM's prioritisation of design. Additionally, there was an ongoing debate in Europe regarding a review of the CIAM's principles. However, due to the prevailing political circumstances and the necessity for expeditious architectural reconstruction, this did not result in any substantial discourse.[56] Kon, who espoused the tenets of social democracy, endeavoured to foster collaboration by re-examining the import of the NAU's continued existence. In the 1949 declaration, he stated that in order to achieve architecture for the people, it was essential to democratise the architectural system, protect architects, protect the people's cultural heritage, democratise education, and collaborate with international architectural movements. It was further argued that it was necessary to be closely involved in the lives of the people and to improve their standards. Nevertheless, the collaboration between architects did not advance, and NAU was disbanded.

Technology, Functionalism and Well-Being

The post-war period in Japan saw a rapid expansion in reconstruction work and the housing market for smaller properties, which in turn led to a shortage of resources and carpenters. This resulted in the introduction of new construction techniques which became a significant issue. The prefabricated construction techniques developed during the war at the Jutaku Eidan and the IAI were also developed in the construction department of the Reconstruction Agency. Additionally, Kunio Maekawa, a student of Le Corbusier, contributed to the development of the prefabricated housing of the Nihon Jutaku Kodan (Japan Housing Cooperation).[57] However, Maekawa experienced difficulties in reconciling the differences between the ideals, social roles and attitudes towards housing of Japanese and French architects, and he continued to raise issues with Nihon Jutaku Kodan.

A member of the corporation later provided the following commentary on his attitude: 'During Maekawa's tenure, there were no citizens who made proposals or who were directly involved.... The architects themselves became increasingly aware of this through their experiences of engaging with the government.'[58] When architects create architecture in response to the needs of citizens, they must be conscious of the quality of the architecture they can provide. As societal expectations of architecture evolve and the role of architecture within society expands, it becomes increasingly intertwined with economic considerations. It is pertinent to question whether technology can genuinely contribute to the happiness of individuals. What can architecture offer in response to the social environment that is required? Maekawa was the sole individual engaged in seeking answers to these questions.

In 1951, the foundations of post-war housing policy in Japan were established with the establishment of the Nihon Jutaku Kodan, Koei Jutaku (Municipal Housing) and the Jutaku Kinyu Koko (Housing Finance Corporation). The Housing Finance Corporation established standard housing plans as conditions for loans, and the '51C Model,' comprising 12–18 tsubo (43–54 m^2) in size, with a dining room/kitchen and two rooms, was adopted for the RC apartment blocks constructed by the Nihon Jutaku Kodan.[59] The Building Standards Law, enacted in 1955, established minimum standards for housing structures, hygiene and living environments. Local governments subsequently initiated the rental and sale of welfare-oriented public housing on a nationwide scale.

Furthermore, large-scale public housing developments were promoted as a means of addressing the reduction in housing size and the deterioration of the urban environment. Maekawa's Harumi Apartments for Nihon Jutaku Kodan were designed in accordance with Le Corbusier's concepts, utilising a skeleton-infill and prefabricated construction methodology. The objective was to create a living space that prioritised well-being, which was based on the modern movement ideologies

Another major influence on post-war Japanese architectural theory and design in the 1950s came from Walter Gropius. In 1954, Gropius visited Japan with the support of the Rockefeller Foundation. After observing the situation in the Japanese architectural community, he argued that rather than unnecessarily adopting foreign technology and design during the post-war transition period, Japan should retain the good aspects of its traditional architectural technology and design. He also pointed out that this would serve as a model for a total approach to architecture in relation to global architectural ideas and design. This total architecture meant that the technology, planning and form of architecture should be deeply connected to lifestyle and social relations. The architect Masachika Kurata, who translated Gropius's book *Scope of Total Architecture* into Japanese as *Seikatsu Kukan no Sozo (The Creation of Space for Seikatsu)*, was one of Kon's students.[60] Kurata appealed to Japanese architects of the time to pay more attention to the relationship between Gropius's theory and the idea of Seikatsu.

Gropius's perspective was expressed in the design of Kiyoshi Seike's minimalist house; and the panel construction method was later adopted by Ken Ichiura in the Nihon Jutaku Kodan projects. However, these architects mainly realised Gropius's ideas in their structural designs. It is difficult to identify the architect who theorised and applied Gropius's ideals in relation to Seikatsu as a turning point in the fundamental perspective of architectural planning and production and put them into practice in public housing projects. Rather, we see the architect Kiyoshi Ikebe as someone who, free from the constraints of Le Corbusier's and Gropius's ideals, sought to re-examine the relationship between architectural technology and human life from the perspective of Japanese tradition, and to re-examine the purpose of architecture from the perspective of the well-being of the people's Seikatsu.

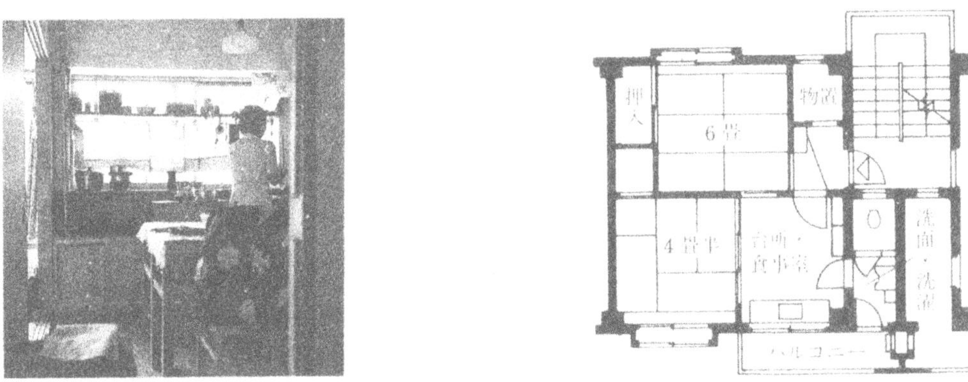

FIGURE 3.15 Plan of 51C model designed by Kodan Housing Corporation with Yoshitake and Suzuki.

Source: Suzuki, Shigefumi, *Suzuki Shigefumi Jukyo ronso, Sumai no keikaku Sumai no Bunka*, Shokokusha, 1988.

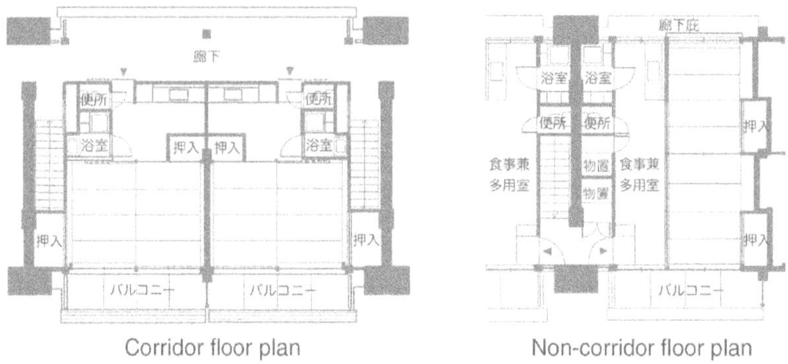

FIGURE 3.16 Plan of Nihon Jutaku Kodan Harumi Danchi Highrise Apartment, designed by Maekawa Kunio office, 1958.

Source: Ueda, Makoto, Harumi Koso Apart ni takusareta oshikousou Shuugoujuutaku no yume, *Shinkenchiku*, Aug. 2008.

Kiyoshi Ikebe's Belief in the Capacity of Technology to Enhance the Quality of Life

A member of NAU, Ikebe was a pioneering figure in post-war Japanese architecture and design. He was responsible for the design of modules, design systems, minimalist housing and industrialised housing. Aware of the transformation in the function of post-war life and architecture, he sought to facilitate the development of well-being by considering architecture not merely as a technical or design-related matter but as a social system centred on life. Ikebe's contributions to housing design theory and educational activities altered the consciousness of residents, thereby facilitating the formation of a social infrastructure that prioritises well-being.

FIGURE 3.17 Exterior photo of Nihon Jutaku Kodan Harumi Danchi Highrise Apartment, designed by Maekawa Kunio office, 1958.

Source: Ueda, Makoto, Harumi Koso Apart ni takusareta oshikousou Shuugoujuutaku no yume, *Shinkenchiku*, Aug. 2008.

From Junzo Sakakura to Kiyoshi Ikebe

Following his graduation from university, Ikebe participated in the reconstruction of Jean Prouvé's Isoare SCAL prefabricated housing, which Junzo Sakakura had received from Charlotte Perriand in 1940.[61] Due to the scarcity of steel, this housing was designed to be constructed from wood using conventional building techniques. From 1943 until the conclusion of the war, it was produced on a large scale for military personnel. Following the conclusion of hostilities, Sakakura undertook a reconfiguration of the design, which was subsequently employed as reconstruction architecture in a number of locations. In 1949, a two-story minimalist house with a vaulted ceiling was constructed as the residence of the president of Nihon Jutaku Kodan. Sakakura designed two standard designs for Nihon Jutaku Kodan housing in reinforced concrete, 53MB and 53MC ($46.2m^2$ and $39.6m^2$, respectively), in the maisonette style, influenced by Le Corbusier's Unité d'Habitation. These were constructed as the Tokyo Metropolitan Kameido Apartments in 1954.[62]

The minimalist house designed by Sakakura, which incorporated a central staircase and a loft, exerted a considerable influence on numerous young architects in the post-war era. This design concept was also carried on in Ikebe's Minimalist House, in which he pursued the creation of a minimalist yet human-like free space. In reflecting on his experience of designing prefabricated housing during the war, Ikebe observed that he had encountered the challenge of understanding the essential quality of space for human beings.[63] This was due to the numerous constraints imposed by standardisation. This was his experience of confronting the human quality of space and the limitations of

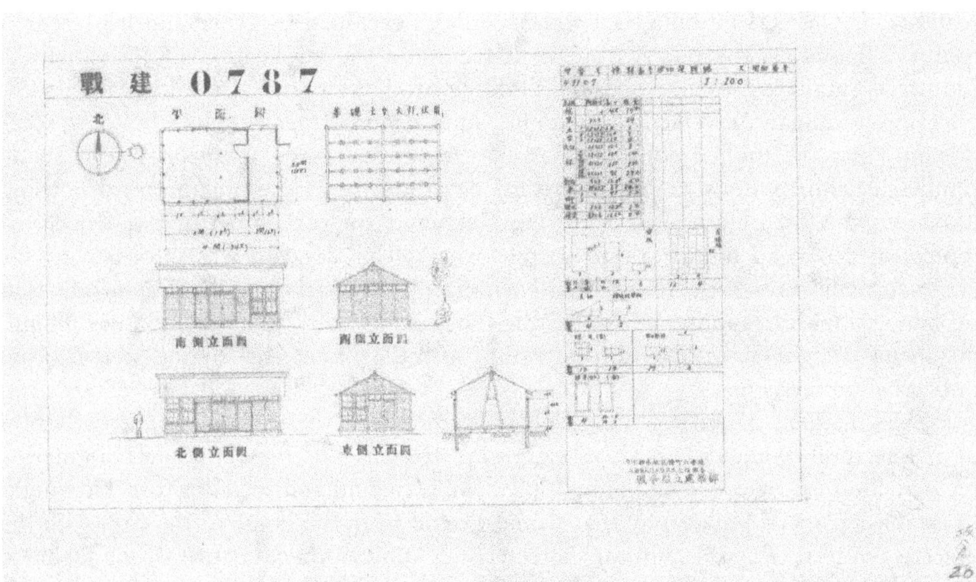

FIGURE 3.18 Senken kenchiku Drawing 0787, Reconstruction of Jean Prouve's ISOARE SCAL prefabrication house with wooden structure by Sakakura.

Source: Kuroishi, Izumi 'Cultural Resilience of Modern Japanese Industrial Design and Housing', presented at 16th International Docomomo Conference, 2020. Original source is Sakakura Collection, Senso Kenchiku 102-01-031, Kokuritsu Kingendai Kenchiku Shiryokan.

standardisation, and he strongly advocated a shift in architectural logic that emphasised well-being, with the focus on the size and quality of the space needed for living, rather than prioritising mass production. Additionally, he emphasised the necessity for designs that considered the minimum volume of a three-dimensional space, as opposed to the two-dimensional designs that were a hallmark of European modernism.[64]

The Living, Production and Social Module System

Ikebe incorporated modular design into his work, considering the changes to living spaces that accompanied industrialisation from the perspective of well-being. Following the war, Japan endeavoured to transition from the conventional Japanese system of measurement to the metric system with the objective of industrialising traditional wooden construction techniques. However, Ikebe perceived this not as a mere matter of numerical values, but as a challenge that would entail the loss of the wisdom and connections to life embodied in traditional carpentry techniques, given the advent of prefabricated housing and the subsequent alteration of living space units.[65] He posited that the standardisation of architecture should be achieved through designs that respect the complex nature of human beings, rather than through industrialisation. He also proposed that the module should serve as the foundation for design freedom. In this way, he sought to develop a spatial logic that would comprehensively address the issues of housing space complexity and production caused by the post-war housing shortage, changes in lifestyle, the limitations of traditional production systems, and the spread of home appliances.

Furthermore, Ikebe aimed to apply this logic to the entire process, from planning to realisation. The GM module (General Module), developed by Ikebe and his research group, is based on the binary system. It facilitates the application of JIS (Japanese Industrial Standards) to conventional building production and also allows for its application to human movement dimensions, industrialised furniture and building components, and the unified consideration of the entire house.[66]Additionally, he made significant contributions to the theoretical development of the prefabricated housing industry, with the objective of achieving a concrete understanding of the concept of 'human order in an industrialized social form.'[67] This concept was informed by his post-war realisation of the transformative impact of industrialised building production on human life. In response, he shifted the focus of his work towards modular design, distancing it from factory-based production, with the aim of challenging preconceived notions about housing.

Ikebe's modular design was not solely concerned with the technical industrialisation of architectural production; it also sought to re-evaluate the role of architects in inventing new lifestyles by coordinating multiple flexible human and social factors. He sought to establish a social philosophy that would extend from the home to the city, with the objective of respecting the cultural characteristics and communal nature of the Japanese living space.[68] Moreover, he posited that the primary objective of architectural design should be to establish a harmonious relationship between people and their environment, rather than focusing on the mere aesthetic aspects of form. He challenged the prevailing modernist architectural approach, which he deemed overly functionalist, and instead advocated for a return to the fundamental principles of human existence and spatial interaction.

The Practical Application of the Modular System

From the late 1950s onwards, Ikebe began to experiment with modular systems in his residential designs. He used geometric diagrams to illustrate a range of concepts, including lifestyle, the human body, behaviour, psychology, social relationships, cultural foundations, building materials and structure. Rather than seeking a universal module or fixed formula, he regarded the module as a means of facilitating communication between the inhabitants, designers, builders, materials and the surrounding environment. He posited that it was crucial to devise a novel module that was conducive to contemporary lifestyles, while also acknowledging the evolution of traditional modules.

He further proposed that the module should serve as a 'language of design.'[69]

To develop the module system, Ikebe proposed four key directions:

1 The emphasis is on the transfer of knowledge from practice to theory.
2 The design process should result in the creation of a flexible logical structure.
3 The integration of human sensory and habitual elements into architectural performance.
4 The module was reinterpreted as a basis for collaborative work to meet economic, technical and social requirements.

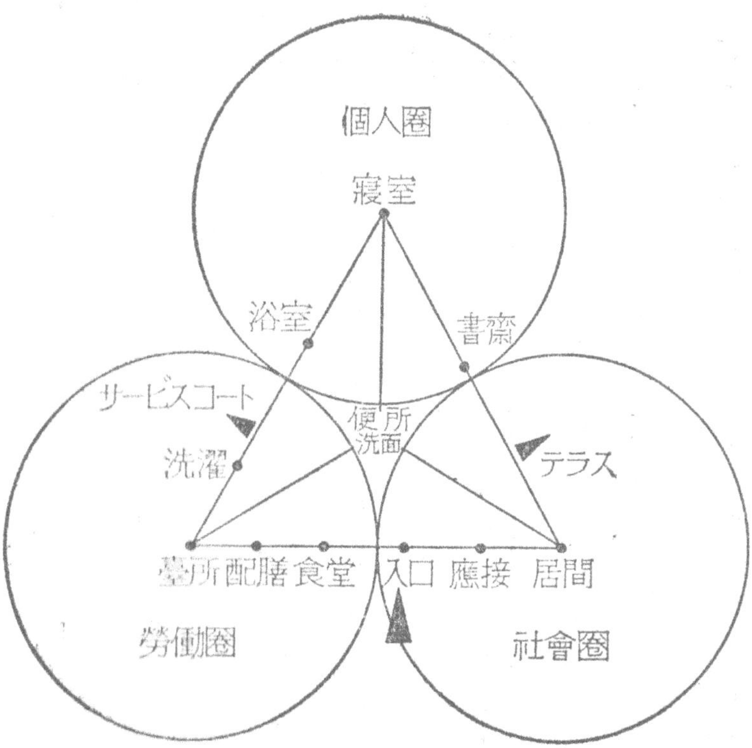

FIGURE 3.19 Kiyoshi Ikebe's diagram of 'language of design.'

Source: Ikebe, Kiyoshi, *Sumai*, Iwanami shoten, 1954.

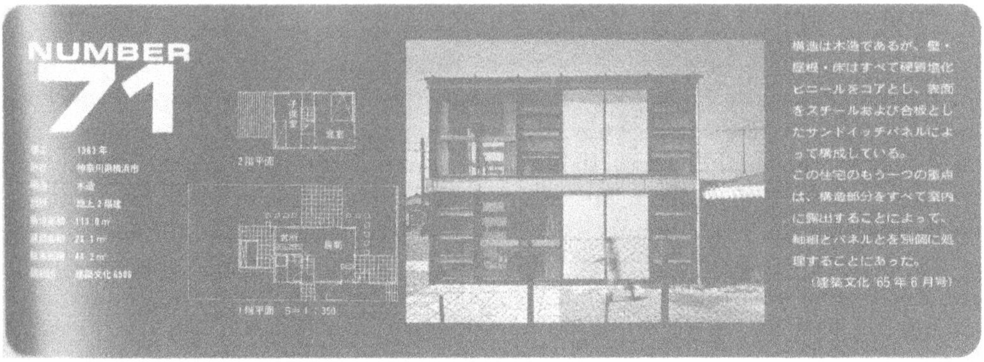

FIGURE 3.20 One of Ikebe's minimum size housing designs, no. 71, in its original form.

Source: Rediscover Ikebe Kiyoshi Zen shigoto no Ashiato kara, Shokokusha, 1997.

He emphasised the importance of using this modular system to facilitate ongoing improvements in design by reflecting the opinions of the residents. The residents of No. 71 had resided in the property for approximately 60 years, during which time they had undertaken four extensions and alterations in response to changes in their family circumstances and their employment status.[70] Throughout this period, they maintained

FIGURE 3.21 Current stage of No. 71, which was expanded four times and is still lived by the original family.

Source: Photo by author.

communication with Ikebe providing an illustrative example of a domestic environment that demonstrated a capacity for ongoing evolution. The approach espoused by this residence was one that was grounded in the philosophy of lifestyle innovation, with a particular emphasis on the promotion of well-being. This was achieved through a process of sincere dialogue with the residents.

Ikebe's Concept of Living and Well-Being

Ikebe asserted that the GM module is efficacious in five respects: the combination of spaces, alteration of quality, organic development, separation and contrast of structures, and modification of the composition system. He further states that it enables the design of living spaces that consider the social quality (well-being) of living spaces.[71] In his book *Sumai*, he further elucidated the conditions for well-being in housing, citing the words of the German architect Gropius: 'The true solution to housing issues can be found in people discussing them.'[72] Thus, housing issues can only be solved when individuals think for themselves. As such, he posited that the housing problem should be addressed as a social and human issue, with consideration given to the three fundamental desires of a free house, a comfortable house and a life with a relaxed feeling, as an integrated whole.

Ikebe also identified four essential functions of housing: living functions, living protection functions, structural and equipment functions, and visual functions. He proposed that housing should be regarded as a unified entity, considering the arrangement of life rather than the configuration of rooms. Furthermore, he divided the fundamental organisation of housing into four domains: the individual, society, work and excretion. He emphasised that housing is the foundation that organises our entire lives, demonstrating that each of these domains is connected as a space. In contemporary housing, he asserted, the focus is on cultivating individual lifestyles and fostering activity. He posited that housing is a necessity for the working class and that it is crucial for individuals to utilise and evolve their housing in an active manner. Additionally, he encouraged readers to adopt a proactive stance, asserting that the resolution of housing issues is contingent upon an individual's comprehension of their own activity structure and its interconnections.

The Promotion of the Concept of Modern Living through Journal Publication

Ikebe collaborated with editor Akebono Watanabe to facilitate the launch of the magazine '*Modern Living*' and was actively involved in its editorial process from 1951.[73] The magazine provided citizens with the opportunity to gain insight into the design and maintenance of their living spaces. It did so by communicating basic information about housing construction and new living space design in an accessible manner, with the aid of illustrative examples and technical data.

Concurrently, he facilitated the expansion of the market for smaller residential units and provided opportunities for young architects to gain employment. Ikebe posited that a house is not a static entity, but rather a dynamic entity that is continuously developed and enhanced by its residents. He further asserted that proactive design activities can significantly enrich people's lives. His assertion that a house is successful if it encourages its residents to develop their lives and that the social significance of design lies in motivating residents suggests new possibilities for housing design based on well-being.[74]

In 1958, architect Arata Isozaki offered a critique of Ikebe's ideas, arguing that housing production was largely controlled by bureaucratic and prefabricated housing industry interests, and that Ikebe's efforts would ultimately be futile.[75] Isozaki's critique reflects the challenges encountered by post-war architects and the housing production system. Nevertheless, Ikebe sought to transform the social significance of architecture by exploring the meaning of life and well-being in architecture in collaboration with residents. Unfortunately, the ideals of Ikebe were not fully comprehended by architects of his own generation or the subsequent generation.

Metabolism Movement and Seikatsu

In the post-war Japanese architectural design movement, the world-renowned Metabolism movement also played an important role in presenting a new architectural view of life. In 1960, to commemorate the post-war recovery, the 'World Design Conference' was held under the leadership of Kenzo Tange and Takashi Asada, and the editor of the architectural magazine '*Shinkenchiku,*' Noboru Kawazoe, invited a group of architects Kisho Kurokawa, Kiyonori Kikutake, Fumihiko Maki, Masato Otaka, and designers Kenji Ekuan and Kiyoshi Awazu to form the group Metabolism. They published the manifesto 'METABOLISM/1960 - Proposals for the City,' presenting the idea of a city in constant renewal, which caused a great stir.[76]

Declaration of Metabolism

At the World Design Conference in 1960, Noboru Kawazoe began his presentation of METABOLISM/1960 with the following statement:

> Metabolism is the name of a group that makes concrete proposals for the shape of society in the future. We believe that human society is a process of creation and development in the universe, from atoms to large nebulae, and we use the biological term 'metabolism' because we see design and technology as an extension of human vitality. Therefore, we do not accept the natural process of history, but actively try to promote it.[77]

The biological metaphors for life force and life activities in the text were developed from the popularism-traditionalism debate that Kawazoe had covered in the architectural magazine '*Shinkenchiku*' between 1953 and 1957. In the 1956 issue of *Shinkenchiku*, Kawazoe published an article entitled 'Aiming to Discover Tradition and the People.'[78] In it, he posed the problem that in post-war Japan, technology and the economy had not yet reached world standards, and that a lifestyle adapted to the climate, weather conditions and cultural forms was needed, while at the same time asking what traditions Japan could be proud of. He also argued that it is human vitality that sustains design, cities and architecture and suggested that in order to replace the abstract world view of architects up to that point and to breathe new life into modern architecture by talking concretely about human images such as images of citizens and families, we should focus on theories of people and theories of materials.[79]

To do this required drawing on replaceable and rebuildable characteristics of wooden architecture proposed by architect Kiyonori Kikutake as the renewability of architecture, combined with the flexible variability of Japanese lifestyle. This theme became a uniquely Japanese architectural concept. Another key was the philosophy of Group Form by Masato Otaka and Fumihiko Maki.[80] This was based on the module concept that Otaka had studied under Ikebe at university and made his life work. It was also shaped by Maki's interest in the invisible and the gentle logic of cities that integrate diverse individuals and the whole, developed through his travels to cities and villages around the world. In talks given to Western architects attending the World Design

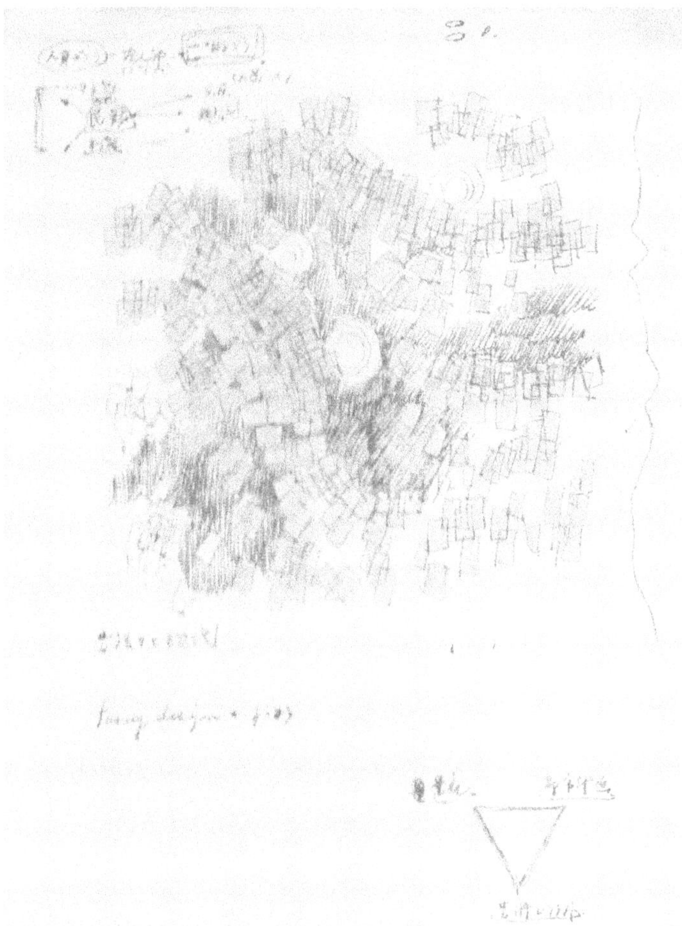

FIGURE 3.22 Otaka Masato's drawing of the concept of 'Group Form,' which explains how units of the same shape come together to Form groups by adapting to the geographical conditions and creating spaces between them with appropriate psychological distances.

Source: Kokuritu Kingendai Kenchiku Shiryokan, *Kenchiku to Shakai wo musubu Otaka Masato no Houhou* PAU, 2016.

Conference, a member of Metabolist and the chief editor of *Shinkenchiku*, Kawazoe argued that 'the difference between Europe and Japan is that we value the idea of change, where both people and nature and architecture are part of nature, and this is what we call "metabolism".'

Kiyonori Kikutake's Design Theory Based on the Idea of Seikatsu in 1969

Kikutake, a leading architect of the Metabolism movement, developed a new direction in architectural concepts and design theory for public housing in the 1960s and 70s. In 1969, he published *Architectural Metabolism: Form, Space and Function* with Shokokusha.[81] In this book, he stated that in order to overcome the limitations of functionalism, the function of space should be abandoned and what is left is seikatsu. He described a methodology of the 'triangular structure of devices' and 'ka-kata-katachi' by dividing spaces into three categories: irreplaceable spaces as 'space devices,' spaces that can be replaced as 'seikatsu devices,' and spaces such as kitchens, bathrooms and storage areas as 'equipment devices.'

'Ka-kata-katachi' refers to the following, respectively.

<ka>: The essential stage, thought, principle and conception. Conception (image) → determination of 'function.

<kata>: The substantial stage, understanding, logic and technology. Clarifying the substance of 'seikatsu.'

<katachi>: The phenomenal stage, feeling and form. Determining 'space and form.'

Kikutake proposed a methodology for design recognition that has three stages: 'katachi' → 'kata' → 'ka', and 'ka' → 'kata' → 'katachi', and they have a three-dimensional spiral triangular structure.

In 1972, Kikutake explained that the tree-like housing plan he had proposed in the Metabolism Movement emphasised common spaces in urban apartment buildings in order to solve the problems of conventional planning theory. He also said: 'Formal planning logic makes it possible to provide collective public services, but the quality of the

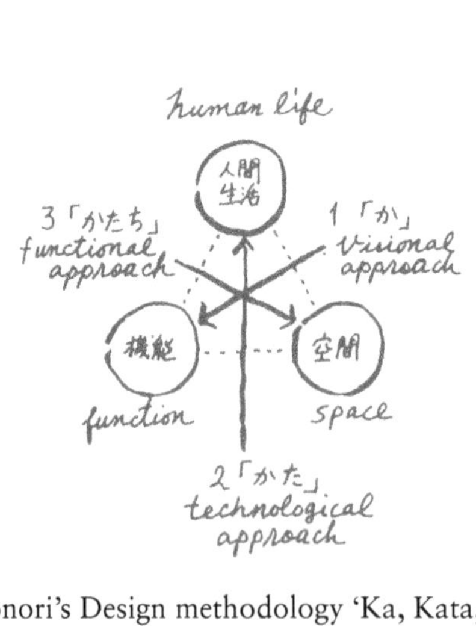

FIGURE 3.23 Kikutake Kiyonori's Design methodology 'Ka, Kata, Katachi.'

Source: Kawazoe, Noboru, etc. *Metabolism to Metabolist tachi*, Bijutsu shuppan, 2005.

environment for those who live directly in it, such as views, isolation and gardens, is inadequate... The planning of the living environment must now be rethought as the relationship between the environment and life from the perspective of individual dwellings and residents.'[82]

He also pointed out that, as a method of design, we should conduct field surveys using the method of Modernology that Wajiro Kon created in his research into the present situation in order to grasp the direct relationship between people's lives and their environment. Based on his survey work, he drew attention to the idea alleyways serve as common spaces. In particular, he discovered the following points regarding their universality and importance as devices for constructing a human environment: 1. People of all ages, from children to the elderly, participate in the space. 2. People have a strong sense of attachment to the space. 3. There is a sense of kinship and mutual support between residents. 4. There are diverse patterns of use. 5. The space is full of different tools for everyday life. 6. There is a sense of freedom from constraints. 7. There are loose restrictions on who can use the space.[83]

He classified the areas of shared space as private, semi-private, semi-public and public, as a link between the areas of everyday life. He argued that it is good to think of architecture as a device that creates sufficient communication between users and planners and suggested that the three device levels of shared space should be considered as life devices, space devices and environmental devices. He also stated that 'architecture is a device for a metabolising environment' and that it is necessary to continue to make modifications in response to the situation in order to create spaces and environments that embrace diverse people.[84]

In sum, Kikutake's design theory does not rely on functionalist categorisation but aims to enrich the perspective of the people who live there by confirming the details of local life and people's daily activities through fieldwork, as well as the relationship with the environment and the diverse and ever-changing spaces that arise between people. This extends Ikebe's philosophy of a comprehensive living system that extends from the individual to society, from the individual space to the family home, and then to activities that extend into the surrounding space and urban space. It is expressed as a high-rise apartment building with various areas that can be realised using modular components.

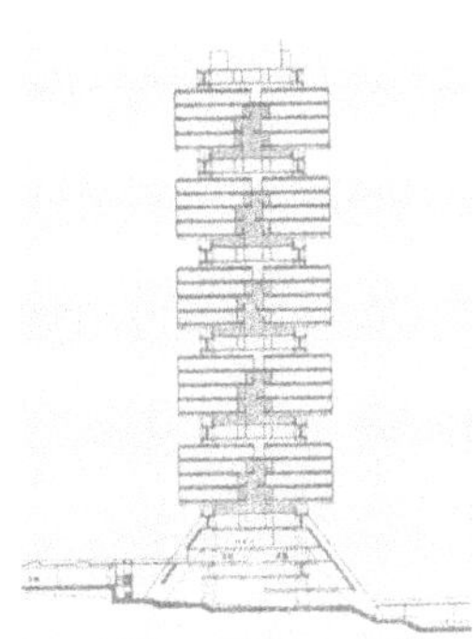

FIGURE 3.24 Kikutake's Tree House design of an urban apartment.

FIGURE 3.25 Space model 3 of Kikutake's Tree House.

Source: Toshi Jutaku, 7202, no. 47, 1972, P37.

Realisations of Metabolism Ideas of Well-Being in Architecture

The principles of Metabolism were implemented in public housing projects such as the Motomachi Apartment (1969–1978) and Tama New Town proposals (1966–1968) by Maekawa's former chief architect, Masato Otaka, and the housing in Peru by Kikutake and Maki between 1969 and 1972. Kikutake and Maki proposed that, in a competition for public housing proposed by the Peruvian parliament, the residents themselves should choose

FIGURE 3.26 Current condition of one of the east corner entrances of Motomachi Apartment designed by Masato Otaka.

Source: Photo by the author.

and live in the various design units proposed by all the participating teams.[85] They designed the units to be loosely arranged around a central square, so that each dwelling unit would have a varied relationship with the whole. However, as the residents continued to live there, all of the architects' works were transformed into spaces that resembled local homes. When they heard this, Maki and Kikutake were delighted, as it was the realisation of the perspective of building from 'Seikatsu' that they had advocated in the Metabolism Movement.

At the World Design Conference in 1960, the imaginative expression of the Metabolism Manifesto and its assertion of a powerful technological image had a great impact on architects from Europe and America. It is also understood in the history of modern Japanese architecture as an example of the futuristic image of post-war Japanese architectural design that attracted worldwide attention. However sometimes, because of the motives behind the group's formation and the great impact of Kawazoe's media strategy, it is seen as a temporary attempt to show off its eccentricity. In Western architectural theory, for example, there are examples of the group's work being interpreted as a peculiar perspective that forcibly introduced the logic of biological life into architecture and fused it with traditional architectural techniques.

The architects in the Metabolism group subsequently went their separate ways and never came together to develop the theory of Metabolism in full, nor did they respond to these evaluations or interpretations. It is clear, however, that these evaluations members of Metabolism's intentions who initially sought to consider the issues of people's living conditions, the issues of individual independence and social relations, and the relationship between housing and the city from the perspective of the well-being of the people living there during Japan's period of social transition.

The post-disaster landscape of the twenty-first century underscored the critical role of housing in supporting both personal dignity and a community-oriented idea of well-being. One of the Metabolist group, architect Kiyonori Kikutake's approach emphasised mutual support and collective well-being over isolated ownership. This perspective became evident in post-earthquake reconstruction efforts that nurtured communal bonds and resilience. Kikutake's philosophy underscores architecture's role as both a foundation for society and an anchor for personal identity, championing a model of well-being that harmonises traditional cultural values with modern social systems.

Well-Being in Public Housing. Inheriting and Taking a New Direction

Kikutake's proposals continue to influence contemporary urban and architectural design, not only due to the visual power of Metabolist imagery. His innovations, grounded in the 'Seikatsu' (lifestyle) of residents, extended the ideas of early thinkers like Ikebe and Wajiro Kon. This emphasis on daily life marked a significant shift from prior Japanese architectural traditions, providing a case study in how architectural creativity could emerge from a well-being perspective rooted in people's everyday lives.

In post-war Japan, architects Komada, Kon, Ikebe and Kikutake addressed not only the physical but also the psychological and cultural dimensions of housing quality. They pursued humane architecture that reflected Japan's cultural identity and evolving social landscape, adapting as societal understandings of well-being expanded.

Prior to and during the war, well-being was largely associated with issues of sanitation, health, and ethical functionalism. However, as post-war democratisation and economic shifts took hold, the concept broadened to include family centred living, technological advancements, individual independence, identity within society, regional and cultural affiliations, physical comfort, leisure and spiritual fulfilment. The focus extended to mutual aid, community belonging, sustainability of tradition, a balance between individual and collective identities, inclusiveness and a connection with nature.

This evolution of 'well-being' reflects not simply the expansion of desires but the complex reconciliation of interests and values amid societal change, echoing Heidegger's notion of dwelling as the 'foundation for the meaning of existence.' Philosopher Ivan Illich described this iterative process as '*conviviality*' – a way for humans to live independently yet coexisting amidst social transformation.[86] Post-war architects in Japan, grappling with the meaning of life itself, envisioned public living spaces as environments of *conviviality*.

Conclusion

This chapter has shown that Japan's public housing policy, both pre- and post-war, was predominantly shaped by administrative priorities, often overlooking the concept of well-being. Particularly in the post-war rush to rebuild the economy, the quality of living environments was deprioritised, resulting in a lack of comprehensive life quality and resident autonomy in housing plans. Yet architects such as Sakae Komada, Wajiro Kon, Kiyoshi Ikebe, Kiyonori Kikutake and Metabolism architects reimagined housing design with the aim of restoring well-being centred on everyday life (Seikatsu). Komada emphasised housing environments that fulfilled both hygienic and spiritual needs, while Kon advocated for designs that transcended physical space to capture a deeper anthropological sense of Seikatsu. Ikebe promoted a modular system that aligned technological tradition and progress with residents' needs, and Kikutake emphasised designs that integrated people's Seikatsu, regional characteristics with advanced technology. These efforts sought to elevate life quality and well-being, which had been largely overlooked in architectural and public housing policies, thereby expanding the role of architects in the pursuit of well-being.

The design philosophy that emerged from these efforts aimed to understand people's Seikatsu holistically, rather than confining them to physical spaces, and to enhance the quality of life. The intention was not to limit Seikatsu issues to individual activities and spatial needs but to recover their connections with the essential meaning of people's lives. This people-centred approach may provide valuable guidance for improving well-being in contemporary housing design. As future housing policy evolves, there is a renewed call for a shift away from government-led, standardised housing plans towards resident-centred, participatory design.

Moreover, the insights of these architects reflect not only the post-war Japanese context but resonate with global architectural trends. Their design philosophy, centring human life within architectural decisions, was a critique of modernism's rationalism and echoed themes of 'total architecture' as re-proposed by Gropius after the war, as well as the critical regionalism of the 1970s and beyond.[87]

Japanese architects' focus on well-being through Seikatsu thus contributes a unique perspective to global architecture, maintaining its significance today. The issues of public housing and urban planning remain central to enhancing residents' quality of life. While government-led planning continues to face challenges, there is an evident need for flexible, community-responsive housing design. The principles of Komada, Kon, Ikebe and Kikutake continue to offer vital insights for designing living environments in collaboration with local communities and citizens, aspiring towards genuine well-being.

Acknowledgement

This chapter would not have been possible without the generosity of Kajima Foundation, and the following archives for allowing access to their collection and permissions for reproduction: Kon Wajiro Archive of Kogakuin University, Japan National Modern Architectural Archive, and National Archives and Research Administration of USA. I am grateful for Prof. Kiyoshi Ikebe's tutorials in my childhood, and for my parents' effort to maintain their house over 60 years.

Notes

1 Gregory, James. 2022. *Social Housing, Wellbeing and Welfare*, Policy Press.
Sparke, Penny. Ioannidou, Ersi. Kirkham, Pat. Knott, Stephen. Scholze, Jana. ed. 2023. *Interiors in the Era of Covid-19: Interior Design Between the Public and Private Realms*, Bloomsbury. The author contributed her text to this volume. 'The Quest for Well-being in Japanese dwellings from late nineteenth century to Covid-19', pp47–59
2 Zhu, Yushu and Holden, Meg. "Housing and psychosocial well-being during the COVID-19 pandemic - *PMC*," https://pmc.ncbi.nlm.nih.gov/articles/PMC10033258/
3 Fukunaga Fumio, Kouno Yasuko eds. 2014. *What is the Post War Period-Dialogues between the studies of Politics and History*, vols. 1 and 2, Maruzen Shuppan.; Dower, John W. 2004. *Embracing Defeat: Japan in the Wake of World War II*, translated by Miura Yoichi and Takasugi Tadaaki, 2 volumes, Iwanami shoten.
4 Inagaki, Eizo. 1978. *Nihon no Kindai Kenchiku* (Japanese Modern Architecture), vols. 1,2. SD sensho, Kajima Shuppan.
Funo, Shuji. 1982. "Kenchiku gaku no keifu-Kindai nihon niokeru sono shitekitennkai (genealogy of architectural study- its historical transformation in Japanese modern period," *Shin Kenchikugaku Taikei, 1, Kenchiku gairon*, Shokoku sha.
5 The author discusses about the idea of well-being in this volume's introduction.
6 Homma, Yoshihito. 2004. *Sengo Jutaku seisaku no kensho*, Shinzansha Publication.
7 Ohmoto, Keino. 1991. *Shogen Nihon no Jutaku seisaku*. Nihon Hyoron sha. "Housing Policy during the Occupation Period (1) The process and meaning of the closure of Jutaku Eidan by GHQ," *The Journal of Tokyo Keizai University* 247 (2005): 133–51. "Modern History of Housing Policies," *History and Ideology*, Tokyo University Press, 1996, 89–120.
8 Hirayama, Yosuke and Ronald, Richard eds. 2007. *Housing and Social Transition in Japan*, Routledge.
Hirayama, Yosuke. Karizumai to Sengo Nihon, Seido sha, 2020.
9 Kuroishi, Izumi. 2023. "Making a Community Around a Table: Reconstruction of Mutual Help System by Tea Parties (Ocha-kai) and Lunch Parties After the Great Eastern Japan Earthquake," *Community Responses to Disasters in the Pacific Rim: Place making in Displacement,* Shu-Mei Huang and Elizabeth Maly, eds., 190–206, Routledge.
Kuroishi, Izumi and Special Committee of the Academy of Lifeology ed. *The Current Situation and Perspectives of Covid-19- proposals from Lifeology*, Kokusai Bunkensha, 2022. The author contributed 'Corona Modernology- Logic of dwelling questioned in the pandemic'
10 Yamane, Yoshio. 2005. *Seikatu Kagaku no 20 seiki* (20th century of Seikatsu science), Kasei kyoiku sha.
11 Yoshio. *Seikatu Kagaku no 20 seiki.*
12 Okouchi, Kazuo. *Kokumin Seikatu no Riron* (Theory of the People's Life).
13 Yoshio. *Seikatu Kagaku no 20 seiki.*

14 Ito, Chuta. Kishida, Hideto. Kiyoshi, Seike. Yosiro, Taniguchi. Gaijiro, Fujishima. 1962. *Kenchiku to Seikatsu* (Architecture and Life), Kagaku Zuihitsu Zenshu, vol. 14, Gakuseisha.
15 Nishiyama, Uzo. Sep. and Oct. 1942 "Seikatsu no kozo to Seikatsu kichi(Structure of life and fortress of life)," *Kenchikugaku Kenkyu*, no. 110 and 111.
16 Honjo, Kazuhiko. 1972. "Sekai no Jutakuseisaku karamita Nihon no baai (Japanese Housing Policy from International viewpoint)," *Kenchiku zasshi* 52 (32): 333–36.
17 Kazuhiko. "Sekai no Jutakuseisaku karamita Nihon no baai."
Honda, Isamu. 1998. "Seikatsu gainenno kentotoseiri-Seikatsu kenkyu no rebyu(Examination of the idea of Seikatsu- Review of the studies about Seikatsu)," *Kokusai Iryo fukushi daigaku kiyo* 3: 13–23.
18 It is reported that 163 cities were affected, with a total of 220,000 buildings destroyed and 8.75 million people affected.
19 The reconstruction plan drawn up by the War Damage Reconstruction Agency had already been prepared in the Planning Bureau of the Ministry of Home Affairs in the year before the war ended, and was put into action immediately by the organisation established after the war.
20 The occupying government basically did not recognise the social and human rights issues of the housing problem in Japan, and took a punitive policy, regarding the shortage of housing and daily necessities for the Japanese people as the 'responsibility of the defeated country'. (Far East Common Engineering Section File 600.1.1947, NARA).
21 Far East Common Engineering Section File 600.1.1947, NARA.
22 Koshizawa, Akira. 2005. *Fukko Keikaku- Bakumatsu/Meiji no taikakara Hanshin Awaji Daishinsai made* (Recovery planning-From the huge fire at the end of Edo and Meiji to the earthquake in Hanshin/ Awaji), Chuko Shinsho.
23 Bruno Taut was a German architect contributed to the Bauhaus education and the designs of German pre-war public housing, immigrated to Japan between 1933 and 1936. His work *Nihon no Kaoku to Seikatsu* (1937) discussed how common people's modest dwellings reflect their rational way of Seikatsu.
24 Charlotte Perian was a French designer who worked with Le Corbusier and Jean Prouve, and was invited by IAI between 1940 and 1942. She designed a reclining chair by using farmer's traditional straw work, and organized an exhibition *Sentaku, Dento, Sozo* (selection, tradition and creation) in 1941.
25 This involved 1/10 scale sketches, full-size drawing production, furniture prototyping, and everything from drawing production to final production. Kappei Toyoguchi, '*Kogei News*'
26 Koizumi, Kazuko. Takayabu, Akira. Uchida, Seizo. 1999. *Senryougun Jutaku no Kiroku*, vols. L 1,2. Sumaino Toshokan.
27 Toyoguchi, K. 1946. "Designing of Occupation Army's Dependent House Furniture," *Kogei News* 14 (2): 8–15.
28 Kaneko, Tokujiro. 1946. "Fukko Jutaku to Kenchikuka kagu(Reccovery House and Architectural Furniture)" *Kogei News* 16 (8): 8.
29 Saito, Nobuharu. 1947. "Kogei sangyo no Tenkan to Honjo no Saiken (Changes in Craft Industry and reconstruction of Honjo office)," *Kogei News* 17 (2): 7–9.
30 Daisuke Magara, Kiyoshi Miyazaki, Takayuki Higuchi. 2008. "The Activities of Shinji Koike in the 1940s," *Society of Design Engineers*, 2BULLETIN OF SSD 55(3): 1–10.
31 SCAP, box 5337, NARA.
Fujita discusses that when the Cold War began, Truman simultaneously tightened restrictions on Japan's socialist movement and strengthened cultural exchange between Japan and the United States. The focus of the occupation policy shifted to an assimilation policy that convinced the Japanese that their independence, security, cultural progress, and prosperity could only be achieved through the American collective security system. President Eisenhower decided to support projects that would introduce American cultural and economic prosperity to Japan (Fujita 2015).
32 Kon, Wajiro. 1971. "Juseikatsu no tameno Jikkenn Jutaku (experimental house for housing life)," *Jukyoron*, Kon Wajiro Zenshu vol. 4, Domesu shuppan: 182–85.
33 SCAP, box 5337, NARA.
34 It received aid from the Rockefeller Foundation immediately after the Great Kanto Earthquake of 1923 to help rebuild medical education institutions and sanitation facilities and was established in 1938 as an agency directly under the Ministry of Health and Welfare.

35 The American 'Basic Principles of Healthful Housing' set out 30 basic principles relating to four elements: physiological requirements, psychological requirements, infection prevention and accident prevention, and established these as the minimum requirements for physical, mental and social health. Winslow CEA, et al. 1938. Basic Principles of Healthful Housing. *American Journal of Public Health Nations Health* 28: 351–72.
36 In Japan, Article 25 of the Constitution of 1947 stipulates that all citizens have the right to a minimum standard of healthy and cultural living, but the right to survival as a human being is not legally guaranteed.
37 Kan Sato, Wajiro Kon, Isao Shibatani, Goro Shinkai, Hiroshi Nakamura, Takashi Hirayama, and Kan Watanabe participated in the exhibition.
38 Nakajima, Akiko, Kobayashi Yotarou, Kikuchi Kuniko, Shimada Kazuko, Shiratori Mariko, Hayafuku Chizuru, Matuo Kuniko, Ymaguchi Haruko. 2000. "Jutaku Eisei Kenkyu no Josei paionia Komada Sakae nikannsurukennkyu (Ei Komada - A Woman Pioneer of Healful Housing)," *Jusouken Kenkyunenpou* (27): 195–206.
39 Tokyo Municipality Housing Office, Japan Architectural Academy, *Toei Takanawa Part Chosakenyu Houkokusho* (Tokyo Municipality Takanawa Apartment Research Study Report,) 1991. It was a four-storey building with 24 units, with two units sharing one staircase, and the units were planned to be 15 tsubo, with 8 tatami mats and 6 tatami mats, a kitchen, toilet and no bathroom. In total, 188 units were built in 9 buildings, but the second phase of construction involved improvements, additions and changes based on the results of a survey of the living conditions of the units in the first phase. The tenants were assumed to be families of various occupations with 3 to 8 members, and although the rent was expensive at 600 yen per month, there were over 220 times as many applicants as there were units. Komada's apartment was in Building 2, Room 301, and had a layout with a 10-tatami mat Western-style room and a 3 tatami mat Japanese-style room, with a wooden floor between the rooms and the kitchen.
40 In the 1950s, the provision of public housing for low-income earners became widespread in the United States, and non-profit organisations such as the National Housing Conference began to become active, but Bauer criticised the large-scale public housing policy of the post-war period, saying that it created economic ghettos.
41 Komada, Sakae, Kobayashi Youtarou, Soda Nagamune, Tamura Kenji, Satake Hiroto. 1968–1969. "Survey Research on the Living Conditions, Health and Mental Health of Urban Residents" 1–3, *Nihon Kenchikugakkai Kanto shibu,* Gakujutukenkyu happyoukai, 39–40.
42 Sakae et al. "Survey Research on the Living Conditions," 40, 1969, 293.
43 Horikoshi, Tetsumi and Horikoshi Hidetsugu. Feb. 2004. "Kenchikukankyou Kogaku no Kenkyuchouryuu no shintento Jidaikubun no Kosatsu: Zouka eisei kara keikakugenron soshite genzai (History of Architectural Planning and Environmental Control Studies in Japan)," *Nihon kenchikugakkai Tokai shibu kenkyuu houkokusho*, 319: 417–22.
44 Kon, Wajiro, *Kon Wajiro Zenshu,* vols. 1–7, Domesu shuppan, 1971. From the 1910s, Kon conducted research into rural life and housing with Kunio Yanagita, and researched changes in urban customs after the Great Kanto Earthquake, which is named Modernologio, as well as housing in Korea and the housing of immigrants.
45 Kuroishi, Izumi. 2014. "Domesticating Others' Space," in *Constructing the Colonized Land: Entwined Perspectives of East Asia around WWII,* Izumi Kuroishi edited and authored, Ashgate: 1–10, 215–252.
46 Kon,Wajiro. 1936. "Seikatsu gaku no Teisho(Proposal for Seikatsu Study)," *Journal Home Economics.*
47 Nihon Gakujutu gakkai. 1941. *Tohoku chihou Nosan Gyoson Seikatsu Kaizen Chosa*, I, II, III, As the background of this study, from the 1910s, Kon conducted ethnographical research into rural life and housing with Kunio Yanagita, and researched changes in urban customs after the Great Kanto Earthquake, as well as housing in Korea and the housing of immigrants. (1924).
48 Kon, Wajiro. 1971. 'Ju Seikatsu (Dwelling)' (1945),*Seikatsu Gaku*, Kon Wajiro Zenshu 5: 129–200.
49 Wajiro. "Ju Seikatsu (Dwelling)."
50 Kon, Wajiro. 1971. "Seikatsu gaku eno Kuso(Imagination for Seikatsu Study) (1951)," *Seikatsu Gaku*, Kon Wajiro Zenshu 5: 16–17.
51 Kon, Wajiro. 1971. "Hitono sumu Jukyo(A House where People Dwell)(1946)," *Seikatsu Gaku*, Kon Wajiro Zenshu 5: 82–86.

"Katei no Ba to shiteno Jukyo(Dwelling as the Place for Family)(1949)," *Seikatsu Gaku*, Kon Wajiro Zenshu, vol. 5, 1971: 87–91.

52 Wajiro, "Hitono sumu Jukyo."
'Katei no Ba to shiteno Jukyo(Dwelling as the place for family)'(1949), *Seikatsu Gaku*, Kon Wajiro Zenshu, vol. 5, 1971: 87–91.

53 Kon, Wajiro. 1971. "Showa no Goningumi jukyo(five members' collective house in Showa)" originally written1944, *Jukyoron*, Kon Wajiro Zenshu, 4. Domesu Shuppan, 162–67.

54 Kuroishi, Izumi. 2016. "Rethinking the Social Role of Architecture in the Ideas and Work of the Japanese Architectural Group NAU," *Review of Japanese Culture and Society* 28: 99–117.

55 Hamaguchi, Ryuichi. 1947. *Hyumanizumu no Kenchiku—Nihon kenchikuno hanseito tenbou* (Architecture of Humanism—Introspection and Outlook of Japanese Architecture), Yukeisha

56 As Masao Maruyama suggested, at the time, Japanese intellectuals readily appropriated Western thought, but ignored its sociocultural foundations.

57 Maekawa's first involvement with Le Corbusier's office was in the design of a minimalist house, and he was also in charge of the presentation at the CIAM in 1929.

58 Nozawa Masamitsu, 2006. "'Toshi eno tegakari wo kenchikuni motomete Maekawa Kunio to toshi(Searching for a clue to approach urban design in architecture: Maekawa Kunio and urban design)," Feb. 1, 2006, http://noz-bw.com/archives/1951

59 Suzuki, Shigefumi. 2006. *Gojuuichi C Hakusho-Watashino Kenchikukeikakugaku Sengoshi*(White paper on51C-Post war history of my architectural planning study), Sumaigaku Taikei 101.

60 Gropius, Walter. 1958. *Seikatsu kuukan no Sozo* (The Creation of space for Seikatsu), translated by Kurata, Masachika, Shokokusha. Original title is Scope of Total Architecture.

61 Yamana, Yoshiyuki, Ikeda, Naoya, Tanigawa, Daisuke. 2006. "Batiman de la Gael kara Senso kumitate kenchikuheno kennkyuukaihatu nikannsurukousatu(Examination of the research from Batiman de la Gael to war time prefabricated architecture)1," *Nihon Kenchiku gakkai taikai Proceedings*, 753–54.
Komada, Tomohiko. 1997. *Kenchikuka Sakakura Junzo no shigoto* (Works of an architect Sakakura Junzo), Kanagawa Kenritsu Kindai Bijutukan: 18–19, 44–45.

62 Tomohiko. *Kenchikuka Sakakura Junzo no shigoto*. Due to this experience of designing, Sakakura was unable to come to terms with the 'unfree' design conditions of the Nihon Jutaku Kodan, and he did not accept any further commissions for Nihon Jutaku Kodan projects. (Sakakura Office HP Memorandum).

63 Nanba, Kazuhiko. 1999. *Sengo Modanizumu Kenchiku no Kyokuhoku* (North Pole of the Post-war Modernism Architecture), Shokokusha.
Kuroishi, Izumi. 2008. "Mathematics for/from sSociety: Module in Modernizing Japanese Architectural Production," *Nexus Network Journal: Architecture and Mathematics* 10 (1): 168–73.

64 Ikebe, Kiyoshi. 1997. "Seikatsu no module wo sagashimasu (Search for the module of Seikatsu)," *Ikebe Kiyoshi Saihakken* (Rediscovery of Ikebe Kiyoshi), Shokokusha, 34–35.

65 Inspired by the translation of Le Corbusier's 'Le Modulor' into Japanese in 1953 [Yoshizaka 1976], an academic committee was established in 1954 to create a national module. The focus of the debate was narrowed down to three points: whether to use the shaku module or the metre module, how to think about the industrialisation and standardisation of architecture, and how to choose a modular coordinate system.

66 The dimensions $X_n = 2^n + 2^{n-1} P_1 + 2^{n-2} P_2 + 2^{n-3} P_3$ (P_1, P_2, P_3 = 0 or 1).

67 Ikebe, Kiyoshi. 1962. "Yooroppa ni okeru Kenchikuseisan no Kogyoka(Industrialization of architectural production in Europe),"*Kenchiku Zasshi* 14 (10): 18–21.

68 Ikebe Kiyoshi. 1949. "Komyuniti no saiken nituite-waruta-guropiusu (Reconstruction of Community: Walter Gropius)," *Kenchiku Zasshi* 756: 29–33. Ikebe explains the significance of Gropius's 'total architecture' as a theory of community.

69 Ikebe, Kiyoshi. 1996. *Dezain no Kagi-Ningen, Kenchiku, Houhou* (Key for design-Human, Architecture and Method), Maruzen.

70 No.71 is the author's home where she had grown up from 8 years old. Her father had to repair and maintain the house to adapt to the family's lifestyle and psychological reactions to the space, sometime opposing to Ikebe's theory. With Ikebe, the family renovated the house 5 times by extending the building, relocating the kitchen, bathroom and stairs, removing walls and changing exterior walls and the roof, and is still living. When the author started learning architecture, Ikebe was delighted to know that his house produced an architect. See Kuroishi (2008).

71 Ikebe, Kiyoshi and Nakahara Youko. 1958. "GM moju-ru niyoru modhura-ko-dhine-shonn (Modular Coordination by GM Module)," *Nihon Kenchikugakkai Kantoshibu* 24: 121–24.
72 Ikebe, Kiyoshi. 1954. *Sumai* (Dwelling), Iwanami Shoten, 10, 11.
73 The first editor in chief of the journal *Modern living* Akebono Watanabe explained that new lifestyles require a new style of home in the age of democracy and rationalism, at its launch in 1951. Ikebe contributed to the journal as the main editor for the architectural section from the beginning and created opportunities for young architects to present their works to the readers who wanted to build their own houses and educated the readers about the basic knowledge of architectural design, planning, structure and facilities.
74 Ikebe, Kiyoshi. 1997. "Jukyo wo tukuri Jukyo wo tukau, soshite Jukyo wa Ningen wo Sasae, Ningen wo Kaeru(Building and Using a House, and It Supports and Changes a Human)," originally published on Shinkenchiku, Jan. 1966, reprinted in *Ikebe Kiyoshi Rediscovered*, Shokokusha, 132, 133.
75 Isozaki, Arata, "Shoujuutaku Sekkeino Mondai:Shoujuutakusakka no Yukuewa(Problems of small House Design: What Is the Future of the Architects of Small Houses," *Kenchiku Bunka*, Jan. 1958, quote from above Nanba, Kazuhiko(1999), 98, 99.
76 Yatsuka Hajime and Yoshimatsu Hideki. 1997. *Metabolizumu- 1960 nendai, Nihon no kenchiku avangyarudo* (Metabolism-Japanese Architectural Avant Garde in 1960s), INAX Sosho, LIXIL.
77 Kawazoe, Noboru, Otaka Masato, Kikutake Kiyonori, Maki, Fumihiko, Ekuan, Kenji, Awazu Kiyoshi, Kurokawa, Kisho. 2005. *Metabolizumu to Metabolisto tachi* (Metabolism and Metabolists), Bijutsu Shuppannsha, 15.
78 Kawazoe, Noboru. July 1956. "Dentou to Minshu no hakkennwo mezashite (Aiming for discovering Tradition and People), *Shinkenchiku*, Shinkenchikusha, 13–16.
79 After the war, the concept of 'tradition' was a forbidden word, but here it was made an issue again, and the concept of 'popular tradition', which differed from the traditional image of the pre-war period, was brought to the fore. See Yatsuka and Yoshimatsu (1997), 46–48.
80 Minohara Kei, Matsukuma Hiroshi, Nakajima Naoto. 2014. *Kenchikuka Otaka Masato no shigoto* (Works by Architect Otaka Masato), Xknowledge, 45–47, 108–09.
Kawazoe, Noboru, Otaka Masato, Kikutake Kiyonori, Maki, Fumihiko, Ekuan, Kenji, Awazu Kiyoshi, Kurokawa, Kisho. 2005. 138–52.
81 Kikutake, Kiyonori. 1969. *Architectural Metabolism: Form, Space and Function*、Shokokusha.
82 Kikutake Kiyonori, *Toshi Jutaku, Special issue Kyoyu Kuukan*, no.47, 7202, Kajima Shuppan, 21–51.
83 Kiyonori, *Toshi Jutaku, Special issue Kyoyu Kuukan.*
84 Kiyonori, *Toshi Jutaku, Special issue Kyoyu Kuukan.*
85 Kawazoe, Noboru, Otaka Masato, Kikutake Kiyonori, Maki, Fumihiko, Ekuan, Kenji, Awazu Kiyoshi, Kurokawa, Kisho. 2005. 124–30, 145–48.
86 Illich, Ivan. 2001. *Tools for Conviviality*, Marion Boyar.
87 Gropius, Walter, 1958. *Scope of Total Architecture*, translated by Kurata, Masachika, Shokokusha.

Bibliography

Arizuka, Reiko. 1996. "Jutaku Eidan Mitsuwa cho Jutakuchi no hensen to kyoju prosesu(Examination of the Transformation of Jutaku Eidan Mitsuwa cho residence and its process of dwelling) 1." Nihon Kenchikuk gakkai taikai gakujutu kougaishu, 343.

Arizuka, Reiko. 1997. "Jutaku Eidan Mitsuwa cho Jutakuchi no hensen to kyoju prosesu(Examination of the Transformation of Jutaku Eidan Mitsuwa cho residence and its process of dwelling) 2." Nihon Kenchikuk gakkai taikai gakujutu kougaishu, 194.

Dower, John W. 2004. *Embracing Defeat: Japan in the Wake of World War II*, translated by Miura Yoichi and Takasugi Tadaaki, 2 volumes, Iwanami Shoten.

Fujita, Fumiko. 2015. *America Bunkagaiko to Nihon (US Cultural Diplomacy and Japan)*.Tokyo: Tokyo University Press.

Fukunaga Fumio, Kouno Yasuko eds. 2014. *What Is the Post War Period-Dialogues between the Studies of Politics and History*, vols. 1 and 2, Maruzen Shuppan.

Funo, Shuji. 1982. "Kenchiku gaku no keifu-Kindai nihon niokeru sono shitekitennkai (geneology of architectural study- its historical transformation in Japanese modern period." *Shin Kenchikugaku Taikei, 1, Kenchiku gairon*, Shokoku sha.
Gregory, James. 2022. *Social Housing, Wellbeing and Welfare*, Policy Press.
Gropius, Walter. 1958. *Seikatsu kuukan no Sozo* (The Creation of space for Seikatsu), translated by Kurata, Masachika, Shokokusha. Original title is Scope of Total Architecture.
Hirayama, Yosuke and Ronald, Richard eds. 2007. *Housing and Social Transition in Japan*, Routledge.
Hirayama, Yosuke. 2020. *Karizumai to Sengo Nihon*. Seido sha.
Homma, Yoshihito. 2004. *Sengo Jutaku seisaku no kensho*, Shinzansha Publication.
Honma, Yoshihito. 2009. *Kyoju no Kinkon*. Iwanami Shinsho, Iwanami Publication.
Honjo, Kazuhiko. 1972. "Sekai no Jutakuseisaku karamita Nihon nobaai(Japanese Housing Policy from International viewpoint)." *Kenchiku zasshi* 52 (32): 333–36.
Horikoshi, Tetsumi and Horikoshi Hidetsugu. 2004. "Kenchikukankyou Kogaku no Kenkyuchouryuu no shintento Jidaikubun no Kosatsu: Zouka eisei kara keikakugenron soshite genzai (History of Architectural Planning and Environmental Control Studies in Japan)." *Nihon kenchikugakkai Tokai shibu kenkyuuhoukokusho* (319): 417–22.
Ikebe, Kiyoshi. 1997. "Seikatsu no module wo sagashimasu (Search for the module of Seikatsu)', *Ikebe Kiyoshi Saihakken*(Rediscovery of Ikebe Kiyoshi), Shokokusha, 34–35.
Ikebe, Kiyoshi. 1996. *Dezain no Kagi-Ningen, Kenchiku, Houhou*(Key for design-Human, Architecture and Method), Maruzen.
Ikebe, Kiyoshi. 1962. "Yooroppa ni okeru Kenchikuseisan no Kogyoka(Industrialization of architectural production in Europe)." *Kenchiku Zasshi* 14 (10): 18–21.
Ikebe Kiyoshi. 1949. "Komyuniti no saiken nituite-waruta-guropiusu(Reconstruction of Community: Walter Gropius)." *Kenchiku Zasshi* (756): 29–33.
Ikebe, Kiyoshi and Nakahara Youko. 1958 "GM moju-ru niyoru modhura-ko-dhine-shonn (Modular coordination by GM module)." *Nihon Kenchikugakkai Kantoshibu* (24): 121–24.
Ikebe, Kiyoshi. 1954. *Sumai* (Dwelling). Iwanami Shoten, 10,11.
Illich, Ivan. 2001. *Tools for Conviviality*. Marion Boyar.
Inagaki, Eizo. 1978. *Nihon no Kindai Kenchiku* (Japanese Modern Architecture), vol.1,2. SD sensho, Kajima Shuppan.
Isozaki, Arata. 1958. "Shoujuutaku Sekkeino Mondai:Shoujuutakusakka no Yukuewa(Problems of small house design: what is the future of the architects of small houses." *Kenchiku Bunka*. Quote from above Nanba, Kazuhiko (1999), pp. 98, 99.
Ito, Chuta, Kishida, Hideto, Kiyoshi, Seike, Yosiro, Taniguchi, and Gaijiro, Fujishima. 1962. *Kenchiku to Seikatsu* (Architecture and Life), Kagaku Zuihitsu Zenshu, vol. 14, Gakuseisha.
Kaneko, Tokujiro. 1946. "Fukko Jutaku to Kenchikuka kagu(recovery house and architectural furniture)." *Kogei News* 16 (8): 8.
Kawazoe, Noboru, Otaka Masato, Kikutake Kiyonori, Maki, Fumihiko, Ekuan, Kenji, Awazu Kiyoshi, and Kurokawa, Kisho. 2005. *Metabolizumu to Metabolisto tachi* (Metabolism and Metabolists), Bijutsu Shuppannsha, 15.
Kawazoe, Noboru, 1956. "Dentou to Minshu no hakkennwo mezashite (Aiming for discovering Tradition and People)." Shinkenchiku, Shinkenchikusha, July, 13–16.
Koizumi, Kazuko, Takayabu, Akira, Uchida, Seizo. 1999. *Senryougun Jutaku no Kiroku*, 2 vols. Sumaino Toshokan.
Komada, Sakae, Kobayashi Youtarou, Soda Nagamune, Tamura Kenji, and Satake Hiroto. 1968–1969. "Survey research on the living conditions, health and mental health of urban residents'1~3." *Nihon Kenchikugakkai Kanto shibu, Gakujutukenkyu happyoukai* 35: A33–A36, 1968-06; and 40: 293–296, 1969-11.
Komada, Tomohiko. 1997. *Kenchikuka Sakakura Junzo no shigoto* (Works of an architect Sakakura Junzo), Kanagawa Kenritsu Kindai Bijutukan, 18–19, 44–45.
Kon, Kajiro.1971. "Katei no Ba to shiteno Jukyo(Dwelling as the Place for Family) (1949)." *Seikatsu Gaku, Kon Wajiro Zenshu* 5: 87–91.
Kon, Wajiro. 1936. "Seikatsu gaku no Teisho(Proposal for Seikatsu study)." *Journal Home Economics*.
Kon, Wajiro. 1971. "Ju Seikatsu (Dwelling)' (1945)." *Seikatsu Gaku, Kon Wajiro Zenshu* 5: 129–200.
Kon, Wajiro. 1971. "Seikatsu gaku eno Kuso(Imagination for Seikatsu Study (1951)." *Seikatsu Gaku, Kon Wajiro Zenshu* 5: 16–17.
Kon, Wajiro. 1971. "Juseikatsu no tameno Jikkenn Jutaku (experimental house for housing life)." *Jukyoron*, Kon Wajiro Zenshu vol. 4, Domesu shuppan, 182–85.
Kon, Wajiro. 1971. *Kon Wajiro Zenshu,* vols. 1–7, Domesu shuppan.

Koshizawa, Akira. 2005. *Fukko Keikaku- Bakumatsu/Meiji no taikakara Hanshin Awaji Daishinsai made* (Recovery Planning-From the Huge Fire at the end of Edo and Meiji to the Earthquake in Hanshin/Awaji), Chuko Shinsho.

Kuroishi, Izumi. 2023. "Making a Community Around a Table: Reconstruction of Mutual Help System by Tea Parties (Ocha-kai) and Lunch Parties After the Great Eastern Japan Earthquake." In *Community Responses to Disasters in the Pacific Rim: Placemaking in Displacement*, edited by Shu-Mei Huang and Elizabeth Maly, 190–206. Routledge,.

Kuroishi, Izumi and Special Committee of the Academy of Lifeology eds. 2022. *The Current Situation and Perspectives of Covid-19- proposals from Lifeology*, Kokusai Bunkensha. The author contributed "Corona Modernology- Logic of dwelling questioned in the pandemic."

Kuroishi, Izumi. 2016. "Rethinking the Social Role of Architecture in the Ideas and Work of the Japanese Architectural Group NAU." *Review of Japanese Culture and Society* 28: 99–117.

Kuroishi, Izumi. 2014. "Domesticating Others' Space." In *Constructing the Colonized Land: Entwined Perspectives of East Asia around WWII*, Izumi Kuroishi edited and authored, pp.1–10, 215–52. Ashgate.

Kuroishi, Izumi. 2008. "Mathematics for/from Society: Module in Modernizing Japanese Architectural Production." *Nexus Network Journal: Architecture and Mathematics*, 10 (1): 168–73.

Minohara Kei, Matsukuma Hiroshi, and Nakajima Naoto. 2014. Kenchikuka Otaka Masato no shigoto, Xknowledge, 45–47, 108–09.

Nakajima, Akiko, Kobayashi Yotarou, Kikuchi Kuniko, Shimada Kazuko, Shiratori Mariko, Hayafuku Chizuru, Matuo Kuniko, and Ymaguchi Haruko. 2000. "Jutaku Eisei Kenkyu no Josei paionia Komada Sakae nikannsurukennkyu (El KOMADA - A WOMAN PIONEER OF HEALFUL HOUSING)." Jusouken Kenkyunenpou 27: 195–206.

Nanba, Kazuhiko. 1999. *Sengo Modanizumu Kenchiku no Kyokuhoku* (North pole of the post war Modernism Architecture), Shokokusha.

Nihon Gakujutu gakkai, 1941. *Tohoku chihou Nosan Gyoson Seikatsu Kaizen Chosa*, I, II, III,

Nishiyama, Uzo. 1942."Seikatsu no kozo to Seikatsu kichi (Structure of life and fortress of life)." *Kenchikugaku Kenkyu*, no. 110 and 111, Sep. and Oct.

Nozawa, Masamitsu. 2006. "Toshi eno tegakari wo kenchikuni motomete Maekawa Kunio to toshi (Searching for a clue to approach urban design in architecture: Maekawa Kunio and urban design)." Feb. 1.

Omoto, Keino.1996. "Modern History of Housing Policies." *History and Ideology*. Tokyo University Press, 89–120.

Omoto, Keino. 2005. "Housing Policy during the Occupation Period (1)The process and meaning of the closure of Jutaku Eidan by GHQ." *The Journal of Tokyo Keizai University*, 247: 133–51.

Ohmoto, Keino. 1991. *Shogen Nihon no Jutaku seisaku*. Nihon Hyoron sha.

Saito, Nobuharu. 1947. "Kogei sangyo no Tenkan to Honjo no Saiken (Changes in Craft Industry and reconstruction of Honjo office)." *Kogei News* 17 (2): 7–9.

Suzuki, Shigefumi. 2006. *Gojuuichi C Hakusho-Watashino Kenchikukeikakugaku Sengoshi* (White Paper on 51C-Post-war History of My Architectural Planning Study), Sumaigaku Taikei 101.

Sparke, Penny, Ioannidou, Ersi, Kirkham, Pat, Knott, Stephen, Scholze, Jana. eds. 2023. *Interiors in the Era of Covid-19: Interior Design Between the Public and Private Realms*. Bloomsbury.

Tokyo Municipality Housing Office, Japan Architectural Academy. 1991. *Toei Takanawa Part Chosakenyu Houkokusho* (Tokyo Municipality Takanawa Apartment Research Study Report).

Toyoguchi, K. 1946. "Designing of Occupation Army's Dependent House Furniture." *Kogei News* 14 (2): 8–15.

Yamamori, Yoshio. 2005. *Seikatsu Kagakuron no 20 seiki*, Kaseikyouikusha.

Yamana, Yoshiyuki, Ikeda, Naoya, Tanigawa, Daisuke. 2006. "Batiman de la Gael kara Senso kumitate kenchikueno kennkyuukaihatu ni kannsuru kousatu (Examination of the research from Batiman de la Gael to war time prefabricated architecture)1." *Nihon Kenchiku gakkai taikai proceedings*, 753–54.

Yatsuka Hajime and Yoshimatsu Hideki, 1997. *Metabolizumu-1960 nendai, Nihon no kenchiku avangyarudo* (Metabolism-Japanese Architectural Avant Garde in 1960s), INAX Sosho, LIXIL.

Zhu, Yushu and Holden, Meg. 2023. "Housing and Psychosocial Well-being during the COVID-19 Pandemic - *PMC*." https://pmc.ncbi.nlm.nih.gov/articles/PMC10033258/

SECTION II

Well-Being, Urban Space and Accessibility

4

DESIGNING FOR WELL-BEING IN LARGE HOUSING ESTATES IN EAST AND WEST BERLIN

Märkisches Viertel and Marzahn

Katharina Borsi

Introduction

This chapter examines key aspects of how well-being was understood, designed and persisted in two large housing estates, Märkisches Viertel (1963–1974) in West Berlin and Marzahn (1977–1990) in East Berlin. Despite the political differences of their respective regimes, the first democratic, the second socialist, the estates share many commonalities. The optimism of post-war planning in rebuilding the city and creating better living conditions for the entire population was common to both. Both estates had a significant role to play in their respective government's efforts to finally address the critical housing shortages that had continued since the end of the war and to ameliorate housing conditions for a large proportion of the population. Both estates followed modernist architectural aesthetics organised according to the principles of modernist urban planning, constructed with pre-fabricated components, and managed by large companies. Both were underpinned by a strong social vision. Märkisches Viertel exemplified the West German welfare state's efforts to distribute the benefits of postwar growth and prosperity by guaranteeing affordable housing for all. Marzahn, the largest project of the East German housing programme, epitomised the vision of socialist classless society. Both estates also carried forward the modernist project of social reform through design, promoting new community identities and visions of a more egalitarian urban life, and a more equitable society.

The malleability of society through spatial form was a persistent belief prevalent amongst both the German welfare state and the socialist GDR, as well as amongst the bureaucrats, architects and engineers who worked on their behalf. For both regimes, the design principles of the estates were believed to directly impact beneficial forms of inhabitation and social interaction – a spatial frame that would engender both personal development and urban community life. Defining the spaces, services and amenities supporting the welfare and happiness of the population was central to both.

This approach was grounded in a continuity of spatial and social reasoning that can be traced back to the emergence of modern housing in the late nineteenth century and

DOI: 10.4324/9781003527930-7

its development in the modernist *Siedlungen* of the 1920s.[1] Both estates adhered to the modernist principles of the separation of functions, and the emphasis on sun, light and air to provide healthy dwellings. Märkisches Viertel and Marzahn can also be understood in the lineage of a transnational discourse in architecture and planning around the concept of community in the 1940s and 1950s, a concept based on a critique of previous functionalist housing as being too focussed on the provision of physiological needs.[2] While light and hygienic, their environment was critiqued as too monotonous, and as perpetuating the problem of estrangement in mass society. Their forms and spaces were seen as lacking a structure that would allow for identification and social cohesion. These debates undelay variations of community building that proliferated across nations in different guises after WW2, from housing estates to New Towns, neighbourhood units, to Soviet micro districts.[3]

Moreover, the conceptions of both Märkisches Viertel and Marzahn were based on another new paradigm of urban thought, a further iteration and critique, of the concept of community prevalent in the period after the war. The concept of 'urbanity through density,' discussed for example at the 11th annual meeting of the Association of German Cities (Deutscher Städtetag) in Augsburg in 1960, exemplified how formal and spatial precepts of the modern city came to be re-evaluated.[4] The former model of the 'structured and dispersed city landscape' that had dominated planning thought from the interwar to the post-war years came to be considered as anti-urban. The disentanglement and loosening of the spatial and programmatic structure with its significant reduction of building densities and the simultaneous augmentation of green areas came to be considered as inadequate for urban life, lacking in opportunities of exchange and encounter and producing isolation and monotony. In East and West, the previous attempts of designing communities were understood as too monofunctional, lacking adequate community infrastructure, and not adequately providing for social exchange and communication.

Significant differences in the relationship between residential satisfaction and well-being, and the context of the respective regimes can be identified in the evolving trajectory of the estates.

Both were exemplar projects that were received extremely well initially, a perception that reverted into its opposite, albeit at different moments in time.[5] Märkisches Viertel shifted from being celebrated as an icon of modernity to its complete rejection as embodying the failures of modernist planning almost as soon as it was built.[6] The large scale of the estate, the perceived monotony of its architecture and the at the time incomplete infrastructure to serve its inhabitants were rendered into a widely publicised vilification as a soulless concrete jungle. Marzahn, until the German reunification seen as a privileged place to live, was, along with the collapse of the GDR, perceived as the material manifestation of the utopian promise of socialism. Along with the seismic changes in the socio-economic context of its inhabitants, this stigmatisation contributed to its declining population, the closure of public services and increasing unemployment.

During the last decades, both estates have been subject to extensive urban regeneration programmes, funded by the EU, the state, the municipality and the housing associations, integrating infrastructural, economic, spatial and social improvement measures.[7] Current urban policy no longer considers Märkisches Viertel and Marzahn as problematic and instead they are viewed as exemplar estate regeneration projects. In academia, they have also seen renewed interest, with revisionist accounts highlighting their significant architectural and urban qualities, while others re-evaluated the everyday lives of residents.[8] At the same time, escalating rents and growing inequality in housing in Berlin have contributed to an emerging debate about their role in promoting sustainable urban development, given their compact organisation providing housing for many, abundant open space and their potential to benefit from public transport links and the development of green heating and energy systems.[9]

This chapter re-examines the architectural and urban design concepts of both estates within the continuity of post-war social and spatial planning in East and West Germany and explores the evolution of the concept of well-being over time.

Märkisches Viertel

Continuities

The Märkisches Viertel was built between 1963–1974 on West Berlin's northern periphery within the framework of social housing (Figure 4.1). The social democratic government had set up a housing programme to address the city's acute housing crisis that had persisted since the war. The ambition of the Märkisches Viertel was also understood as a signal communicating Berlin's investment in its future despite its precarious position of isolation. The original plan for the new district envisioned 14,000 residential units, later expanded to 17,000 to accommodate 50,000 inhabitants. By 2022, the district housed approximately 41,000 residents.[10]

The urban concept, primarily developed by the architects Georg Heinrichs and Hans Christian Müller, with guidance from the senate building director Werner Düttmann, prescribed a range of parameters such as the height of the buildings and principles of formal organisation. A group of 25 architects were invited to contribute, all below 35 years of age but all with demonstrated expertise.[11] The variations of the buildings outlined in plan are indicative of the shared formal principles. The dwelling ranges and sizes were pre-set by the prevailing social housing standards.

Finally achieving adequate housing provision for all, the mass provision of a good standard of living, supplemented by extensive green space and community facilities and infrastructure was the priority. Modern baths and kitchens, recessed balconies, central heating and lifts supplied an unprecedented level of residential comfort for its residents, who often came from at the time dilapidated, un-refurbished tenements built at the end of the previous century.

For the architects, the question of form was considered as central. Many of the design principles of the estate, particularly the principles underlying the formation of its buildings, are in direct continuity to Hans Scharoun.[12] After WW2, Scharoun's 'dwelling cell,' a building cluster for a defined number of inhabitants, constituted the building block of his concept of the neighbourhood; realised, in parts, in his estate Charlottenburg Nord.[13] Looking back on the modernist Siedlung Siemensstadt he planned in 1930, directly adjacent to Charlottenburg Nord, he critiqued the restrictions imposed on the design. He argued that he and his collaborators were forced to argue rationally and respond to the 'demands for light, air, and the demands of the tenants for the principally equal quality of the dwelling.'[14] By contrast, in the planning of dwelling cells in the 1950s, Scharoun argued that he ought to exceed these technical-organisational demands in favour of a focus on man himself. Instead of considering the relationship between dwelling to man; he argued that the relationship between dwelling, man, cell and community ought to be the basis of design. As opposed to beginning with programme or function, he promoted instead beginning with a 'Gestalt' an idea as image and driving concept. While

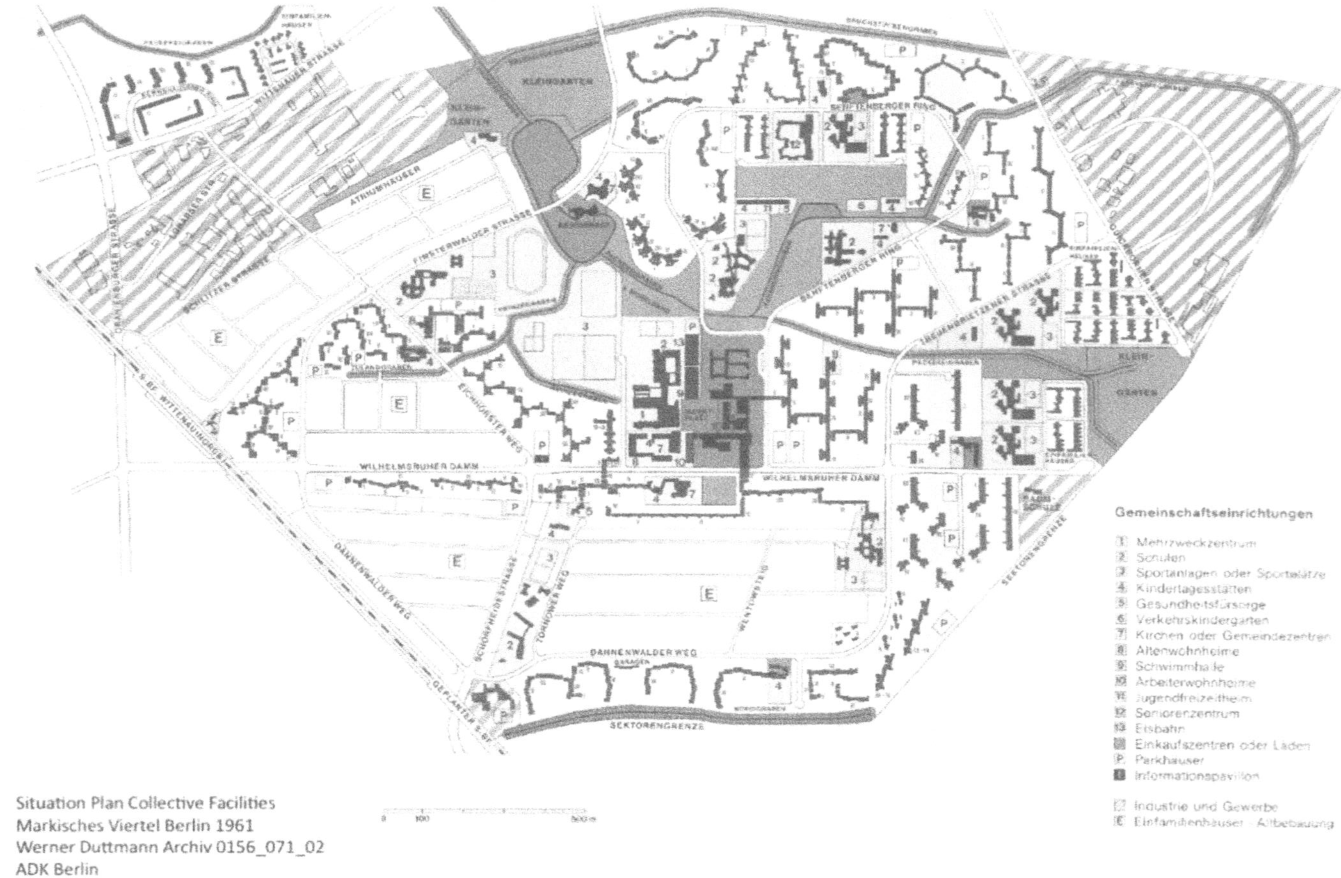

FIGURE 4.1 Situation Plan with Collective Facilities Märkisches Viertel, 1961.

Source: © Akademie der Künste, Berlin, Werner Düttmann Archiv 0156_071_02.

this exemplifies Scharoun's belief in the power of form to induce social relationships, it reflects the wider transnational rationale of spatial layouts explicitly designed to promote identification and social coherence of neighbourhoods. Echoing Scharoun, Düttmann, Heinrichs and Müller explained that it was the monotony and lifelessness of the previous Siedlungen that the design of Märkisches Viertel was meant to overcome. The austere, rational layout of 'Zeilenbau' (row building) was understood to be lacking a 'soul' – thus not seen as conducive to establishing community formation and identification.[15]

As the situation plan in Figure 4.1 shows, the estate is configured as three development arms with residential buildings branching off from the centre, where retail, culture, education, sports and services were nested. The arms were articulated as connected chains of staggered high-rise residential buildings that enclose the existing and newly built areas with smaller residential buildings. The individual sculptural housing complexes arrayed along the arms repeat this gesture and articulate space-forming concave and convex spaces. They are formal variations of Scharoun's dwelling cells.

In Scharoun's dwelling cells in Charlottenburg Nord, the plasticity of the space shaped by the staggered curvature of the adjacent residential buildings was understood as a structure, one that affiliated symbolism and meaning with the enclosure. For Scharoun, the shape of the enclosure itself was understood to generate social cohesion amongst its inhabitants. Scharoun named this figure a 'Gehöft' – a term commonly used for the typically partially enclosed yard in farmsteads. The urban planners of Märkisches Viertel explicitly referred to Scharoun and prescribed the design principle of space forming 'Gehöfte.'[16] Also the staggered spatial organisation in plan and section followed Scharoun's design principles. In addition to forming enclosures, these allowed variation, multiplied sightlines, enhanced daylight and rendered the apartments visually more generous. Heinrichs, Müller and Düttmann shared Scharoun's belief in the power of form to directly affect community formation and social cohesion. Programmatically, these enclosures were seen as 'extended backyards' – leisure spaces for both children and adults, unaffected by traffic.

For Düttmann, the figural 'opening up' of the buildings also had another important meaning in their inversion of the dark courtyard enclosed by the nineteenth-century tenement. At a time before the tenement came to be positively re-evaluated, the courtyard had become synonymous with the unsanitary, overcrowded housing condition of the nineteenth-century city; its lack of air and light encapsulating the conditions upon which modern housing was understood to provide a solution to. For Düttmann, this 'symbol of social injustice,' needed to be 'broken up' to provide light, sun and air equally for all dwellings, an ambition complemented by the design of large-scale green and open spaces.[17]

The scale, density and height of buildings, in conjunction with the declared ambition of interlinking different functions such as living, relaxation, shopping and sport, was the further evolution of Scharoun's concept of the neighbourhood, superimposing the new paradigm of urbanity through density. The tall sculptural buildings were also conceived in response to the scale of the landscape, a fortress of density juxtaposed against the flat green landscape surrounding it. This expressive urban monumentality was understood to provide a crystallisation point for the northern periphery of Berlin, by the power of its architecture.

What Scharoun and the designers of Märkisches Viertel shared, was the social utopia of much of modernist planning, the inscription of social relationships through form. In this perspective, well-being was administered through the very provision of light and airy dwellings, through enabling social ties and facilitating encounters at different scales.

Dwellings and Clusters

Märkisches Viertel shows a real strength in the experimentation with the design of the dwellings, their optimal grouping and their sectional integration with the adjacent void space; design principles derived from Scharoun.

Chen Kuen Lee, a pupil and collaborator of Scharoun, showed his allegiance clearly in his design rationale for the overall grouping of his buildings and the dwelling plans. In his case, a large void space was defined between the different buildings, but with a scale is too large to be perceptible at ground level. The staggered outline of the buildings in plan is primarily read as a dynamic façade (Figure 4.2).

The design experimentation in Lee's buildings appears to focus primarily on the dynamic variegation of his floorplans and their assembly into the overall figure. Both the angular folds in plan and its staggered heights, ranging from nine to 18 floors, show

FIGURE 4.2 Housing Block by Chen Kuen Lee.

Source: Photograph by the author.

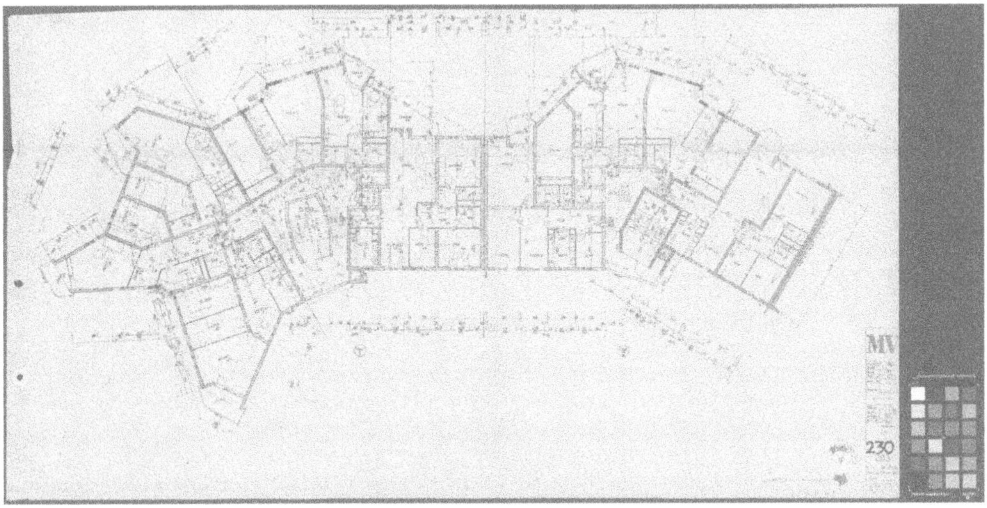

FIGURE 4.3 Chen Kuen Lee. Plan for Märkisches Viertel, 1967.
Source: © Akademie der Künste, Berlin, Lee Archiv 0139_018.

formal similarities to Scharoun's Charlottenburg Nord. Lee's main focus was the articulation of a variety of different dwelling plans, their array and orientation organised to maximise access to light and sun; and a purposeful turning away from each other. In the plan shown in Figure 4.3, the larger dwellings are punched across the building to allow light and air from two sides; whereas the smaller dwellings are rotated to fan out, as if to open up the interior of the rooms towards the outside. The angled walls provide dynamic sightlines and perceptual generosity but also ensure privacy of terraces and living rooms.

Many of his dwelling plans have a generous entrance foyer, often linked to a dining space – central for Lee as space of communication and engagement – which was typically provided in addition to the living room. Again, similar to Scharoun, Lee integrated workplaces along windows in many living and bedrooms; showing the continued emphasis of the dwelling as a space of work, concentration and personal development.

The theme of structures creating *Gehöfte*, the partially enclosed voids articulated by the building lines, allowing 'living into' the green and leisure spaces and 'living out into' the public realm of the street sees a range of permutations.[18] In addition to Lee's project, the urban figures of the architects of the Scharoun school, Heinz Schudnagies, Peter Pfannkuch and Jo Zimmermann, as well as Shadrach Woods, articulate the concept most clearly, in that their curved and staggered building lines frame large green and play spaces. As a consequence, they appear as housing complexes with clearly delineated insides and outsides, but less conducive to drawing movement into and across the ground plane or activating the adjacent urban realm.

Stranz's articulation of the complex sculptural urban figure was derived through careful calibration, negotiating sightlines and maximising sunlight (Figure 4.4). Describing

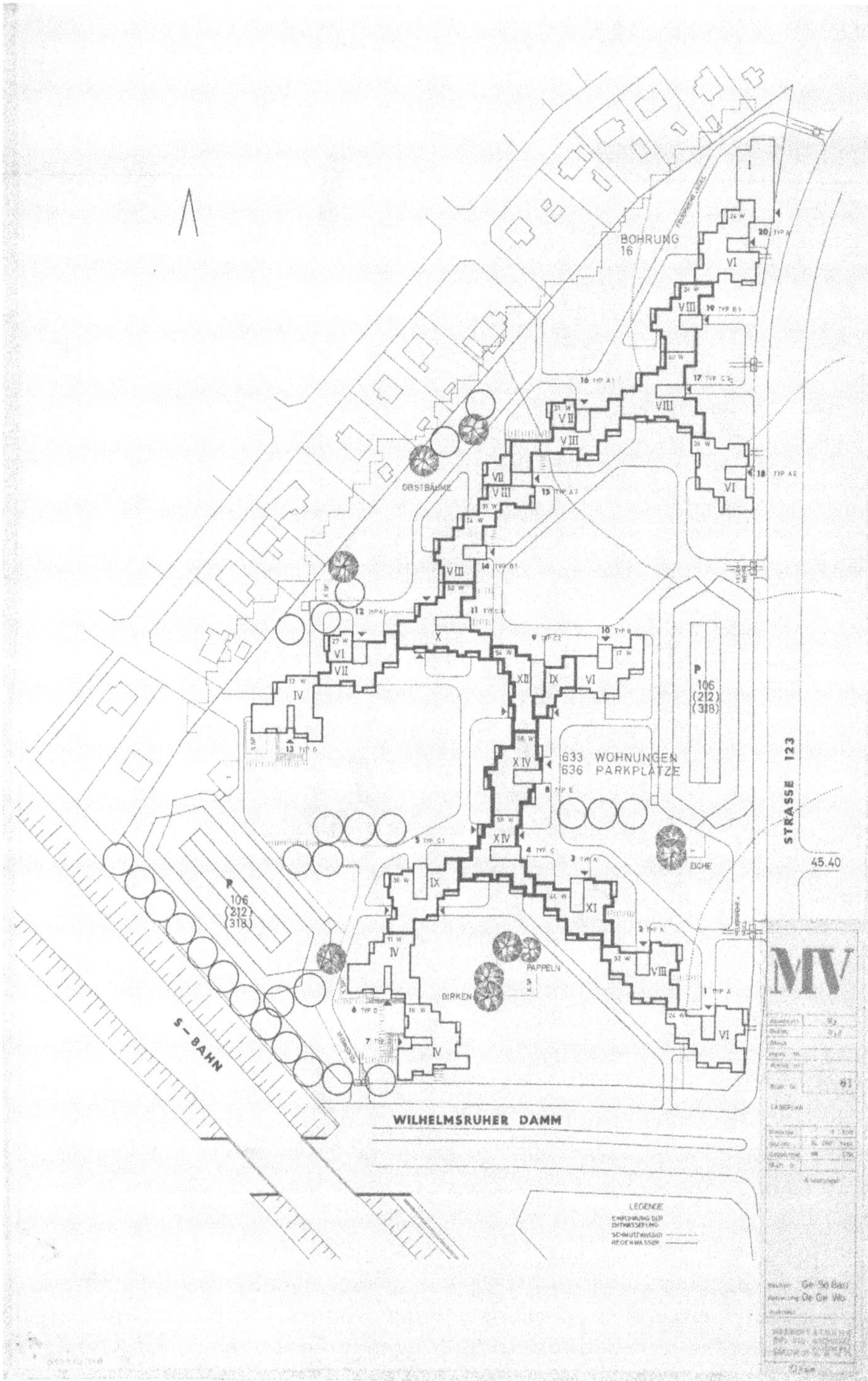

FIGURE 4.4 Herbert Stranz: Situation Plan Märkisches Viertel, Wilhelmsruher Damm, Finsterwalder Straße, Berlin-Reinickendorf, 1964

Source: © Architekturmuseum der TU Berlin, Inv. Nr. HST 009,001.

it as a structure, not a house, he claimed that it was designed through 'applied sun' and adapted to different site conditions. His larger dwellings are organised to face all directions to allow for a maximum of light, air and sun. The smaller dwellings, which he described as either 'early morning- morning – midday dwellings' or 'midday- afternoon-evening dwellings' face primarily east and west.[19] In contrast to Lee's angles, in Stranz's plans, it is the rotations, orientations and grouping of rooms that not only maximise the access to sun, light and air but also afford multiple uninterrupted sightlines and allow a perceptual individuality and generosity of space. In his organisation of the plans, the communal spaces are often linked and serve as through rooms to the individual rooms of retreat. He described his dwellings as being 'structured into sub dwellings' allowing the 'separation of the individual in sleeping towers... or sitting together, on the balcony, the dining room and living room which are play spaces.'[20]

In contrast to Lee, Stranz' amoebic urban figure articulates much more clearly differently configured concave urban spaces (Figure 4.5). While Stranz declared that his sculptural form is democratic, since it expresses 'the individuality of the dwelling that is emphasized within the arrangement,' at the urban scale, its curved outline diversifies the sought after 'living into' and 'living out of' the dwellings into adjacent void spaces.[21] Stranz describes how the building frames leisure spaces of varying character: a market space facing the road, allotments enclosed within, a green space with a large playground,

FIGURE 4.5 Courtyard of Herbert Stranz Housing Project Märkisches Viertel.

Source: Photograph by the author.

and an area designated for playing chess. Apart from the significantly larger areas assigned to car parking, most of these still have the same use today and are well occupied, providing a variegated series of public spaces as well as reducing the impression of the large form.

Also the rectilinear staggered building complexes in Märkisches Viertel explored the negotiation between the clustering of rooms, their orientation, views and the assembly of dwellings with defining external shared spaces.

The 'General Living Area' (Allgemeines Wohngebiet), designed by Heinrichs and Müller, houses differently sized apartments, studios for artists as well as commercial and manufacturing spaces. Its adjacency to the district centre was understood to require a high density, with a maximum height of 18 storeys, and the range of commercial programmes was meant to extend and disperse the central area.[22]

The buildings are lifted off the ground to allow pedestrian movement underneath into a richly detailed and terraced internal park green and playgrounds (Figure 4.6). Play areas are situated where the distances between buildings are larger, quieter terraces with trees and pedestrian walkways are situated in closer proximity to the residential buildings. Today, the park-like courtyards with a variegated landscape feel protected yet large enough to not feel overlooked. The interweaving of paths below the building and the distribution of services and retail at ground level make them well integrated with the

FIGURE 4.6 Courtyard of Allgemeines Wohngebiet Märkisches Viertel.

Source: Photograph by the author.

adjacent cluster of buildings around the market square, rendering the project more urban than others.

Düttmann's cluster of dwellings is situated at the edge of the district; a staggered line of tall buildings in an east west orientation and a cluster of lower buildings framing a green space at the southern end of the plan (Figure 4.7). The distribution of his tall buildings forms large spatial sequences that give variation to the adjacent void spaces. True to his dictum of 'breaking open the dark nineteenth century courtyard of the tenement'; the dwellings are organised to maximise their orientation to the outside. The staggered outlines achieve orientation in several directions for a number of the dwellings; and generally, a sense of individuality and privacy for the large terraces. In the blocks with fewer floors, where views over the landscape were not provided, the l-shaped building layouts configured a courtyard with planting.

The description above is indicative of the design explorations of all complexes in Märkisches Viertel. The design imperative of structuring buildings into *Gehöfte*; and the living into and living out of the internal and external spaces was a central design principle realised by all. With variations in their degree of enclosure, the *Gehöfte* articulated perceptual urban interiors, offering diversity in the shared green spaces across the district.

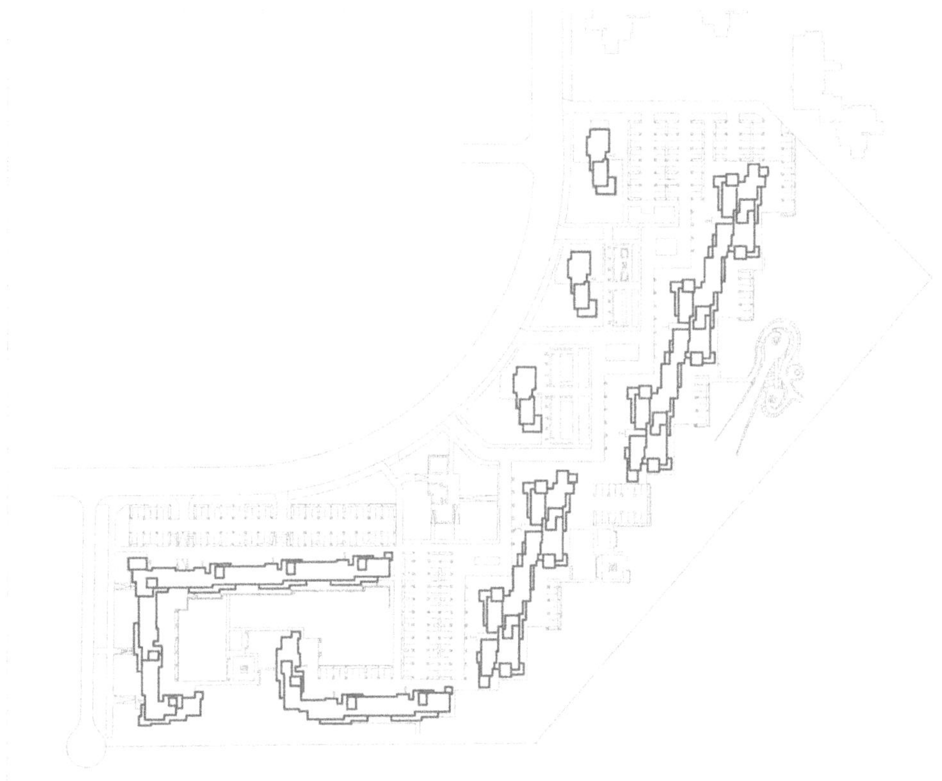

FIGURE 4.7 Werner Düttmann Situation Plan, Märkisches Viertel. Drawn by author.

Source: Akademie der Künste, Berlin, Werner Düttmann Archiv, ADK, 548.

The Centre and the Continuous Ground

The centre of Märkisches Viertel, as the social core, was given particular significance in providing urban vitality and intensity. Despite the active building site for the current redevelopment of the centre at the time of writing, and an array of visually very diverse and some mediocre buildings, aspects of the original aspirations are still visible.

A public square adjacent to a shopping centre functioned as the heart of the district, grouping the other key central functions around it: a comprehensive school, a large public swimming pool and the Catholic Church of St. Martin, with its community centre, kindergarten and an old people's home, as well as the Fontane Haus, a cultural and social centre assembling a wide range of programmes, including a large auditorium; exhibition hall, library and restaurant. [23] At the time of its inception, and still today, the spatial organization of this area, along with the breadth of its program, was designed to bring together the entire population. In plan, it provides a network of pedestrian streets and passages between and also across buildings, that weave into the surrounding landscape and into the adjacent housing complex designed by Müller and Heinrichs. Architecture's contribution to the centre as a place of exchange and communication relies not so much on its architectural expression as on its capacity to cohere and organise rooms for movement, encounter and engagement between the inside and outside of its buildings.[24]

While the centre was designed with urbanity, density and vitality in mind, it is linked to the different housing projects via a continuous shared, predominantly green realm. It is on this ground plane that the spatial and programmatic interweaving envisioned by the architects becomes evident. Meandering footpaths traverse the green spaces around and between the buildings, including their respective Gehöfte, sports areas, lake, and park. This ground plane offers a distinctive quality that contributes to an overarching sense of cohesion.

The areas in yellow in the situation plan show collective facilities, such as schools, kindergartens, and various sports and leisure facilities. Play and sports grounds are distributed evenly across this landscape; which is also modulated in height. The quality of the green spaces today, the result of intensive investment and maintenance over the last decades, invites movement across the terrain and thus links to the multiplicity of facilities and community infrastructures. Today this offer has been further diversified, evidence of a continuous investment into the social infrastructure of the district. The 'extended backyards' of the *Gehöfte*, and the expressive articulation of the housing forms that form those, punctuate this landscape.

The cohesive spatial organisation and the corresponding programme of social infrastructure support the view that Märkisches Viertel exemplifies how a paternalistic welfare state provided for its citizens and offered housing in the context of public service. However, this perspective hides the degree to which architecture contributed to the successful persistence of the estate as an exemplar of successful dense urban housing.

The above reading suggests that many of the design principles envisaged by Heinrich, Müller and Düttmann are still legible today. The overall effect of the plan is to provide a cohesive environment, in which the relative similarity of the buildings' expression produces a sense of cohesion and continuity across the large distances between the different parts. The quality of the shared continuous ground is central in delivering this spatial and perceptual continuity. The extensive experimentation with the meandering sculptural forms contributes to a sense of variation and interest, and, as argued above, at times provides pockets of more intense activation and use for the wider district as much as for the respective inhabitants.

The experimentation with the layout of dwellings, negotiating the spatial restraints of the parameters of social housing with maximising sun, light and air, as well as a sense of privacy, individuality and generosity has been widely acknowledged, both within the profession of architecture as well as by the inhabitants of Märkisches Viertel, even at the time when the estate came into the crossfire of public criticism.[25]

Marzahn

Housing in the GDR

Berlin Marzahn, the German Democratic Republic's largest housing development, was the flagship of the state's Housing Construction programme. Launched by Head of State Erich Honecker in 1973, the goal of the programme was to finally solve the country's housing crisis, primarily through the construction of new housing complexes using prefabricated building methods. The programme, the largest of the socialist party was considered the basis of its social policy.[26]

Since the 1950s, East Germany had focussed on the industrialisation of construction and prefabricated, standardised housing slabs. Large state-owned companies, under the tight control of central government, became the designers and builders of nearly all East German housing. The desperate need for housing meant that the GDR constructed apartments as quickly and as cheaply as possible in the 1950s and 1960s. Meanwhile, the existing building stock was decaying, and many of the existing flats were lacking adequate sanitary facilities. The quantitatively ambitious Housing Programme sought to address the continued acute housing shortage and finally provide adequate sanitary housing for the entire population, thereby addressing the rising critique and dissatisfaction across the population resulting from the ongoing inadequate housing provision.[27]

This was particularly significant given the prominence housing was given in GDR ideology. It figured centrally in the state's vision of the itself and official definitions of home, identity and citizenship.[28]

Housing was understood as the ground upon which a truly communist society would emerge. The historically conditioned social inequality of classes and strata was supposed to be superseded by fundamentally equitable housing in socialism. Regardless of profession or income, everyone was meant to live in the same flats, under the same conditions.

The scale of the neighbourhood in particular was understood as the spatial frame enabling a socialist way of life; an ideological construct the adherence to which, it was presumed, provided well-being. As GDR sociologist Alice Kahl described, the culture of social relationships in regard to housing was meant to free the population from economic pressures and support a communist way of life.[29] In particular, the socialist woman was to be supported in her development to be fully engaged in socialist life, which meant full-time employment and ideally multiple motherhood. We will come to see that this had a significant impact on the design of the neighbourhood and the social infrastructure required to provide full day care across all stages of childhood.

The development of new residential areas was seen as a central building block of socialist society, with Marzahn as its flagship project. While the reality of much GDR housing differed in terms of material quality and preferential allocation along party lines, the above highlights the optimism that underpinned the planning of Marzahn as a means of enabling a socialist way of life.

Marzahn, the Neighbourhood of Residential Areas and the Planning of Urbanity

Following the initiation of the GDR Housing Programme in 1973, the City Council of East Berlin initiated a long-term development concept for the eastern part of the city, and the decision to establish the residential area for Marzahn was formally authorised by the highest party organs of the Socialist Unity Party of Germany (*Sozialistische Einheitspartei Deutschlands)*, the ruling party in the GDR, in 1975.

For the state, the significance of the housing program lay primarily in achieving a sufficient number of homes. The planners of housing estates, the German Construction Academy, Institute for Urban Planning and Architecture (Deutsche Bauakademie – Institut für Städtebau und Architektur, henceforth DBA) were given relatively free reign. Given the prestige and scale of Marzahn, its planners had significant freedom in defining the parameters of design but needed to work within the logic of prefabricated housing units called the *Platte* (slab) and their assembly into residential areas with prescribed community infrastructure.

The majority of Marzahn was built with the WBS 70 system (Wohnungsbauserie 70th series), an updated version of the *Platte* developed in the early 1970s by the German Academy of Architecture and the Technical University of Dresden. WBS 70 delivered what was termed a 'complete comfort apartment' (Vollkomfortwohnung), meaning it had central heating, a fully equipped bathroom with endless warm water, and often a balcony and an elevator. Responding to the need for a better and more diverse housing offer, WBS 70 used a larger panel size than its predecessors which enabled more cost-efficient production and allowed more spacious and better-lit living spaces. Produced to deliver 5, 6 and 11 storeys, its plans could be flexibly configured to house a combination of dwellings between one and five rooms. Based on a grid of six-by-six meters, areas could be added horizontally and vertically to adapt the dwelling plans. Moreover, the outline of the floor plans could be adapted to the functional and urban demands by vertical and horizontal combination of functional units. This also meant that dwellings could be oriented facing the short edge of the slab, avoiding the 'mute' open corners of previous slab construction.

The Platte was assembled and grouped to form residential areas (the Wohnkomplex, later called Wohngebiet) for approx. 4000–5000 residents. The residential area and its assembly of slabs along with the accompanying programme of public buildings for learning and education, consumption, medical and social services, sports and culture, its green space provision and traffic infrastructure were based on a careful calculation of the material and cultural needs of the population. A version of this socio-spatial diagram had already been enshrined in the Sixteen Principles of Urban Design, which were the primary model for urban planning in the GDR between 1950 and 1955, strongly influenced by soviet planning. Along with the GDR Housing Programme, an even stronger emphasis on the neighbourhood as the basis of planning emerged in the 1960s and 70s. The SED's Central Committee's Department of Construction as well as the DBA were increasingly focussing on holistic planning, based on sociologically determined needs of the citizen.[30] Sociological studies of GDR neighbourhoods examined residential satisfaction, questions of social integration into the new living environment, social coexistence on site and the use of supply and infrastructure facilities.[31] These fed into the increasingly complex guidelines governing the ratios and dimensions of housing and the thus defined needs of the community. The whole came to be codified in 1974, in the 'Komplexrichtlinie für die städtebauliche Planung und Gestaltung von Neubauwohngebieten' [Complex Guidelines for the Planning and Design of New Housing Districts].[32]

Both the *Platte* and the public buildings were prefabricated and standardised and rendered the residential area into a kit of parts with minor variations. These 'complete' neighbourhoods became the ubiquitous housing experience in the GDR, housing around one-quarter of the population, a significantly higher proportion then the west German population housed in large-scale housing estates.[33] The repeated implementation of this building arrangement led to structural and spatial monotony, which was reinforced by the typically grey facade. Nonetheless, in Marzahn and elsewhere, moving into the Platte was considered a privilege by the first wave of residents. For most, this implied a significant rise in dwelling standards that included indoor baths and showers, hot water and central heating, as well as well-designed, comparatively spacious, well-lit dwellings and a range of community infrastructure.

It was within these parameters and the limited range of standardised building types, drawn from the catalogue of the *Komplexrichtlinie* that the architects and planners of Marzahn had to forge a district of an unprecedented scale. Despite the limitations of their fundamental building blocks, they worked hard in attempting to realise a more varied, denser and more urbane version of the neighbourhood, one that aimed to enhance social interaction and vitality.

Roland Korn, Heinz Graffunder and other members of the DBA envisaged a departure from the previous housing construction. They critiqued the previous housing construction in Berlin and elsewhere as being without scale, oppressive, and uninhabitable. In the East, just like in the West, the previous concept of the neighbourhood was understood as inconducive to the generation of the new paradigm of vibrant urban life. A sociological-environmental study for the planning of Marzahn exemplified this paradigm shift. It provided guidelines that encouraged planners to design not only for housing needs but also to address the material, seasonal, and cultural aspects of life, as well as the health and well-being of its residents.[34]

Accordingly, the planners believed that a dense and diverse spatial organisation could generate more vibrant social relationships, no longer simply cohering the residents of a neighbourhood. The design intention in the residential areas aimed to avoid monotony through the combination of various types, arrangements and heights of buildings.[35] The main and numerous sub-centres, with their extensive social amenities and medical facilities, were envisaged as dense, lively and active environments of interaction and social exchange. In contrast to the monotonous housing districts of the previous decades, the quality that was sought was urbanity and density, spontaneity and vitality, similar in design intent to the conception of Märkisches Viertel.[36] Moreover, as Torsten Lange has shown, Marzahn was intended as a total environment, through integrated design across all scales, from buildings, landscapes, art and street furniture, in order to establish a network of differentiated places of encounter and social communication.[37]

The Urban Plan

The aerial view of Marzahn shown in Figure 4.8 is based on an urban plan by Korn, who was then the chief architect of East Berlin; it emerged as the basis for the development following an internal urban planning competition. The implementation and further development took place under the supervision of Graffunder, who became chief architect of Marzahn's construction management in July 1976. Working with an extensive team of architects, engineers, and planning officials, Korn and Graffunder envisioned a development that would holistically meet its future residents' needs by integrating infrastructure such as public transportation, shopping centres, schools, playgrounds, nurseries and medical clinics within the newly built housing complexes. The scale and prestige of the project allowed them to exceed the standard programmatic recommendations and to add purposefully designed buildings and urban elements. Over time, many of the design concepts, particularly the public realm and social infrastructure, came to be curtailed due to limited economic means, and the technical standards of the housing construction curtailed in exchange for the production of more housing.

The plan for Marzahn, projected to house at least 48,000 apartments for 137,000 residents, was structured into three 'living areas,' separated by traffic arteries. The new district was bound by several roads and railway lines, as well as topographical features, and set within in a sea of existing single-family houses. Each of the three areas was planned to have its own centre, with the centre in the middle serving as the primary district centre. In addition, there was to be a leisure and recreation park, and industrial areas were occupying the edges of the site.

The plan of living area no 3 (Figure 4.9), in the middle of the overall plan, shows how the area is structured as an assemblage of seven residential areas, subdivided by roads and transport infrastructure. The seven residential areas are clustered around a

FIGURE 4.8 Dieter Urbach, Aerial View Marzahn, 1978.

Source: ©IRS Erkner/Wissenschaftliche Sammlungen, Bestand Wolfgang Urbanski, C_26_01-01.

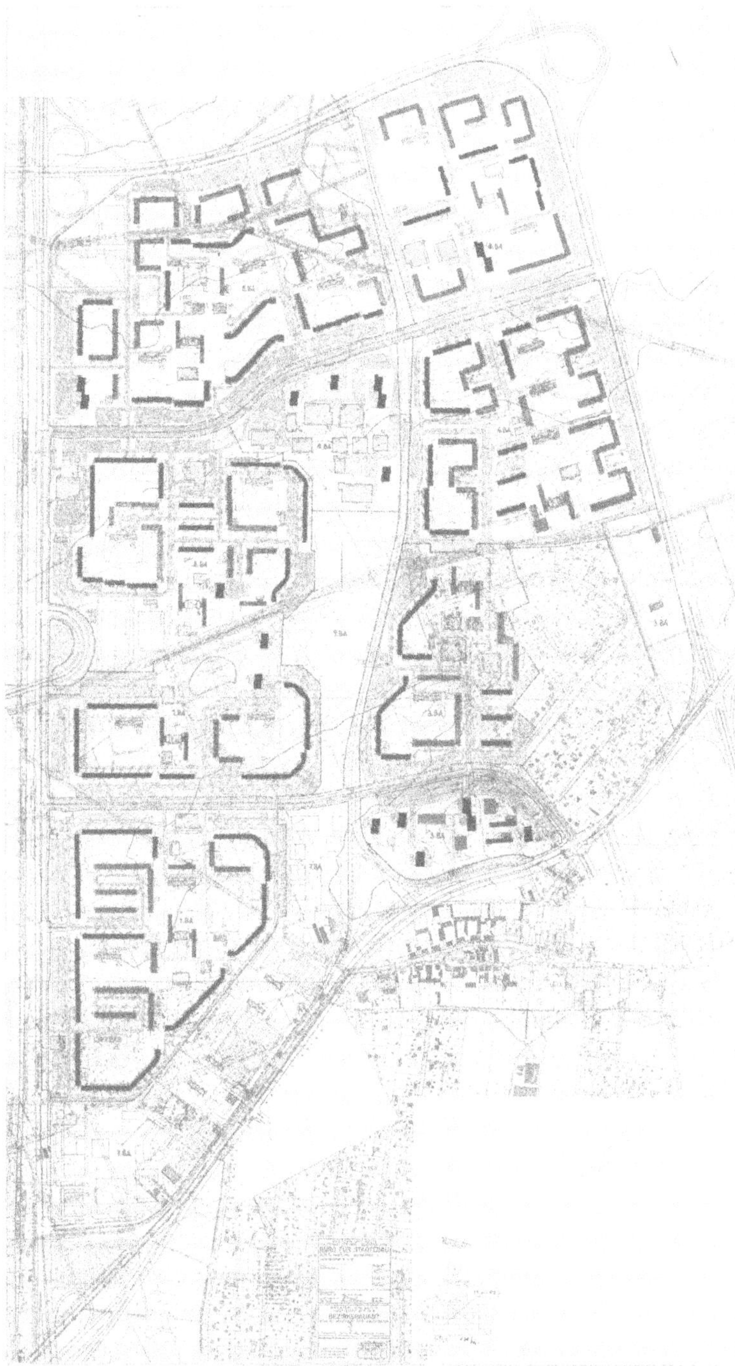

FIGURE 4.9 Heinz Graffunder, Berlin-Marzahn, Living Area 3, 1978.

Source: ©IRS Erkner/Wissenschaftliche Sammlungen; Bestand ISA, Abteilung Wohngebiete, Sig. A_05_01_04-01, https://stadt-raum-geschichte.de/item/f62cd10c-dfd9-4da7-81d9-f17c17e6ad51.

central axis. Each shows variations in the size and grouping of the *Platten* according to the conditions of the site, their arrangement and distribution showing a broader variation than the typical layout suggested in the *Komplexrichtlinie*. Each residential area is arranged as an open cluster defining an interior, their edges defined by straight or meandering slabs, separated by access roads. Their community buildings are loosely grouped in their centre.

Given its size, Marzahn was assigned the status of a superordinate residential area centre, allowing additional recreational and supply facilities. The southern part of the axis, shown only faintly in this plan, is the main centre of the overall district, the pedestrian boulevard 'Marzahner Allee,' lined by shops and connecting a leisure and cultural centre in the north with a retail and service centre to the south. In the middle of the plan lies a large park with a cluster of larger buildings at its northern end, serving as a secondary centre. It concentrated the community functions of its two adjacent residential areas, complemented by a healthcare centre, a two-story restaurant complex, a pharmacy, a department store, a shopping hall, four pavilions, and a swimming hall.

The plan is a composition of a series of nested relationships, the clusters of the residential areas enclosing their own neighbourhood centres, the grouping and assembly of these clusters framing the central axis of the park and the two larger centres, all connected through a continuous landscape of greenery, sports field and play areas, interspersed with public and community buildings.

Sociologist Fred Staufenbiel had predicted that the distribution and clustering of facilities and programmes across the area would enable social contacts and promote socialising and encounters between the residents across the entire residential area.[38] While the casual observation of patterns of occupation and social exchange in Marzahn cannot empirically confirm Stauffenbiel's statement, it appeared intensive enough to support at least some of this claim.

The Civic Centre

The 'Marzahner Promenade,' a boulevard that stretches between the 'Marzahner Tor' shopping centre from the south to the societal 'Freizeitforum' the leisure forum, to the north, constituted the main centre. It was designed as a spatially, formally and programmatically coherent ensemble. The scale and prestige of Marzahn allowed for this centre piece and the extensive service provision of its programme.

Tall, 11-story slabs line the boulevard, with their chamfered corners grouped to allow sightlines and spatial connections between the promenade and the adjacent residential units (Figure 4.10). The slabs support the structure of the promenade into five segments, and while subject to a shared set of design principles, each shows variations in the design of the continuous shared public realm. The spatial sequence is articulated through changing spatial geometries in plan, and different levels of walkways, gardens and rows of shops along the eastern row of slabs define the promenade in section. The character of a unified ensemble is further developed through the use of the octagon as a motive. This appears in the chamfered corners of the slabs, the shape of the squares, in the street furniture elements and the planting scheme, as well as in the shape of the stairs, terraces and the fountain along the promenade and the large squares near the *Marzahner Tor* and the *Freizeitforum*.

FIGURE 4.10 View of a square along Marzahner Promenade.
Source: Photograph by author.

Both the *Marzahner Tor* and the *Freizeitforum* were multipurpose buildings, designed as internal open landscapes connecting the different programmes, but they also promoted communication between different users in their circulation spaces, a concept echoing the logic of the Boulevard. Today, a contemporary shopping centre has replaced the *Marzahner Tor*, and with its interiorised functions, detracts from the life of the boulevard.

The density of the centre, its design articulation as well as the broad range of commercial, cultural and social amenities was a purposeful attempt to create urbanity, diversity and intensity. In various planning documents, both architects and sociologists declared the necessity of the centre of providing a social space of encounter and communication. Much of it has been preserved and restored. While not as vibrant as hoped for by Marzahn's planners, it continues to have a strong perceptual unity, is well used, and contributes significantly to lending identity and coherence to the district as a whole.

The Residential Area

The excerpt of the situation plan showing the residential area 4BA at a larger scale (Figure 4.11), situated in the north-eastern part of the living area no 3, exemplifies how the architects and planners sought to imbue variation and coherence into the residential

FIGURE 4.11 Institut für Städtebau und Architektur, Detailed Situation Plan Living Area 3, 1979.

Source: ©IRS Erkner/Wissenschaftliche Sammlungen, Bestand ISA, Abteilung Wohngebiete, Sig. A_05_01_04-03, https://stadt-raum-geschichte.de/item/45f2ac87-a6a1-4554-986e-8e204259e7a2.

areas with the prescribed catalogue of elements. The residential area is composed of four urban blocks divided by access roads. Each of the urban blocks is defined by linear or meandering slabs, forming courtyard-like spaces: green areas in which playgrounds and children's facilities are nested. These clusters in turn frame the 'societal centre' of the residential unit with its community infrastructure. The slabs facing inwards, towards the centre of the overall area, are taller with 11 storeys, in order to provide density and urbanity. Those that border the edge are 6 storeys high, to mediate the transition to the landscape and the surrounding single-family houses. The loose grouping and meandering forms underscore the attempt to undercut the monotonous regularity of previous housing units. As usual, the Kindergarten and crèche building are situated within the urban blocks, close to the residential slabs. The other community infrastructure – the sports hall, the school and the school dining hall, often located at the edges of a residential unit, are here clustered in the south eastern urban block, and in combination with the residential unit restaurant, the shopping facility and the recycling facilities form the societal centre. This spatial organisation sought to ensure a comprehensible structure of the neighbourhood, such that, according to Graffunder, the residents in their 'Kiez,' the term used for a neighbourhood in the nineteenth-century tenement structure, become known to each other.[39]

This seemingly socio-functional diagram of the socialist housing complex is often reduced to a critique of undifferentiated housing provision, a technocratic approach aimed solely at fulfilling basic housing needs. However, the plan conveys the care with which the life of the community was to be promoted, and recognition of the significance of integrating well-designed green space into housing areas.

The plan communicates a continuous dense ground plane of planting and surfaces providing variation and coherence. The careful layout of different green areas and zones for activities, subtly differentiated by planting, yields a continuous, variegated active ground plane. The schools and kindergartens are surrounded by different gardens; different surfaces indicate a variety of play spaces – from ballgames, frolicking grounds; sandboxes and playgrounds, and different sport fields surround the sport hall. Unusual is also the provision of some private gardens for residents. The green space inside the northwestern urban blocks is structured by two play areas with different geometries; a roller-skating ring and a ball games area, and the area between the free-standing slabs shows variations in planting and a 'floor ornament.' The mini centre is highlighted by its geometric planting, an ornamental square with a fountain, with an annotation that reads 'fountain art,' a ground ornament and 'play art.' The only area left white in the centre of the plan, not showing paths, planting or functional assignation is annotated as a 'free areas according to the conception of healthcare' – although it has pencilled in some potential workshop spaces.

The density of the graphic notation in the green void space underscores the vision of the housing slab as the background to a rich community life. The plan communicates the principal design objective of the estate – its density and variety visualise a shared realm aspiring to support a cohesive community with a range of needs, an area conducive to movement and encounter. While much of the richness of the design came to be curtailed in the execution, today, extensive investment and ongoing maintenance render aspects of this shared collective realm legible.

Today, the residential area reads much more quietly than what the almost bewilderingly dense annotation of the green plan suggested. However, the paths, playgrounds and remaining community buildings are well used, and the intensive planting and landscaping in the courtyards promote a sense of spatial cohesion and mediate the large scale of the surrounding slabs. The refurbishment of the housing stock, providing new balconies and colourful facades in place of the original grey, has significantly improved the appearance of the residential complexes.

The courtyards are woven into the continuous shared green realm across much of the estate, with play spaces and community infrastructure distributed across it. Judging by the degree to which it is used by the inhabitants, the quality and expanse of this green

FIGURE 4.12 Courtyard Marzahn.

Source: Photograph by the author.

space – a rarity in Berlin – contributes significantly to the spatial and social cohesion of the estate overall. (Figures 4.12 and 4.13). This is particularly noticeable when encountering gated courtyards of some of the privatised residential areas. The fence not only disrupts the continuity of the shared ground plane, it perceptually disrupts the coherence of the district as a whole. There is no evidence that these gated green spaces are more effectively utilized.

The reading above has shown a number of similarities to that of Märkisches Viertel.

The scale and density of Marzahn provides a degree of urbanity and vibrancy, even if it is much less intense than what was hoped by its original designers. The density of the centre and the range of its social, cultural, retail and service provision further help to promote a degree of urban life missing in other, smaller housing estates. The variegation of the design of the centre, the sequence of squares and rhythms of adjoining buildings along Marzahner Promenade, in conjunction with the restored public realm is central both for identification with the district as much as providing the infrastructure for sustaining urban life. For Marzahn planners, it was this vitality and communication, social engagement at neighbourhood and district level, that was seen as the socialist 'good life.' Within the ideology of the GDR, well-being was mandated by the state, and by extension designed for by the planners.

FIGURE 4.13 Garden Courtyard in Marzahn.

Source: Photograph by the author.

Stigmas and Revivals

Both housing estates were subject to extensive and multifaceted stigmatisation at a local and national level. Describing the dramatic shift from celebrated icon of the welfare state to the scapegoat of modernist planning, Florian Urban has shown that the vitriolic critique against Märkisches Viertel that abounded in the media in the 1970s was essentially not a debate about architecture.[40] Left-wing activists, filmmakers and reporters were central in the portrayal of Märkisches Viertel as bleak and desolate, its architecture being made directly responsible for the socially fractured social relationships it appeared to generate. The perceived inhospitality of its environment was coupled with a critique on lacking infrastructure and services and the poor quality of public realm. The latter had been delayed in its implementation and was still in the process of development years after the first tenants had moved in. While the estate was decidedly socially mixed at the time, its portrayal as a place of fear and loneliness was inextricably linked to its labelling as a lower-class quarter.[41] One of the noted effects of this process of stigmatisation was that it drove in response a process of identity and community formation, the very qualities it was critiqued as lacking.[42]

Märkisches Viertel became the emblem subsuming all the different strands of criticism levelled at modernist mass housing and urban planning. In addition to the alienating effect perceived in modernist urban structures, these included the critique on top-down autocratic decision-making; the large-scale planning of mass housing and the tenement demolitions this often entailed, with its consequences of forced relocation from the old centre and the disruption of old neighbourhood structures.

Once the community infrastructure and the public realm were completed and post-completion construction problems of the buildings were resolved, residential satisfaction increased and the external image of the estate became more positive. In a survey of Märkisches Viertel in 1971, 87% of inhabitants stated that they were either very satisfied or satisfied with their housing situation; while a survey of the 1980s showed that 69% of residents were 'pleased' or 'very pleased' with their environment.[43] Moreover, contemporary recollections from first-time residents offer a moving testimony to the pride and joy they felt in their new apartments – the light-filled interiors, the spaciousness, the comfort of central heating, hot water, and indoor toilets, as well as the proximity to green spaces.[44] These recollections are often accompanied by comparisons to previous living conditions – whether in barracks, emergency accommodations, or the dark, cramped, and often overcrowded tenements with coal heating and shared toilets on the stair landing.

From the 1980s onwards, the Märkisches Viertel underwent a process of continuous improvement to its living environment, partly driven by residents' protests against the estate's infrastructural issues mentioned above. Werner Düttmann argued that the protests and criticisms of the incomplete social infrastructure and the structural defects of buildings mobilised the residents into developing their own initiatives and participation in the planning dialogue.[45] This galvanization saw the gradual remediation of construction faults such as leaking roofs and deficient insulation, and improvements in the external appearance of green and public shared space. Particularly, the design of entrance porches and adjacent extensive landscaping resolved many of the tenants' concerns about the scale and lack of identifiable access to some of the large buildings. These changes to the external appearance based on consultation with the resident community were very positively received and further consolidated identification with the estate. In the last decades, the estate has seen extensive investment in measures improving energy efficiency, as well as significant investments in social infrastructure and the design and maintenance of the public realm.

Since the German reunification in the 1990s, Marzahn has been stigmatised through its symbolic affiliations with the collapsed regime of socialism superimposed onto the more general critique against its monotonous, repetitive seriality. The radical socio-cultural and economic changes triggered by German reunification in 1990 had major impacts on Marzahn: its image shifted abruptly from one of the most privileged areas to live in to being framed by the West as a zone of urban marginality and social dysfunction.

This image stood in strong contrast to perceptions within Marzahn prior to reunification. A longitudinal sociological study throughout the 1980s noted that 76% were happy in their apartments, and 73% had a sense of well-being in Marzahn.[46] This high degree of residential satisfaction is also reflected in more recent interviews and oral histories. Similar to the experience of the first residents of Märkisches Viertel, also the inhabitants of Marzahn underscored how desirable it was as a place to live. Being allocated an apartment in the newly constructed settlement was seen as a privilege, both due to the significant improvement over the often decaying inner-city dwellings they were leaving, as much as in being able to participate in the new socialist utopia that the GDR officials and their information channels perpetuated. Moreover, a study of 2013 confirmed a strong sense of identity and place attachment during the GDR period also due the state-administered emphasis on personal and communal responsibility for the area.[47] Inhabitants were expected to help with the building and initial beautification of the area and maintain the housing stock they lived in. This created close contact between people living in the same block and enabled them to establish new social networks, some of which remain into the present. The same study made very little mention of the surveillance by the secret police that invariably infused the informal networks of social contact.

The seismic shift that followed the regime change in 1990 entailed entirely new conditions and uncertainties. The closure of many enterprises resulted in subsequent mass unemployment – a completely new phenomenon for East Germans. At a time when movement was no longer restricted, and employment opportunities made relocation necessary for many, a significant number settled in new locations.

Insecurity over the future of the estate accelerated the significant population decline at Marzahn. Many housing units were sold to private investors. Some of the companies were partially owned by the city and some blocks remained in the hands of the workers' building cooperatives which had existed in the GDR. The privatisation of the housing stock along with transition to a housing market where rents were not subsidised led to significant increases in rents. Combined with the progressively worsening reputation of Marzahn, this led to an even greater decline of the population. Not surprisingly, the social cohesion of the area suffered as a result of these dramatic changes.

The regeneration projects of 2002 and 2008, part of the larger, federal project Urban Reconstruction East, was an attempt to prevent further social and financial stagnation of the district. The most decayed buildings were demolished, some were reduced in size, the remaining buildings were renovated, and trees were planted. Over the last decade, regeneration has continued, and the grey face of the Platte is now colourful, insulated, and often has added balconies. The green space between buildings has seen extensive landscaping and the community infrastructure has been renovated.

Today, the population of Marzahn is growing again. Despite rising rents and changing demographics, identification with the district and satisfaction with the living environment is high. Current residents value the estate as a very green and peaceful area, where the housing stock has recently been well renovated and made visually appealing, and where one can reach the inner city and nature outside the city in a matter of minutes with a car or with efficient public transport systems.[48]

Conclusion

Despite the stark differences in the social-political context of the two estates, the description above has shown extensive similarities between the two. In each case, a strong state – one in the name of welfare, the other in the name of socialism – has sought not only to address acute housing shortages but to significantly enhance the access to good quality housing to many, and thus provide more equitable living conditions across its population.

As has been testified by the voices of inhabitants east and west; the basic provision with housing amenities we take for granted today, such as kitchen, bathrooms, central heating, and an adequate amount of self-contained space, was seen as a privilege by the first inhabitants. It forms the basis of the possibility of a socially just city and the well-being for its citizens. Märkisches Viertel and Marzahn have contributed significantly to one of the biggest objectives of well-being in the provision of safe and healthy housing. With their large scale, both estates continue to provide housing for a significant part of Berlin's population and continue to offer relatively affordable accommodation at a time of challenging housing markets. While both estates are not without socio-economic challenges, these are not significantly different to other areas in Berlin that concentrate medium and low-income households.[49]

The stigmas associated with large-scale housing estates continue to linger. As flagship projects of their respective regimes, for many Märkisches Viertel and Marzahn continue to embody the social utopias of modernism, and in the case of the latter, that of socialism. While we might not share the modernist vision of form by itself cohering communities and inculcating positive social contacts, the description above identifies a degree of continuity in the spatial performance of both estates between the time of their conception and the present.

While the intensive ongoing regeneration of the estates had a significant role to play in their relative success, their architecture and morphologies continue to provide a good spatial frame for a large population. Both estates were designed as an integrated urban environment, in which housing clusters, green space and the public realm were cohesively employed to link an extensive array of programmes and facilities in support of the community, even if the initial realisation fell short of the designer's original ambitions. Both epitomise the value of a shared common realm, underscoring the importance of the multi-scalar conception of housing. The focus on urbanity and density in both estates, with it aims to promote vitality, communication and encounter, is still legible in parts today, even if what transpired was a more muted form of vibrancy than the optimistic urban intensity the planners envisaged in their original plans. The literature has shown that the quality of the provision across these scales, that of the dwelling, the housing cluster and the district, had significant impact on resident satisfaction and identification with their respective estates.

In Märkisches Viertel, the primary focus of the design experimentation sought to maximise the quality of the dwelling space seeking to achieve relatively generous, light filled rooms for all within the spatial limitations of social housing. In Marzahn with the prescribed housing plan of the WBS 70, the primary design focus lay in providing variety in the arrangement and grouping of slabs, and a well-designed shared green realm between. However, this difference is also reflective of the fundamentally different housing culture within each regime. The extremely varied hyper-articulation of individual dwellings in Märkisches Viertel that sought to elevate the housing standard of a segment of the population highlights the radicality of the very concept of the socially undifferentiated housing provision in Marzahn.

The concept of social equality and corresponding principle of the same housing conditions for the entire population of the GDR appears to have been highly valued by Marzahn inhabitants. While the lack of choice may have played a role, it seems that the social ties within this community – despite being partly state-administered – were strong. This is in stark contrast to the social polarization inherent in the very concept of social housing. The ongoing stigmatisation of Marzahn obscures the radical significance of what housing policy in the GDR sought to achieve, and, at least in parts, realised.

The description above also summarises some of the consequences of stigmatisation, where an externally produced narrative had consequences on the self-perception, and by extension well-being, of the estates' inhabitants. It is here that the difference between the two estates becomes crucial as a lesson for investigating housing and well-being: it is impossible to define residential well-being without an extensive understanding of the respective context, and the reality of its inhabitants.

This is also relevant in our assessment of the scale and the forms of Märkisches Viertel and Marzahn, which are in marked contrast to current conceptions of housing and neighbourhoods. However, as the account above showed, it is not the height or the density of buildings that are responsible for a lack of well-being. Florian Urban has shown that very similar housing models are successful in different global contexts and as diverse in their significance and connotations as its many different cultural contexts.[50]

Our current planning paradigm tends to be focussed on smaller scale developments, with more varied building forms and morphologies, and with mixed tenures. In parts, this is the result of the general disenchantment with large-scale modernist planning as exemplified by Märkisches Viertel and Marzahn; just as their designs were based on a critique on what went on before. Also, the integration of community involvement in planning can be understood, in parts, as being due to changing sensibilities, in parts based on a critique against the autocratic planning exemplified in Märkisches Viertel and Marzahn.

Nonetheless, this chapter has argued that the architecture of both estates, once brought to an adequate standard, has supported well-being and community cohesion. Today, we continue to deploy formal and spatial experimentation at the scale of the neighbourhood and that of the dwelling. Given that we continue to use spatial arrangements and adjacencies to imbue light and air, but also vitality and variety, social cohesion and neighbourly interaction, we should remember that the efforts that go into good design are valuable.

Acknowledgements

I would like to thank the Kajima Foundation for funding this research. This chapter would not have been possible without the generosity of the following archives, who granted access to their collections and permissions for reproduction, as well as the archivists' for their expertise and support: Juliane Kreißl, Tanja Morgenstern and Celia Alfes, Baukunstarchiv, Akademie der Künste, Berlin; Claudia Zachariae and Franziska Schilling, Architekturmuseum TU Berlin; and Anja Pienkny, Leibniz-Institut für Raumbezogene Sozialforschung (IRS), Erkner. A thank you also to Katharina Merz und Hans Düttmann for permission to access and reproduce works from the Werner Düttmann archive, Baukunstarchiv, Akademie der Künste.

Notes

1 Katharina Borsi, *The Berlin Tenement and the City* (Abingdon, England; New York, NY: Routledge, 2025); Katharina Borsi, "Hans Scharoun's 'Dwelling Cells' and the autonomy of architecture," *The Journal of Architecture* 7–8, no. 23 (2018), https://doi.org/10.1080/13602365.2018.1513418.

2 Kenny Cupers. 2015. "The Cultural Center," *Journal of the Society of Architectural Historians* 74 (4), https://doi.org/10.1525/jsah.2015.74.4.464, https://dx.doi.org/10.1525/jsah.2015.74.4.464.

3 Annemarie Sammartino. 2017. "The New Socialist Man in the Plattenbau: The East German Housing Program and the Development of the Socialist Way of Life," *Journal of Urban History* 44 (1), https://doi.org/ https://journals.sagepub.com/doi/full/10.1177/0096144217710231.
4 Steffen Krämer. 2007. ""Urbanität durch Dichte" – Die neue Maxime im deutschen Städte- und Siedlungsbau der 1960er Jahre," https://doi.org/10.11588/artdok.00006641, https://archiv.ub.uni-heidelberg.de/artdok/6641/.
5 Florian Urban. 2018. "Large Housing Estates of Berlin, Germany," in *Housing Estates in Europe. The Urban Book Series* eds. I. Tammaru D. Hess, and M. van Ham, Cham, Switzerland: Springer; Christiane Reinecke. 2020. "Into the Cold: Neighborliness, Class, and the Emotional Landscape of Urban Modernism in France and West Germany, " *Journal of Urban History* 48(1).
6 Urban, "Large Housing Estates of Berlin, Germany."
7 Senatsverwaltung für Stadtentwicklung Berlin. 2010, "Fachkonferenz 'Stadtumbau in Großsiedlungen' Fontane-Haus im Märkischen Viertel, Berlin-Reinickendorf Mittwoch, 08.07.2009". https://www.nachhaltige-erneuerung.berlin.de/fileadmin/_migrated/content_uploads/Fachkonferenz_SU_in_Grosssiedlungen_01.pdf
8 Jascha Braun, *Großsiedlungsbau im geteilten Berlin. Das Märkische Viertel und Marzahn als Beispiele des spätmodernen Städtebaus* (Berlin: Gebr.Mann Verlag, 2018). Christine Hannemann, *Die Platte Industrialisierter Wohnungsbau in der DDR* (Wiesbaden: Vieweg+Teubner Verlag, 1996). Eli Rubin. 2014/2006. "Amnesiopolis: From Mietskaserne to Wohnungsbauserie 70 in East Berlin's Northeast," *Central European History* 47 (2), https://doi.org/10.1017/S0008938914001277.
9 Ronald van Kempen et al., eds., 2005. *Restructuring Large Housing Estates in Europe: Restructuring and Resistance Inside the Welfare Industry,* Bristol: Bristol University Press.
10 Amt für Statistik Berlin-Brandenburg. 2023. *Statistischer Bericht. A I 5 – hj 2/22. Einwohnerregisterstatistik. Berlin 31. Dezember 2022.* Potsdam.
11 25 architects were involved in the realisation of housing projects, many of them came to be well known: Karl Fleig, René Gagès, Ernst Gisel, Werner Düttmann, Georg Heinrichs, Hans Christian Müller, Lothar Juckel, Chen Kuen Lee, Ludwig Leo, Peter Pfankuch, Hansrudolf Plarre, Heinz Schudnagies, Herbert Stranz, O. M. Ungers, Schadrach Woods, Astra Zarina, Siegfried Hoffie, Erwin Eickhoff, Jo Zimmermann and the building department of the housing company Deutsche Gesellschaft zur Förderung des Wohnungsbaues.
12 Hans Scharoun was collaborator and mentor to Düttmann and many of the architects contributing to the Märkische Viertel. See: Georg Heinrichs and Hans Christian Müller Werner Düttmann. 1963. "Märkisches Viertel, Berlin-Reinickendorf," *Bauwelt* 54.
13 Katharina Borsi. 2018. "Hans Scharoun's 'Dwelling Cells' and the autonomy of architecture," *The Journal of Architecture* 7-8 (23), https://doi.org/10.1080/13602365.2018.1513418.
14 Hans Scharoun. 1962. "Charlottenburg-Nord. Sechzig Jahre Entwicklung der "Siemensstadt" von der Randbebauung zum Wohngehöft," *Neue Heimat* 2.
15 Georg Heinrichs and Hans Christian Müller Werner Düttmann. 1963. "Märkisches Viertel, Berlin-Reinickendorf," *Bauwelt* 54.
16 Hans Christian Müller, Brigitte Jacob, and Wolfgang Schäche. 2004. ""Es ist unglaublich, ein solches Viertel gebaut zu haben" Ein Gespräch mit Hans Christian Müller," in *40 Jahre Märkisches Viertel. Geschichte und Gegenwart einer Grossiedlung*, ed. Brigitte Jacob and Wolfgang Schäche. Berlin: Jovis.
17 Werner Düttmann. undated. *Märkisches Viertel Description. Archiv Düttmann 0156_071_02*, Akademie der Künste, Berlin, Baukunstarchiv.
18 See the descriptions by the different architects in M.S., "Berlin Märkisches Viertel – Ein Zwischenbericht," *Bauwelt* 46/47 (1967).
19 M.S., "Berlin Märkisches Viertel – Ein Zwischenbericht." p. 1192
20 M.S., "Berlin Märkisches Viertel."
21 M.S., "Berlin Märkisches Viertel."
22 M.S., "Berlin Märkisches Viertel," p.1191
23 For the ideological role of Cultural Centres see Cupers, "The Cultural Center."
24 See Braun, *Großsiedlungsbau im geteilten Berlin. Das Märkische Viertel und Marzahn als Beispiele des spätmodernen Städtebaus.*

25 The Düttmann Archive held in the ADK Baukunstarchiv Berlin contains letters to Düttmann by residents, upset by the negative media portrayal and expressing thanks for the quality of their apartments. See also "Oswald Mathias Ungers im Interview," in *40 Jahre Märkisches Viertel – Geschichte und Gegenwart einer Grosssiedlung*, ed. Brigitte Jacob and Wolfgang Schäche (Berlin 2004).
26 Hannemann, *Die Platte Industrialisierter Wohnungsbau in der DDR.*
27 Marilyn Rueschemeyer. 1988. "New Towns in the German Democratic Republic," *International Journal of Sociology* 18 3–4, https://doi.org/ https://www.tandfonline.com/doi/abs/10.1080/15579336.1988.11769961.
28 Emily Pugh. 2014. *Architecture, Politics, and Identity in Divided Berlin.* Pittsburgh: University of Pittsburgh Press.
29 Alice Kahl. 1989. "Wohnkultur in der DDR – soziale Ergebnisse und Erfahrungen des Wohnungsbauprogramms," in Kultur Und Gesellschaft: Gemeinsamer Kongreß Der Deutschen, Der Österreichischen Und Der Schweizerischen Gesellschaft Für Soziologie, Zürich 1988, Beiträge der Forschungskomitees, Sektionen und Adhoc-Gruppen. ed. H.-J. Hoffmann-Nowotny, *Zürich: Seismo Verl*, pp. 486-488. https://nbn-resolving.org/urn:nbn:de:0168-ssoar-146779.
30 Rubin, "Amnesiopolis: From Mietskaserne to Wohnungsbauserie 70 in East Berlin's Northeast."
31 Hannemann, *Die Platte Industrialisierter Wohnungsbau in der DDR.* Sigrun Kabisch et al. 2022. "Measuring residential satisfaction over time: Results from a unique long-term study of a large housing estate," *Housing Studies* 37 (10), https://doi.org/10.1080/02673037.2020.1867083, https://www.tandfonline.com/doi/full/10.1080/02673037.2020.1867083?src=recsys.
32 Bauakademie der DDR. 1976. *Komplexrichtlinie für die städtebauliche Planung und Gestaltung von Neubauwohngebieten.*
33 In 1994, every fourth person was living in a large scale housing estate in the new federal states of the former GDR, in the old federal states only every sixtieth person lives in an estate with more than 2500 residential units. Bauwesen und Städtebau Bundesministerium für Raumordnung, *Großsiedlungsbericht 1994* (1994).
34 Pugh, *Architecture, Politics, and Identity in Divided Berlin.*
35 Braun, *Großsiedlungsbau im geteilten Berlin. Das Märkische Viertel und Marzahn als Beispiele des spätmodernen Städtebaus.*
36 As Annemarie Sammartino demonstrated, East German planners were influenced not only by modernist principles and soviet planning, but also by the new urbanism of Jane Jacobs. Sammartino, "The New Socialist Man in the Plattenbau: The East German Housing Program and the Development of the Socialist Way of Life."
37 Torsten Lange. 2015. "Komplexe Umweltgestaltung [complex environmental design]. Architectural theory and the production of the built environment in the German Democratic Republic (GDR), 1960-1990, " University College London.
38 Sammartino, "The New Socialist Man in the Plattenbau: The East German Housing Program and the Development of the Socialist Way of Life."
39 See Sammartino, "The New Socialist Man in the Plattenbau: The East German Housing Program and the Development of the Socialist Way of Life."
40 Urban, "Large Housing Estates of Berlin, Germany."
41 Reinecke, "Into the Cold: Neighborliness, Class, and the Emotional Landscape of Urban Modernism in France and West Germany ".
42 Alexander Wilde. 1989. *Das Märkische Viertel,* Berlin: Nicolai.
43 in Reinecke, "Into the Cold: Neighborliness, Class, and the Emotional Landscape of Urban Modernism in France and West Germany"; Urban, "Large Housing Estates of Berlin, Germany."
44 Brigitte Jacob and Wolfgang Schäche, eds., *40 Jahre Märkisches Viertel: Geschichte und Gegenwart einer Großsiedlung,* Berlin: Jovis verlag.
45 Brücke-Museum, *Düttmann on the planning of the Märkische Viertel,* Landesarchiv Berlin.
46 The study was conducted by sociologist Loni Niederländer at the Humboldt University's Institute for Marxist-Leninist Sociology. In: *Rubin, "Amnesiopolis: From Mietskaserne to Wohnungsbauserie 70 in East Berlin's Northeast."*
47 Open Society Foundation. 2014. *Europe's White Working Class Communities: Berlin.*
48 Open Society Foundation, *Europe's White Working Class Communities*

49 Zeiher, Johannes, Kathleen Häßler, Dr. Jonas Finger, and Dr. Sabine Hermann (Senatsverwaltung für Wissenschaft, Gesundheit, Pflege und Gleichstellung Berlin).2022. Gesundheits- Und Sozialstrukturatlas Berlin (https://www.berlin.de/sen/gesundheit/ service/gesundheitsberichterstattung/gesundheit-und-sozialstruktur/)
50 Florian Urban. 2012. *Tower and Slab: Histories of Global Mass Housing*. Abingdon, Oxon; New York, NY: Routledge.

References

Berlin-Brandenburg, Amt für Statistik. 2023. *Statistischer Bericht. A I 5 – Hj 2/22. Einwohnerregisterstatistik. Berlin 31. Dezember 2022.* (Potsdam).

Borsi, Katharina. 2018. "Hans Scharoun's 'Dwelling Cells' and the Autonomy of Architecture [In En]." *The Journal of Architecture* 7–8 (23): 1104–42. https://doi.org/10.1080/13602365.2018.1513418.

Borsi, Katharina. 2025. *The Berlin Tenement and the City*. Abingdon, England; New York, NY: Routledge.

Braun, Jascha. 2018. *Großsiedlungsbau Im Geteilten Berlin. Das Märkische Viertel Und Marzahn Als Beispiele Des Spätmodernen Städtebaus*. Berlin: Gebr.Mann Verlag.

Bundesministerium für Raumordnung, Bauwesen und Städtebau. 1994. *Großsiedlungsbericht.*

Cupers, Kenny. 2015. "The Cultural Center." *Journal of the Society of Architectural Historians* 74 (4): 464–84. https://dx.doi.org/10.1525/jsah.2015.74.4.464

DDR, Bauakademie der. 1976. *Komplexrichtlinie Für Die Städtebauliche Planung Und Gestaltung Von Neubauwohngebieten..*

Düttmann, Werner. Undated. *Märkisches Viertel Description. Archiv Düttmann 0156_071_02.* Akademie der Künste, Berlin, Baukunstarchiv.

Foundation, Open Society. 2014. *Europe's White Working Class Communities: Berlin.*

Hannemann, Christine. 1996. *Die Platte Industrialisierter Wohnungsbau in Der Ddr*. Wiesbaden: Vieweg+Teubner Verlag.

Jacob, Brigitte, and Wolfgang Schäche, eds. 2004. *40 Jahre Märkisches Viertel: Geschichte Und Gegenwart Einer Großsiedlung*. Berlin: Jovis Verlag.

Kabisch, Sigrun, Janine Poessneck, Max Soeding, and Uwe Schlink. 2022. "Measuring Residential Satisfaction over Time: Results from a Unique Long-Term Study of a Large Housing Estate." *Housing Studies* 37 (10). https://doi.org/10.1080/02673037.2020.1867083. https://www.tandfonline.com/doi/full/10.1080/02673037.2020.1867083?src=recsys.

Kahl, Alice. 1989. "Wohnkultur in Der DDR- Soziale Ergebnisse Und Erfahrungen Des Wohnungsbauprogramms." In *Kultur Und Gesellschaft: Gemeinsamer Kongreß Der Deutschen, Der Österreichischen Und Der Schweizerischen Gesellschaft Für Soziologie, Zürich 1988*, Beiträge der Forschungskomitees, Sektionen und Adhoc-Gruppen. Edited by H.-J. Hoffmann-Nowotny, Zürich: Seismo Verl, pp. 486–488. https://nbn-resolving.org/urn:nbn:de:0168-ssoar-146779.

Kempen, Ronald van, Karien Dekker, Stephen Hall, and Iván Tosics, eds.. 2005. *Restructuring Large Housing Estates in Europe: Restructuring and Resistance Inside the Welfare Industry.* Bristol: Bristol University Press.

Krämer, Steffen. 2007. ""Urbanität Durch Dichte" – Die Neue Maxime Im Deutschen Städte- Und Siedlungsbau Der 1960er Jahre." https://doi.org/10.11588/artdok.00006641. https://archiv.ub.uni-heidelberg.de/artdok/6641/.

Lange, Torsten. 2015. "Komplexe Umweltgestaltung [Complex Environmental Design]. Architectural Theory and the Production of the Built Environment in the German Democratic Republic (Gdr), 1960-1990." University College London.

M.S. 1967. "Berlin Märkisches Viertel – Ein Zwischenbericht." *Bauwelt* 46/47: 1189–211.

Müller, Hans Christian, Brigitte Jacob, and Wolfgang Schäche. 2004. ""Es Ist Unglaublich, Ein Solches Viertel Gebaut Zu Haben" Ein Gespräch Mit Hans Christian Müller." In *40 Jahre Märkisches Viertel. Geschichte Und Gegenwart Einer Grossiedlung*, edited by Brigitte Jacob and Wolfgang Schäche, 158–75. Berlin: Jovis.

Pugh, Emily. 2014. *Architecture, Politics, and Identity in Divided Berlin*. Pittsburgh: University of Pittsburgh Press.

Reinecke, Christiane. 2020. "Into the Cold: Neighborliness, Class, and the Emotional Landscape of Urban Modernism in France and West Germany." *Journal of Urban History* 48 (1): 163–81.
Rubin, Eli. 2014. "Amnesiopolis: From Mietskaserne to Wohnungsbauserie 70 in East Berlin's Northeast." *Central European History* 47 (2/06). https://doi.org/10.1017/S0008938914001277.
Rueschemeyer, Marilyn. 1988. "New Towns in the German Democratic Republic." *International Journal of Sociology* 18 (3–4). https://doi.org/https://www.tandfonline.com/doi/abs/10.1080/15579336.1988.11769961.
Sammartino, Annemarie. 2017. "The New Socialist Man in the Plattenbau: The East German Housing Program and the Development of the Socialist Way of Life." *Journal of Urban History* 44 (1).. https://doi.org/https://journals.sagepub.com/doi/full/10.1177/0096144217710231.
Scharoun, Hans. 1962. "Charlottenburg-Nord. Sechzig Jahre Entwicklung Der "SiemensStadt" Von Der Randbebauung Zum Wohngehöft." *Neue Heimat* 2: 18–32.
Schmidt, Lisa Marei. 2024. "Düttmann on the Planning of the Märkische Viertel." Brücke Museum. Werner Düttmann. Building. Berlin. https://wernerduettmann.de/.
Senatsverwaltung für Stadtentwicklung Berlin. 2010. "Fachkonferenz 'Stadtumbau in Großsiedlungen' Fontane-Haus im Märkischen Viertel, Berlin-Reinickendorf Mittwoch, 08.07.2009". https://www.nachhaltige-erneuerung.berlin.de/fileadmin/_migrated/content_uploads/Fachkonferenz_SU_in_Grosssiedlungen_01.pdf
Urban, Florian. 2012. *Tower and Slab: Histories of Global Mass Housing*. Abingdon, Oxon; New York, NY: Routledge.
Urban, Florian. 2018. "Large Housing Estates of Berlin, Germany." In *Housing Estates in Europe. The Urban Book Series*, edited by I. Tammaru, D. Hess, and M. van Ham. Cham, Switzerland: Springer.
Werner, Düttmann, Georg Heinrichs, and Hans Christian Müller. 1963. "Märkisches Viertel, Berlin-Reinickendorf." *Bauwelt* 54: 390–93.
Wilde, Alexander. 1989. *Das Märkische Viertel*. Berlin: Nicolai.
Zeiher, Johannes, Kathleen Häßler, Jonas Finger, and Sabine Hermann (Senatsverwaltung für Wissenschaft, Gesundheit, Pflege und Gleichstellung Berlin). 2022. *Gesundheits- Und Sozialstrukturatlas Berlin* 2022. https://www.berlin.de/sen/gesundheit/service/gesundheitsberichterstattung/gesundheit-und-sozialstruktur/

5

THE IMPACT OF HOUSING ACCESS POLICIES ON WELL-BEING IN SPAIN

Montserrat Pareja-Eastaway

Housing Policies and Their Effect on Well-being: An Introduction

The concept of well-being has become a prominent topic in social sciences, characterised by its cross-disciplinary relevance and multidimensional nature (Jarden and Roache 2023). The relationship between housing and well-being has been extensively explored in the literature (McClatchey et al. 2023; Rice and Drane 2020; Riva et al. 2022) with renewed emphasis following the COVID-19 lockdowns on the critical importance of the physical environment where people live, study, and work (D'Alessandro and Appolloni 2020). Health and well-being measures are strongly correlated with factors such as housing service provision, tenants' experiences of property quality, and neighbourhood characteristics (Rolfe et al. 2020).

A significant research gap exists in analysing the relationship between the consequences of housing policies (or their absence) and well-being. The underlying hypothesis is that a certain level of well-being directly results from the implementation of housing policies. For example, Leifheit et al. (2022) suggest that the observed correlation between housing insecurity and low levels of well-being in the US stems from specific policy decisions made in the past (Leifheit et al. 2022) and Nix et al. (2024) conclude that housing policies mandating health-related requirements are essential in reducing the disease burden associated with poor housing conditions (Nix et al. 2024).

Housing is a multifaceted good that provides access to various functions. The meaning of home and its contribution to well-being is closely tied to housing policies, which play a crucial role in shaping the accessibility, affordability and quality of housing for individuals and communities (Smith 2005). Housing policies significantly impact home affordability, influencing individuals' ability to establish and maintain a stable home environment. Affordable housing policies aim to ensure that diverse individuals, regardless of socioeconomic status, can access housing that meets their needs. The availability of affordable housing contributes to community stability and fosters a sense of home for residents. These policies also influence living standards by addressing issues related to safety, health and overall well-being. Similarly, regulations and guidelines established by

DOI: 10.4324/9781003527930-8

housing policies help create homes that provide a secure and healthy environment. Therefore, housing quality directly affects the meaning of home, as a safe and well-maintained physical space is essential for individuals to feel comfort and belonging. The absence of policies guaranteeing affordability can prevent housing from triggering positive outcomes in other dimensions of well-being.

The development of various welfare states in Europe after World War II (WWII; 1939–1945) and the Spanish Civil War (1936–1939) aimed to improve the population's quality of life through public or publicly guaranteed provision of essential goods such as education, health, and housing. These policy efforts led to the current 'European social model,' which represents the consolidation of decades of government intervention in these areas. Despite housing being a vital asset, housing policies have been considered as one of the 'wobbly pillars' of the welfare state (Torgersen 1987) due to their relative inability to establish a robust housing system capable of providing residential solutions to all segments of the population, unlike health or education systems.

The significant housing deficit following the armed conflicts, combined with the need to rebuild existing housing stock, directed housing policies in Europe primarily towards supply, namely, new housing construction by the public sector or with private sector support. In most European countries, massive social housing construction, mainly for public rent, aimed to provide relief to low-income families. Newly built areas, known as housing estates, emerged as distinct geographical areas planned by the state or with state support (Dekker and van Kempen 2005).

Spain presents a case where post-Civil War housing access was understood differently than in most European countries. Instead of focusing on the subsidised rental market, the public sector promoted homeownership by subsidising both supply and demand. Unlike in Europe, social housing in Spain was viewed as homeownership. In addition, many of the publicly owned dwellings built in the periphery of cities initially rented were privatised – mostly acquired by the residents - along time. This strategy had a very significant impact on the well-being of families. The scarcity of a robust and sufficiently large segment of social housing provided by the public sector led to family networks and relationships acting as a safety net in citizens' housing careers (Allen et al. 2004). These family networks act as a support in the absence of formal alternatives, which can have both positive and negative repercussions.

Spanish public authorities shared the goal of affordable housing provision with their European neighbours but also aimed to reinforce the real estate sector as an economic driver with a significant multiplier effect on the broader economy. By the end of the twentieth century, Spain's social sector or publicly owned rented dwellings represented less than 1% of the housing stock, much lower than in other European countries.

In this chapter, I argue that Spain's historical trajectory of housing policies favouring access has significantly impacted its citizens' well-being, shaping their current challenges and opportunities. Housing's role as an economic driver in Spain has diminished its importance as a key asset for citizens' welfare. Well-being in Spain has been deeply affected by the (lack of) housing policies targeting lower-income segments, and this has also encouraged bottom-up initiatives to provide alternatives to public access delivery of social housing, reinforcing the notion of well-being. Therefore, I emphasise the importance of family networks and communities as safety nets, given the inconsistencies of public policies in ensuring adequate housing for all and the negative effects on households' overall perception of well-being. This chapter will also provide examples of how well-being is considered in top-down policies and more community-based initiatives.

Welfare States in Europe. The Role of Housing and the Consideration of Well-being

In his 1990 book, The Three Worlds of Welfare Capitalism, Esping-Andersen outlined a typology of welfare states for the Western world (Esping-Andersen 1990). The classification is based on the degree of decommodification of social rights. Later, the author expanded his analysis to include the role of families and the participation, especially of women, in the provision of welfare services (Esping-Andersen 2000).

A society's welfare regime is defined by the joint and interdependent way welfare is produced and distributed by its key actors: the State, the market, the family, and the Third Sector or non-profit sector, as well as the relationships established between these agents. Under this premise, Esping-Andersen identifies three types of welfare states (see Figure 5.1). Despite potential limitations and simplifications, Esping-Andersen's theories offer a complex, accurate and insightful view of welfare systems and their sometimes-conflicting relationship with housing systems (Stephens 2020).

Depending on the characteristics of each scheme, aid for housing access takes different forms. For example, liberal regimes provide limited assistance to working-class individuals or families, depending on their eligibility based on several income-related criteria. Conservative regimes, which are based on traditional values, intervene only when families' capacity to access housing is insufficient. Social democratic regimes, on the other hand, are universal and promote equal access to housing for all social strata, regardless of income.

Countries such as Italy, Spain, Portugal and Greece are not represented by this classic typology, although Esping-Andersen later emphasises the relevance of family networks as substitutes for or complements to the state (Esping-Andersen 2000). Likewise, the countries of Central and Eastern Europe, which have transitioned from planned to capitalist economies, are not included. Thus, some academics characterise Southern Europe as a set of countries where the welfare system is rudimentary, and family and personal

FIGURE 5.1 Welfare estate typologies.

Source: Esping-Andersen 1990.

networks fill a large part of the gaps in public policy (Allen et al. 2004; Leibfried 1993), while Central and Eastern Europe is often referred to as a region of 'transition regimes' or ultra-homeownership countries (Hegedus et al. 1992).

The specificities of public policies, family and personal relations and family culture in Southern Europe have contributed to the definition of a 'Mediterranean welfare model.' Many authors agree that Mediterranean countries require an alternative model in which welfare services that contribute to household well-being are integrated into the family system. As Mignone (2005) points out, this phenomenon has implications such as the increased importance of kinship relations, delayed independence for young people, and declining birth rates (Mignone 2005).

Figure 5.2 illustrates the relative convergence of welfare states in certain countries in 2023. On the one hand, the Swedish social democratic tradition is assimilated by countries like Germany and the Netherlands, which are more liberal. These countries, with pre-transfer poverty rates between 37 and 42%, manage to reduce these rates to between 14 and 16% through public welfare state interventions. On the other hand, Southern Mediterranean countries show slightly higher pre-transfer poverty rates than those of more interventionist countries, around 45%. However, despite maintaining higher post-transfer poverty rates than Germany, Sweden and the Netherlands, evidence suggests that even a rudimentary welfare state in these Southern Mediterranean countries contributes to significantly reducing poverty rates, to between 18.8 and 20.4%.

Welfare states are decisive in shaping each country's housing systems (van der Heijden 2013). The convergence of supply (developers, builders, intermediaries or rental housing owners) and demand (primarily households and their preferences and needs), along with the institutions involved, is framed within the context and cultural values typical

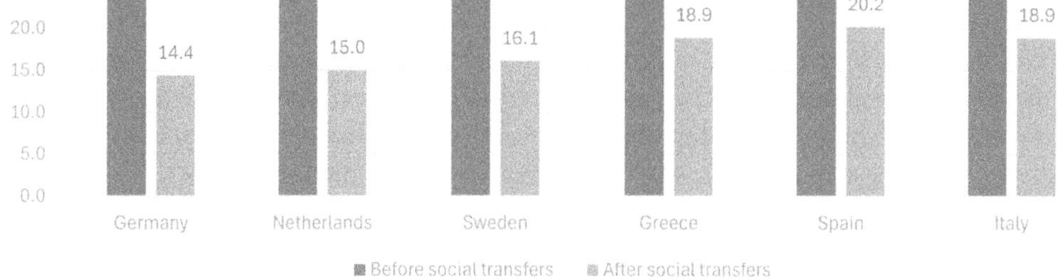

FIGURE 5.2 At-risk-of-poverty rate (*) before and after social transfers by poverty threshold. Several countries. 2023.

Source: EU-SILC, 2023.

(*) Percentage of persons living in households where the equivalised total disposable household income is below 60% of median equivalised disposable income of all households.

of a specific welfare state. These values reflect the sentiments of a society and are thus dynamic and subject to change.

Since housing has never been an integral component of the public welfare systems that have characterised European welfare states since 1945, the tension between market forces and public housing policy orientations has been evident throughout the second half of the twentieth century and continues today. In Spain, this tension is apparent when reviewing the sector's evolution since the late 1940s, affecting the market's structural composition, pricing and rental levels, spatial distribution, and the institutional characterisation of the agents involved (Pareja-Eastaway and Sánchez-Martínez 2017a).

Despite being part of the group of countries with rudimentary welfare states, Spain exhibits certain peculiarities in housing, particularly the strong commitment of the dictatorship to the real estate sector over several decades. The government's lack of active involvement in broadly providing quality-of-life standards between 1939 and 1975 resulted in inadequate public protection. This led to the emergence of a welfare state largely dependent on family networks of help and cooperation (Allen et al. 2004; Navarro 2004) with limited success in protecting the right to housing (Bosch et al. 2023a). Although stronger policies in education and health significantly contributed to the well-being of Spanish households and families, the deep and exacerbated social divide between rich and poor, a legacy of decades of dictatorship with weak welfare provisions, translated into significant disparities in well-being. Opportunities were not equally distributed, and being born into a working-class family significantly diminished one's chances of success in both work and housing careers.

Housing Systems, Housing Policies and Well-being

The analysis of the relationship between welfare states and housing provision has led to the identification of four distinct housing models or systems, considering the evolution of welfare systems worldwide and their influence on housing provision choices (Kemeny and Lowe 1998).

Firstly, it is argued that all housing provision systems are driven by the same underlying imperatives, leading to either present similarities or eventual convergence. This idea forms the basis of the 'convergence' theories of housing provision systems. However, there is no clear consensus on what these systems will converge towards, whether in terms of predominant tenure types or the role of social housing. Implicitly, the trajectory of welfare states is also assumed to converge under certain assumptions (Donnison 1967; Harloe 1995; Hegedüs et al. 1996). To summarise, key characteristics include the growing dominance of homeownership, the expansion of the private rental sector, and the *residualisation* of social housing, with the intervention of a minimalist state.

Conversely, other theories emphasise the differences between housing systems and propose typologies, derived from cultural, ideological, political or other relevant theories, as a basis for understanding these variations. These are known as 'divergence' theories in housing provision. This approach places fundamental importance on discerning patterns and typologies of housing systems, paying careful attention to historical and cultural contexts as well as the trajectories or path dependencies of different institutions, policies, and actors.

Proponents of the divergent view of housing provision identify multiple aspects where countries do not overlap. Examples include the varying roles of social housing within different housing systems, the influence of significantly different starting points in social housing provision, or the feasibility of making the public rental sector profitable and economically viable (Hoekstra 2010).

The third group of theories, known as capital-led or capitalism-directed theories, explain social housing provision through the lens of the capitalist system (Schwartz and Seabroke 2008). According to this perspective, each variety of capitalism is associated with a specific welfare system, which in turn corresponds to a particular housing regime. As the system evolves, ranging from minimal to extensive state intervention, different varieties of capitalism emerge, leading to different models of housing systems.

Finally, bottom-up theories identify new processes, accelerated by the global financial crisis and the COVID-19 pandemic, that are based on emerging welfare benefits introduced by new actors (households, civil organisations, local collective actions) primarily at the local level. These new processes promote innovative mechanisms of social innovation. In housing, illustrative examples include self-provided (collective) housing, cohousing, citizen protests the banking system, housing cooperatives and energy cooperatives (Blessing 2012).

As we will see, Spain evidences the case of a divergent model after the war period where affordability was not the main target of public policies but the reinforcement of the real estate sector, key for the economic development of the country, with direct implications for the well-being of society. Facilitating access to homeownership became the rule while the provision of affordable housing was left in hands of the family and social networks. However, since European countries are currently addressing more efforts to promote homeownership than reinforcing the rented sector, private or public, similarly to what Spain experienced in the past, they are witnessing the emergence of bottom-up strategies based on grassroots movements or activism to ease housing access after the Great Financial Crisis. A preliminary conclusion would be that when public authorities fail in their role of facilitating access to housing, society self-organises to maintain a minimum level of well-being for its citizens.

Evidence of Housing Systems Performance

The different trajectories of European housing systems play a fundamental role in contemporary analyses of tenure and the significance of home and well-being. The distinctive characteristics of housing demand and supply in each country, along with the evolution of public policies in this area, determine which issues define each situation. Specifically, the combination of public intervention and market forces to facilitate housing provision for the lowest incomes has led to the existence of social housing stocks with very different characteristics across countries, reflecting different conceptions of the social housing sector. The nature of social housing '... depends on the impact of past policies and the current strength of organizational, regulatory, and market structures' (Whitehead 2003, 151). It is also worth noting that terms like 'social rent' are not always synonymous with public rent. In fact, many social housing managers are non-profit entities, such as the well-known 'housing associations' in the Netherlands or the UK, which play a crucial role in providing affordable rental housing and are not necessarily public companies, as might be assumed in Spain.

Public spending on social protection in housing objectively and comparably demonstrates the values and priorities of states in the housing sector. Despite varying starting

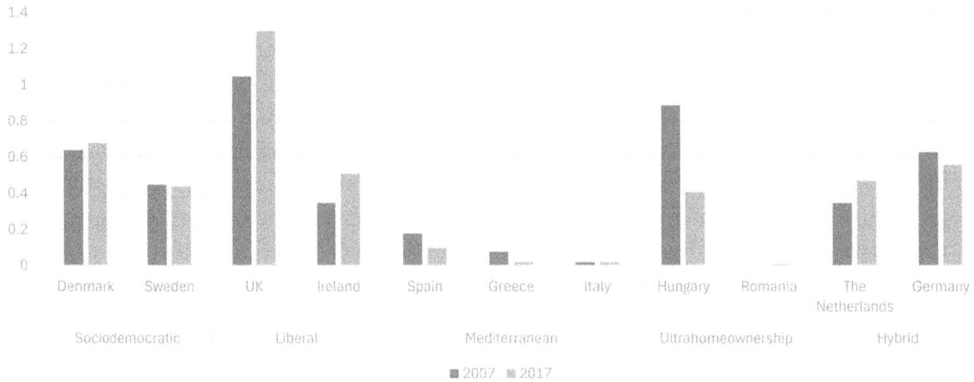

FIGURE 5.3 Spending on social protection in housing. Percentage of GDP. Several countries.

Source: Eurostat.

points and housing dynamics across Europe, selecting countries that represent different welfare states, actors, policies, and trajectories highlights the significant variation in percentages of spending on social protection in housing (see Figure 5.3).

The latest data published by Eurostat indicate that while spending on social protection in housing in Spain represents 0.15% of GDP, in the UK, the Netherlands, and Sweden, it represents 1.3, 0.39 and 0.44%, respectively. Despite its low percentage, Spain's spending is still above that of Greece and Italy, both of which have an expenditure of 0.03% (Ministerio de Transportes Movilidad y Agenda Urbana 2020).

The tenure regime allows for easy comparison of the diverse housing systems in which populations live at a given time. Figure 5.4 shows the distribution of the population in 2023 by tenure – whether ownership or rental – in six European countries representing different housing system trajectories and, consequently, different welfare states. The great

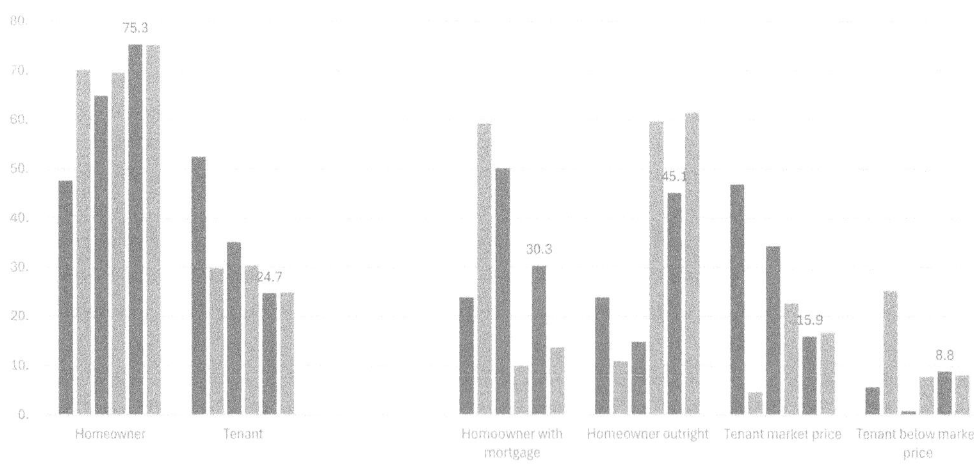

FIGURE 5.4 Distribution of population by tenure status. 2023. Several countries.

Source: EU-SILC, 2023.

variability in dominant tenure types, results from a complex interplay of resources, actors and policies unique to each country. Of those selected, only Germany has a higher percentage of its population living in rental homes than in owned ones. Greece, Italy and Spain have the highest percentages of populations living in fully paid-off homeownership (between 45 and 60%). Conversely, all countries except the Netherlands show almost insignificant percentages (less than 10%) of people living in rental homes with below-market rents. Germany and Sweden have the highest percentages of people living in private rentals, at 53.3 and 35.1%, respectively.

This snapshot of tenure composition in several European countries illustrates the consequences of factors related to different levels of government and their implications for welfare policies and citizen well-being. It also reflects the degree of 'decommodification' of housing, the influence of pressure groups (political corporatism), the public-private fragmentation in the provision of 'traditional' welfare services such as education or health, and the articulation of the market and state in each country. Of all the possible relationships and synergies established between these actors and outcomes, the academic literature has provided significant insights, particularly concerning the relationship between social housing and the characteristics of each country's welfare state, especially from the perspective that considers housing a social right, provided either universally or selectively (Bengtsson 2001; Kristensen 2002; Schöning 2020).

Housing Policies, Welfare and Well-being

The housing policies adopted in the past play a crucial role in shaping the current mix of tenure regimes and the position of housing within the broader welfare system. As previously mentioned, in response to the post-WWII housing deficit, most European countries focused on the creation of large-scale social rental housing estates by promoting construction through subsidies. Simultaneously, access to housing was facilitated through various rent control mechanisms. Although the promotion of social housing was initially widespread and strongly supported by public authorities across Europe since the 1950s, the subsequent evolution of this housing stock has taken on distinct characteristics in each country. According to Van de Heijden (2013), this evolution largely depends on changes in general housing policy, which include:

- The promotion of homeownership for all citizens, not just those with higher incomes.
- The reduction of subsidies, especially those targeting the housing itself, and an increase in household spending on housing.
- The abandonment of rent control mechanisms.
- A relative increase in subsidies aimed at individuals, particularly those in low-income brackets (van der Heijden 2013).

Currently, there is significant debate regarding the role of housing within the modern welfare state. Many experts (Kristensen 2002; Malpass 2008; Scanlon et al. 2014; Schöning 2020) discuss the implications of the *residualisation* of social housing and the shift towards a welfare system based on homeownership. They argue that the rise in homeownership not only contributes to the decline of social housing but could also act as a Trojan horse within the welfare state. High levels of homeownership enable governments to reduce public spending and shift responsibility for individual and family well-being onto citizens themselves. If this trend continues, there could be serious consequences for the future of social housing. The significant reduction in social policies aimed at ensuring housing access may result in fewer incentives to support the (public) rental sector, creating a challenging environment for ensuring the well-being of all citizens.

As we will see, these models contribute to explain the Spanish case and the current dynamics in housing markets, policies, and the well-being of Spanish citizens. While Spain was once considered an outlier in public policy after the wars, exemplifying a 'divergent' model of housing provision, the convergence of housing-related issues now means that Spain is increasingly adopting similar housing policies to those of its European neighbours, despite its different starting point.

Housing Access in Spain and Its Impact on Well-being

Housing plays a crucial role in personal and family development and is a key factor in the social integration and cohesion of neighbourhoods and cities. Housing is a decisive driver of household's well-being. Despite its importance in the above-mentioned areas, housing has not traditionally been treated as a central element of social policy in Spain. Instead, it has been viewed primarily as a driver of economic development (Pareja-Eastaway and Sánchez-Martínez 2012; Trilla 2001).

The housing system in Spain differs significantly from those of other European countries. Spain's welfare state, and particularly its housing policies, has taken a distinct path, shaping a unique framework for public policy. This divergence has led to specific characteristics in Spain's housing system, including an imbalance in tenure types, minimal public housing, and a real estate sector that heavily influences the economy.

One of the key differences between Spain and other European countries, particularly those with a social democratic tradition that has recently shifted towards liberalism, is their starting point. While other countries have built up substantial stocks of protected or social housing units to address market failures, Spain has lacked such a social housing stock, leading to significant gaps in support for vulnerable populations. As Trilla (2001) points out, Spain's housing system has been liberal throughout its history, leaving little room for a more supportive, continuous public strategy for housing access (Trilla 2001).

Spain's political trajectory is also unique. The complexity of the housing system in twenty-first-century Spain is largely a result of the evolution of housing policy since the end of the Civil War (1936–1939). From early post-war interventions focused on addressing housing deficits and poor living conditions, to more sophisticated tax relief and direct subsidies for families, Spain's housing policies have evolved along two main lines: supply side interventions, such as direct support for housing construction, and demand-side interventions, such as financial aid to families, particularly for first-time homebuyers.

The affordability crisis became widespread in Spain following the 2008 Global Financial Crisis, exacerbated by the COVID-19 pandemic in 2020. The percentage of persons living in households in Spain where the total housing costs, net of housing allowances, represent more than 40% of the total disposable household income, net of housing allowances (the so-called 'housing cost overburden' rate) slightly decreased between 2014 and 2023 (from 10.9% in 2014 to 8.2% in 2023) (see Figure 5.5). For the EU (27), that percentage decreased from 11.7% in 2014 to 8.9% in 2023.

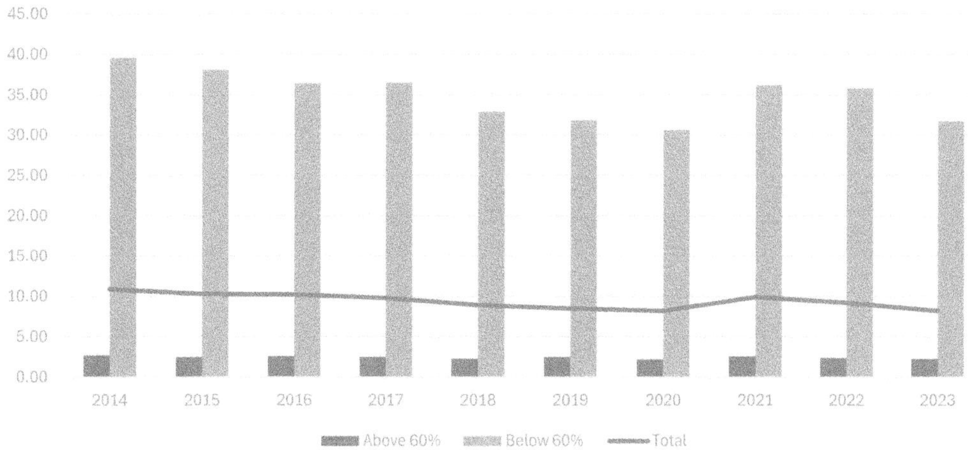

FIGURE 5.5 Housing cost overburden rate in Spain (2014–2023).

Source: EU-SILC 2014–2013.

The differences in housing cost overburden rates between Spanish households and those across the EU (27) for households below the poverty line (with an income below 60% of the median household income after housing costs) are significant. In Spain, the housing cost overburden rate for households below the poverty line decreased from 39.6% in 2014 to 31.7% in 2023. This significant reduction of 7.9 percentage points indicates a relative improvement in housing affordability for low-income households over the last decade. In contrast, for the EU (27), the housing cost overburden rate for similarly low-income households remained relatively stable, starting at 33.1% in 2014 and slightly increasing to 33.6% in 2023. This 0.5 percentage point rise suggests that, on average, low-income households in the EU did not experience the same degree of improvement in housing affordability as seen in Spain.

To provide a wider picture of the overall well-being of Spanish households, to their financial situation analysis, two additional indicators have been considered, on the one hand, the material deprivation (Eurostat, 2024 ilc_pw01) for the housing dimension and, on the other hand, the overall life satisfaction (Eurostat, 2024 ilc_pw01).

Individuals being 'materially deprived' are those at the state of housing deprivation, defined as the state of suffering one or more of the following dwelling problems: (a) leaking roof/damp walls/floors/foundation or rot in window frames; (b) accommodation too dark; (c) no bath/shower; and (d) no indoor flushing toilet for sole use of the household. The figures reveal a notable disparity in deprivation levels between those below the poverty line in Spain and the EU (27). In Spain, 30.8% of individuals below the poverty line experience deprivation in at least one essential item, compared to 19.4% in the EU (27). This indicates that low-income households in Spain face a significantly higher risk of deprivation than their counterparts in the broader European Union. The difference of 11.4 percentage points reflects a gap in living standards and social protection between Spain and the EU average, highlighting potential weaknesses in social welfare programs or structural economic factors that disproportionately affect vulnerable groups in Spain (see Figure 5.6).

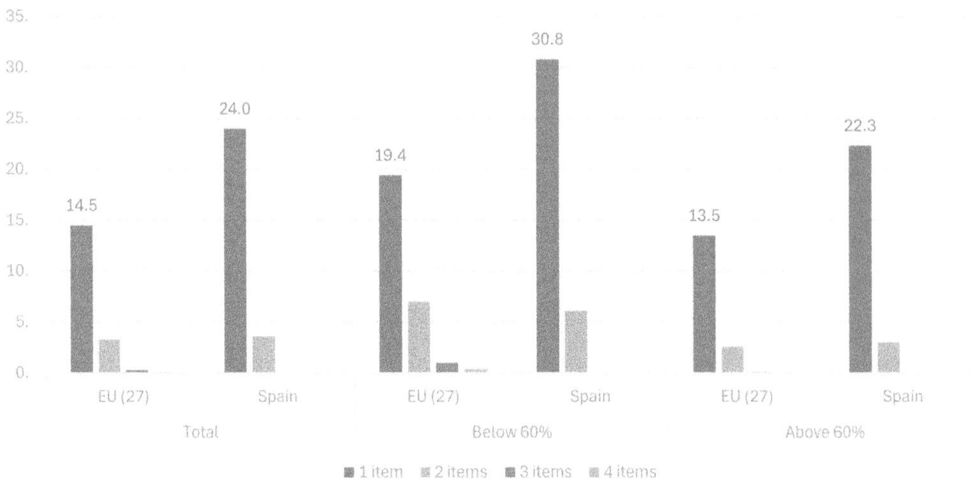

FIGURE 5.6 Material deprivation for the 'Housing' dimension by poverty status and by number of items of deprivation.

Source: EU-SILC, 2023.

One of the most important aspects of subjective well-being is an individual's satisfaction with life in general. In 2023, the rate of overall satisfaction with life in Spain, based on a scale from 0 (not at all satisfied) to 10 (completely satisfied), was at 7.2 on average. As it can be seen in Figure 5.7, the first quintile (lowest income group) consistently has the lowest satisfaction, while the 5th quintile (highest income group)

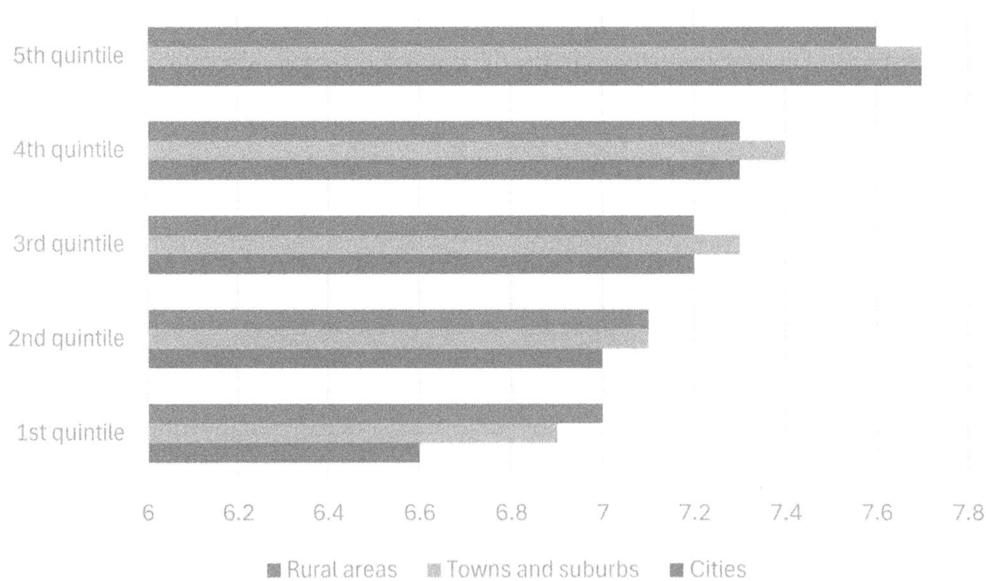

FIGURE 5.7 Overall life satisfaction by income quintile and degree of urbanisation in Spain 2023.

Source: EU-SILC, 2023

shows the highest satisfaction levels. Satisfaction levels rise progressively from the first quintile (around 6.6–7) to the fifth quintile (around 7.6–7.7), indicating that income is a strong determinant of well-being. In cities, satisfaction starts at 6.6 in the first quintile and increases to 7.7 in the 5th quintile. Ci ties show the largest disparity between the lowest and highest income groups. In towns and suburbs, satisfaction ranges from 6.9 (first quintile) to 7.7 (fifth quintile), with slightly higher scores compared to cities in the lower quintiles. Interestingly, satisfaction in rural areas is consistently higher in the lower quintiles (starting at 7), but by the fifth quintile, it reaches 7.6, slightly lower than cities and suburbs.

The overall degree of satisfaction in Spain is closely linked to income, with wealthier households consistently reporting higher satisfaction across all areas. However, lower-income households in rural areas tend to report higher satisfaction than their urban counterparts, suggesting that factors beyond income, such as lifestyle or community support, may play a role in rural well-being.

The persistent problem of housing affordability in Spain with all its consequences on well-being of households has geared public efforts to increasingly focused on improving the quality, quantity, and accessibility of the rental sector, which had been neglected for decades.

The effects of these measures on community cohesion at the neighbourhood level require further study. Increased residential mobility is likely, which could blur established spatial and family/community ties that were previously strengthened by homeownership. The territorial dispersion of new rental housing may disrupt traditional spatial relationships, while simultaneously increasing cultural and economic diversity within neighbourhoods.

For many years, the rising homeownership rate had a significant spatial impact on cities and neighbourhoods. Household mobility in Spain was minimal, with many families remaining in the same home they purchased at the start of their household formation, often after marriage. This limited mobility contributed to a strong sense of community, with individuals often living near their parents, relatives and friends. These close-knit networks played a vital role in the development of households, facilitating access to jobs, elder care, schooling, and leisure activities, as well as housing. Consequently, the housing system helped preserve a collective memory tied to specific locations.

Historical Case Studies of Housing Policies and Their Impact on Well-being in Spain

Post-War Housing (1940s-1970s). The case of Sant Roc, Badalona.

The 1960s saw speculative real estate movements and rapid urban expansion, often resulting in poorly planned housing estates lacking essential infrastructure and services. These neighbourhoods were often situated in polluted areas near factories and lacked environmental controls. The Sant Roc neighbourhood in Barcelona is an example of this phenomenon. Built between 1962 and 1965 to house people from slums and new internal immigrants, Sant Roc comprised 3,395 dwellings across various types of blocks, some as tall as 14 stories. Despite the joy many felt at moving into a new apartment, the neighbourhood suffered from poor construction quality, and by the 1990s, many buildings were affected by structural problems that required replacement.

FIGURE 5.8 Balconies affected by concrete pathology in Sant Roc.
Source: Photo by Montserrat Pareja-Eastaway.

Despite the width between blocks, basic infrastructures were not built, not even planned: sewers, streets with sidewalks, lighting, traffic lights, paving, green areas and services. Despite housing conditions were not the best, the arrival in the neighbourhood was for many a great joy for a new apartment. Enthusiasm for a change of life, full of expectations and dreams, of being part of a community, of a neighbourhood. These dwellings were lately privatised following the trend in the rest of Spain and the neighbourhood, although kept some private rented units, was dominated by homeownership.

In the late Franco era, there was growing awareness of the poor conditions in neighbourhoods like Sant Roc and a rising workers' movement demanding better housing and social services. Sant Roc has been partially renovated due to the concrete pathology affection. The neighbourhood is inhabited by different groups, with a particular relevance of Roma families. For many years, the social-economic position of the inhabitants decreased as people who improved their social, economic and cultural position left the area. Many foreign immigrants (especially from outside the EU) with scarce financial resources have entered the area. Social cohesion and its impact on well-being has been negatively influenced by problems between some of these population groups. Sant Roc remains stigmatised due to the high concentration of marginalised populations, including low-income immigrants, most of them attracted by the low housing prices or rents.

FIGURE 5.9 Daily life in Sant Roc.

Source: Photo by Montserrat Pareja-Eastaway.

Family support or social networks of family or acquaintances usually emerged as a substitute for an unambitious welfare state with a reduced weight in public policies. The social coverage provided by the family through intergenerational aid, both in kind and in cash, compensates for the lack of public action to guarantee a certain standard of living. This is particularly true when looking at housing in certain Southern European countries (Allen et al. 2004).

Democratic Transition and Housing Reforms (1970s–1990s). The Case of Orcasitas, Madrid.

The transition to democracy in Spain in 1975 and the 1978 Constitution marked a turning point for social policy, including housing. This period saw the establishment of the foundations of the Spanish welfare state and significant housing policy reforms. Compared to other European countries, Spain's welfare state was distinctive due to its ongoing decentralisation and the outsized influence of the real estate sector on the economy (Bosch et al. 2023b; Pareja-Eastaway and Sánchez-Martínez 2017b; Trilla and Bosch 2018).

Orcasitas, a neighbourhood in Madrid's Usera district, is a prime example of the housing regeneration efforts during Spain's democratic transition. Originally settled by internal migrants in the 1950s, Orcasitas consisted of barracks and self-built dwellings. In the 1970s and 1980s, these were replaced with decent, affordable housing, with residents playing a key role in the neighbourhood's redevelopment. The housing stock in Orcasitas is, thus, relatively young, with good technical quality and reasonable size (most dwellings have five or six rooms and are between 81 and 100 square metres) They are located in multi-family dwellings with between 20 and 50 dwellings and respond to the later privatised ownership.

The regeneration of Orcasitas included not only new housing but also improved infrastructure, commerce, and services. The neighbourhood association was instrumental in the design of both the housing and the urban layout, and today, Orcasitas remains a strong community with a distinct neighbourhood identity. This transformation from a slum area to a respectable neighbourhood demonstrates the success of the regeneration efforts and the importance of resident involvement in urban development. Orcasitas shows a relative strong social cohesion, and most people are satisfied living there (Pareja-Eastaway et al. 2007).

Contemporary Social Innovation in Housing Access: The case of La Borda, Barcelona.

In recent years, austerity measures have significantly impacted housing policy and the well-being of Spanish citizens, particularly in terms of access to affordable housing. Issues such as temporary housing and disruptive gentrification have highlighted the need

FIGURE 5.10 General view of the Orcasitas neighbourhood.

Source: Photo by Montserrat Pareja-Eastaway.

FIGURE 5.11 Public space in the Orcasitas neighbourhood.

Source: Photo by Montserrat Pareja-Eastaway.

for new housing policies that consider urban effects more carefully. Social innovation in housing has emerged as a response, seeking not only to facilitate access to housing but also to foster a sense of community and shared values.

La Borda is an international example of how residents can commit to values and norms that differ from those dominating the housing market. La Borda is a residents-led housing cooperative to access decent, non-speculative housing that places its use value in the centre, through a collective structure. This project can be aligned under the Collaborative Housing label as it involves collaboration in both their development and management. Processes of co-design along the shaping of the La Borda project contribute to better satisfy resident's needs reflecting their own values and priorities (Brysch et al. 2023).

The community started the initial project in 2012 driven immersed in the process of recovery of the industrial premises of Can Batlló in the Sants neighbourhood of Barcelona. The project is located on a public land of social housing, with a leasehold of 75 years.

La Borda is an international example of resident's commitment to other values and norms of those that dominate the housing market. The creation of a cooperative is an innovative endeavour to provide affordable housing in a context of heated housing prices

FIGURE 5.12 Collective space at La Borda.

Source: Photo by Lluc Miralles.

FIGURE 5.13 Inner corridors and stairs at La Borda.

Source: Photo by Lluc Miralles.

as the one Barcelona is. Spain has not a large tradition in housing cooperatives. During the 70s, although being not mainstream, cooperatives were created and worked as housing developers, maintaining the ownership of the houses. Following the Danish model, La Borda is a housing cooperative where the ownership remains in the cooperative and not in the inhabitant.

The intergenerational community at La Borda includes 45 adults and 13 children living in 28 flats of various sizes. The cooperative's democratic organisation not only provides affordable housing but also offers additional benefits such as capacity building, leadership opportunities, and a sense of belonging. By actively participating in the future of their accommodation, residents enhance their well-being and satisfaction with their living environment (Girbés-Peco et al. 2020).

Discussion. Well-being in Spanish Housing Policy Contexts

The relationship between housing policies and well-being is an intricate and multi-dimensional issue, reflecting a broader debate on how welfare states influence quality of life. This discussion is particularly pertinent in Spain, where historical and policy contexts have shaped the current housing landscape.

Well-being is a nuanced concept, encompassing physical, mental, and social health. Housing significantly impacts well-being through factors like property quality, service provision, and neighbourhood characteristics. Research suggests that specific housing policies – or the lack thereof – directly affect well-being. The housing system acts as the backbone of the relationship between sustainable urban development and the growing social polarisation caused by the phenomenon of globalisation. Thus, one of the local elements that will define the possibilities of avoiding the risk of social exclusion and, in turn, achieving neighbourhoods rich in diversity and socially cohesive is precisely housing, which in turn is a constitutional right. Context-related particularities – institutional factors, path dependency, roots of traditions, specific characteristics – define the local capacity to face the various challenges of the twenty-first century, including the consideration of well-being at home.

European welfare states post-WWII aimed to enhance quality of life through public services, including housing. If we accept that transfers from the welfare state have acted as a counterpart to the trend initiated by globalisation, internationalisation, and growing liberalism, those 'rudimentary welfare states' required of other mechanisms to ensure a certain degree of well-being of population. This way, many of the activities that could not be carried out by the public sector have been transferred to other agents of a diverse nature as they would otherwise have been completely ignored. Spain's welfare model aligns more with the Mediterranean or rudimentary welfare system, where family and personal networks play a crucial role in welfare provision. In a similar vein, Spain's housing system reflects a divergence from the more social democratic models found in other parts of Europe.

Spain's approach diverged from the broader European trend of focusing on social housing. Instead, Spain emphasised homeownership, aiming to stimulate the real estate sector as an economic driver. Unlike many European countries that developed substantial social housing stocks, Spain's housing policies historically favoured homeownership. This resulted in a minimal public rental sector and a reliance on family networks to fill housing gaps.

Housing is one of the main integration mechanisms in the city for newly arrived families. Most European countries have offered a public provision of housing as an instrument to guarantee integration. However, the importance of the family as a complementary institution in the provision of housing, along with other elements, are some of the attributes that are usually associated with the housing systems of Southern European countries and help to explain the uniqueness of some processes linked to territory and housing. Thus, in past eras of rural-to-urban immigration, 'the significance of housing as a mechanism of integration into urban society meant that housing was the primary objective in family strategies for survival in the city' (Allen et al. 2004, 61). The relevance of these phenomena is undeniable in the context of the arrival of the non-EU population in the country. At the same time, the weakness of the welfare state in Spain and the inclusion of other mechanisms beyond the public policy of provision in the interpretation of the welfare system (i.e. informal networks, the family, etc.) makes the housing system a fundamental axis of analysis for the evaluation of the well-being of households residing in Spain.

Three examples have illustrated the varying role of community and engagement in the provision of housing in Spain.

During the 1960s, rapid urban expansion and speculative real estate developments led to the creation of poorly planned housing estates, such as Sant Roc in Badalona. Designed to relocate people from slums and new immigrants, Sant Roc consisted of densely packed, poorly constructed blocks with inadequate infrastructure. While many residents initially welcomed the new apartments, the lack of essential services – such as sewers, streets and green areas – led to significant structural problems by the 1990s. Despite some initial joy and a sense of community, social cohesion and well-being of residents suffered due to the area's stigmatisation and the influx of marginalised populations, including low-income immigrants. The absence of robust public welfare meant that family and social networks played a crucial (informal) role in supporting residents, compensating for the limited public action in providing a decent standard of living.

The Spanish democratic transition in the seventies marked a shift towards improved social policies, including housing reforms. Orcasitas in Madrid exemplifies this change. Originally consisting of self-built dwellings and barracks, Orcasitas underwent significant redevelopment in the 1970s and 1980s, replacing old structures with modern, well-designed housing. This regeneration not only improved housing quality but also upgraded infrastructure and services. Residents' involvement was key to this transformation, fostering a strong sense of community and enhancing social cohesion. Orcasitas demonstrates how effective urban planning, and resident participation can improve living conditions and well-being.

In recent years, austerity measures have strained housing policies, prompting innovative approaches to housing access. La Borda, a resident-led cooperative in Barcelona, represents a new model in affordable housing. Located on public land and designed with a 75-year leasehold, La Borda emphasises collaborative development and management. This cooperative model prioritises non-speculative housing and fosters a strong sense of community through democratic organisation. With 28 flats accommodating a diverse, intergenerational group, La Borda not only provides affordable housing but also promotes leadership, capacity building, and a collective sense of belonging, significantly enhancing residents' well-being.

In summary, well-being is closely intertwined with the policies that govern housing. Thoughtful and inclusive housing policies can contribute to creating environments where individuals feel secure, connected, and able to build a meaningful sense of home. Conversely, inadequate or discriminatory housing policies can undermine these foundations, impacting the well-being and sense of belonging for individuals and communities. Therefore, a holistic understanding of the meaning of home and well-being must consider the broader policy frameworks that shape the housing landscape. Housing policies in Spain have evolved from poorly planned post-war estates to more inclusive and community-oriented models. The cases of Sant Roc, Orcasitas and La Borda highlight the critical role of infrastructure, resident involvement, and innovative approaches in shaping the well-being and social cohesion of communities.

References

Allen, Judith, James Barlow, Jesús Leal, Thomas Maloutas, and Liliana Padovani. 2004. *Housing and Welfare in Southern Europe*. Blackwell Publishing Ltd.

Bengtsson, Bo. 2001. "Housing as a Social Right: Implications for Welfare State Theory." *Scandinavian Political Studies* 24 (4): 255–75. https://doi.org/10.1111/1467-9477.00056.

Blessing, Anita. 2012. "Magical or Monstrous? Hybridity in Social Housing Governance." *Housing Studies* 27 (2): 717–38.

Bosch, Jordi and Carme Trilla. 2023a. "Sistema d 'Habitatge i Estat Del Benestar. El Cas Europeu." 1–8.

Bosch, Jordi, Universitat Pompeu Fabra, and Carme Trilla 2023b. "Sistema d 'Habitatge i Estat Del Benestar. El Cas Europeu." 8–9.

Brysch, Sara Lia, Adrià Garcia i Mateu, and Darinka Czischke. 2023. "The Process of Value Setting through Co-Design: The Case of La Borda, Barcelona." CoDesign. https://doi.org/10.1080/15710882.2023.2277724.

D'Alessandro, D., and L. Appolloni. 2020. "Housing and Health: An Overview." *Annali Di Igiene Medicina Preventiva e Di Comunita* 32 (5): 17–26. https://doi.org/10.7416/ai.2020.3391.

Dekker, Karien, and Ronald van Kempen. 2005. "Large Housing Estates in Europe: A Contemporary Overview." In *Restructuring Large Housing Estates in Europe Restructuring and Resistance Inside the Welfare Industry*, 18–45. Policy Press. https://doi.org/10.1332/policypress/9781861347756.003.0002.

Donnison, D.V. 1967. *The Government of Housing*. Penguin Books.

Esping-Andersen, Gosta. 1990. "The Three Worlds of Welfare Capitalism." In *248. Princeton*: New Jersey: Princeton University Press.

Esping-Andersen, Gosta 2000. "The Sustainability of Welfare States into the Twenty-First Century." *International Journal of Health Services* 30. https://about.jstor.org/terms.

Girbés-Peco, Sandra, Mar Joanpere Foraster, Liviu Catalin Mara, and Teresa Morlà-Folch. 2020. "The Role of the Democratic Organization in the La Borda Housing Cooperative in Spain." *Habitat International* 102 (August). https://doi.org/10.1016/j.habitatint.2020.102208.

Harloe, Michael. 1995. *The People's Home? Social Rented Housing in Europe and America*. Wiley-Blackwell.

Hegedüs, Joseph, Ivan Tosics, and Stephen K. Mayo. 1996. "Transition of the Housing Sector in the East Central European Countries." *Review of Urban and Regional Development Studies* 8 (2): 101–36.

Hegedus, Joseph, Ivan Tosics, and Bengt Turner. 1992. *The Reform of Housing in Eastern Europe and the Soviet Union*, edited by Joseph Hegedus, Ivan Tosics, and Bengt Turner. Routledge.

Heijden, Harry van der. 2013. *West European Housing Systems in a Comparative Perspective*. Delft: IOS Press.

Hoekstra, Joris. 2010. *Divergence in European Welfare and Housing Systems*. Deflt University of Technology.

Jarden, Aaron, and Annalise Roache. 2023. "What Is Wellbeing?" *International Journal of Environmental Research and Public Health*. https://doi.org/10.3390/ijerph20065006.

Kemeny, Jim, and Stuart Lowe. 1998. "Schools of Comparative Housing Research: From Convergence to Divergence." *Housing Studies* 13 (2): 161–76.

Kristensen, H. 2002. "Social Housing Policy and the Welfare State: A Danish Perspective." *Urban Studies* 39 (2): 255–63. https://doi.org/10.1080/00420980120102957.

Leibfried, Stephan. 1993. "Towards a European Welfare State?" In *New Perspectives on the Welfare State in Europe*, edited by Catherine Jones, 245–80. Routledge.

Leifheit, Kathryn M., Gabriel L. Schwartz, Craig Evan Pollack, and Sabriya L. Linton. 2022. "Building Health Equity through Housing Policies: Critical Reflections and Future Directions for Research." *Journal of Epidemiology and Community Health* 76 (8): 759–63. https://doi.org/10.1136/jech-2021-216439.

Malpass, Peter. 2008. "Housing and the New Welfare State: Wobbly Pillar or Cornerstone?" *Housing Studies* 23 (1): 1–19.

McClatchey, Rachael, Katie McClymont, Emma Griffin, and Laurence Carmichael. 2023. "Community Led Housing, Health and Wellbeing: A Comprehensive Literature Review." *International Journal of Housing Policy*. https://doi.org/10.1080/19491247.2023.2232200.

Mignone, Enzo. 2005. "Urban Social Change: A Socio-Historical Framework of Analysis." In *Cities of Europe. Changing Contexts: Local Arrangements, and the Challenge to Urban Cohesion*, edited by Yuri. Kazepov, 67–89. Oxford: Blackwell Publishing.

Ministerio de Transportes Movilidad y Agenda Urbana. 2020. "Observatorio de Vivienda y Suelo. Boletín Especial de Vivienda Social." Madrid. https://apps.fomento.gob.es/CVP/.

Navarro, Vicenç. 2004. *El Estado Del Bienestar En España*. Madrid: Tecnos.

Nix, Emily, Andrew Ibbetson, Ke Zhou, Michael Davies, Paul Wilkinson, Ramona Ludolph, and Helen Pineo. 2024. "Getting to Effective Housing Policy for Health: A Thematic Synthesis of Policy Development and Implementation." *Cities and Health* 8 (3): 486–503. https://doi.org/10.1080/23748834.2024.2328951.

Pareja-Eastaway, Montserrat, and Ma Teresa Sánchez-Martínez. 2012. "La política de vivienda en España: lecciones aprendidas y retos de futuro. Revista de Economia Galega." 21 (2): 203–32.

Pareja-Eastaway, Montserrat, and Teresa Sánchez-Martínez. 2017a. "More Social Housing? A Critical Analysis of Social Housing Provision in Spain." *Critical Housing Analysis* 4 (1): 124–31. https://doi.org/10.13060/23362839.2017.4.1.331.

Pareja-Eastaway, Montserrat, and Teresa Sánchez-Martínez. 2017b. "Social Housing in Spain: What Role Does the Private Rented Market Play?" *Journal of Housing and the Built Environment* 32 (2): 377–95. https://doi.org/10.1007/s10901-016-9513-6.

Rice, Louis, and Mark Drane. 2020. "Indicators of Healthy Architecture—a Systematic Literature Review." *Journal of Urban Health* 97 (6): 899–911. https://doi.org/10.1007/s11524-020-00469-z.

Riva, Alessia, Andrea Rebecchi, Stefano Capolongo, and Marco Gola. 2022. "Can Homes Affect Well-Being? A Scoping Review among Housing Conditions, Indoor Environmental Quality, and Mental Health Outcomes." *International Journal of Environmental Research and Public Health*. https://doi.org/10.3390/ijerph192315975.

Rolfe, Steve, Lisa Garnham, Jon Godwin, Isobel Anderson, Pete Seaman, and Cam Donaldson. 2020. "Housing as a Social Determinant of Health and Wellbeing: Developing an Empirically-Informed Realist Theoretical Framework." *BMC Public Health* 20 (1). https://doi.org/10.1186/s12889-020-09224-0.

Scanlon, Kathleen, Christine Whitehead, and Melissa Fernández Arrigoitia. 2014. "Social Housing in Europe." *Social Housing in Europe* 1–465. https://doi.org/10.1002/9781118412367.

Schöning, Barbara. 2020. "Paradigm Shifts in Social Housing after Welfare -State Transformation: Learning from the German Experience." *International Journal of Urban and Regional Research* 44 (6): 1023–40. https://doi.org/10.1111/1468-2427.12914.

Schwartz, H, and L Seabroke. 2008. "Varieties of Residential Capitalism in the International Political Economy: Old Welfare States and the New Politics of Housing." *Comparative European Politics* 6 (3): 237–61.

Smith, Susan J. 2005. "States, Markets and an Ethic of Care." *Political Geography* 24 (1 SPEC. ISS): 1–20. https://doi.org/10.1016/j.polgeo.2004.10.006.

Stephens, Mark. 2020. "How Housing Systems Are Changing and Why: A Critique of Kemeny's Theory of Housing Regimes." *Housing, Theory and Society* 37 (5): 521–47. https://doi.org/10.1080/14036096.2020.1814404.

Torgersen, Ulf. 1987. "Housing: The Wobbly Pillar under the Welfare State." *Scandinavian Housing and Planning Research* 4 (1): 116–26. https://doi.org/10.1080/02815737.1987.10801428.
Trilla, Carme. 2001. La Política de Vivienda En Una Perspectiva Europea Comparada. Fundación La Caixa. www.estudios.lacaixa.es.
Trilla, Carme, and Jordi Bosch. 2018. El Parque Público y Protegido de Viviendas En España: Un Análisis Desde El Contexto Europeo. Fundación Alternativas. Vol. 197. Fundación Alternativas.
Whitehead, Christine. 2003. 'Restructuring Social Housing Systems'. In Forrest, Ray and Lee, James (Eds.) *Housing and Social Change. East-West Perspectives*, 1–296. Routledge.

6

NISHIYAMA UZO*

Writing for Housing and Planning for Well-Being in Post-War Japan

Carola Hein

The concept of well-being has been at the heart of planning and housing proposals for a long time but recently the concept has come to the fore. The World Health Organization (WHO) defines well-being as 'a positive state experienced by individuals and societies.' According to their website:

> Similar to health, [well-being] is a resource for daily life and is determined by social, economic and environmental conditions. Well-being encompasses quality of life and the ability of people and societies to contribute to the world with a sense of meaning and purpose. Focusing on well-being supports the tracking of the equitable distribution of resources, overall thriving and sustainability. A society's well-being can be determined by the extent to which it is resilient, builds capacity for action, and is prepared to transcend challenges.
>
> *(Glossary of Terms 2021, https://www.who.int/activities/promoting-well-being)*

A key feature for well-being is access to good quality housing in a neighbourhood with appropriate social amenities and connectivity.

Global Histories of Housing and Well-being and the Impact on Tokyo

Planners around the world have been exploring the relationship between urban conditions, housing, and well-being for many years even if they did so using varied vocabulary. In 1898, Ebenezer Howard's garden city concept, expounded in his 1898 *To-morrow: A Peaceful Path to Real Reform*, was a comprehensive societal program translated into a design for housing and urban form. Howard's ideas were essentially a response to what he saw as a need for well-being, which he considered to include access to nature, open space, and clean air and water. Although the concept of the garden city was eventually translated into many languages and its spatial form spread around the world, it lost its connection to a political and social program.

DOI: 10.4324/9781003527930-9

In 1918, Fukuda Shigeyoshi, a technical officer of the City of Tokyo, developed the visionary *New Tokyo Plan* for a deconcentration of the metropolis over the next 50 years. Fukuda's proposal resembled Howard's diagram no. 5 of city growth, with open country nearby and rapid communication lines. Fukuda used Howard's idea to plan a large metropolis, rather than a town of 55,000 inhabitants, and proposed decentralising commercial, rather than residential, functions and moving them to the rim of the city. In his plan, Fukuda limited the city's size to ten kilometres from the Imperial Palace in Tokyo, which at the time corresponded to a one-hour commute and proposed the development of subcentres and satellite cities. His aim was to control travelling time and provide healthier living conditions than those found in a large, dense industrial metropolis. Proposing decentralising commercial functions – rather than residential – may have built on local, traditional concepts, notably the traditional *machi,* socio-spatial units, de facto small towns that made Japanese cities so liveable.[1]

Throughout the 1920s and 1930s, as unrestrained growth spread across Tokyo, lifestyles were changing and new housing developments were needed. Meanwhile, Japanese planners kept track of discussions among their Western counterparts and consulted with practitioners in Europe and America. Fukuda, for example, after the Kantō earthquake discussed the rebuilding plan for Tokyo with the German planner Fritz Schumacher (1869–1947). Ishikawa Hideaki (1893–1955), at that time an engineer in the Home Ministry assigned to the town planning of Nagoya, travelled to Europe in 1923 to seek advice about his city's master plan. While there, he consulted the British architect and planner Raymond Unwin (1863–1940).[2] Eventually, garden city concepts, along with examples of socialist municipalities and housing districts that developed in the 1920s, arrived in Japan. The traditional Japanese understanding of cities as composed of distinct urban units may have influenced the reception of these ideas.[3]

The neighbourhood unit is a central concept of twentieth-century planning, closely associated with the American urban planner Clarence Perry (1872–1944), who proposed the concept in the early part of the century. Residential neighbourhood units, often organised around cul-de-sac streets, have since become central planning features in many countries around the world, intended to allow children to play safely in streets and neighbours to interact. These neighbourhoods allowed for urban development in units, disconnected from the larger urban context. Many of these projects failed, however. In the United States and elsewhere, modern neighbourhood planning – e.g., Levittown, the name given to several large suburban housing developments built in the United States by Levitt & Sons – have been residential subdivisions for single-income brackets that rapidly lost their attractiveness for many reasons, including homogeneity.

The Dōjunkai Foundation, Housing and Well-being in Tokyo

Certain characteristics of urban development in Japanese cities have persisted over time, shaping the growth of modern housing districts into structures that are distinctly Japanese. Planners had few legal tools to implement large-scale plans, and they faced widespread opposition to any attempts at comprehensive planning. For these reasons, their preference was for small-scale, machi-like patterns. Japanese planners appropriated ideas from different origins, with housing being a key consideration, resulting notably in the Dōjunkai apartments. These apartments, especially the larger complexes, illustrate how

European and North American town planning ideas – most notably those from Ebenezer Howard's garden city concept and in Berlage's Amsterdam Zuid project – were adapted to local approaches to city making. Constructed under the supervision of the Dōjunkai Foundation in various locations in Tokyo and in Yokohama following the Great Kantō Earthquake of 1 September 1923, 15 reinforced concrete apartment complexes were completed between 1925 and 1934. These complexes were designed as models for future neighbourhoods, serving as prototypes for residential developments both in terms of construction technology (reinforced concrete) and modern amenities, such as flush toilets and central heating. Additionally, they contributed innovative ideas to the community lifestyles and the urban units that have traditionally existed in a Japanese city.[4]

An examination of the Dōjunkai Apartments reveals they are representative of a uniquely Japanese evolution of modern urban form. These apartment complexes have been understudied as singularly Japanese, and they are not only examples of the many ways Japanese architects tweaked foreign concepts to suit local needs. Most importantly, these apartment complexes built upon the traditional organisation of Japanese cities in small socio-spatial units: the *machi*. Following the Great Kantō Earthquake of 1923, the Dōjunkai Foundation led the construction of social housing districts, after the Great Kanto Earthquake in Tokyo. It completed sixteen reinforced concrete apartment complexes in various locations in Tokyo and Yokohama between 1924 and 1934. The Dōjunkai Apartments were designed as models for future neighbourhoods, as prototypes for residential developments and models of modern life and well-being. Japanese architects and planners considered these groups of multi-unit housing as pioneers, in terms of both construction technology and material – concrete – and the amenities they contained. This is evident most notably in the Daikanyama Apartments (1927–1930), by then the most 'suburban' of the fifteen sites in Tokyo identified by the Dōjunkai Foundation. The implementation of foreign ideas, including the garden city concept, depended largely on the availability of implementation tools. One instrument in particular offered planners a way to modernise in keeping with existing Japanese practices: notably land readjustment (*kukaku seiri*), a key tool for redeveloping agricultural land and reorganising urban areas.

The Role of Nishiyama Uzō in the Debate of Housing and Well-Being in Japan

Since the very beginning of establishing city planning as a discipline in Japan in the late nineteenth century, the country's leaders had seen innovation not primarily as an issue of aesthetics but as one of economic dominance and transportation. Their urban plans and legislation focused on infrastructure, especially road construction. They focused less on other aspects, such as building typologies. By the 1930s, Japanese planners, theorists and historians were studying the town planning history and traditions of other countries to see what they might connect with Japanese practice, as noted above.[5] Among the leaders in Japanese urban planning thought with a great interest in well-being was the architect/planner Nishiyama Uzō (1911–1994), historian-theorist, humanist, and avowed Marxist, who was educated as an architect between 1930 and 1933 (Figure 6.1). Nishiyama was a prolific writer, who published many books and whose extensive articles[6] were reprinted in three volumes in 1968. Spanning a period of enormous political and spatial changes,

FIGURE 6.1 Nishiyama as a honorary professor after retirement from Kyoto University.
Source: Uzō Nishiyama Memorial Library.

'Nishiyama's work helped shape Japanese housing and planning in the twentieth century and drew attention to the role of housing in inclusive living, that is, community-oriented housing that can accommodate a variety of needs and interests.'[7] Nishiyama dedicated several books to the question of housing, including two volumes in a series that focus on housing planning (*Jūtaku keikaku*) and theory of residence (*Jūkyo ron*), as well as his reflections on urban and regional planning (*Chiiki kūkan ron*) and architecture (*Kenchiku ron*), all of which speak to the larger question of well-being from the architectural to the planning scale.[8] Through his writings (and as a teacher), he influenced an entire generation of Japanese urban planners and architects, to pay attention on the question of housing and well-being notably in the post-war period.

Nishiyama's publications span from the 1930s to the 1990s, an era of enormous political change and transformation of urban space of Japanese cities. By the 1930s, when he was a student in Kyoto, Japan had shaped its own approach to modern architecture and urbanism and was no longer dependent on direct intervention from foreigners. Nishiyama maintained an abiding interest in the development of housing throughout his life, and he produced abundant, detailed sketches of buildings and innovative analytical drawings and maps to document Japan's changing housing types over the centuries.[9] His unique drawings provide meticulous accounts of neighbourhoods, floor plans, sections and construction details of traditional Japanese townhouses (machiya) and tenement houses, wooden and other apartments, as well as mansions in both metropolises and villages. He also carefully examined the changing lifestyles and everyday objects of the Japanese and this included drawings and photographs of traditional Japanese townhouses and row houses (*nagaya*) (Figures 6.2 and 6.3).

FIGURE 6.2 Drawing by Nishiyama of the interior of a traditional machiya townhouse in Kyoto in 1936 showing the narrow and deep corridor used for multiple purposes including as kitchen, and providing access to the rooms.

Source: Uzō Nishiyama Memorial Library.

In line with the idea that well-being is important for everyone, Nishiyama resisted the idea that architecture was an elitist medium and instead focused on its social aspects, particularly in the architectural magazine *DEZAM*. Humanist approaches were at the core of his practice, as is clear as early as a 1948 article, 'The Architecture of Humanism'[10] where he explained,

> We must manage our residential sphere on the surface of the earth where the land meets the sky, but transform this contact area into a three-dimensional, optimally rich environment; without wastage, use all the blessings provided from the sky (especially the emission of solar energy) and natural resources from the ground; and create the best residential configuration on the earth's surface.[11]

For Nishiyama, the urban and regional scales provided the context for his concept of the structure of life, an idea that is closely related with housing, transportation and well-being. Nishiyama's ideas on urban organisation resonate with traditional concepts of Japanese community structures. He connected these concepts with foreign ideas that he was very familiar with, including Clarence Perry's neighbourhood concept.

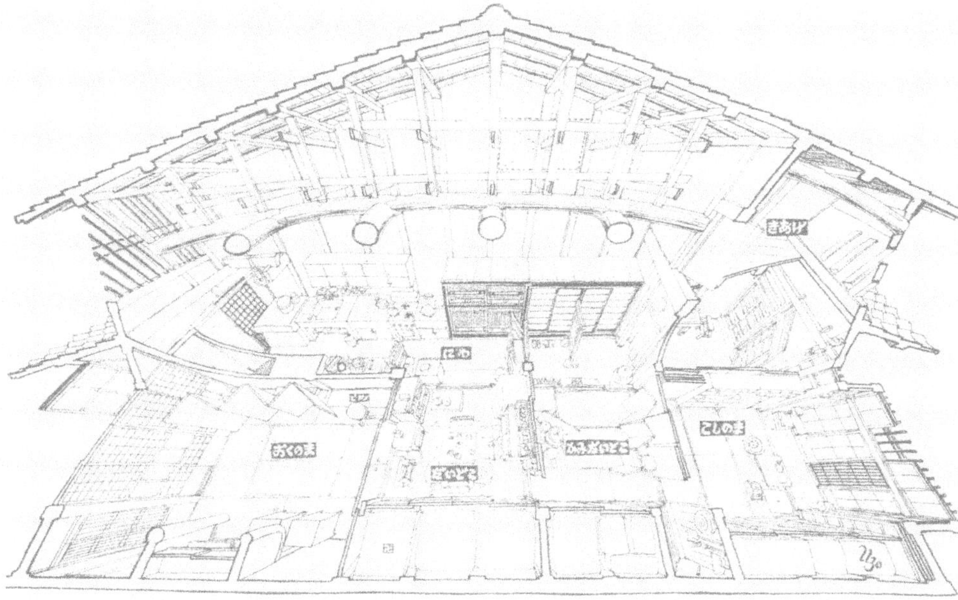

FIGURE 6.3 Nishiyama's innovative depiction of a traditional Japanese house from above, depicting both the architectural structure as well as the use of the various spaces. Transforming lifestyles are captured through the presence of a Piano in the room at the lower left.

Source: Uzō Nishiyama Memorial Library.

Throughout his life, Nishiyama maintained an abiding interest in the development of housing. Through abundant, detailed sketches of buildings and innovative analytical drawings and maps, he created a careful analysis of Japan's changing housing types over the centuries.[12] His unique drawings offer detailed accounts of neighbourhoods, floor plans, sections and construction details of traditional Japanese town houses, row houses, apartments, mansions and wooden apartments in the large metropolises and villages alike. He also carefully examined changing lifestyles and everyday objects of traditional Japanese people from the earliest times of Japanese construction to postwar practices. Through his publications, Nishiyama provided detailed and carefully documented insight into changing lifestyles, as through his drawings and photographs of traditional Japanese row houses, the *nagaya,* and established fertile ground for future design for liveable spaces (Figures 6.4 and 6.5).

In 1942, Nishiyama was examining the problem of the big city as a locale for a concentrated workforce, trying to find a new organisational form for the Japanese city. As part of that project, as he analysed the major urban planning discussions in the West, he selected material to present without regard to political context, whether capitalist America, socialist Russia or fascist National-Socialist Germany. He compiled his findings and interpretations in an article titled 'The structure of life-units (or spheres)' (*Seikatsu kichi no kôsô*).[13] Nishiyama presented and critiqued plans by Ebenezer Howard, Le Corbusier and Ludwig Hilberseimer in capitalist Britain, France and Germany, rejecting them as

FIGURE 6.4 Photo of recently built row houses in Osaka's Sumiyoshi ward (Kagaya) taken in 1935 by Nishiyama.

Source: Uzō Nishiyama Memorial Library.

FIGURE 6.5 Photo taken in 1936 of the rear side of row house lanes (back alley) in Osaka's Nishikujo area by Nishiyama.

Source: Uzō Nishiyama Memorial Library.

simply reorganising the city without solving the density problem and for merely transposing capitalist American cities into Europe, more for aesthetic reasons than in response to social needs. Plans by the Soviet planner Milyutin for a linear city, in contrast, appeared to him to be an attempt to build a 'comprehensive whole,' but he did not agree with its separation of work and home. Nishiyama remained unsatisfied with many foreign proposals and instead searched for a way to make city life meaningful as a whole in both new and existing cities.

Nishiyama Uzō and the Concepts of Machi and Life-Spheres

In his extensive work, Nishiyama captured Japanese traditions of living and dwelling and reshaped them. In his work, he captured the unique tradition of *machi* (meaning neighbourhood as well as small town), local self-management and the absence of metropolitan-scale planning – and ultimately, he helped bring community-based planning practices into postwar urban development. Japanese cities were traditionally separated into socio-spatial units, de facto small towns, which were under the control of the military class, temples and shrines, or the townsmen, each with their own regulatory and even police powers. Monofunctional districts existed for samurai and their retainers, and for merchants; there was also the geisha district (e.g. Kazue-machi, Kanazawa) or shopping district. These *machi* composed the city. The idea and practice of *machi*, as a small city and as an urban unit, has resonated with the rapid transformation and modernisation of Japanese cities since the Meiji restoration and has influenced the way in which the Japanese imported foreign concepts. Specifically, as Japanese planners projected comprehensive plans for large urban regions, they included the notion of small units composing a city. Thus, planners found ways to coexist with and adapt to longstanding traditions: of self-governing neighbourhood groups, of small-scale land use and land ownership patterns and of planning tools adapted to small areas.

Nishiyama developed several projects concerning the organisation of the city in decentralised, self-governed neighbourhoods (in the tradition of *machi*), which he called 'life spheres' or 'life units.' Specifically, he built upon historical practices of Japanese cities and contemporary urban theory, including the ideas of the German geographer Walter Christaller, to propose an organised distribution of cities throughout the Japanese mainland. Christaller, whose writings were first introduced in Japan in the 1930s, analysed urban services in regional contexts and developed a theory about the distribution, number, size and location of specific urban functions (such as housing, working, education, leisure) in space that planners could use in locating and planning new cities that also reflected the concept of life units. Such an organisation of cities into basic life units was in line with the historic development of Tokyo, or Edo as the city used to be called. One of the largest cities in history, Edo had historically housed up to 1 million inhabitants. This large number of people had been traditionally organised in different neighbourhoods and wards, an organisation that could be used to structure the modern metropolis.[14]

In his writings, Nishiyama outlined an organisation close to western concepts of zoning: most of the city would be a network of small monofunctional urban units (industrial, cultural and harbour facilities) located along major lines of transportation, principally railway lines, and separated from other urban areas by green strips. Exclusively residential districts were located at a larger distance, themselves centres for surrounding villages. Nishiyama's plan reserved the city centre for administrative, economic, financial and commercial central functions. According to him, cities and particularly megacities had to have a working city centre. (This is a surprising statement, as Japanese cities did not traditionally have a centre – in Tokyo, the centre was the shogunal palace that was not accessible to the public – and also the idea of the centre was an aspect that Western modernists had largely ignored in the pre-war era.)

Nishiyama calculated distances between the different units in temporal terms, not the spatial terms that Ishikawa used. Distances between large cities of between 100 and 500 hundred kilometres could be travelled by high-speed trains and planes, whereas highways and trains connected smaller cities over distances of between 30 and 50 kilometres. Ordinary streets and trains led to villages, and it took a person about an hour to travel 20 kilometres. Even the villages, however, should be at a maximum traveling time of three hours from the capital.

Nishiyama also allocated room for recreational leisure and vacations, a universal demand in an urbanised world. The notion of day-trips gets a new meaning here. What was originally conceived as a way to organise trips to work, now provided structures to facilitate times on and off work. Nishiyama argued that, with the possibility of day trips anywhere in Japan, the capital should expand rather than remain small, while the creation of urban units separated by green belts, the life units, would ensure that nature would be embedded in the metropolis. (For Nishiyama, the green zones were furthermore an important element in guaranteeing the urban food supply.) The idea of day trips from the capital to any place in the country is virtually a reality today. It has effectively led to further concentration, even though some had argued it could help to promote decentralisation.[15]

Nishiyama thus tried to maintain the multifunctionality of big cities while making them more liveable. He stressed the need for balanced growth with an appropriate number of workplaces, welfare facilities, and the like, in order to prevent sprawl.[16] Nishiyama was keenly aware that cities would not be able to grow endlessly. He essentially proposed to urbanise national space and to structure the various scales of settlements, from rural populations in hamlets to regional hubs to mega-cities. He imagined megacities of 7.5 million with appropriate green spaces, or 18.7 million at 100 people per hectare.[17] Nishiyama correctly assessed the fact that the Tokyo area would grow, although he under-estimated its population growth and over-estimated the density. In 2016, the Tokyo Metropolis was about 13.6 million people with a density 6,158 people per square kilometre, while the larger metropolitan area stood at approximately 37 million inhabitants and 2,662 people per square kilometre (thus approximately 62 or 26 per hectare).[18] His predictions were based on a peak population of about 122 million, which is close to Japan's population of 126 million today.[19]

Just like his Western counterparts, he opposed unnecessary traffic and suggested the creation of small urban units. However, he did not criticise the big city itself. On the contrary, and this is typical of Japanese planners, he tried to find a way to maintain the multifunctionality of big cities while making them more liveable. Nishiyama's book, (*Seikatsu kichi no kōsō*)[20] 'The Structure of The Base of Life,'[21] sets the foundation for Nishiyama's urban thinking and reflections and demonstrates the close relationships that he saw between society and housing and between housing and urban planning. When Nishiyama wrote the original text, he was examining the problem of the big city as a locale for a large-scale, modern, concentrated workforce, trying to find a new organisational form for the Japanese city. The text explores the organisation of cities through urban units that cater to specific needs of the population in terms of work, housing, education, culture and transportation, hence the title 'The Base of Life.'

Driven by his desire to connect work and life, Nishiyama argued that the structural elements of the city, conceptualised as life spheres or life units, should be organised around elementary schools and workplaces, as argued by many other planners in Japan and elsewhere. They needed to be carefully organised, separated by green areas and connected by transportation. He thus affirmed the organisation of cities in small units as the base for living. The text originally appeared in *Kenchikugaku kenkyū* (Research on architecture) in 1942, when Japan was deeply involved in World War II and continuing to expand across Asia and the Pacific. Within Japan, rationing and food shortages had become common and over a million children were evacuated from cities to more rural areas. Introducing the text in a 1968 compilation, Nishiyama acknowledged the original context of the text, which explained the then-typical references to Japanese aspirations of leadership in Asia, while also assessing the needs of wartime defence. But Nishiyama did not discuss the politics of Imperial Japan, or distance himself from it; instead, he focused primarily on cities and society as a modern challenge.

Nishiyama's goal was a qualitative reform of cities for an industrialised society, with a new social life. What seemed most important to him is that a city should have a true social structure. He rejected what he perceived as purely aesthetic or economic choices and privileged social concerns. In his view, the modern metropolis, with its capitalist and chaotic form, needed substantial rethinking. This mindset and his own political affiliation could have led him to embrace urban planning ideas applied in the Soviet Union. But while Nishiyama explored and discussed those ideas in his 1942 article, he advocated a different approach. Taking up the contemporary idea of a necessary, legally proscribed space that provides all the functions of daily life, he proposed a *life space*, the life units mentioned above, and argued that it would engage traditional Japanese practices (samsara, meaning the circle of life) and leading ideas of contemporary urban planning at the time.

Nishiyama argued for maintaining mega-cities. Moreover, he proposed that such cities be planned rather than left to unchecked capitalist development. Nishiyama outlined an organisation close to Western concepts of zoning: most of the city would be a network of small monofunctional urban units (industrial, cultural and harbour facilities) located along major lines of transportation, principally railway lines, and separated from other urban areas by green strips. Exclusively residential districts were located at a larger distance, themselves centres for surrounding villages. Nishiyama's plan reserved the city centre for administrative, economic, financial and commercial functions. He believed that cities, particularly megacities, needed a working city centre. This is a surprising position, as Japanese cities did not traditionally have a centre: in Tokyo, the centre was the shogunal palace that was not accessible to the public. Also, the idea of the centre was something that Western modernists had largely eliminated in the pre-war era.

In keeping with his holistic view of planning and well-being, Nishiyama calculated distances between different units in temporal terms. Distances between large cities of between 100 and 500 kilometres could be travelled by high-speed trains and planes, whereas highways and trains connected smaller cities over distances of between 30 and

50 kilometres. Ordinary streets and trains led to villages, and it would take a person about an hour to travel 20 kilometres. Even the villages, however, he believed should be at a maximum traveling time of three hours from the capital.

Nishiyama also allocated room for recreational leisure and vacations, a universal demand in an urbanised world. The notion of day trips gets a new meaning here. Nishiyama argued that with the possibility of day trips to anywhere in Japan, the capital should expand rather than remain small, while the creation of urban units separated by green belts, the life units, would ensure that nature would be embedded in the metropolis. For Nishiyama, the green zones were also an important element in guaranteeing the urban food supply, a need that is essential in peace but also in war times.[22] The idea of day trips from the capital to any place in the country is virtually a reality today. It has effectively led to further concentration of people who gather in the main cities and take advantage of fast travel to the provinces rather than the other way around, even though some had argued it could help to promote decentralisation.[23]

The Role of Nishiyama Uzō in the Debate of Housing and Well-Being in Japan after 1945

Nishiyama thus tried to maintain the multifunctionality of big cities while making them more liveable. Nishiyama was keenly aware that cities would not be able to grow endlessly. He essentially proposed urbanising the national space and structuring the various scales of settlements, from rural populations in hamlets to regional hubs to mega-cities. He imagined mega-cities of 7.5 million with appropriate green spaces, or 18.7 million at 100 people per hectare.[24] Nishiyama correctly predicted that the Tokyo area would grow, although he underestimated the extent of its population growth and overestimated the density. In 2016, the Tokyo metropolis was about 13.6 million people with a density 6,158 people per square kilometre, while the larger metropolitan area stood at approximately 37 million inhabitants and 2,662 people per square kilometre (thus approximately 62 or 26 per hectare).[25] His predictions were based on a peak population of about 122 million, which is close to Japan's population of 126 million today.[26] Nishiyama acknowledges that some of the key features of his plan, particularly the organisation of life units, were not realised after the war, mostly due to what he identified as capitalist tendencies for agglomeration that did not necessarily acknowledge the everyday needs of citizens.[27] He knew that his plans had become outdated, but insisted that the need for planning remained.

Nishiyama was instrumental in the development of postwar housing typology (Figures 6.6). Particularly influential was his insistence on the separation of eating and sleeping spaces. He translated his findings from history into housing proposals for the future. Looking at the traditional separation of spaces in Japanese houses with hard surfaces (pounded earth) from those with soft ones (tatami), he argued for a separation of tatami rooms for sleeping from living/dining/kitchen areas (LDK) with wooden floors.[28] The new organisation of housing led to characteristic post-war housing projects: *n*LDK apartments, with *n* indicating the number of bedrooms added to the core of Living and Dining-Kitchen.[29] For Nishiyama urban form was key, but questions of aesthetics, the design and the scale of buildings, were also a key interest. In his extensive writings on housing, he tied these architectural proposals into broader urban plans for towns across

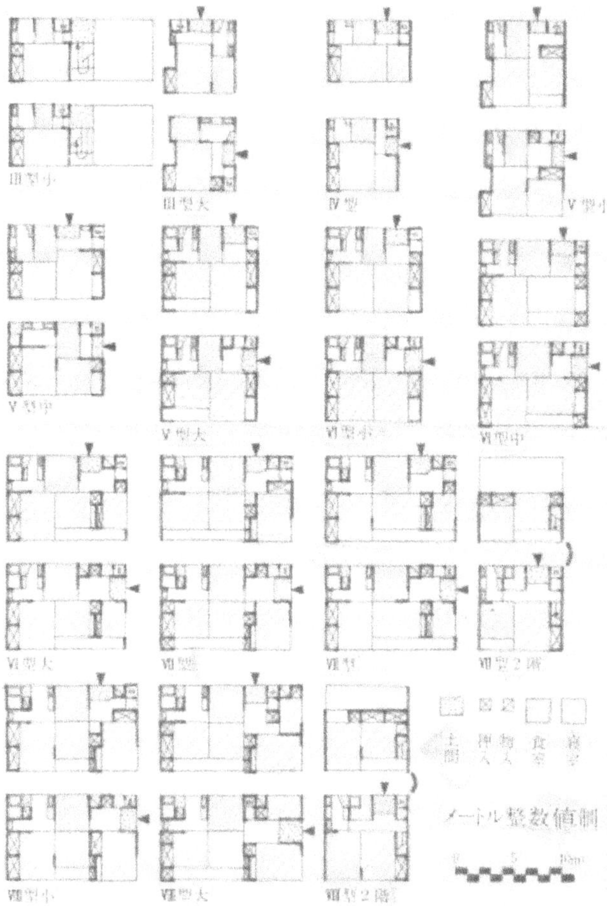

FIGURE 6.6 Apartment floor plans for mass-produced with depiction of tatami rooms and other spaces, drawing by Nishiyama.

Source: Uzō Nishiyama Memorial Library.

Japan including some of his most intriguing visionary projects, some of which are also part of his book *Chiiki kûkan ron* (Reflections on urban, regional and national space).

As professor at Kyoto University from 1961 to 1974 and vice president of the Architecture Institute of Japan in 1959, Nishiyama influenced an entire generation of Japanese urban planners and actively participated in developing Japanese architecture and cities. That period saw important urban changes. The postwar reconstruction and high growth period of the 1950s and 1960s included urban extension and redevelopment, and the 1968 New City Planning Act rethought urban practice, aiming to direct rapid urban growth with areas where growth was to be controlled and others where it was promoted. His influence was particularly strong in Western Japan, the so-called Kansai area.[30] At the height of his career, in the late 1960s, major shifts were occurring that went beyond urban area: new towns were built and comprehensive national plans established, both initiatives that Nishiyama had discussed throughout his career.[31] This was also a period when the country was shifting to community planning (*machizukuri*), in which he was an active player.

In his proposals for Kyoto, Nishiyama cited the 'vision' of motorisation that brought cars to Japan, which did not separate traffic functions or have an appropriate street network, and where people simply used traditional roads that had been a place for community activities. Streets were another room to play in and to meet, like an extension of the home. But few people discussed the negative effects of car traffic like noise, air pollution, and the need for parking spaces. Despite the negative connotation of the word *bijon* (vision), Nishiyama strongly recommended that planners develop a vision by mapping out basic principles and giving an overall aim to individual initiatives.

In the post-war period, Nishiyama continued to observe changes in housing and urban space. He also added his own voice and observations to changing modern living, from the first temporary housing in old train wagons to low- and high-rise modern housing. His observations on tatami living and the need to separate different functions within the house – already spelled out in 1942 – are yet another indication of the continuity of his thinking since the 1940s and the impact of his work on Japanese housing. Nishiyama's proposals for high-rise housing with tatami-equipped apartments illustrate the changing Japanese lifestyle (Figures 6.7 and 6.8).

The 1960s were a crucial period, when Japan became a key player on the global stage in general and in urban planning in particular. Major international events – the 1964

FIGURE 6.7 Municipal apartment housing in Osaka in 1956.

Source: Uzō Nishiyama Memorial Library.

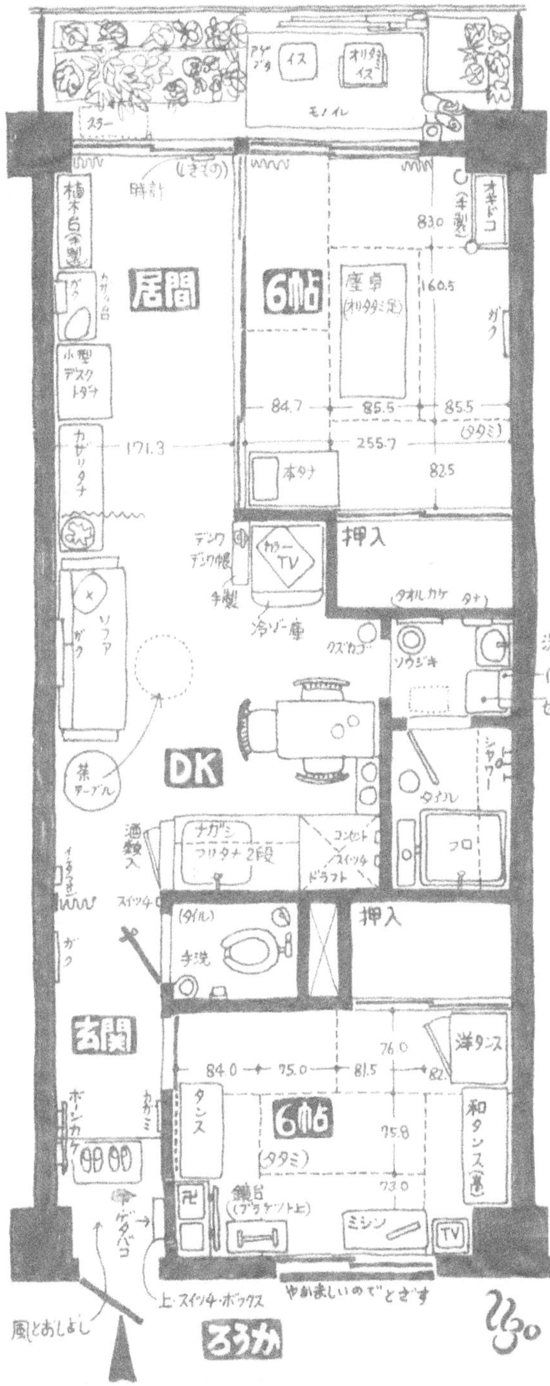

FIGURE 6.8 Drawing of the floor plan of a post-war high-rise apartment (47 m^2) that belonged to Nishiyama's friend K in 1967, featuring two tatami rooms and the use of each space published in his series on housing in Japan.

Source: Uzō Nishiyama Memorial Library.

Olympics and the 1970 Osaka World Expo – were firsts in Asia, and they played a major role in establishing Japan as a world leader in planning and architecture. The close connection between's theories, reflections and historical studies of the pre-war/war periods and the plans and visions of the 1960s is visible in the publication of the material after the war. The principles that he developed in the pre-war and war years – on national planning, spatial distribution, careful organisation of cities and control of sprawl/spread – would become the foundation for his proposals in the 1960s and 1970s. In the 1940s, he developed his ideas about urban structure in separate units that cater to everyday needs, surrounded by green areas that also serve as sites for food production or to the development of urban cores. This continuity is also visible in his terminology. The term 'kombinaato,' an industrial complex, appears in his writings of the 1940s and again in his plans for Osaka Expo '70.

The 1960s were an important decade for Nishiyama. He was involved as an advisor in national projects, including, beginning in 1963, in the master planning for the Osaka Expo '70. His urban design project for Kyoto, featuring a high-rise axis through the centre of the ancient city, published in 1965, created a lot of controversy.[32] Nishiyama continued to work on visionary proposals, following up on his theoretical analysis. He continued to argue for a specifically Japanese approach that took into account the particularities of hilly geography and population increase. Together with his students, he launched the concept of 'Image Planning' (*Kōsō Keikaku*) and suggested a model core of a future city at the Tokyo World Design Conference in 1960.[33] His goal in these visionary proposals was to show the contradictions in urban living space, including potentially negative features or what he termed 'inferno.'[34] In his desire to respond to the particular needs of the Japanese cities, he also proposed '*Iepolis*' (Home City),[35] a city limited to pedestrian traffic and mechanised public transportation. The car had to stay on the outskirts, reflecting Nishiyama's goal of meeting modern needs while maintaining housing traditions, such as the practice of inhabitants and visitors removing their shoes on entering a dwelling from outside.

Both proposals, Image Planning and Home City, build upon the traditional structure of Japanese cities, and on the concept of a network of compact cities with central cores and marketplaces. They VL_ were at the heart of his 1965 integrated plan for Kyoto, consisting of an analysis of the current conditions of the former Japanese capital and a proposal for an extension.[36] Land control, including the division of land into autonomous units and the construction of a central plaza, as he had proposed in the 1940s, was another key feature of his plans. He suggested a skyscraper axis in the ancient city that strangely echoes Le Corbusier's proposal for a city of 3 million inhabitants, the Cité Voisin, to be built over the centre of Paris, destroying a central north-south area of the existing urban structure. As such, it surprisingly contrasted with Nishiyama's earlier negative assessment of Le Corbusier's work and other aspects of his own writings while also incorporating his notion of displaying 'inferno' to the masses.[37]

As Andrea Urushima has shown, Nishiyama proposed making the Osaka site a model city core, and suggested erecting buildings that could be used after the event as the heart of a new city area with key urban functions.[38] The concepts of 'Image Planning' as the shift from theoretical planning to plans for compact cities, and 'Iepolis' were first launched at the Tokyo World Design Conference in 1960. This was a unique opportunity to invest public money in urban construction as Nishiyama had been advocating, and the ultimate confirmation of the ideas he had elaborated in the 1940s. Nevertheless, the final exhibition project was built by Tange Kenzo, the internationally known architect of Japanese national identity.

Instead of Nishiyama's organised construction, the country saw urban sprawl of a haphazard nature, and the large-scale projects that he could have led were largely assigned to and identified with Tange.[39] His intervention in favour of the neighbourhood, *machi*, was not a direct reaction to wartime destruction; it transcended this period and had a strong influence on *machizukuri*, the movement for neighbourhood or community planning, which includes social as well as physical aspects. As Nishiyama had pointed out earlier, there is a special quality to the neighbourhood, its social and functional diversity, and its meaning for the Japanese in terms of identity that is distinctive of the traditional *machi*. *Machizukuri,* as local participation in decision-making or small-scale urban amelioration programs, was a first step towards a more humanised planning. It does not, however, replace Nishiyama's central project: a comprehensive vision based not only on economic concepts but on a set of social and political ideas for a balanced society with a focus on community and the experience of ordinary people.

Conclusion

In later years, Nishiyama remained engaged with planning practice and pragmatically adapted his writing, shifting from a top-down planning approach focused on national policies to a more bottom-up one. His disappointment with urban planning practices characterised by proximity between government officials and the construction industry led him to support grass-roots initiatives. Over time, he came to support movements against high-rise construction and expressways and for the preservation of traditional houses in both urban and rural contexts. As Nakabayashi Hiroshi has emphasised, Nishiyama's reflections on urban and regional planning were published in 1968, but he continued to work into the 1990s and that time needs further research.[40] In particular, his role in pushing for the preservation of historic Japanese cities through the *Santo Shimin* Forum (Nara, Kyoto, and Kamakura residents planning movement) deserves further investigation.

Nishiyama's arguments on well-being have shifted over time in relation to changing societal and spatial conditions. His thoughts are today of renewed importance. While his experience of the food shortages of World War II and its aftermath was formative, his work is relevant to ongoing debates on sustainability, autonomous cities, and circular economies, demonstrating the importance of reflecting on the past for future practice and human well-being.

Notes

* This article builds upon Hein, Carola. "Nishiyama Uzō: Leading Japanese Planner and Theorist." In Uzo Nishiyama, Reflections on Urban, Regional and National Space: Three Essays, with an Introduction by Carola Hein. New York. London: Routledge, 2017.

1 On the importance of the concept of *machi* in the transformation of Japanese cities see also: Carola Hein. 2008. "Machi: Neighborhood and Small Town. The Foundation for Urban Transformation in Japan," *Journal of Urban History* 35(1): 75–107. https://doi.org/10.1177/0096144208322463

2 On Ishikawa see: Sumie Shoji. 1993. "The Life of Ishikawa Hideaki," *Toshikeikaku/City Planning Review (special issue)*, no. 182. Raymond Unwin and Barry Parker (1867–1947) planned the garden city of Letchworth (1904).
3 For leading theories on garden cities, see: Ebenezer Howard et al. 2003. *To-Morrow: A Peaceful Path to Real Reform,* London: Routledge, (original 1898), Ebenezer Howard and Frederic James Osborn. 1965. *Garden Cities of To-morrow,*Cambridge, Mass.: MIT Press (originally published 1902). On a Japanese garden city see also: Watanabe Shun'ichi. 1980. "Garden City Japanese Style: the case of Den-en Toshi Company Ltd., 1918-28," in *Shaping an Urban World, Planning in the Twentieth Century*, eds. Gordon E. Cherry, London: Mansell.
4 For an examination of Japanese terms connoting "neighborhood," see Yorifusa Ishida. 1996. "Japanese Equivalents for French 'Quartier' in Professional and Popular Languages," *Kogakuin Daigaku kenkyūjohō* (81): 213–20.
5 Shoji, "The Life of Ishikawa Hideaki," 15–30.
6 Sumie Shoji. 1993. "The Life of Hideaki Ishikawa," *Toshikeikaku/City Planning Review (special issue)*, no. 182.
7 Uzō Nishiyama.1967. "Humanism no kenchiku [The Architecture of Humanism]," in *Kenchikuron [Theories on Architecture]*, ed. Uzō Nishiyama, Tokyo: Keisō Shobō.
8 Uzō Nishiyama. 1968. *Chiiki Kūkan Ron (Reflections on Urban, Regional and National Space)*, Tokyo: Keisō Shobō; *Jūtaku Keikaku (Housing Planning)*, (Tokyo: Keisō Shobō, 1967); *Kenchikuron (Architecture Theory)*, (Tokyo: Keisō Shobō, 1967); Nishiyama Uzō, ed. 1968. *Jūkyoron (Theory of Residence),* Tokyo: Keisō Shobō.
9 Nishiyama Uzō. 1987. *Nihon no sumai*. Tokyo: Keisō Shobō.
10 Uzō Nishiyama. 1967 "Humanism No Kenchiku (The Architecture of Humanism)," in *Kenchikuron (Architecture Theory)*, ed. Uzō Nishiyama, Tokyo: Keisō Shobō.
11 BOOK Ch. 10, p. 286.
12 Uzō Nishiyama, 1987. *Nihon No Sumai,* Tokyo: Keisō Shobō.
13 Uzō Nishiyama. 1968. *Chiiki Kūkan Ron (Reflections on Urban, Regional and National Space),* Tokyo: Keiso shobo.
14 Nishiyama references the size of the Tokyo wards, Ch. 9, p. 243.
15 Carola Hein and Philippe Pelletier. 2006/2009. *Cities, Autonomy and Decentralization in Japan,* London, New York: Routledge.
16 Uzō Nishiyama. 1971. *Toshikeikaku to Machizukuri [Urban Planning and Community Design]*, vol. 2, Tōkyō and Kyōto: Chōbunsha.
17 Ch. 9, p. 252.
18 Tokyo Metropolitan Government: About Our City: Tokyo's History, Geography and Population (http://www.metro.tokyo.jp/ENGLISH/ABOUT/HISTORY/history03.htm, (accessed 28 December 2016); Tokyo 2020東京都の人口（推計） [Population of Tokyo estimated] 22.12.2016 http://www.toukei.metro.tokyo.jp/jsuikei/2016/js16cf0000.pdf; World Population Review, Tokyo Population 2016 http://worldpopulationreview.com/world-cities/tokyo-population/ (accessed 28 December 2016).
19 Ch. 9, p. 244.
20 *Chiiki Kūkan Ron (Reflections on Urban, Regional and National Space),* Tokyo: Keiso shobo, 1968.
21 In earlier writings, I have translated this as "The structure of life-units."
22 Garon, Sheldon. 2000. "Luxury Is the Enemy: Mobilizing Savings and Popularizing Thrift in Wartime Japan," *The Journal of Japanese Studies* 26 (1): 41–78.
23 Carola Hein and Philippe Pelletier. 2006/2009. *Cities, Autonomy and Decentralization in Japan,* London: Routledge.
24 Ch. 9, p. 252.
25 Tokyo Metropolitan Government: About Our City: Tokyo's History, Geography and Population (http://www.metro.tokyo.jp/ENGLISH/ABOUT/HISTORY/history03.htm, (accessed 28 December 2016); Tokyo 2020 東京都の人口（推計） [Population of Tokyo estimated] 22.12.2016 http://www.toukei.metro.tokyo.jp/jsuikei/2016/js16cf0000.pdf;
World Population Review, Tokyo Population 2016 http://worldpopulationreview.com/world-cities/tokyo-population/ (accessed 28 December 2016).
26 Ch. 9, p. 244.
27 Ch. 1, p. 23.

28 Uzō Nishiyama. 1942. "Jūkyo Kūkan No Yōto Kōsei Ni Okeru Shinshoku Bunriron. (Theory of Separation of Bedding in the Usage Structure of the Residential Space.)," *Kenchiku gakkai ronbunshū* 25.
29 Carola Hein, 2016. Tatami: Floor Cover, Building Block and Lifestyle, Het Nieuwe Instituut, http://platform.hetnieuweinstituut.nl/en/tatami-floor-cover-building-block-and-lifestyle-carola-hein
30 Carola Hein. 2000. "Nishiyama Uzō and the Spread of Western Concepts in Japan," 10+1 (20); Andrea Yuri Flores Urushima, 2007. "Genesis and Culmination of Uzō Nishiyama's Proposal of a 'Model Core of a Future City' for the Expo 70 Site (1960-73)," *Planning Perspectives* 22 (4). Andrea Yuri Flores Urushima. 2011. "The 1970 Osaka Expo: Local Planners, National Planning Processes and Mega Events," *Planning Perspectives* 26 (4); Carola Hein. 2008. "Machi: Neighborhood and Small Town-the Foundation for Urban Transformation in Japan," *Journal of Urban History* 35 (1); 2003. "The Transformation of Planning Ideas in Japan and Its Colonies," in *Urbanism – Imported or Exported? Foreign Plans and Native Aspirations*, ed. Joe Nasr and Mercedes Volait, (Chichester: Wiley).
31 Kosei Hatsuda, 2011. *Toshi No Sengo* (Post-war city), Tokyo: Tokyo University Publisher.
32 Uzō Nishiyama. 1965. "A Plan for Kyoto," *Japan architect* 105.
33 The World Design Conference Organization. 1961. *World Design Conference 1960 in Tokyo,* Tokyo: Bijutsu Shuppansha.
34 Thanks to Professor Nakabayashi Hiroshi for pointing to the notion of "inferno." Andrea Yuri Flores Urushima has also addressed this theme: "Everyday unavoidable modernization and the image of hell: visual planning in the writings of Nishiyama Uzō," *Alternative Visions of Post-war Reconstruction: Creating the Modern Townscape*, ed. John Pendlebury, Erdem Erten, Peter Larkham (London: Routledge, 2014), pp. 90–107.
35 Uzō Nishiyama, H. Mimura, and T. Katayose. 1960. "Home City," *Kindai Kenchiku* 14.
36 Nishiyama, "A Plan for Kyoto."
37 Shinya Katagata. 2008. "Ch. 3: Kōsōkeikaku: Kūkan No Ronri to Yosoku," in *Nishiyama Uzō No Jūtaku, Toshiron: Sono Gendaiteki Kenshō*, eds. Shōji Sumita and Nishiyama Uzō Kinen Sumai Machizukuri Bunko, Tokyo: Nihon Keizai Hyōronsha.
38 Andrea Yuri Flores Urushima. 2007. "Genesis and Culmination of Uzō Nishiyama's Proposal of a 'Model Core of a Future City' for the Expo 70 Site (1960-73)," *Planning Perspectives* 22 (4).
39 André Sorensen. 2002. *The Making of Urban Japan. Cities and Planning from Edo to the 21st Century,* London: Routledge.
40 Hiroshi Nakabayashi. 2008. "Ch. 4: Chiiki Seikatsu Kūkan Keikaku-Ron to Keikan Keikaku-Ron/ Nakabayashi Hiroshi," in *Nishiyama Uzō No Jūtaku, Toshiron: Sono Gendaiteki Kenshō*, eds. Shōji Sumita and Nishiyama Uzō Kinen Sumai Machizukuri Bunko, Tokyo: Nihon Keizai Hyōronsha.

SECTION III

Well-Being, Ideological and Personal Affluence

7

THE IMPACT OF WELL-BEING ON HOUSING POLICIES AND THE CONSUMPTION OF DURABLE GOODS IN POST-WAR WEST GERMANY

Nodoka Nagayama

Introduction

Against a backdrop of serious housing shortages after World War II (WWII), many nations turned to social housing policies to rapidly increase the housing supply and raise housing standards. These policies were largely a success and created an additional economic benefit: ownership rates of durable consumer goods rose along with the housing supply. During the 1950s and 1960s, indicators of domestic well-being were somewhat different than they are today. Present-day evaluations of well-being tend to focus on social and psychological thriving, rather than simple economic stability. In postwar Europe as well, there was a renewed emphasis on what I refer to as 'non-material well-being,' achieved through factors like family time, relaxation, reductions in housework (especially for women), social mixing, a sense of community and entertainment. However, popular conceptions of well-being also included the satisfaction of material desires as a key element – in particular, the secure enjoyment of a domestic living space and possession of durable consumer goods. Indeed, it may be impossible to decouple the purchase of consumer goods from the desire to satisfy physical, social and psychological needs. In other words, households in the postwar decades may have sought to meet non-material needs (e.g. less demanding labour environments, more leisure time and more family bonding) through the satisfaction of material needs (e.g. housing and durable consumer goods).

However, West Germany serves as an interesting counterexample to this trend. Among the former Axis nations, West Germany was the quickest to engage in reconstruction and benefit from the 'economic miracle' of the postwar period. And yet, despite this economic prosperity, many West German households were slow to adopt domestic durable goods like refrigerators and washing machines. This suggests that they may have been pursuing well-being in non-consumer contexts, or directing their spending towards non-durable goods and services. This chapter addresses the counterintuitive purchasing habits in West Germany via two questions. First, in the wake of WWII, what kinds of well-being were being pursued? And second, what role did social housing and durable consumer goods play in West Germans' understanding of well-being?

DOI: 10.4324/9781003527930-11

In order to parse the relationship between housing, durable goods and well-being during the postwar period, it is necessary to understand the intentions and effects of social housing policies at the time. The goal of postwar municipal housing policies was not only to increase the housing supply (though that was, of course, important); public debates on social housing also revealed a preoccupation with the design of specific components of the home, such as kitchens and bathrooms, with the belief that design changes could improve residents' overall quality of life. In other words, housing debates functioned as a forum for discussing and defining the overarching concept of non-material well-being. In this respect, social housing policies helped increase both housing standards and non-material well-being at the same time.

Social housing in the 1950s was often subsidised and/or rent stabilised, which meant that households were able to direct more of their wages towards other expenditures. Indeed, data from the period reveals high levels of discretionary spending at all income levels. Even so, there were relatively low ownership rates of domestic durable goods in West Germany, with many households delaying purchase of goods like washing machines and televisions. I argue that this decision not to purchase major appliances, despite the ability to do, serves as one of the signals that West Germans did not closely associate non-material well-being with domestic durable goods. However, by analysing ownership rates of domestic durable goods according to social status and income, this chapter reveals the distinct ways in which each socioeconomic class pursued non-material well-being, as well as the differences in their spending patterns.

The Effects of Social Housing Policy on Material and Non-Material Well-Being

In the aftermath of WWII, standards of living in West Germany rose remarkably as a result of economic growth and the implementation of state welfare policies, one of the most important of which was housing policy. The creation and implementation of new housing policies raised housing standards by both ameliorating the quantitative shortage of housing and improving the quality of domestic facilities.

Housing policy at the federal level had two main pillars. One was the provision of subsidies to companies undertaking residential social housing construction (*sozialer Wohnungsbau*). During the 1950s, public funds were injected into the construction of rental housing as a matter of priority, which resulted in the mass provision of rental housing at the national level. The other pillar of housing policy was the economic regulation of housing (*Wohnungszwangswirtschaft*) through the reinforcement of rent controls and tenant protections, which remained in place until 1960. Housing policy at the federal level also included the implementation of model housing projects – experiments designed to help raise housing standards – and the provision of subsidies to relevant research organisations. These policies were partly financed by counterpart funds under the Marshall Plan. According to Grünbacher,[1] the Economic Cooperation Administration (ECA), an agency of the Marshall Plan, pushed for a higher standard of living than was usual at the time, partly by financing housing for underserved populations like miners and refugees.

West Germany's policy of funding social housing and aiding residential construction had a decisive impact on improving residential conditions in the country. Von Saldern[2] notes that qualitative improvements in housing had been a goal of social housing construction since the 1920s. However, these goals fell into abeyance during the Great Depression and the period of Nazi dictatorship. The drive towards qualitative improvement finally resumed in the second half of the 1950s, with the standard of domestic facilities rising again during the 1960s and 1970s. In terms of specific domestic facilities, bathrooms became much more common in the 1950s and 1960s, and kitchen formats and locations were more widely discussed. This was a period of intense analysis of the best layouts for raising housing standards.

Within these governmental debates on social housing construction, two facets of well-being emerged as particularly important to policymakers – one based on harmony within the home, and the other on harmony within the broader community. On the domestic front, much stress was placed on familial bonding and lightening housewives' workload, and policymakers felt that the right housing design choices could facilitate those aspects of well-being.[3] Three federally funded research groups were tasked with determining the ideal home layout: the Institute für Bauforschung in Hannover, Forschungsgemeinschaft Bauen und Wohnen in Stuttgart and Arbeitsgemeinschaft für zeitgemäßes Bauen in Kiel.[4] Layouts were tested via model housing development projects (funded, as previously discussed, by counterpart funds from the Marshall Plan), and the results of these projects were publicised in the two-volume *Neuer Wohnbau* (*New Residential Construction*) in 1952 and 1958. The book's editor, Hermann Wandersleb, was Chief Secretary of the Federal Ministry for Housing, Urban Development and Regional Planning. He hoped to use the experiences gained from the ECA model housing projects to benefit social housing construction.

A major point of discussion was the format to be adopted for the kitchen. Until WWII, housing developments in Germany typically featured an 'eat-in kitchen' (*Wohnküche*) – a shared space that is used not only for cooking but also for eating meals, and perhaps supervising children's homework, doing crafts or playing games at the kitchen table. However, postwar discussions of social housing construction advocated for a dedicated kitchen space separate from the other rooms (*Kochküche* or *Arbeitsküche*). This debate on kitchen format had been ongoing since the 1920s, giving rise to the Frankfurt Kitchen, a prototype of the dedicated kitchen that was designed to improve workflow efficiency for housewives. While the kitchen itself is a material asset, these discussions also reflected non-material aspects of people's lives. For example, the second volume of *New Residential Construction* (1958) discusses the kitchen in terms of the need for discrete spaces for cooking, family relaxation and sleeping.[5] It recommends housing plans with a separate kitchen, living room and bedrooms on the grounds that cooking should not interfere with family relaxation, or family relaxation with sleeping. This approach was intended to counteract the collapse of family life brought about by WWII and help reconstitute the nuclear family.

In addition, policymakers began to consider well-being not only in the context of domestic interior space but also in the broader realm of entire residential neighbourhoods. In West Germany, well-being in this larger sense was tied to the idea of 'social mixing.' It has already been pointed out by Harlander and Kuhn (2012) and Oba (2019) that postwar West German housing policies aimed to achieve a social mix – that is, a balance of different socioeconomic backgrounds in the same residential area – which spurred far-reaching debates, for instance, in the city of Stuttgart. These debates on social mixing stemmed in part from previous failures in housing policy. During the first half of the

1950s, city authorities in Stuttgart had provided simply equipped municipal housing (*Einfachwohnung*) to refugees from East Germany, who were seen as 'other' by the local resident population. This othering was exacerbated by the fact that refugee housing was concentrated in one block of one area of the city, thus stymying any social mixing and leading many local residents to look down on social housing.[6]

Under these circumstances, city council debates centred on how to better design municipal housing, as well as how to make this housing available to the general public (not just refugees) so as to dispel the negative image that had been built up around it. Discussions held at the Stuttgart City Council Technical Committee meeting in 1954 stressed the need to construct social housing in the same residential areas where the general population lived in order to achieve a social mix of specially subsidised apartment dwellers, for example refugees, and other kinds of residents. But despite the best of intentions, the limitations of social mixing were soon revealed during a public debate on housing for foreign workers (*Gastarbeiter*) in Sindelfingen, a city near Stuttgart. In 1964, Daimler Benz, a large automobile company, planned to employ 1,400 *Gastarbeiter* from Spain. Although it asked the city to prepare beds for them in existing social housing estates, the company was not able to secure enough beds and was instead forced to build new housing near the factory. According to minutes from a 1965 meeting of the Sindelfingen City Council, council members asked the company to have the *Gastarbeiter* isolated from German residents, thus foreclosing any possibility of social mixing.[7]

The definition of well-being – and especially non-material well-being – that prevailed in West Germany after WWII can also be gleaned from the arguments of those who opposed housing policymakers. For example, around 1960, Stuttgart city authorities announced a plan to clear some woodlands in order to build housing developments and resolve the housing shortage. However, the plan was successfully opposed by a conservationist civic group, *Schutzgemeinschaft Deutscher Wald*, on the grounds that the woodlands were needed to maintain air quality in the low-lying basin area of the city.[8] Moreover, around 1965, when the city of Stuttgart announced the construction of the Hannibal housing development in a forest area near Schönberg, civic groups such as the *Schwäbischer Heimatbund* and *Schönberger Bürgerverein* protested the plan on the grounds that the city's woodlands needed to be retained as a leisure amenity – though in this case, the city administration rejected the argument, and high-rise apartments were ultimately built near Schönberg.[9] Around the same time, the Stuttgart city administration broached plans to construct a 'satellite city' in the neighbouring town of Renningen; however, the plan fell through because of strong concerns in Renningen about the loss of valuable farmland.[10] As all of these cases demonstrate, for people opposing the residential plans of the 1950s and 1960s, well-being included fresh air, leisure opportunities and preservation of farmland, serving as a precursor to contemporary debates on which facets of well-being to prioritise in urban development.

Active and aggressive new housing policies, including policies on the construction of social housing, enabled West Germany to achieve not only a rise in housing standards but also increased consumption of domestic durable consumer goods – another material desire and economic goal at that time. Almost half of the new housing units in the 1950s came with public subsidies and/or rent control, meaning that housing was affordable even for lower-income earners.[11] During this same period, wages were rising faster than prices, and the ongoing constraints on housing costs allowed for increased spending on

TABLE 7.1 Monthly expenditures of households of people with paid employment in West Germany

Year	*1950*		*1953*		*1956*		*1959*	
	DM	%	*DM*	%	*DM*	%	*DM*	%
Food	132.54	46.4	170.11	42.7	201.95	40.5	228.8	39.2
Drink, cigarettes	16.48	5.8	24.8	6.2	33.4	6.7	39.29	6.7
Housing	29.85	10.5	37.19	9.3	47.24	9.5	58.68	10.0
Furniture, housekeeping	13.28	4.6	27.72	7.0	39.6	7.9	49.47	8.5
Electricity, gas, fuel	15.46	5.4	19.99	5.0	28.05	5.6	27.37	4.7
Clothes, shoes	38.81	13.6	58.4	14.7	71.84	14.4	78.8	13.5
Body, health	12.21	4.3	17.58	4.4	22.27	4.5	27.91	4.8
Education, culture, entertainment	20.62	7.3	31.65	7.9	40.0	8.0	52.27	9.0
Transport	6.18	2.1	11.15	2.8	14.44	2.9	20.94	3.6
Sum of living costs	**285.43**	100	**398.59**	100	**498.79**	100	**583.53**	100
Other spending	8.61		9.78		12.86		18.65	
Total expenditures	**294.04**		**408.37**		**511.65**		**602.18**	

Source: Bundesministerium für Ernährung, Landwirtschaft und Forsten (Ed.). 1960. *Die Frau im Staat, in Haushalt und Familie*. Bonn, B-IV-4. Translated by the author.

other goods. Table 7.1 provides a breakdown of monthly expenditures throughout the 1950s for West German households with paid employment. While overall expenditures rose year on year, housing expenses did not increase as a proportion of total expenditure. Instead, the data shows marked rises in expenditures on clothing, furniture and household-related goods (including durable consumer goods), which suggests that the low, fixed level of housing expenses facilitated higher and more flexible spending in other areas.

I argue that the West German housing policy in the 1950s spurred consumption of domestic durable consumer goods, at least among certain classes and income levels, and hastened the attainment of material sufficiency for the postwar population. Even so, the next section will discuss ongoing resistance to the acquisition of certain durable goods, despite the ability to afford them.

The Effects of Class and Income on Consumer Choice and Purchasing Behaviours

As mentioned above, after WWII, popular conceptions of well-being included the satisfaction of material desires, including the possession of durable consumer goods. In Japan, for example, people referred to three specific domestic durable goods – televisions, washing machines and refrigerators – as the 'three Sacred Treasures' due to their high level of desirability and status as a symbol of affluence.

However, these 'Sacred Treasures' were not necessarily universally desired in the 1950s and 1960s, as evidenced by the case of West Germany. According to Jun Suzuki, ownership rates of televisions, washing machines and refrigerators were significantly lower in West Germany than in Japan. In 1964, only 41% of West German households owned a television, compared to 88% in Japan; likewise, 38% of West German homes had an

TABLE 7.2 Ownership rates of durable goods in three-person households in West Germany in 1962/1963, by class

Social status	*Ownership rates in %*								
	Cars	*Television sets*	*Refrigera-tors*	*Washing machines (automatic and non-automatic)*	*Record players*	*Tape recorders*	*Cameras*	*Video cameras*	*Projectors*
Public servants	35.2	50.1	75.9	37.9	24.8	8.4	71.3	3.0	12.1
Employees	43.1	48.4	78.9	38.5	26.6	7.7	68.6	3.1	13.9
Workers	25.0	48.6	63.0	39.4	20.5	6.2	53.5	0.8	4.0

Source: Statistisches Bundesamt (Ed.). 1966. *Wirtschaft und Statistik*. Vol. 8, p. 470. Translated by the author.

electric washing machine, compared to 61% in Japan. This is somewhat surprising given that economic recovery was achieved earlier in West Germany than in Japan.[12] The delay in the acquisition of durable consumer goods thus raises the question of whether West Germans were pursuing (and attaining) well-being outside of the satisfaction of material desires.

The low rates of acquisition for these household appliances cannot be easily attributed to household income or pricing. On the contrary, this was a period of high economic growth, with wages rising relative to prices; many consumers thus had the material means to purchase durable consumer goods. In order to understand West German purchasing patterns and lifestyle choices at this time, it is necessary to look beyond overall income and analyse ownership rates of household appliances by social class.

According to German historian Jan Logemann, 'class and occupational milieu, not just income, seemed to determine consumption patterns, belying the claim of a 'leveled middle-class society' in postwar West Germany.'[13] In his book *Trams or Tailfins*, Logemann analyses the spending patterns of middle-class and working-class residents of West Germany based on statistics published by the Federal Statistical Office of Germany in 1966. Logemann builds on the research of American sociologist Richard Hamilton (1975), who noted that postwar working-class households typically avoided buying major durables (with the exception of television sets); overall, they placed considerably less value on status symbols and more value on home entertainment. Table 7.2 illustrates some of these class-related differences through ownership rates of common durable goods in 1962/1963. The categories of social class are given as 'public servants' (*Beamte*), 'employees' (*Angestellte*) and 'workers' (*Arbeiter*).

Table 7.3, by contrast, shows the ownership rates of durable goods by both social class and income level. Unsurprisingly, class and income are highly correlated, with public servants comprising the largest percentage of high-income earners (800–1200 DM), salaried employees being mostly middle-income (600–800 DM) and workers being mostly low-income (300–600 DM). Even so, income and class alone fail to fully explain ownership rates for these goods.

Among public servants and employees, ownership rates for durable goods rose when their income levels reached mid-level and above; however, ownership rates among

TABLE 7.3 Ownership rates of durable goods in three-person households in West Germany in 1962/1963, by class and income

Monthly net income in DM in 1961 /Social status of head of household	*Number of households*	*Ownership rates*									
		Cars		*Television sets*		*Refrigerators*		*Automatic washing machines*		*Washing machines*	
	All	*%*	*Number*	*%*	*Number*	*%*	*Number*	*%*	*Number*	*%*	*Number*
300-600											
Public servants	584	19.2	112	44.7	261	63.4	370	7.4	43	22.9	134
Employees	1,244	29.2	363	44.8	557	67.4	838	9.9	123	23.6	294
Workers	8,575	20.7	1775	44.9	3850	61.0	5231	6.6	566	30.2	2590
600-800											
Public servants	937	30.4	285	56.4	528	81.2	761	13.2	124	28.1	263
Employees	2,405	41.6	1000	49.6	1193	78.5	1888	10.9	262	27.4	659
Workers	5,467	26.9	1471	52.7	2881	65.0	3554	7.7	421	33.4	1826
800-1200											
Public servants	1,043	48.4	505	47.5	495	78.2	816	13.0	136	26.1	272
Employees	2,395	51.7	1238	49.1	1176	85.4	2045	18.4	441	22.9	548
Workers	2,297	36.4	836	52.6	1208	65.5	1505	10.0	230	35.4	813

Monthly net income in DM in 1961/ Social status of head of household	*Ownership rates*									
	Record players		*Tape recorders*		*Cameras*		*Video cameras*		*Projectors*	
	%	*number*	*%*	*number*	*%*	*number*	*%*	*number*	*%*	*number*
300-600										
Public servants	20.0	117	7.4	43	68.2	398	1.0	5.84	6.8	39.712
Employees	25.3	315	6.5	81	62.1	773	2.2	27.368	8.4	104.496
Workers	20.2	1732	5.2	446	52.5	4502	0.5	42.875	2.6	222.95
600-800										
Public servants	23.1	216	6.6	62	70.7	662	3.0	28.11	11.8	110.566
Employees	26.2	630	7.0	168	68.7	1652	2.2	52.91	10.7	257.335
Workers	19.0	1039	7.4	405	55.5	3034	1.3	71.071	5.2	284.284
800-1200										
Public servants	29.1	304	10.5	110	73.6	768	4.1	42.763	15.3	159.579
Employees	27.6	661	9.1	218	71.9	1722	4.4	105.38	20.0	479
Workers	25.1	577	7.0	161	52.6	1208	1.0	22.97	6.4	147.008

Source: Statistisches Bundesamt (Ed.) 1966. *Wirtschaft und Statistik*. Vol. 8, p. 470. Translated by the author.

workers did not substantially change, even when their incomes rose. Thus, it is not necessarily the case that ownership rates increased in tandem with income. Instead, workers demonstrated a distinctive tendency towards non-ownership in comparison with other social classes. This pattern extended to many goods, including private automobiles, records, cameras, video cameras, projectors and washing machines. By contrast, the television ownership rate among workers was two points *higher* than the rate among public servants and employees (see Table 7.2). Among high-income workers in particular, the television ownership rate was over three points higher than that for public servants and employees (see Table 7.3). This suggests an aspirational trend among workers for television ownership in particular, despite their lack of interest in other domestic durable goods.

Given that the postwar increase in wages did not always correspond to spending on durable consumer goods, what *did* West Germans spend their money on? Data on monthly household spending shows that expenditures on food, clothing, luxury foods, alcohol and tobacco were quite popular, especially among workers – even as their overall spending remained lower than that of the other classes, regardless of income level (see Table 7.4). In other words, workers did not engage in a great deal of spending overall; however, when spending occurred, the trend was towards outlays on food and related luxury foods, alcohol and tobacco.[14]

Regarding the consumption of the middle class, on the other hand, Logemann points to a 'bourgeois ethos of consumption,'[15] with spending focused on education and related cultural expenses that reinforced traditional social distinctions. High-income public servants tended *not* to purchase televisions, despite having the material means to do so and higher overall spending patterns than the other classes, which suggests the possibility that they were deliberately pursuing well-being independent of durable goods. Indeed, the spending breakdown in Table 7.4 reveals that, compared to middle-income public servants, high-income public servants devoted a higher percentage of their income to clothing and footwear, personal hygiene and health, education and entertainment and personal devices.

The categories of 'body and health' and 'education, culture, and entertainment' were particularly popular among public servants, even compared to high-income members of the other social classes. However, it should be noted that the label 'education and entertainment' conflates two quite different activities that are worth examining individually. Outlays on education (*Bildung*) included school fees and boarding school expenses; the purchase of books, newspapers, magazines, works of art and writing materials; and tickets for the theatre, cinema, concerts, museums and exhibitions. Outlays on entertainment, meanwhile, included the purchase of televisions, radios, tape recorders, record players, cameras, home movie equipment, musical instruments, toys, camping goods, sporting goods, tickets for sporting events and fees for entertainment. When viewed separately, entertainment expenses were higher than education expenses among all social classes and income levels. One of the reasons for this probably was the wide availability of public education, which kept education expenditures down – though high-income public servants and employees still spent slightly more on education than workers (even high-income ones).

The ownership rates of durable consumer goods and the patterns of consumption mentioned above raise the question of the relationship between non-ownership of goods like

TABLE 7.4 Private consumption in three-person households in West Germany in 1962/1963

Monthly net income in DM in1961/ Social status of head of household	*Food, luxury foods, alcohol and tobacco*		*Clothes, shoes*		*Rent, etc.*		*Electricity, gas, fuel, etc.*		*Other housekeeping*		*Monthly net income in DM in1961/ Social status of head of household*	*Transport, news transmission, etc.*		*Body, health, etc.*		*Education, culture, entertainment*		*Personal equipment, etc,*		*All private consumption*	
	DM	%	DM	%	DM	%	DM	%	DM	%		DM	%	DM	%	DM	%	DM	%	DM	%
300–600											300-600										
Public servants	275,27	41.3	79,76	12	80,18	12	32,61	4.9	73,52	11	Public servants	43,08	6.5	26,83	4	42,47	6.4	12,55	1.9	666,27	100
Employees	280,17	37.7	90,49	12.2	84,07	11.4	33,57	4.5	79,79	10.7	Employees	77,85	10.5	23,98	3.2	52,15	7	21,08	2.8	743,15	100
Workers	283,76	43.2	81,33	12.4	64,65	9.8	28,84	4.4	72,00	11	Workers	52,15	7.9	20,26	3.1	41,37	6.3	12,23	1.9	656,59	100
600–800											600-800										
Public servants	303,03	38.1	85,81	10.8	93,42	11.7	35,45	4.5	99,88	12.5	Public servants	76,31	9.6	28,71	3.6	56,23	7.1	17,61	2.1	796,45	100
Employees	316,19	37	103,92	12.2	97,56	11.4	37,12	4.3	98,65	11.5	Employees	88,08	10.3	32,03	3.8	55,76	6.5	25,53	3	854,84	100
Workers	323,26	42	97,32	12.7	76,17	9.9	30,00	3.9	84,29	11	Workers	64,86	8.4	25,41	3.2	49,89	6.5	18,18	2.4	769,38	100
800–1,200											800-1200										
Public servants	374,68	37.1	119,17	11.8	113,26	11.2	42,32	4.2	113,71	11.3	Public servants	90,59	9	44,51	4.4	83,24	8.3	27,08	2.7	1008,56	100
Employees	358,19	33.6	125,50	11.8	121,13	11.4	42,19	4	130,20	12.2	Employees	135,20	12.7	41,76	3.8	76,91	7.2	35,53	3.3	1066,61	100
Workers	356,34	40	119,97	13.5	74,37	8.4	33,19	3.6	126,54	14.2	Workers	66,40	7.5	28,07	3.2	58,49	6.6	27,39	3	890,76	100

Source: Statistisches Bundesamt (Ed.). 1966. Wirtschaft und Statistik. Vol. 8 August, p. 469. Translated by the author.

refrigerators and televisions and outlay on non-material well-being. The working class undeniably spent more on food, luxury foods, alcohol and tobacco and less on household appliances. This can be partially explained by differences in employment rates of married women among the different classes. The employment rate for married women was considerably higher among workers than the other social classes: only 7.2% of women married to public servants were employed, compared to 15.9% of women married to workers in 1950.[16] We can surmise that employed women had less time to perform housework and thus less time to use domestic durable goods like washing machines. They also tended to spend more money on food, luxury foods, alcohol and tobacco that did not necessitate the use of a refrigerator—in other words, ready-made foods and dining outside the home. Table 7.5 shows that, in many of the socioeconomic categories, lower ownership rates of refrigerators corresponded to higher spending on food, and vice versa.

Non-ownership of televisions among high-income public servants, on the other hand, likely had a different explanation. This group did not necessarily eschew all durable goods; on the contrary, they displayed the highest ownership rates for record players, tape recorders and cameras (see Table 7.3). Thus, it is likely that the television was viewed as a more 'common' or 'lowly' form of entertainment compared to the more traditional record player. Moreover, high-income public servants frequently sought entertainment outside the home, through more expensive or exclusive experiences that satisfied their need for psychological or physical well-being. Cameras were portable and thus could be brought along to these experiences, while televisions could not.

To summarise, the growing consumption of durable consumer goods across multiple sectors of West German society attests to the country's growing wealth during the two decades following WWII. However, increased wealth did not always result in increased consumption of all durable consumer goods. Some households deliberately avoided

TABLE 7.5 Food consumption in three-person households in West Germany in 1962/1963

Monthly net income in DM in 1961/Social status of head of household	*All private consumption*	*Food, luxury foods, alcohol and tobacco*		*Ownership rates of refrigerators*
	DM	*DM*	*%*	*%*
300–600				
Public servants	666,27	275,27	41.3	63.4
Employees	743,15	280,17	37.7	67.4
Workers	656,59	283,76	43.2	61.0
600–800				
Public servants	796,45	303,03	38.1	81.2
Employees	854,84	316,19	37	78.5
Workers	769,38	323,26	42	65.0
800–1,200				
Public servants	1008,56	374,68	37.1	78.2
Employees	1066,61	358,19	33.6	85.4
Workers	890,76	356,34	40	65.5

Source: Statistisches Bundesamt (Ed.). 1966. *Wirtschaft und Statistik*. Vol. 8, p. 469. Data compiled by the author.

high-ticket items, despite their ability to afford them, as we saw with both workers and high-income public servants. Indeed, as incomes rose, well-being was often pursued by purchasing psychological and physical experiences outside the home, like entertainment and dining. Interestingly, the characteristic spending patterns of each class held steady even after incomes increased.[17]

Washing Machines in West Germany: A Case Study in the (Non-) Consumption of Durable Goods

Analysing the reasons why people did not consume or possess certain goods reveals much about the lifestyles that postwar consumers were choosing. Though lifestyles changed rapidly during the postwar recovery period, ownership rates of major appliances, like washing machines and refrigerators, were lower in West Germany than in Japan. While the previous section compared purchasing habits across various socioeconomic groups within West Germany, this section takes a closer look at the generally lower consumption of domestic durable consumer goods in West Germany. The central question is: what led consumers in West Germany to decide *not* to buy these domestic durable consumer goods when many of their peers in other developed nations did? I argue that the answer lies in part in the nature of German housing developments, dating back to the second half of the nineteenth century. This section takes the electric washing machine as a case study for why ownership of durable goods was not more actively pursued in West Germany.

A number of factors were at work in delaying the spread of the at-home electric washing machine in West Germany. One probable cause for the low ownership rate stemmed from the country's cultural history and established laundry practices. In German cities, laundry was traditionally not done at home but was instead outsourced to professional clothes-washing businesses or facilities (*Wäschereien*). According to the Stuttgart City Directory, the city had over 150 more *Wäschereien* listed in the 1950s than in the 1920s, despite the advent of at-home electric washing machines.[18] Although the numbers dipped slightly in the decade that followed, there were still 147 *Wäschereien* in operation in 1963, as well as a number of businesses offering clothes drying and ironing services. Convenience was a major selling point for these businesses; speakers at the 1958 conference of the Federation of Laundry Businesses, for example, advised that housewives should have their clothes washed at the *Wäschereien* in order to ease their domestic workload.[19] Of course, the at-home electric washing machine also promised to reduce the amount of time and effort required to complete household chores; but if that work was already being outsourced in West Germany, then the machine would have had less appeal, especially if households had the discretionary funds to spend on laundry services.

A second probable factor for the slow uptake in washing machines is that many women worked for *Wäschereien* – over 90,000 in 1958 (see Table 7.6). Choosing not to purchase a washing machine was therefore also a choice to protect women's work opportunities.

A third probable factor was the prohibition against hanging washing on balconies. A 1960 newsletter from the Solingen Savings and Building Association (*Spar- und Bauverein Solingen*), one of the agencies involved in social housing construction in the central West German city of Solingen, forbade drying laundry on balconies.[20] Instead, it recommended decorating the space with flowers. I argue that these aesthetic regulations would have made West German households more hesitant to wash clothes at home, and thus to

TABLE 7.6 Service sector in West Germany on September 30, 1958

Sector	*Employees*		
	All	*Women*	*Women/all×100 in %*
Photography	17,484	13,314	76
Laundry, dye works, chemical cleaning	107,573	90,763	84
Cleaning of buildings	26,730	20,815	78
Porter	431	80	19
Restaurant	381,454	286,256	75
Living	28,723	13,446	47
Public pool	6,244	3,676	59
Hairdresser	148,869	111,900	75
Art, theatre, music, film, radio, literature, show, sport	81,025	36,816	45
Housekeeping	618,626	617,387	100
All	1,417,159	1,194,453	84

Source: Bundesministerium für Ernährung, Landwirtschaft und Forsten (Ed.). 1960. *Die Frau im Staat, in Haushalt und Familie*. Bonn, A-3-13. Translated by the author.

purchase washing machines for that purpose. Such a directive demonstrates how postwar housing policies were governed not only by material concerns about also by aesthetics and the psychological well-being of residents.

A fourth probable factor is that housing complexes often had common laundry areas. Such areas had been a feature of social and public housing developments in Germany since the second half of the nineteenth century.[21] Open to all residents, they functioned as places of both work and socialisation for the housewives who used them. These spaces were so popular that even after domestic washing machines came into widespread use, some residents continued to use their common laundry areas as assembly halls or 'laundry museums.'

Sometime after 1963, the number of *Wäschereien* began to decline; indeed, though the 1975 Stuttgart City Directory lists 'laundries,' there is no specific category for *Wäschereien*. I maintain that during the first half of the 1960s, consumers became aware of technical innovations in durable consumer goods through facilities outside the home, but did not see an immediate need to adopt them (for the reasons discussed above). Eventually, though, they came to acknowledge the usefulness and convenience of having these goods within the home.

The delay in the spread of the washing machine in West Germany reveals much about domestic life, women's labour and housing policies in the postwar period. Residents did not feel pressured to immediately purchase washing machines because they were able to achieve domestic comfort and lightened workloads by outsourcing laundry to *Wäschereien*. Housewives were also interested in protecting their distinctive practice of washing clothes in common laundry areas, which served an important social and community function in addition to the more obvious pragmatic function. Developments within the realm of public and social housing, including municipal regulations governing the use of domestic space, ultimately supported and reinforced these habits.

Longer-Term Outlook on Non-Material Well-Being in Social Housing

The examples mentioned above for the pursuit of non-material well-being indicate distinct features at specific time points in the 1950s and early 1960s. While each of the small case studies is situated within the longer-term development of well-being – that is within the 30-year period from the 1950s to the 1970s when social housing construction took place—it is not possible to conclude that there was a significant shift from material to non-material well-being in post-war West Germany solely based on the material presented so far.

How, then, can we position the nature of non-material well-being around 1960, as discussed in this book within a broader historical context? The ownership rates of washing machines, as discussed in Section 4 of this book, continued to rise after the early 1960s, reaching 74.5% by 1973. Similarly, the prevalence of television sets in West Germany as a whole rose to 87.2% by 1973.[22] Thus it is also not possible to simply argue for a shift from material to non-material well-being based on the ownership rates of durable consumer goods alone.

Noteworthy here is whether various elements considered to embody the pursuit of non-material well-being in the early 1960s – such as the preservation of forests as a source of fresh air and recreational spaces; the ideal of social mixing; the provision and enjoyment of opportunities for education, culture and entertainment; the provision and use of spaces for communal interactions within residential areas; and the aesthetic sense regarding the use of balconies – were ephemeral either as the needs of contemporary consumers or methodologically in the surviving documentation, so that they would vanish amidst the subsequent developments – such as the rise in ownership rates of durable consumer goods and the intensification of housing estate developments.

The discussions on forest preservation and social mixing in the housing debates of the 1950s (as mentioned in Section 2) are even more prominent in the public debates now, which again include the overarching issue of housing. The activities of nature conservation organisations can of course be placed within the history of the growing environmental movement in twentieth-century Germany. The ideal of social mixing has not materialised as expected, and social segregation has arguably progressed post-unification, nonetheless it had been institutionalised in housing policies across West German cities. For example, in the 2010s, a new system was introduced in the city of Hamburg to promote balanced urban development. This system mandates that one-third of the new housing supply, consisting of 30–40 units or more, must be provided as social rental housing.[23] Similar initiatives have also been undertaken in other cities such as Stuttgart and Solingen. Therefore, the discussions related to well-being today can indeed be seen as an extension of the housing discourse in the 1950s and early 1960s.

In respect with the elements constituting non-material well-being mentioned in Sections 3 and 4, such as opportunities for education, culture and entertainment, the provision of communal spaces for residents which facilitated communication, and the aesthetic sense regarding the use of balconies, it is not possible to analyse the overall West German developments after the early 1960s. Instead, by examining the results of a survey conducted among residents of a newly constructed social housing estate in Stuttgart in 1970, we can consider how these elements were valued or overlooked within housing estates at that time.

The housing estate 'Lauchhau,' supplied by the Stuttgart Housing Estate Company (*Stuttgarter Wohnungs- und Siedlungsgesellschaft*) which was again sponsored by the city of Stuttgart between 1968 and 1970, provided 442 housing units consisting of 2–6 rooms across 9 buildings of 4–21 floors on a 5.31-hectare plot of land. The estate employed prefabricated construction methods based on the most sophisticated industrial knowledge at the time, and state-of-the-art technology was used for heating facilities. Additionally, the latest sociological research materialised in the floor plan when the layout of each housing unit included a 'multipurpose room.' While conventional West German social housing at the time typically featured individual rooms for children, a parents' bedroom and a living room, the Lauchhau project included spaces without designated uses. In 1970, a survey was conducted among newly arrived residents of the estate by the city authorities, with 320 out of 361 households responding.[24] Of these, 62% were answered by women. According to the survey results, the estate was predominantly inhabited by households in their 20s–40s, with 72% of households having a 'housewife' (*Hausfrau*). The survey categorised the heads of households into 'lower class' comprising unskilled and skilled labourers, 'middle class' including other employees, and 'upper class' consisting of self-employed individuals, higher-ranking civil servants, mid-level professionals and managerial staff. In total, 33% of respondent households belonged to the lower class, 42% to the middle class and 25% to the upper class. Thus, the profile of the estate suggests a slightly lower-middle-class population.

At the time, the estate featured not only the multipurpose rooms in residential buildings but also community facilities. While various events and spaces were provided, such as mother-and-baby classes, events for preschoolers, sewing classes, women's gatherings, gatherings for the elderly and informational evenings (which invited architects, politicians and so on), participation rates in these activities, except for sociological-baby classes (64%), events for preschoolers (22.5%) and informational evenings (17.8%), were generally low, mostly below 5%. Despite efforts to encourage community interaction, it appeared that residents did not fully utilise these facilities and services, with exceptions along the gendered lines of care work.

The city of Stuttgart recognised that existing community services for its citizens were not sufficient at the time and conducted a general survey asking: 'What additional facilities are absolutely desired within the housing estate premises?' As options for responses, they presented 'sports clubs,' 'libraries' and so on. Although the city had not yet invested in the field of education, culture and entertainment by 1970, they acknowledged the need for opportunities in sports and literacy/reading. Through this question, the city wanted to inquire about what self-organised services were needed or desired as adjunct facilities to the community centre of the housing estate. However, respondents seemed to perceive the question as asking what was needed in general within their local housing estate premises. The survey results showed that the top choice was 'libraries' at 20%, followed by 'sports clubs' at 18.8% and then options not listed, such as 'shops, post offices, bars, cafes, pools, walking paths,' at 11.9%. As I have shown in Section 4 of this book, the proportion of spending on 'education and culture' was higher for higher-income professionals and salarymen compared to other groups. In the Lauchhau project in 1970, the city also seemed to be aware of the necessity of libraries as part of the category of 'education and culture' within the estate premises. Nevertheless, the percentage of respondents who answered 'absolutely want a library/library room' was lower than the proportion of upper-class residents (approximately 25%). There appeared to be a discrepancy between the city's and the residents' outlook regarding shared facilities. The mention of 'coffee house' and 'pub' (*Café* and *Kneipe*) in free responses suggests that while the city was not considering providing these within the estate at the time, there were residents who desired such opportunities within the housing estate in 1970. For example, working-class men might have been used to frequent bars in older or more naturally grown neighbourhoods as intergenerational spaces of social interaction and political organisation.

The survey shows that even in 1970, when the ownership rate of durable consumer goods increased, the municipality, as the entity responsible for formulating housing policies, carried out or designed housing development with a focus on facilitating inter-residential communication and educational facilities – which had been preferred by the higher-income public servants and employees within the housing estates during the early 1960s. However, there was a tendency in the city's housing policy not to prioritise options favoured more strongly by the working class, who tended to spend more money on food outside of the house/indulgences (luxury foods, alcohol and tobacco) than another social status in 1966 (Table 7.4). In 2013, a discount store of the 'Netto'-chain for food, drink and household goods started to be operated directly near the housing estates, but the issue was addressed by private enterprise outside the framework of housing policies. Leaders of local civic organisations such as 'Children's House' (*Kinderhaus*) and 'Citizens Association' (*Bürgerverein*), feared the spread of underage drinking due to the opening of the discount store[25]. Additionally, 'book boxes' (Baumbibliothek) had been placed along the walking paths within the housing estate premises by the municipality (see Figure 7.1).

FIGURE 7.1 Tree library in the housing estate 'Lauchhau.'

Source: Author.

While the realisation of a library may not have materialised, the underlying principle of advancing literacy for education and entertainment seems to have endured.

Regarding laundry, 82.5% of respondents in the Lauchhau estate survey owned washing machines, and 79.7% of them used their washing machines in the bathroom. The percentage of respondents who answered 'hanging laundry' when asked 'how do you generally use your balcony?' was 40.9%. This indicates the balcony being utilised as a place for housework, but it is also noteworthy that 59.1% do not primarily consider the balcony as such a functional space. The data of the survey does not allow inferences to the social status of the respondents and their respective uses of the balcony, e.g. a continuity of hanging laundry in middle-class households.

A strong attachment to the communal laundry facilities within housing estates was observed not only in the Weegerhof estate in Solingen, pointed out in Section 4, but also in the Hallschlag municipal housing estate in Stuttgart and the Heeper Fichten housing estate in Bielefeld. In the case of Hallschlag in Stuttgart, when demolition plans were proposed by the city in the 1980s, protests by citizen groups led to its renovation as a community centre.[26] Similarly, in the Heeper Fichten estate, the former laundry room is used as a meeting place. The memory of the laundry room as a space for communication and interaction has continued in Bielefeld since the 1980s and this function remains today.

Therefore it can be concluded that many of the communal and/or spatial elements believed to embody the pursuit of non-material well-being in the early 1960s were not immediately eliminated, even amid the increase in the ownership rate of durable consumer goods and the intensification of housing estate development towards individual needs thereafter.

Conclusion

Around the 1950s, housing policymakers expected that a sufficient housing supply and better housing standards would facilitate family relaxation and reductions in housework. However, failures in housing policy and opposition to residential construction led to the pursuit of well-being outside the home, in the form of fresh air, entertainment and social mixing. In West Germany in the 1960s, residents across social classes and income levels frequently pursued well-being in ways that did not involve the consumption of durable consumer goods. Detailed analysis of spending by class and income has revealed that, though workers spent less overall than other social classes, their spending was proportionally higher in the areas of food, luxury foods, alcohol and tobacco. This suggests that workers were pursuing non-material well-being through non-domestic dining and leisure experiences rather than the purchase of durable consumer goods. Furthermore, the relatively low ownership rates of televisions among high-income public servants and employees – groups that clearly had the means to purchase a television – suggests that they may have been deliberately forgoing these appliances in favour of spending on non-domestic entertainment and education. Finally, the low ownership rates of washing machines in West Germany (when compared to countries like Japan) reflect unique cultural factors, such as the widespread availability of clothes washing businesses and policies forbidding the display of laundry on balconies, which delayed the adoption of the personal washing machine within the home. The choice to delay or avoid purchase of these domestic durable consumer goods can be viewed as a sign of consumers' desire for non-material forms of well-being in the postwar era, despite increased wages and higher spending power across class lines.

In the 1970s, there was both progress in residential development and an increase in durable consumer goods ownership. So the lived experience in the three post-war decades cannot be simply characterised as a shift from material well-being to non-material well-being. However, when we focus on housing policy, environmental policy and certain regional policies aimed at solving issues below the federal or state level, elements that prompted the pursuit of non-material well-being in the 1950s and 1960s, such as forest conservation and social mixing, were taken into consideration in policy formulation in the following decades. Various forms of non-material well-being pursued by different social groups around 1960 were the basis for services considered important by policymakers in the 1970s, for example in the field of education. Later, after the era of social housing came to an end, (commercial) spaces for grocery shopping and buying luxury foods, alcohol and tobacco were incorporated in areas near the estates. Former communal laundry rooms are presently being utilised for other community purposes and maintained as social spaces. In other words, the planned or contested elements of non-material well-being did not disappear but were appropriated by different actors in or near the housing estates.

Today, in an ageing society, non-profit organisations in Germany are making attempts to provide residential services to the senior residents of these estates. The efforts seen in Section 4 of this book, by both municipal and non-profit organisations, to achieve non-material well-being, seem related to the development of residential welfare services today.

Notes

1 Grünbacher 2012: 703–08.
2 Von Saldern 1995: 234, 253f.
3 Nagayama 2017: 161–66.
4 Wandersleb 1958: 14.
5 Wandersleb 1958: 28–38.
6 Nagayama 2021: 78–70.
7 Sindelfinger Gemeinderat 1965.
8 Staatsarchiv Ludwigsburg 1960–1966; Stadtarchiv Stuttgart [StA Stuttgart] 1–703.
9 Schwäbischer Heimatbund 1963; StA Stuttgart 20/1-258.
10 StA Stuttgart 14/1-1374.
11 Heuer 1985: 174; Iino 1989: 133.
12 Suzuki 2013: 259.
13 Logemann 2012: 105.
14 Logemann 2012: 102.
15 Logemann 2012: 104.
16 Niehuss 2001: 229.
17 Logemann 2012: 102f.
18 Adressbuch der Stadt Stuttgart 1928; 1951; 1955; 1957; 1963; 1975.
19 StA Stuttgart 20/1-1006.
20 Blätter für Wohnungswesen 1960, 12, 6.
21 Bullock and Read 1985: 133; Zimmermann 1991: 68.
22 Kramper, 2000: 27.
23 Oba 2019: 241–42.
24 StA Stuttgart: 50/1-12.
25 Stuttgarter Zeitung, February 22, 2013.
26 Förderverein Gegegnungszentrum Hallschlag e.V. (Without year).

References

Bullock, N. and Read, J. 1985. *The Movement for Housing Reform in Germany and France, 1840–1914*. Cambridge: Cambridge University Press.

Bundesministerium für Ernährung, Landwirtschaft und Forsten, ed. 1960. *Die Frau im Staat, in Haushalt und Familie*. Bonn.

Grünbacher, A. 2012. "Cold War Economics: The Use of Marshall Plan Counterpart Funds in Germany, 1948–1960." *Central European History 45* (4): 679–716.

Förderverein Gegegnungszentrum Hallschlag e.V. (Without year). Vom Waschhaus zum Begegnungszentrum. Amtschimmel gegen Bürgerwillen. (Without place)

Hamilton, Richard 1975. "Affluence and the Worker: The West German Case." *American Journal of Sociology* 71 (2): 144–152.

Harlander, T., and Kuhn, G., eds. 2012. *Soziale Mischung in der Stadt*. Stuttgart: Krämer Verlag.

Heuer, Jürgen H. B. 1985. *Lehrbuch der Wohnungswirtschaft*. Frankfurt am Main: Fritz Knapp Verlag.

Iino, Yumiko. 1989. Nishi doitsu tyotiku syourei/zaikei seisaku no tenkan to kojin tyotiku kouzou. *Syoken kenkyu* 88: 83–159.

Kramper, Peter. 2000. "From Economic Convergence to Convergence in Affluence? Income Growth, Household Expenditure and the Rise of Mass Consumption in Britain and West Germany, 1950–1974." (Working Paper No. 56/00 Department of Economic History London School of Economics).

Logemann, Jan 2012. *Trams or Tailfins? Public and Private Prosperity in Postwar West Germany and the United States*. Chicago: University of Chicago Press.

Nagayama, Nodoka. 2017. Dai niji taisen go nishi doitsu ni okeru kyojyu suijyun no koujyo to jyutaku seisaku—Stuttgart shi ni tyakumoku shite. *Seijyo daigaku keizai kenkyu* 218: 159–182.

Nagayama, Nodoka. 2021. 1950nen dai nishi doitsu ni okeru toudoku syussinsya no tame no jyutakukensetsu—Stuttgart shi no jirei. *Geschichte* 14: 64–81.

Niehuss, Merith. 2001. *Familie, Frau und Gesellschaft: Studien zur Strukturgeschichte der Familie in Westdeutschland, 1945–1960 (*Schriftenreihe der Historischen Kommission bei der Bayerischen Akademie der Wissenschaften, 65). Göttingen: Vandenhoeck & Ruprecht.

Oba, Shigeaki. 2019. *Gendai doitsu no jyuutaku seisaku: Toshi saisei senryaku to kouteki kainyu no saihen (Modern German Housing Policy: Urban Renewal Strategy and Reorganization of Public Intervention)*. Tokyo: Akashi Shoten.

Schwäbischer Heimatbund, ed. 1963. *Schwäbische Heimat: Magazin für Geschichte, Landeskultur, Naturschutz und Denkmalpflege* 14.

Sindelfinger Gemeinderat. 1965. "Niederschrift über die Verhandlungen des technischen Ausschusses des Gemeinderats, 23. September 1965." In *Protokollbuch der Stadt Sindelfingen*. Sindelfingen.

Spar- und Bauverein Solingen eG, ed. 1960. *Blätter für Wohnungswesen*, *12*, 6.

Staatsarchiv Ludwigsburg. 1960–1966. *Schutzgemeinschaft Deutscher Wald, Landesverband Baden-Württemberg e.V.* = PL 429 I Bü 67.

Stadtarchiv Stuttgart. 1957–1974. *Bundes- und Länderverwaltung, Landesverteidigung, Militärische Anlagen und Gebäude, Militärische Gebäude und Anlagen außerhalb des Stadtgebietes Stuttgart* = 14/1–1374.

Stadtarchiv Stuttgart. 1958–1963. *Förderung des Wohnungsbaus durch Bund und Länder, Einzelne Wohnungsbauprogramme, Wohnungsbauprogramme 1959 und 1960* = 20/1–703.

Stadtarchiv Stuttgart. 1961. ""Was erwartet die Großstadt von der Raumordnung?" Vortrag des OB Dr. Klett, Stuttgart, in Waiblingen am 18.5.1961. "In *Raumplanung (Bundes-und Landesplanung), Regionalplaner-Tagungen des Landes Baden-Württemberg* = 20/1–258.

Stadtarchiv Stuttgart. 1956–1958. *Organisationen und sonstige Einrichtungen, Vereinigungen und Verbände der Wirtschaft, Deutscher Wäschereiverband* = 21/1–1006.

Stadtarchiv Stuttgart. 1970–1972. Unterlagen der Arbeitsgruppe Stadtentwicklung und Regionalplanung 50/1–12.

Statistisches Bundesamt, ed. 1966. *Wirtschaft und Statistik*. Vol. 8. Wiesbaden

Stuttgarter Zeitung. February 22, 2013. "Das Zauberwort heißt Netzwerk". https://www.stuttgarter-zeitung.de/inhalt.vaihingen-das-zauberwort-heisst-netzwerk.84cd86e7-2a32-4127-9905-af53118cd2a8.html, accessed 25 May 2024.

Suzuki, Jun. 2013. *Shingijutsu no shakaishi (A History of Modern Japan)*. Tokyo: Chūō Kōron Shinsha.
Von Saldern, Adelheid. 1995. "Von der ‚guten Stube' zur ‚guten Wohnung.' Zur Geschichte des Wohnens in der Bundesrepublik Deutschland." *Archiv für Sozialgeschichte* 35: 227–254.
Wandersleb, Hermann, ed. 1958. *Neuer Wohnbau*. Vol. 2. Ravensburg: Otto Maier.
Wandersleb, Hermann, ed. 1952. *Neuer Wohnbau*. Vol. 1. Ravensburg: Otto Maier.
Zimmermann, Cremens. 1991. *Von der Wohnungsfrage zur Wohnungspolitik*, Göttingen: Vandenhoeck und Ruprecht Verlag

8

POST-WAR HOUSING AND THE CONCEPT OF WELL-BEING

A Comparison of the US and China

Benjamin Gianni

Typical of many countries, the US and China both faced severe housing shortages emerging from World War II (WWII). In both countries, governments played an important, but indirect, role in addressing these shortages and housing played a key role in reorganising cities. The difference in approaches – as manifested in the types of housing constructed, how, where and by whom – reflects both the difference in contexts and the contrasting ways in which well-being was defined.

Notwithstanding the vastly different economic and political milieux, 1949 was a particularly significant year for both China and the US. The Communist Revolution of 1949 led to the founding of the Peoples' Republic of China and marked the beginning of the shift from a disaggregated, post-imperial, bottom-up economy to a soviet-style, command economy. This, in turn, occasioned a major reorganisation of Chinese society with significant implications both for the structure of cities and the production of housing. In the US, the Housing Act of 1949 was largely responsible for the type and location of housing, as well as the means by which it was produced in the post-war decades.

The US

Emerging from WWII, housing shortages in the US were seen both as a challenge and an opportunity. Government support for the construction of housing was intended both to address supply and to generate peacetime employment for war workers and returning veterans. It was widely acknowledged that housing production would have a significant knock-on effect on the demand for construction materials and consumer goods, including furniture, fixtures, appliances and automobiles. New infrastructure – roads, pipes, water and sewage treatment plants, schools, etc. – was also required to support housing. This translated to jobs for many of those to whom this housing would be directed, namely, younger, first-time homebuyers, many of whom were returning veterans.

Housing shortages were particularly acute in US cities, to which a significant number of households gravitated during the Depression and the wartime years. Housing starts dropped precipitously with the market crash of 1929 and had just begun to recover when

DOI: 10.4324/9781003527930-12

resources were re-directed to the war effort in 1942. Through the 1930s and 1940s, households were forced to double up, money was scarce and maintenance suffered. As such, the housing stock was not only depleted but in poor condition after the war. Affordable dwellings frequently lacked central heating and indoor plumbing.

The first three of the six sections or 'titles' comprising the Housing Act of 1949[1] had a significant impact on the shape of the built environment in the US following the war. Titles I and III were focused on the replacement of existing housing while Title II largely underwrote the construction of new housing on previously undeveloped land.

Title I: Slum Clearance and Community Development and Redevelopment

Enabling what came to be referred to as *urban renewal*, the programs introduced under Title I targeted urban housing, empowering cities to expropriate, clear and sell off property in 'distressed' neighbourhoods to make way for replacement housing. The program authorised $1 billion in loans to help cities acquire slums and blighted land for public or private redevelopment. It also allotted $100 million annually for a five-year period for grants to cover two-thirds of the difference between the cost of acquiring, clearing and improving land and whatever revenue cities were able to generate through resale.

Title I was intended to help cities upgrade their housing stock and recover a portion of the tax base that they had been losing to suburban municipalities since the 1920s. It focused on mid- and high-rise, multi-unit housing for the middle class.[2] As the program preceded the introduction of condominium designation, however, apartments were not available for purchase.[3] An aversion to renting, coupled with a general distaste for cities and apartment-style living compromised the program's success. Both in their form and location, the buildings produced under Title I were largely out of synch with the demographic in search of housing, namely, younger, aspiring middle-class families with children.

Examples of Title 1 housing include Detroit's Lafayette Park, designed by Mies Van der Rohe, the Lake Meadows complex on Chicago's south side, and the towers designed by IM Pei in Philadelphia (Society Hill Towers), New York (Silver Towers) and Pittsburgh (City View Apartments).

Title II: Amendments to National Housing Act

Title II of the 1949 Housing Act re-authorised the federal guarantees on loans to homebuilders and buyers introduced in the Housing Act of 1934 – part of a package of programs intended to stimulate the Depression-era economy. Access to capital was key to transforming the homebuilding industry, which, prior to WWII, was both disaggregated and inefficient. Access to federally guaranteed loans made it possible for homebuilders to work at a much larger scale, i.e. to purchase large tracts of undervalued farmland on the urban periphery, install infrastructure and construct housing more quickly. To further contain costs for both builders and occupants, limits were placed on size of homes these loans could underwrite.

While size, location, economies of scale and speed of production significantly reduced the price of suburban homes, qualified homebuyers also benefitted from guaranteed, long-term, self-amortising mortgages, which reduced the monthly obligation to be competitive with rental rates for similar properties. Down payments were also reduced – or waived in the case of veterans. In addition to increasing supply and stimulating the economy, then, federal programs were intended to move as many households as possible to ownership. Tantamount to self-sufficiency, home ownership has long been considered a key component of well-being in North America.

Where the production of suburban housing was concerned, builders like Levitt & Sons honed their skill at mass production during the war. The small, self-contained houses the firm constructed for defence workers were virtually identical to those that appeared in the first generation of post-war suburban subdivisions (see Figures 8.1 and 8.2). In addition

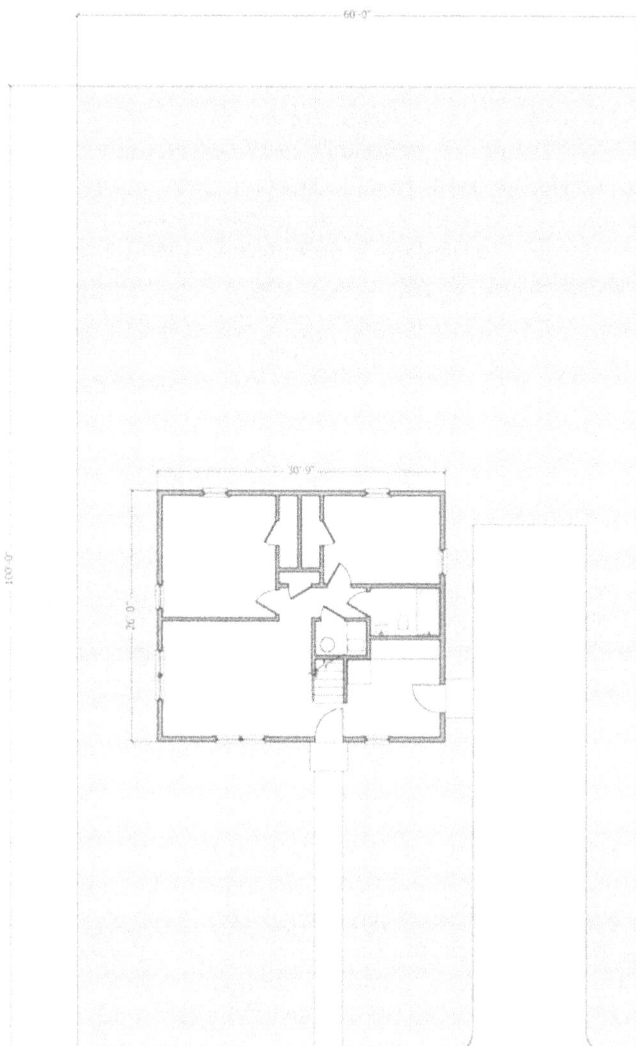

FIGURE 8.1 Ground floor plan of the classic 'Cape Cod' house offered by Levitt & Sons. in the early phases of their 1949 development in Levittown, NY. Houses occupied 60' × 100' lots. The ground floor included a kitchen, 3-piece bathroom, two bedrooms and a combined living/dining room. Houses come complete will all appliances and a stair to an unfinished attic, which could be easily divided into two additional bedrooms as needed.

Source: Author.

FIGURE 8.2 Aerial view of Cape Cod-style starter homes in Levittown, NY, 1951.
Source: Getty Images.

to access to inexpensive, cleared, and well-drained farmland, builders benefitted from pre-cut and standardised materials (e.g. 4 × 8 sheets of plywood), and from time- and cost-saving techniques like slab-on-grade construction. Levitt & Sons were infamous for having 'transformed the farmer's field into a factory floor,' completing a house every sixteen minutes when production was in full swing. By 1958 some 13 million new homes had been constructed in the US – 11 million (85%) of which were located in suburbs, and most of which had benefitted from incentives under Title II.[4] Without question, then, the various provisions and programs of Title II were the most successful of those approved under the US Housing Act 1949, both in terms of the volume of housing they underwrote and their longer-term impact on cities and urban form. Federally funded highway construction also greatly facilitated the build-out of the suburban periphery.

While suburban development continued apace into the 1960s, it became increasingly difficult for builders to deliver inexpensive starter homes for first-time homebuyers. Among other things, this reflected a significant increase in the cost of land and of the cost of infrastructure to service it. The market responded by shifting to 'trade-up' homes, targeting buyers that had purchased starter homes a decade earlier. Demand for these larger homes reflected both steady increases in household income and size as families expanded. 'Trade-up' homes included additional bedrooms, en suite master bathrooms, family rooms and two-car garages. Having dipped to an average of 817 sq. ft. in 1946 (from 1150 sq. ft. in the late 1930s when only families of means could afford to build), new homes in the US averaged 1289 sq. ft. by 1960 and 1680 sq. ft. by 1970.[5] Offsetting these increases in size, however, were decreases in the width of lots, as garages were tucked into or under homes.

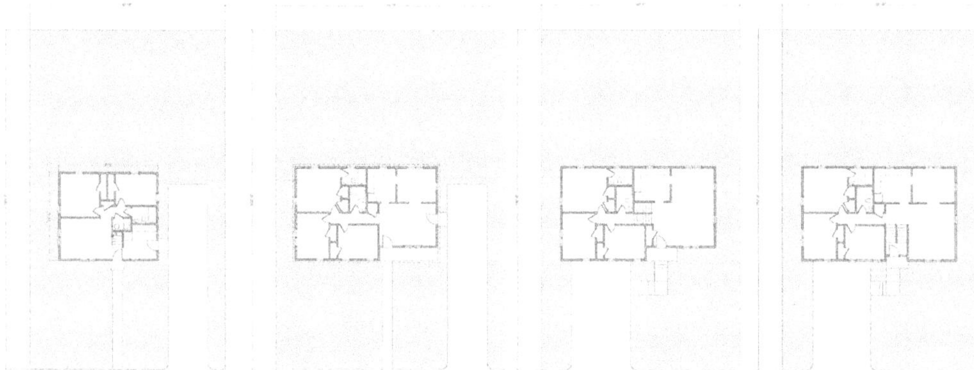

FIGURE 8.3 Suburban housing styles in the US in the post-war decades. Lot sizes increased from an average of 40' wide in the 1920s to 70' wide for the 1-story, post-war ranch house. Throughout the next several decades lot widths narrowed while floorplates increased with the inclusion of two-car garages, family/great rooms and ground-floor master suites.

Source: Author.

The average size of new single-family homes dropped to 1500 sq. ft. in the early 1970s as builders introduced freehold townhouses as affordable alternatives for first-time homebuyers. From a high of 2.36 million in 1973, housing starts dropped to 1.3 million in 1975, reflecting the recession brought on by the OPEC crisis. The average size of new homes continued to increase, however, through the late 1970s and 1980s, breaking 2000 square feet by 1990. Annual housing starts remained below the mid-1970s high, averaging 1.37 million annually through the mid-1990s. Among other things, this reflected a precipitous rise in interest rates in the 1980s.

Title III: Low-Rent Public Housing

Title III of the Housing Act of 1949 reinstated the federal subsidies for rent-geared-to-income housing for 'temporarily disadvantaged' families approved under the US Housing Act of 1937. These subsidies had been redirected to war-worker housing in 1939 before being suspended altogether in 1941 with the introduction of war measures.[6] Under Title III, the federal government provided municipal housing authorities funds to acquire and clear land and to construct low-rent housing. In tandem with Title I, the initiative was intended to enable cities to redevelop so-called distressed neighbourhoods, move low-income residents into higher-quality units, stem the spread of urban blight and generally make the urban core more palatable to investment. Arguably, rehousing the poor was a means to a larger end, namely, the economic revitalisation of cities.

To avoid unfair competition with private developers, the program focused on the replacement of substandard housing rather than on increasing the overall housing supply. Municipal authorities were required to demolish or renovate one existing dwelling unit for every new unit of subsidised housing they constructed. Severe restrictions were placed on the size and cost per square foot of units – restrictions that became even more strict as funding was renewed in subsequent years. As a result of opposition to subsidised housing from residents and politicians, units produced under this program tended to be aggregated into large ensembles – the path of least resistance being to locate new subsidised housing adjacent to existing subsidised housing. In many cities, entire neighbourhoods gave way to large-scale ensembles or 'projects,' tantamount to ghettos. Being different in form and height than the housing they replaced, these ensembles tended to stigmatise residents. This was especially true of African American tenants, who were largely barred from acquiring homes in the suburban subdivisions underwritten by Title II. Households caught in the urban core, where jobs were increasingly scarce in the post-war decades, were unable to acquire property and accumulate wealth.

While funding under Title III covered land acquisition, clearance and construction, it made no provision for operating subsidies. Local authorities depended on rental revenues to maintain and operate their housing. As buildings aged, vacancies increased, and the median income of tenants dropped, expenses outpaced operating revenues and many ensembles fell into disrepair.

Among the more notorious examples of housing produced under Title III were the Pruitt-Igoe complex in St. Louis and the Robert Taylor and Cabrini-Green Houses in Chicago, both of which have since been demolished.

China

Context

In the immediate post-war period, China struggled to emerge from an extended period of instability and uncertainly. The so-called Century of Humiliation began with the 1842 Treaty of Nanking that ended the Opium Wars, significantly weakened the power of the central government, and paved the way for the establishment of Treaty Ports to facilitate international trade. Foreign countries set up extraterritorial governments – or concessions – in some fifty cities across China over the next half-century. Shanghai, Guangzhou, Tianjin, Ningbo and Xiamen were among the earliest of these Treaty Ports.

Having lost territory to the Japanese in 1895 and again in 1905, China's ruling Qing Dynasty was toppled in 1911 by revolutionaries led by Sun Yat Sen. For the next four decades central authority waivered in response to military takeovers, challenges from regional warlords, additional Japanese incursions and an ongoing civil war between the nascent Republic of China and the Chinese Communist Party. During the Nanjing Decade (1927–1937), most of China was under the control of the Kuomintang (KMT), led by Chiang Kai-shek. In 1941 the Japanese took control of the Treaty Ports which, until then, had been largely immune from internal political turmoil – some 90% of the country's population being rural.

Emerging from WWII, then, there was widespread appetite for change in China and for the prospect of new beginnings. Pervasive poverty, a decimated and underdeveloped economy and support from the expanding Soviet bloc gave Mao Zedong's Chinese Communist Party (CCP) the leverage necessary to wrest control from the KMT, which had been forced to collaborate with the CCP during the war.

As was the case with the US, housing shortages in China were especially acute in cities due to redistributions of population during the war and to the fact that virtually no housing had been constructed from the mid-1930s onward. With the expropriation of private property under the newly established communist regime, the state assumed responsibility for housing all citizens, both rural and urban.

Between 1950 and 1952, some 240 million acres of arable land were redistributed to some 75 million peasant families. Rural residents were subsequently organised into collectives that took responsibility for housing and other services, and through which households reported to the central government.[7] Such reporting was facilitated by a system of household registration (*hukou)*, implemented in cities in 1951 and expanded countrywide by 1958. Under this system, households were classified according to two criteria: geographic location and rural/urban status, i.e. whether located in a rural area or within the boundaries of a recognised city. One's access to services – including education, housing and health care – was limited to the area in which one had *hukou*. The system was used to determine the mechanisms through which citizens would be tracked and cared for and, by extension, the nature of the services to which they would have access. Envisioned as a means by which to secure social and political order, the *hukou* system effectively curtailed physical mobility. Under this system, it was not possible to relocate – not even from a rural area to a city within the same province – without the express permission of the government.

During China's first Five Year Plan (1953–1957) the state assumed control of most industries and businesses, the majority of which operated in or around Treaty Port cities. Under this plan, existing businesses, service providers, health care and educational institutions were restructured into collectives or state-owned enterprises. Citizens with urban *hukou* largely reported to the central government through these entities – i.e. their employers – which assumed responsibility for virtually all aspects of daily life. During the same period, significant investment was made in new industries and industrial facilities. The bulk of this investment was directed towards inland cities, i.e. away from the coastal cities in which existing factories were largely located.

Throughout the 1950s, then, cities were partitioned into *danwei* or work units, each associated with different state-owned enterprises. Larger work units included factories, warehouses, workshops, offices, housing, social services, child-care facilities, public toilets and bath houses, social spaces, schools, cafeterias, sports facilities and grocery and dry goods stores. Wages accounted for only a small portion of employee compensation, the bulk taking the form of housing and other services provided by the state through the employer.[8]

Housing in the Post-War Decades

In most work units, unmarried individuals were accommodated in dormitories while married couples were assigned apartments – or rooms in shared apartments. Larger *danwei* also included areas of informal housing to which families were assigned pending construction of formal housing. The amount of space allocated to households varied with their size and the rank of residents in the company hierarchy. As both male and female heads of households worked, children were tended in collective day-cares from the age of six months.

As China's Soviet-backed industrial initiatives were launched in the 1950s, a general call was made for citizens to relocate to the inland cities in which new, large-scale, industrial operations were being established. A key example, the *Dongfanghong* Tractor Factory – one of the largest state-owned enterprises initiated under the First Five-Year Plan – was located in the city of Luoyang, the ancient capital of the Eastern Han Dynasty.[9] With 40,000 employees, the work unit accommodated some 100,000 residents, including children and retired workers. The *danwei*'s 12 residential districts were served by five elementary schools, 3 middle schools and 2 secondary schools. Still in operation today, it remains one of the largest factories in the world, and the complex has been home to successive generations of families.

Soviet influence is evident in the design of the first generation of housing in Luoyang's *Dongfanghong* work unit. Managers and their families were assigned to three-room apartments in Complex 9, whose low-rise, red-roofed buildings were organised around courtyards. As additional housing was constructed, however, courtyards were abandoned in favour of the established Chinese practice of organising buildings into repetitive, east/west (south-facing) rows. Recalling the configuration of Beijing's *hutongs* and the *lilongs* of Shanghai, the width of the laneways separating these buildings varied with their height to enable all units to receive at least one hour of sunlight each day. Successive generations of housing ranged from three to six stories and were typically organised as point-access walk-ups with four to six units per floor per landing (see Figure 8.4).

FIGURE 8.4 Satellite image of several of the residential complexes of the Dongfanghong Tractor Factory in Luoyang's Jianxi District. While the earliest housing to be constructed was organized around courtyards, successive generations were configured into east/west rows. Also visible are patches of informal housing, which continue to operate as temporary dwellings for households in transition.

Source: Apple Maps.

Frequently shared by multiple households, space in apartments was reallocated as families expanded. With each two children, households were given access to an additional room, such that a family of six might occupy all three rooms of a given apartment. As the space allocation in the First Five-Year Plan was a modest 4 square meters per person, rooms averaged about 8 square meters each – roughly 3.2 meters × 2.5 meters.[10]

As illustrated below, early, Soviet-style units in *Dongfanghong*'s Complex 9 included small kitchens and toilet rooms – relatively rare for housing constructed in the post-war decades. Bathing was done in a collective bathhouse while laundry was done at home, using sinks and buckets. Unmarried individuals took meals in communal cafeterias while most families prepared food at home, sharing kitchens as necessary.

In larger cities – and outside of newly established industrial districts generally – municipalities played a greater role in housing. In Shanghai, for example, the exodus of foreign residents and business owners during the WWII enabled local tenants to become *de facto* landlords. With a population of some five million emerging from the war, however, demand vastly outstripped supply and a significant number of residents occupied informal dwellings – especially in the industrial districts beyond the foreign concessions.

With the abolition of private property under the communist regime, the Shanghai municipal government took control of existing housing under a newly formed housing and property bureau. In addition to managing the allocation of this housing, the bureau undertook the construction of several residential complexes with support from the state and the Soviet Union. These complexes – or worker villages – replaced shantytowns along the Wusong and Huangpu rivers and were often undertaken in tandem with adjacent factories.

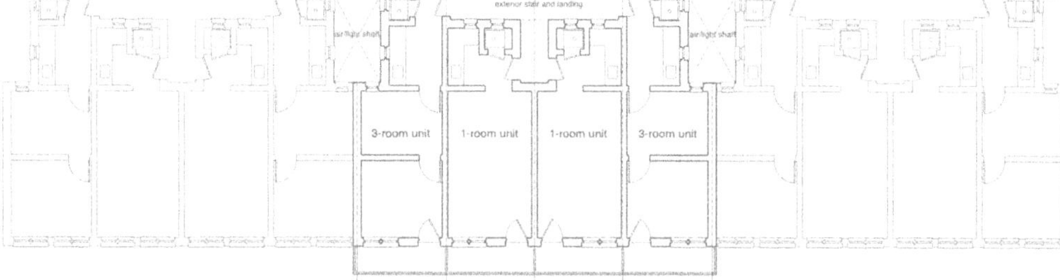

FIGURE 8.5 Schematic plan of a multiple point-access building with four units per floor per module like those in Dongfanghong's Complex 9. Each module includes two 1-room units and two 3-room units, each of which includes a small kitchen and toilet room. Air shafts inserted between modules brought light and ventilation to interior rooms. Kitchens and toilet rooms in 1-room units vented onto the open stairwell. The buildings followed a 3.2 m bay system.

Source: Author.

Several types of enterprises operated in Chinese cities in the post-war era. These included:

- State-owned enterprises (SOEs) of various sizes and types – some newly formed and others resulting from the consolidation of existing factories.
- Collectives of various sizes (e.g. garment producers' collectives).
- Private businesses (e.g. service providers).

Individuals unable to procure housing through an employer could apply to the municipal housing bureau. In Shanghai, couples without children were frequently assigned space in existing *shikumen* houses where they were allocated rooms in shared apartments. Couples with children could apply for units in the newly constructed municipal housing compounds.[11] As housing shortages were more severe in Shanghai than elsewhere, however, families of four were frequently assigned one-room apartments.

Unlike larger *danwei* complexes, buildings in these worker villages did not typically include toilets (available elsewhere in the compound), nor were central bathhouses provided (bathing was done at home, using buckets). Units, typically six or eight to a floor in a multiple point-access configuration, shared small kitchens arrayed along the north side of the corridor (see Figure 8.6). Units (and balconies) faced south.

Municipal worker villages included kindergartens, primary schools, communal toilets, food stores and other collective infrastructure. For all intents and purposes, these villages operated as work units, but with residents reporting to different employers.

The bulk of industrial investment, including the construction of housing for workers, occurred during the First Five-Year Plan. By this point, land reform had been largely completed, agricultural production was up and the rural economy was recovering. Responding to the call of industrialisation, however, some 42 million newly 'self-sufficient' peasants moved off the land to work in industrial centres between 1953 and 1957,[12] significantly increasing the percentage of the population dependent on state-owned enterprises. With investment greatly outpacing revenues, however, the central government

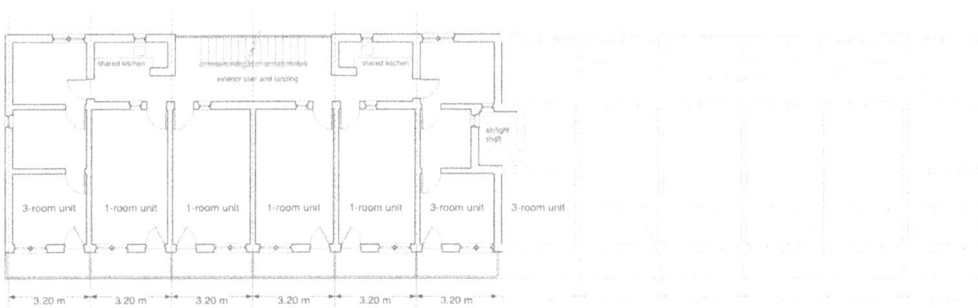

FIGURE 8.6 Schematic plan of a typical residential building constructed by the city of Shanghai in the early 1950s. Each module included four to six 1-room units – each averaging 16 square meters – and two 3-room units at about 26 square meters. Units included neither kitchens nor toilet rooms, although shared kitchens were available along the corridor.

Source: Author.

TABLE 8.1 Urbanisation levels in China 1949–2015

Year	*Urbanisation level (%)*	*% Change*
1949	10.6	
1957	15.4	+4.9
1961	18.4	+3.0
1962	14.0	–4.4
1965	17.9	+3.9
1978	17.9	–
1984	23.0	+5.1
1991	26.4	+3.4
2010	49.95	+20.5
2015	56.1	+6.15

Source: Gu (2017).

set higher – and ultimately unrealistic – targets for output during its 2nd Five-Year Plan (1958–1962). Known as the *Great Leap Forward,* the economic program forced agricultural collectivisation and promoted rural industrialisation with the goal of increasing grain and steel production. As a result, some 20 million 'surplus workers' were moved off the land and into newly established industrial centres.

An acute contraction in the Chinese economy, however, accompanied by a precipitous drop in agricultural output and widespread famine, impelled the central government to reverse course in 1961. Under a program of 'readjustment, consolidation, strengthening and improvement,' investment in industrialisation was severely curtailed. In total, 29 million industrial workers were laid off between 1961 and 1964, 90% of whom returned to rural areas. As a result, China's urbanisation rate dropped from 18.4% in 1961 to 14% in 1962. To further address housing shortages and reduce the burden placed on the state by state-owned enterprises, some 40 million urban youth (*Zhiquig*)[13] were also relocated to rural areas between the mid-1950s and 1978. This was done under a spectrum of initiatives including the ideologically oriented 'Up to the Mountains and Down to the Countryside' (UMDC) movement which was launched in parallel with the Cultural Revolution in 1966. As a result, the country's urbanisation rate, which had edged back up by almost 4% by 1965, remained at a steady 17.9% between 1965 and 1979 (see Figure 8.7).[14]

Ongoing reductions of investment in 'non-productive' assets throughout the 1960s and 1970s resulted in cuts both to the allowable cost per sq. ft. for housing and to the overall percentage reserved for housing within the capital funds allocated to enterprises.[15] Heading into the 1980s, housing shortages were further exacerbated by a Reform Era policy that permitted youth displaced under the UMDC programs to return to the cities they'd vacated. The population of Shanghai, for example, increased from 5.7 to 10 million between 1978 and 1993,[16] placing extraordinary pressure on an already overburdened housing supply. In response, the city leased land on the east bank of the Huangpu River (*Pudong*) on which to construct housing.[17] As was the practice both for *danwei* housing and the laneway housing of the Treaty Port era, this housing was organised into parallel, south-facing rows. At six stories, however, these walk-up buildings were taller than earlier housing and units were largely self-contained, i.e. included kitchens and bathrooms. Among other things, this reflected the fact that this housing did not benefit

FIGURE 8.7 Housing adjacent to the Century Boulevard (世纪大道), which cuts diagonally through Shanghai's Pudong district. The area shown is immediately south of Lujiazui Finance and Trade Zone, which sits directly opposite the Bund.

Source: Apple Maps, retrieved July 2024.

from the same level of collective infrastructure as housing in Shanghai's earlier worker villages. Given its relative inaccessibility during this period, however, housing in Pudong was significantly less desirable than smaller, less-well-equipped accommodations on the west bank (*Puxi*).[18]

Among the many changes associated with the 'Era of Reform and Opening,' launched in 1979, was the transfer of housing from enterprises and municipalities to tenants. This was done in a leasehold arrangement, where the government maintained ownership of the land. The transfer of title for individual units, however, was only possible where units were fully self-contained, i.e. included bathrooms and kitchens.

In larger cities, well-placed ensembles of non-compliant housing, i.e. units with shared kitchens and toilets, were targeted for redevelopment. At two to three stories high, much of this housing was low density. Notable exceptions aside,[19] most residents not only welcomed but also courted redevelopment. In exchange for a room in a shared unit, displaced residents were offered title to larger, self-contained units in newer buildings, whether in the redeveloped complex or elsewhere in the city. Households with older children were frequently able to negotiate title to multiple units – one for the parents and one for each of the children. Property value based on location – both of vacated units and those to which displaced residents were offered title – also figured into the compensation that residents could negotiate.

On the Concept of Well-Being

In both post-war China and the US, the state played a large role in the supply of housing; in both cases, it was indirect. In China, funds flowed through the state-owned enterprises that assumed responsibility for housing employees and their families. Municipal agencies took up the slack in cities, managing the allocation of existing housing. In the US, the bulk of new housing was realised with the help of Title II programs, i.e. with aid in the form of guaranteed, low-interest loans to builders and long-term, low-interest mortgages for qualified buyers. Local Federal Housing Administration offices worked with homebuilders to set limits for the size and price of the homes for which government-backed mortgages were available. Emphasis was placed on housing for younger families with limited incomes. The only housing directly constructed and managed by public authorities was the rental housing produced under Title III.

As China shifted from a market- to a command-economy under the Communist regime, housing took second place to 'productive' assets such as factories and industrial facilities. In the US, by contrast, housing was embraced as a commodity to be produced and as a mechanism to transition from a top-down, wartime economy to a market-driven peacetime economy. With demand outstripping supply, housing was seen as an important trigger for the production of a range of upstream construction materials and downstream consumer goods.

As builders like Levitt & Sons demonstrated that they could produce homes for purchase – primarily single-family houses in large-scale, suburban subdivisions – that could compete in price with similarly sized rental properties, the emphasis shifted from an increase in the overall supply of housing to the production of housing for purchase.[20] This reflected a longstanding, middle-class preference for homeownership and self-contained dwellings in North America. Moreover, the focus on small, detached housing versus dwellings in multi-unit buildings was inevitable inasmuch as freehold properties were the only dwelling types that qualified for mortgages. The condominium designation, which extended ownership to apartments in multi-unit buildings, was not in use in the US until the last quarter of the twentieth century.

This taps into a larger concept of well-being in the US, i.e. that both individual households and society as a whole were better served by property ownership than by renting (or, in the case of China, than by accessing housing through an employer). Ownership took pressure off the state. Not only did 30-year, self-amortising mortgages bring down the monthly cost of owning, but they also made it possible for most homebuyers to hold title to their homes by the time they retired. This substantially reduced the state's obligation to subsidise rental housing for seniors with limited savings.

Just as homeownership was considered to be key to a stable, politically engaged middle class, long-term debt was promoted as a stabilising factor – contributing to the larger well-being of society. Workers were seen to be less likely to strike or cultivate revolutionary ideas if they carried housing debt. Homeowners were also more likely to be invested in the larger, long-term stability of their communities, if only to protect their assets. Indeed, throughout much of history, property ownership was a prerequisite to participating in the political process.

And at the limit, although it was by no means clear emerging from the Depression, housing was seen as a means of wealth creation. Not only could individuals bequeath assets to heirs, but, if and as property values increased over time, families would benefit from the unearned increment. Equity in one's home also provided funds against which to borrow if emergencies arose – further protecting the state from the need to intervene.

In the case of the US, then, one might posit that the well-being of the whole was measured by the self-sufficiency of the parts, namely, individual households. In China, by contrast, the opposite could be said to have been true, namely, that if the country as a whole prospered, individual households would benefit. From this perspective, Chinese households might be seen to have made sacrifices for the larger good, i.e. short-term pain for longer-term gain.

Indeed, when comparing the size and quality of post-war *danwei* accommodations to American, post-war starter homes, it may be tempting to and jump to conclusions regarding the subordination of the part to the whole. At 750 square feet (70 square meters), the 2-bedroom American version was more than four times the size of its four-person *danwei* equivalent. Moreover, it included a kitchen (replete with appliances), a 3-piece bathroom, and a private yard. Starter homes like the Levittown 'Cape Cod' were also easily expandable, obviating the need to move or negotiate with employers for additional space as the household expanded.

In reality, however, *danwei* accommodations were vastly superior to the dwellings to which most Chinese had access in the first half of the twentieth century. Prior to the Communist Revolution in China, some 90% of the country's population lived in rudimentary rural dwellings while those in larger cities (foreigners excepted) frequently occupied self-built dwellings without heat, plumbing, electricity and privacy. The infrastructure, resources and services available to the average resident under the *danwei* system were vastly superior to what was previously available. Of particular importance were schools; emerging from WWII, some 80% of China's 550 million citizens were illiterate – with rates as high as 95% in rural areas.[21] By 1962, the national literacy rate had jumped to 48% for individuals over the age of 15.[22]

It might be argued that the housing to which the average Chinese worker had access in the immediate post-war period resembled the housing in that many North Americans occupied during the Depression and war years, when households were forced to double up, food was rationed, and funds for maintenance were in short supply. Units in less affluent districts of North American cities lacked indoor plumbing and central heating well into the post-war era. Indeed, it was the poor state of urban housing that Titles I and III of the 1949 Act were intended to redress. As noted, support for this was arguably motivated less by concern for the well-being low-income residents than by the need to enhance the appeal of cities as factories obsolesced, industries contracted and/or relocated and middle-class residents decamped to the expanding suburbs.

In this respect, the funding for urban housing – both middle-class and subsidised – made available through Titles I and III of the 1949 Housing Act was intended to offset the effects of Title II, which accelerated the build-out of low-density suburbs. While Titles I and III were meant to replace substandard rental housing in underperforming urban neighbourhoods, Title II was intended both to increase the overall supply of housing and to augment the percentage of homeownership.

In considering the relative merits of the American and Chinese approaches to post-war housing, it is also crucial to consider context. Emerging from WWII, China was a country of 550 million people compared with a modest 150 million in the US. Secondly, the level of urbanisation was much lower in China – 10.6% in 1949 compared to 64% in the US – reflecting, among other things, a significant difference in industrial capacity. Per capita GDP in the US was $1083 in 1949[23] compared to less than $50 USD in China.[24] Equally important is that the US benefitted economically from WWII, both from the sale of supplies and on the interest on the loans it made for their purchase. As measured in constant dollars, the gross national product of the US grew from $88.6 billion in 1939 to $135 billion in 1944.[25]

50 Years Onward

When considering the relative merits of approaches to housing and their impact on overall well-being in the post-war period, it's important to acknowledge where things stand at present. Despite a significant downturn in production and an attendant drop in the overall well-being of China during the 1960s and 1970s, both the dwelling space per occupant and the percentage of homeownership have increased exponentially since the end of WWII. From an average of 4 square meters of residential space per person in the post-war decades, China now averages 41 square meters – a tenfold increase. Similarly, homeownership in China, virtually non-existent in the immediate post-war period (except in the form of rural collectives) now hovers around 90%. While most of these gains have been made since the 1990s, units could not have been transferred to residents had they not been constructed by state-owned enterprises in the first place. By comparison, the rate of homeownership in the US stands at about 65%, and per-capita residential space has doubled since the mid-1950s.[26]

Secondly, as successful as suburban homebuilding was in addressing supply and moving people to ownership in the post-war period, many Americans were unable to benefit from the programs that supported it. Contracts for homes in subdivisions like Levittown frequently prohibited their use or occupation by 'any person other than members of the Caucasian race,' and covenants ensured that houses would not be resold to African Americans.[27] Several generations later, steep financial barriers have put the descendants of excluded households at a further disadvantage where homeownership is concerned. Compared to their white counterparts, for example, African Americans have been less able to benefit from the intergenerational wealth that is increasingly necessary to enter the housing market. The US now ranks 50th among countries in percentage of homeownership, well behind many formerly socialist countries.

Finally, it should be noted that both China and the US now face challenges where housing affordability is concerned – reinforcing that the status of housing as a market commodity and investment vehicle can interfere with its basic function as shelter. Without ongoing state intervention, the percentage of homeownership is likely to drop in both countries, as is the size and stability of the middle class.

Well-Being and the 'Moderately Prosperous' Society

Grounded as it was in the Marxist idea of class struggle, the Communist Revolution in China was motivated by the idea of a classless society. In China, class struggle took two forms: the wresting and redistribution of agricultural lands held by feudal lords, and, to a lesser extent, the seizing of industry from capitalists to redistribute to workers. In relatively short order, the Chinese peasantry was reorganised into land-owning and largely self-sufficient rural collectives while industry was expanded and restructured into state-owned enterprises and collectives. As industrialisation was a pre-condition of capitalism, it was necessary for China to industrialise to progress to socialism, which Marxism envisioned as an advanced form of capitalism. The larger goal was a classless, industrialised society where workers controlled the means of production and the work of each would benefit all.

The persistence of the communist vision among key Communist Party officials posed challenges for reformers, notwithstanding the economic collapse and devastating famines of the 1960s and 1970s. In his capacity as Paramount Leader, Deng Xiao Ping evoked the term *Xiaokang Shehui* to usher in the Era and Reform and Opening in 1979.[28] Confucian in origin, the term roughly translates to a 'moderately prosperous' or 'basically well-off society.' In modern economic terms, this may be characterised by an all-encompassing, 'functional middle class.' Implying, as it did, a relatively equitable distribution of resources among the population at large, the idea was palatable to communist hardliners.[29] Being evolutionary, not revolutionary, *Xiaokang* was intended to recast the Chinese communist project in the light of a longstanding cultural paradigm that transcended the parameters of the Cultural Revolution. *Xiaokang* was the basis on which China's economy would modernise in the Reform Era, with the expectation that modernisation would be a collective endeavour. Consistent with the idea of a classless society, it continues to be important to the Communist Party of China (CPC) that the poor not be too poor nor the rich too rich.

Also implicit in *Xiaokang* is the idea that economic advancement is not the sole focus of society, i.e. that prosperity – and by extension, well-being – cannot be understood in purely economic terms. It must be balanced with larger, often conflicting, collective goals for which self-interest must defer to something akin to enlightened self-interest. Otherwise stated, it is often one's best – and longer-term – interest to attend to larger, collective interests.

In an article entitled *Toward a Fully Harmonious Society that Puts Wellbeing First*,[30] Japanese scholar Takashi Maeno observes that:

> The tendency under the expansionary system of the past was to aim mainly for physical and economic forms of wellbeing, which in its crudest sense meant seeking visible forms of value such as money, goods, and status. In the study of wellbeing, these are called positional goods that deliver satisfaction through comparison with other people.
>
> I have come to call the current social model that has arisen from capitalism a 20th-century version of the game of survival of the fittest. This is a society based on the law of the jungle in which individuals compete in a struggle for survival and try to bring each other down. As the losers are always forced out, inequalities of wealth expand relentlessly… The goals of such a society are the positional goods of money, material possessions, and prestige, with their acquisition being what defines happiness and identifies winners.
>
> …
>
> Nationalism and societies based on survival of the fittest pose risks for humanity as a whole and for global sustainability, such as exacerbating conflicts of religion, nationality, and ideology and the potential for a relentless increase in inequality as well as

environmental degradation, food shortages, and unforeseen pandemics of contagious disease. Moreover, being driven by individual self-interest makes it difficult under this model to take the broad view and adopt long-term measures. Even when confronted with problems that demand urgent action, we lack the power to do anything about them.

...

What I am proposing in response is a 21st-century fully harmonious symbiotic society, one in which people are considerate of one another and that achieves society-wide harmony while allowing each person to express their individuality and creativity... While it might look chaotic at first glance, it is like a forest that exists in a state of balance and is rich in diversity.

The term 'harmonious society' (*Hexie Shehuì*) was introduced into the political discourse of Reform-Era China by President Hu Jintao in 2004. The term was coined at a plenary session on social inequality at the 16th Congress of the CPC, which was staged in response to concerns about the widening wealth gap and social injustice during a period of unchecked economic growth.[31] Like *Xiaokung*, the idea of a harmonious society has a long history in China and can be traced to Confucianism. In this context, it was intended to reinforce the idea is that economic growth cannot be seen as an end in itself, but rather in the context of the broader advancement of society where the gains of some are not made at the expense of others.

From the Western perspective, it is tempting to see the paragon of 'harmony' as a banner under which to suppress dissent (dissonance), especially given the heavy-handed policies associated with the Cultural Revolution. At the same time, however, harmony suggests that cooperation need not be predicated on sameness or blind adherence to a single set of principles (e.g. Marxist ideology), but rather that divergent perspectives be kept in balance. In this respect, differences of opinion, lifestyle, etc. are not only tolerated but seen as a fundamental component of balance – *yin* and *yang*.

In the US, the paradigms of autonomy, self-sufficiency and freedom to do as one chooses often trump visions of collectivity. Fundamental to each of these paradigms is elbowroom. Paradoxically, then, what holds Americans together is what separates them, namely, space. This space – both physical and political – enables individuals to engage in the pursuit of happiness with minimal interference from or impact on others. Where this space is compressed and cooperation becomes necessary, as is the case in cities, Americans have long sought alternatives.

Throughout much of the second millennium CE, a key difference between the so-called New World and 'older' worlds such as Europe and China was the availability of land. There were two aspects to this: the amount of land per capita – in particular, arable land – and the terms under which it could be acquired, occupied and/or worked. Not being under the control of feudal lords and/or constrained by formalised systems of deeds, titles and cadastral parcels, land in much of North America was seen being there for the taking. As such, the subdivision and distribution of property among the *many* in a non-hierarchical (albeit patriarchal) fashion in North America was the basis on which a model for a new post-feudal and post-urban experiment with democracy could be orchestrated.

Distrustful of cities, which he disparaged as 'pestilential to the morals, the health, and the liberties of man,' Thomas Jefferson envisioned the US as a nation of yeoman farmers. All (white, male) citizens would be allocated land through the subdivision of territories into 36-square-mile townships, each divided into 160-acre plots (quarter sections). Landownership at this scale enabled self-sufficiency and supported participatory democracy, as the vote was limited to those owning property.[32] Land – and by extension, the franchise – was to be divided among the many, who would disperse across an expanding nation.

In the mid-nineteenth century, self-sufficiency morphed into a proto-suburban vision of the rural cottage – a rustic, frequently self-built dwelling on privately owned land. By the early twentieth century, it took the form of the freehold, suburban bungalow, connected back to the city by an expanding trolley system. Frederick Law Olmsted, best known for the design of New York City's Central Park, proclaimed that 'no great town can long exist without great suburbs,' which he believed had the potential to be 'the most attractive, the most refined and the most soundly wholesome forms of domestic life, and the best application of the arts of civilization to which mankind has yet attained.'[33] Implicit in this are control over one's property, access to nature and an abundance of elbowroom.

Reacting, among other things, to the Great Depression, Frank Lloyd Wright's vision for Broadacre City[34] consisted of a continent-wide constellation of low-density settlements, peppered with factories and businesses linked by highways and airports. In service of self-sufficiency, all citizens would be granted title to at least one acre of land on which to build dwellings and grow food. Wright considered renting – then, as now, the default option for most residents of large, North American cities – to be tantamount to indentureship, notwithstanding the fact that voting rights had been, by then, extended to non-property owners. Prefiguring today's work-from-home culture, he was optimistic that automobility and telecommunications would obviate the need both for cities and suburbs. As historian Robert Fishman notes, Wright envisioned that, together, 'Edison and Ford would resurrect Jefferson,'[35] i.e. that technology would enable Americans to realise Jefferson's founding vision of radical dispersion, separation and self-sufficiency.

Oh, give me land, lots of land under starry skies above

Don't fence me in

…

And I can't look at hovels and I can't stand fences

Don't fence me in[36]

Separation in the US is both predicated on an abundance of space and fuelled by deep-rooted anti-urban sentiment. But while separation might facilitate harmony (or at least minimise the potential for conflict), such harmony is not grounded in cooperation. To the extent that it exists, cooperation has less to do with what people elect to undertake together than what they agree not to do, namely, interfere with or encroach upon each other's space. And given its tendency to foster segregation, separation can breed polarisation and threaten collective well-being.

However diluted or compromised in its post-war, suburban incarnation, the frontier mentality is alive and well in the 'collective' vision of Americans, as are the principles of individualism, private property and self-sufficiency. This is not the case in China, where the frontier had long been settled and where, up through the middle of the twentieth century, the countryside remained the purview of peasants. As was the case in medieval Europe, freedom, in China, has traditionally been associated with cities, which were places of exchange, erudition, administration, cooperation and opportunity. Within the feudal traditions of both Europe and China, it was necessary for one to escape the countryside – and the bonds of indentureship – to be free. The adage 'city air sets you free' references a medieval German practice whereby runaway serfs were released from service to their feudal lords if they managed to live in a city for at least a year and a day.[37]

The equating of cities and freedom is in stark contrast to the American vision of the landscape as a place into which to escape. Despite having been wrested from feudal lords by the CPC, agricultural land in China is still largely viewed as a place to move from, rather than to.[38] The city is the cradle of civilisation and the nexus of opportunity and social mobility. It is the mechanism through which citizens negotiate diversity and forge a whole that is greater than the sum of its parts. And while this may be easier in China, where the urban population is relatively homogeneous, the group of yeoman farmers envisioned by Thomas Jefferson was quite homogeneous by current standards.

In sum, distinct histories and divergent perspectives on autonomy and collectivity shape the ways in which well-being – and by extension housing – is understood in the Chinese and American contexts. This is reflected in the forms housing takes, the locations in which it is built, and the terms of reference under which it can be occupied.

Notes

1 Titles IV, V and VI of the Act covered housing research, farm housing, and 'miscellaneous provisions, respectively.
2 The terms of reference were altered in the mid-1950s to underwrite clearance for the construction of non-residential uses such as hospitals, educational and cultural institutions.
3 While the condominium designation, i.e. the legal right to own an apartment in a multi-unit residential building, was introduced in the US in the 1960s, it did not come into widespread use until the 1980s. Reasons for this include the longstanding predilection for detached homes and reticence by lending institutions to offer mortgages on non-freehold units.
4 "Levittown," *Digital History*, https://www.digitalhistory.uh.edu/disp_textbook.cfm?smtID=2&psid=3427. Accessed 12 February 2024.
5 Comen, E. 2016 (updated 2021). "The Size of a Home the Year You Were Born," *24/7 Wall St.* https://247wallst.com/special-report/2016/05/25/the-size-of-a-home-the-year-you-were-born/. Accessed July 2024.
6 The War Powers Acts of 1941 and 1942, coupled with the Controlled Materials Plan introduced by the US War Production Board in 1942.
7 Ho, Peter. 2005. *Developmental Dilemmas: Land Reform and Institutional Change in China*. Routledge.
8 Russo, Alessandro. 2020. *Cultural Revolution and Revolutionary Culture*. Durham, NC: Duke University Press. p. 253.
9 Six of the 157 large-scale industrial projects initiated under the First Five-Year Plan were located in Luoyang, in China's Henin Province.
10 Lu, Junhua, Rowe, Peter G., and Zhang, Jie. 2001. *Modern Urban Housing in China, 1840–2000*, Munich, London, New York; Prestel Verlag, 126.
11 An example is the Caoyang New Village in Shanghai's Putuo district.
12 15.4% of 647 million in 1957 (99.6 million) vs. 10.6% of 542 million in 1949 (57.4 million) represents an increase of approximately 42 million. See Gu Chaolin, Hu Lingqian, Cook Ian G, 2017. "China's urbanization in 1949–2015: processes and driving forces." Chinese Geographical Science, 27(6): 847–59. doi: https://doi.org/10.1007/s11769-017-0911-9

13 A distinction is made between the *Huixiang Zhiqing* (rural youth who had migrated to large, established cities in the 1950s and were encouraged to return under *Youth Reclamation* programs such as those operating in Beijing and Shanghai) and the *Zhiqing* (urban youth sent to rural areas beginning in the mid-1960s under the UMDC movement, which stressed re-education in support of the larger Cultural Revolution and which, itself, had several phases). See Weiyi, Wu, and Hong, Fan, "The Rise and Fall of the "Up To The Mountains And Down To The Countryside" Movement: A Historical Review," in the *Rosenberg Quarterly*, https://rozenbergquarterly.com/the-rise-and-fall-of-the-up-to-the-mountains-and-down-to-the-countryside-movement-a-historical-review/. Accessed 7 July 2024.

14 Gu Chaolin, Hu Lingqian, and Cook Ian G. 2017. "China's urbanization in 1949–2015: processes and driving forces." *Chinese Geographical Science* 27 (6): 847–59.

15 Lu, Junhua, Rowe, Peter G., and Zhang, Jie. 2001. *Modern Urban Housing in China, 1840–2000*, Munich, London, New York; Prestel Verlag, 198.

16 Source: https://www.macrotrends.net/global-metrics/cities/20656/shanghai/population. Accessed 11 June 2024.

17 Enabled by another Reform Era policy that gave rural collectives more flexibility about how to use – or even dispose of – their land. It should be noted that this housing was constructed prior to 1990, when Premier Li Peng officially announced the policy of Pudong's opening and development.

18 In the 1980s, it was not uncommon for Shanghainese to declare that they "would rather have a room in Puxi (the west bank) than a suite in Pudong. (宁要浦西一张床, 不要浦东一套房). Given the severity of shortages, well-located housing was often a consideration when arranging marriages.

19 See Shao, Qin, *Shanghai Gone: Domicide and Defiance in a Chinese Megacity, Rowman & Littlefield Publishers; 1st edition (20 February 2013)*. The author compellingly chronicles redevelopment in Shanghai during the early years of the Reform Era, describing the draconian ways in which some residents were displaced and the nebulous legal framework they were forced to negotiate to seek recourse. She makes a strong case for power of place, the importance of location, and the value of social networks.

20 Returning GIs, for example, could become homeowners in Levittown, NY with nothing down and monthly payments of only $65. See Rybczynski, Witold, "The Pioneering "Levittowner," https://realestate.wharton.upenn.edu/wp-content/uploads/2017/03/556.pdf, retrieved, February 2024.

21 "辉煌60年:"扫盲"字眼的消失 一个落后时代的远去" *[60 years of glory: The disappearance of the word "literacy" and the passing of a backward era]*. www.gov.cn. 6 September 2009. Retrieved 21 June 2023, and "新中国扫盲运动——人类历史上的奇迹" *[New China's literacy Movement – a miracle in human history]*. www.sohu.com. 24 May 2018. Retrieved 21 June 2023.

22 及玥 *(25 October 2019)*. "教育事业70年：从文盲率80%到义务教育巩固率 94.2%" *[70 years of education: from 80% illiteracy rate to 94.2% retention rate of compulsory education]*. news.cctv.com. Accessed 21 June 2024.

23 https://countryeconomy.com/gdp/usa?year=1949. Accessed 30 June 2024.

24 Some sources put it as low as $10 USD. See https://www.ceicdata.com/en/china/gross-domestic-product-per-capita. Accessed 1 July 2024.

25 See Tassava, Christopher J., *The American Economy during World War II,* Economic History Association. https://eh.net/encyclopedia/the-american-economy-during-world-war-ii/#:~:text=The%20gross%20national%20product%20of,1943%20(Milward%2C%2063). Accessed 1 July 2024.

26 See https://www.aei.org/carpe-diem/new-us-homes-today-are-1000-square-feet-larger-than-in-1973-and-living-space-per-person-has-nearly-doubled/#:~:text=With%20the%20average%20new%20house,using%20the%20average%20size%20house. Retrieved 30 June 2024.

27 Sandweiss, Naomi. 2020. "The Kings of Suburbia," *Tablet* (online) magazine, 1 September 2020, https://www.tabletmag.com/sections/community/articles/kings-of-suburbia. Accessed 2 July 2024.

28 Inaugurated in 1979, the *Era of Reform and Opening* initially focused on the reform of rural collectives and the creation of four special economic zones in which to experiment with alternative economic models and to attract foreign investment. The second phase, in the 1990s, shifted the focus toward urban reform with the creation of stock and real estate markets, in addition to the reform of State-Owned Enterprises.

29 Where the idea of a middle class is concerned, it is perhaps not surprising that China liberalized its housing market and opened up ownership to a broad spectrum of its population. In many countries, including the US, property ownership is the basis on which the middle-class wealth and stability are predicated.

30 Maeno, Takashi, 2020. "Toward a Fully Harmonious Society that Puts Wellbeing First," Hitachi Review 69 (2): 136–37, https://www.hitachihyoron.com/rev/column/ei/vol13/index.html. Accessed 30 June 2024.

31 Social Inequity was seen to be the result of collusion between entrepreneurs and officials. See Zhong, Wu. "China yearns for Hu's 'harmonious society'," *Asia Times*, 11 October 2006, https://web.archive.org/web/20061103063705/http:/atimes.com/atimes/China/HJ11Ad01.html. Accessed 1 August 2024.

32 Most states during this period limited the vote to white males owning at least a fifty-acre plot of land. See Onuf, P, "Thomas Jefferson: The American Franchise," Miller Center, University of Virginia. https://millercenter.org/president/jefferson/the-american-franchise. Accessed 9 July 2024.

33 See *Subdivisions and Suburban Communities*, National Park Service, https://www.nps.gov/frla/learn/historyculture/suburbs.htm. Accessed 18 July 2024.

34 First introduced in his 1932 book, *The Disappearing City*.

35 Fishman, R. 1982. *Urban Utopias in the 20th Century*, The MIT Press.

36 *Don't Fence Me In*, 1934, music by Robert Fletcher and words by Cole Porter. The song was made popular by Bing Crosby.

37 Hart, M., and van der Heijden, M. 2011. "'City Air Sets You Free' Autonomy and Rivalry in the Early Modern Northern Netherlands," in *Living in the City*, Routledge.

38 It bears noting that the rate of rural-to-urban migration in China has declined in recent years, resulting in an oversupply of urban housing. Among the issues at play are the difficulties in negotiating a change of *hukou*, the exorbitant cost of housing in cities (most of which, until very recently, was only available for purchase), and advances in technology and connectivity that provide greater flexibility in earning a living in rural areas.

9

HOUSING SECURITY AND POLICY OVER THE LONG RUN, JAPAN 1600–2000

Mitsuo Kinoshita

Introduction

Well-being, or decent living standards, cannot be achieved without adequate housing. Therefore, what level of housing is considered adequate, or respectable, and how it is provided and secured socially and politically reflects the historical characteristics of a society in a given period vividly. In this chapter, we will examine these points through the case of seventeenth- to twentieth-century Japan and discuss what kind of social ideology formed the history of dwelling and well-being in Japan from a long-term perspective.

Before starting our historical discussion, we should look at the attitude of contemporary Japan as it seems that the Japanese people are now the 'coldest' nation in the world as far as their attitude towards a governmental housing safety net and the right to dwelling is concerned. According to the International Social Survey Programme 2016, in which 35 countries participated, people were asked whether it should or should not be the government's responsibility to provide decent housing for those who cannot afford it (ISSP Research Group 2018: 66–67). While in 34 countries, 60% or more, and in 21 countries, 80% or more people answered that it should be the government's responsibility, only 37.6% of people in Japan showed a positive attitude towards it. Furthermore, in 2006, when the Diet was discussing the bill of the Basic Act for Housing (*Juseikatsu kihonho*), the Director-General of the Housing Bureau of the Ministry of Land, Infrastructure, Transport and Tourism was asked how the right of dwelling was secured in this act and answered, '[d]welling right has not yet acquired a national consensus to be stipulated by law' (Minutes of the Committee: 8; Honma 2009: 119–22).

Are these negative attitudes towards governmental housing security and dwelling rights a new phenomenon? Back in 1927, when insufficient housing was gradually recognised as a social problem in Japan, the social bureau of Osaka city complained in a housing annual report that '[f]or the Japanese, dwelling has been a moral matter for a long time, and this traditional national character created a low interest in housing problems until these days' (Kingendai Shiryo Kankokai 1996: 11). A hundred years later, this 'traditional' low interest in housing security and dwelling rights still seems to persist in

DOI: 10.4324/9781003527930-13

the twenty-first century, suggesting that a long-term perspective is required, not only stretching from modern times but also including the early modern days, to analyse the issue of housing security in Japan.

While the history of the housing system in post-war Japan is well-researched by Yosuke Hirayama and Yoshihito Honma (Hirayama 2013; Hirayama 2020; Honma 2004; Honma 2009), who insist that housing policy tends to be strongly market-based, analysis of the characteristics of housing security and policy in the early modern and modern era, especially that of rural areas, remains to be carried out.[1] To discuss these points and explore the historical background of the Japanese 'cold' attitude towards housing issues, this study first demonstrates what the general standard of housing was in early modern rural Japan, how it was secured by the autonomous villages and the authorities (the Tokugawa shogunate and the lords[2]), and whether the level of housing security changed after Japan turned from a decentralised lordship state to a centralised modern state from the 1870s onwards.

Since historical documents that directly explain how adequate or decent housing was defined by early modern and modern Japanese villagers scarcely remain, we will tentatively substitute the median size of an ordinary peasant's house for the general standard of housing and for respectable standards of living. On the other hand, we have clear evidence that they regarded living in a hut dwelling as an unrespectable lifestyle. By utilising the size of an ordinary house and people's attitude towards living in a hut, this paper explores what 'well-being,' an obscure notion in a historical context, was in the everyday life of rural dwellers in seventeenth- to twentieth-century Japan.

General Standard of Housing in the Seventeenth- to Twentieth-Century Japan

Historically, housing has become problematic in urban areas, especially in the industrialised modern period. However, when discussing housing security from a long-term perspective, we should focus on rural societies since in early modern Japan, 90% of people lived in rural areas (6% of the country was urbanised in 1,600 and 10% in 1874), and even in 1920, urbanisation level was approximately at 20% (Saito 1998: 172; Saito and Takashima 2016: 370). The mean household size of a peasant family in the eighteenth century was approximately five people, not so different from European societies, but differed in generational depth. While the main household type in Europe was a nuclear family, among Japanese peasants, we find a strong trend of the three-generational family of six–seven people (Laslett and Wall 1972; Saito 1998), and even in 1954, 44.6% of the population still lived in three-generational cohabiting households (Comprehensive Survey of Living Conditions 2021).

Since no national statistics of early modern Japanese housing exist, we have to estimate the general standard of housing – that is, the ordinary size of a peasant house – from fragmentary cases. Table 9.1 shows 11 cases of village house sizes in five provinces from 1644 to 1843. Though there was a wide gap within individual villages and between the villages, it seems that the median laid in about 15 *tsubo* (48.6 square meters)[3], meaning that the general standard of housing equated to 7–10 square meters per person if we set the household size at five–seven people. Usually, half of a rural house was occupied by an earthen floor called *doma*, which was used as a kitchen and a working space. For instance, in Okazaki village, mentioned in Table 9.1, one of the 13.5-*tsubo* houses in the 1840s was composed of two rooms, 4 and 3 *tsubo*, respectively, and a *doma* (Tani 1990).

TABLE 9.1 House size in early modern rural Japan

Year	*Province*	*County*	*Village*	*Household*	*House size (tsubo)*		
					Maximum	*Median*	*Minimum*
1644	Shinano	Saku	Shitakaize	31	27	14	8
1644	Kawachi	Wakae	Wakae	225	49.5	9	1.5
1644	Kawachi	Tanboku	Saraike	58	21	6	2
1644	Kawachi	Furuichi	Usui	44	55	11.5	1.5
1645	Shinano	Ina	Ogawa	34	90	27	3
1645	Shinano	Chikuma	Shimohata	39	48	15	4
1654	Shinano	Saku	Hara	28	45	15	4.5
1654	Shinano	Saku	Usuda	46	54	18	6
1718	Mutsu	Aizu	Ishibushi	25	48	18	8
1795	Yamato	Yoshino	Tawara	41	33.75	13.5	2
1843	Yamashiro	Soraku	Okazaki	51	18	12	6

Source: Kusano (1995); Kinoshita (2019b); Oishi (1967); Takao (1958); Takao (1961); Tani (1990).

Furthermore, modern nationwide statistics show that the area of floor space per person equalled to approximately 10 square meters from 1886 to 1940 (Figure 9.1). Combining them with Table 9.1 data, these facts suggest that the general standard of housing did not change drastically for about 300 years from the 1640s onwards. Early modern and modern Japan's view of an adequate, decent house size seemed to be static, and only

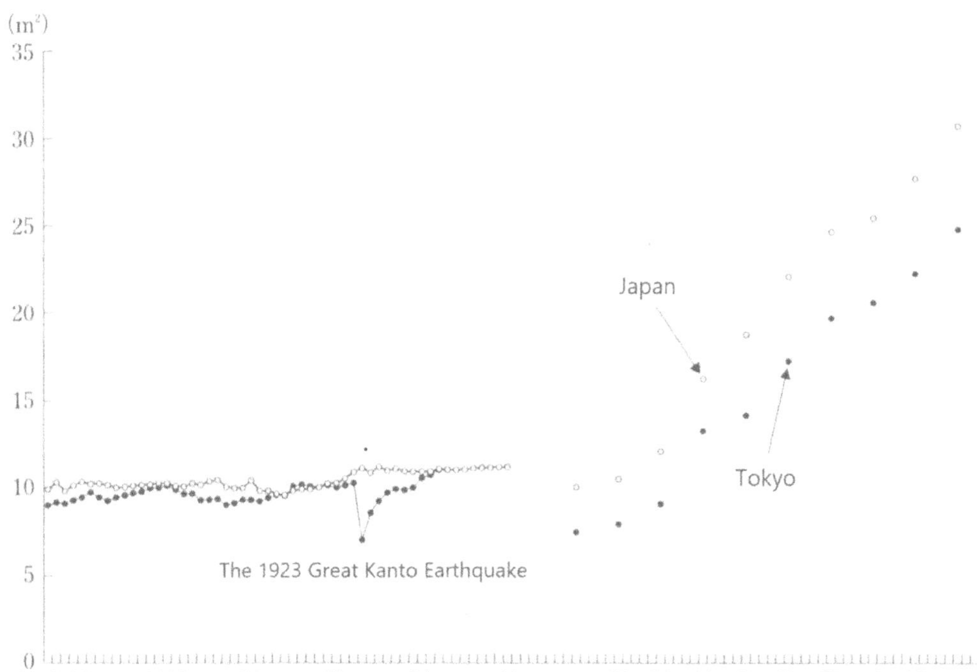

FIGURE 9.1 Area of floor space per person, 1886–1993.

Source: Tachibanaki (2003: Figure 7.2).

after the rapid economic growth starting in the 1950s did the housing standard trends begin to change.

Housing tenure structure differed between cities and villages. Since the rental housing rate accounted for 70–80% in Osaka from 1659 to 1860 (Osakashi 1989: 530, 1990: 249), most early modern urban dwellers lived in rented houses, and the high level of private renting in urban areas continued until Japan lost World War II (hereafter WWII) in 1945 (Hirayama 2020: table 3.1). On the other hand, again, this is supported by scarce evidence, early modern villagers tended to be homeowners. In Tawara village (Yoshino county, Yamato province), all forty-one households owned their houses in 1795, and in 1864, among forty-three households, thirty-four were homeowners (Kinoshita 2019b: table 2; Kataoka family: 4-5-96). According to the 1920s national survey of the landowner system customs, no prefecture reported a social custom that required landowners to provide or lend houses to tenant farmers, which meant that even the tenants had to prepare dwellings by themselves (Tsuchiya 1982).

After heavy air raids of WWII devastated Japanese cities, people dealt with extreme housing shortages by building barracks. This trend drastically changed the housing tenure in urban areas. While the ratio of homeownership in 24 cities was only 22.3% in 1941, it increased to 67% in 1948, and since the 1960s, the nationwide owned housing rate has kept at around 60% until now (Hirayama 2020: 72–75). For urban dwellers, WWII marked a major turning point in their tenure structure, but in the eyes of villagers, it seemed that the 'traditional' homeowning culture eventually prevailed in the post-war times.

Housing Security in Early Modern Japan

Poor relief in early modern rural Japan depended heavily on the households' ability for self-reliance, or self-help. Though the autonomous villages – which were delegated primary responsibility for relief by the Tokugawa shogunate – and the lords granted short-term, limited amounts of aid to the 'deserving,' both parties were reluctant to provide allowances on a long-term, sufficient base even if their communal members or subjects were in desperate need (Kinoshita 2019a).

This self-help attitude towards the poor relief also appears to have penetrated the housing security sector. In the aftermath of natural disasters, the authorities and the local communities usually provided emergency food aid for the victims. However, when people lost their homes as a result of tremendous floods, great earthquakes, or fires, neither the lords nor the Tokugawa shogunate nor the autonomous villages attempted to assist the victims in rebuilding their houses and left the reconstruction of housing to the self-reliance of those affected by the natural disasters.

In 1742, huge floods of eighteen rivers hit Shinano, Kozuke, Musashi, Hitachi, Shimousa, Kazusa and Awa provinces, damaging 4,094 villages and washing away 18,175 houses. As the central government, the shogunate ordered ten lords to rebuild the broken dikes but paid no attention to providing housing aid for the flood victims in these areas. The Kawagoe domain, where 28 villages were damaged and 353 houses were lost, granted some formal relief called *osukui*, which seemed to be restricted to food aid and did not include housing reconstruction. On the other hand, local communities lent or gave food aid to the victims from their communal granaries or funded by wealthy members' charities. In Kugedo village (Iruma county, Musashi province), where 171 households (866 people) lived, 122 households (530 people) were starving as a result of the floods, so the village lent barley from their granary to forty households (109 people) and provided charity alms in barley and Japanese barnyard millet to 63 households (233 people) for six months, on the base of 4 *go*[4] for each person per day (Saitamaken 1984: 909–27). While the standard amount of alms in early modern rural Japan was 1 *go* per person per day – a very limited amount given that an adult ate 5 *go* of grains daily (Kinoshita 2019a) – the Kugedo's food charities seemed to be abundant, but housing aid was not provided even in this 'kind-hearted' village.

In some cases, housing support could be arranged, but it was usually provided on a hut (*koya*) level, not a house level. When Mount Asama erupted in 1783, damaging 55 villages and destroying 1,151 houses, a wealthy inhabitant of Hoshimata village (Agatsuma county, Kozuke province) built an emergency hut measuring 30 *tsubo* (97.2 square meters), 12 *ken* (21.6 meters) in length, and 2.5 *ken* (4.5 meters) in width, for 50–60 people (estimated to equal to ten households, with 3 *tsubo* per household). It was dedicated to those who evacuated from Kanbara village, a neighbour of Hoshimata, and food aid was also granted for two weeks. Haneo village in Agatsuma county pleaded with their lord to provide each household 1 *ryo* in gold to build a 6-*tsubo* (19.44-square-meter) hut for each family (Watanabe 2003). For early modern villagers, preparing a *koya* for the victims was regarded somewhat as the responsibility of their communities or authorities, but, on the contrary, rebuilding one's house was left to each household's effort even in a dire situation, and it was not considered a communal responsibility or lord's or shogunate's duty. As the relief (*osukui*) expenditures in the shogunate finance were collectively called 'loans and allowances for foods, seeds, farming equipment and emergency huts construction' (*fujiki-tanekashi nogudai narabini osukui sonohoka koya-gake haishaku*) (Ono 2008), the shogunate, either as an individual lord or the central government, attempted to lend or grant aids for constructing huts, but not houses.

Utilising the market economy was taken for granted in the self-help housing security. During the 1847 Great Zenkoji Earthquake of Shinano province, 9,337 houses were completely destroyed or washed away, 2,802 houses were partially destroyed and 3,120 houses suffered severe damage in the rural areas of Matsushiro domain alone (Naganoken 1982: 232–40). Though the lord of Matsushiro spent 16,000 *ryo* to grant food aid to the victims in his community, the domain implemented no support for the dwelling even when more than 15,000 houses had to be rebuilt (Naganoken 1989: 135–36). On the other hand, five months after the earthquake, the shogunate (as a lord), the Matsushiro domain and the Zenkoji domain ordered their subjects not to raise unfairly the price of timber and wages of day labourers and craftsmen such as carpenters when people were building their emergency huts, suggesting that the authorities usually left the reconstruction of housing basically to the market economy (Naganoken 1982: 679–80).

Based on these facts, under disastrous conditions, in early modern Japan, no housing policy, or housing system, existed, means of housing security were limited to a communal or authoritative provision of an emergency hut, and maintaining and reconstructing one's house heavily depended on the market economy and people's self-help. In 1834 and 1843, Ogaito village (Hirose county, Yamato province) estimated the construction of an 11.25–12.50-*tsubo* (36.45–40.50-square-meter) house cost 250 *monme* in silver (approximately 4 *ryo*[5]), which meant that building cost of an average-standard 15-*tsubo* house could be around 300–325 *monme* (approximately 5 *ryo*) (Koryocho 2001: 557–59,

563–65). Considering that the median annual income among 41 households of Tawara village (Yoshino county, Yamato province) in 1807 was 670 *monme* (Kinoshita 2017: 134–35), for an ordinary peasant, building a new house could cost half an annual income. Furthermore, in Ichinoe-shinden village (Katsushika county, Musashi province), where 53 households inhabited in 1842, 46 households carried out renovation of their houses, ranging from 6 to 55 *tsubo* (median 16.2 *tsubo*), at least one time from 1838 to 1847 (Nakamura 2015: chap. 6). The market-based self-help of housing security required early modern villagers to invest half of their annual earnings to construct a decent 15-*tsubo* dwelling and repair it at least once every ten years to keep it in proper condition.

These self-help attitudes towards housing security, especially of the lords and the shogunate, show a sharp contrast with early modern lordship state Prussia, where the demesne lords granted timber provisions to their subjects (tenant farmers) when the farmers had to repair or reconstruct their houses, especially in case of fires (Iida 2013, 2019).

Admittedly, in Japan, rare cases existed in which rebuilding allowances were supplied by the authorities. For instance, when almost all of the houses in Subashiri village (Sunto county, Suruga province), where people made a living by hosting travellers to Mount Fuji, collapsed or burned down as a result of the 1707 Great Eruption of Mount Fuji, reconstruction aid was provided by the shogunate (as the central government) for each house on the base of 0.5–1.0 *ryo* per *tsubo* (Oyamacho 1991: 858–65). After the 1783 Great Eruption of Mount Asama, the shogunate (as a lord) lent reconstruction expenses to the victims in Karuizawa, a post town of the Nakasendo Highway in Shinano province, allocating 5–9 *ryo* to each household whose house was destroyed or burned down (Watanabe 2003: 17–19). Perhaps these special treatments were arranged because both places were not typical agricultural villages but held economic and communication importance, respectively. Similarly, in 1802, a wealthy member of Sukegai village (Tsuga county, Shimotsuke province) helped a fire victim in the same community by providing them with some food and timber (Hirano 2022). Such as this case, housing assistance from a communal leader or a wealthy member could be confirmed in early modern rural Japan, but it depended on the suppliers' goodwill and was not a systematic relief.

Moreover, *koya*, a hut, itself symbolised the historical characteristics of housing security and social ideology in early modern and modern Japan. First, a communal custom to provide an emergency hut for a suffering village member lasted not only through the modern era but until the 1950s. In 1884, villagers of Kanmaki village (Katsuge county, Yamato province) prepared a *koya* for a single elderly woman who was living in extreme poverty and granted her food aid daily (Makiura family: 34-5–35). In 1950, a fire burned down six houses in the Kochi community (total population of 737 people), one of the communities that comprised Kowashigawa village of Ketaka county, Tottori prefecture. Three days later, the entire community was involved in building four emergency huts of 6 *tsubo* by cutting down timber and thatch from their communal forest. Though most of the victims reconstructed their new houses within a year, here again, thanks to self-reliance illustrated by buying old timber, one family managed to continue living in the same hut, as shown in a picture shot in 1954 (Figure 9.2), even after four years had passed since the fire occurred (Nishiyama 1968: 181–86). Mutual assistance, local commons and the size of 6 *tsubo*, the same size as the 1783 Haneo village's case, imply the long-term characteristics of communal housing security in rural societies. At the same time, the tradition of self-help attitude continued to impose on people living in 6-*tsubo*

FIGURE 9.2 An emergency hut in Tottori prefecture, 1954.

Source: Nishiyama (1968: 186).

huts, which were far from the size of a 15-*tsubo* house (considered a decent size), if they could not overcome misfortunes on their own.

In addition, though providing an emergency hut for a victim of a natural disaster could imply demonstrating the local communities' hospitality or kindness on the one hand, on the other hand, for those to whom this kindness was shown, living in a *koya* meant social ostracism. For early modern and probably modern villagers, *koya* was a symbol of bankruptcy, which was considered to be a source of shame for the rural population.

In early modern Japan, the liability to pay tax to the lords was not imposed on an individual person or household but on the individual village. Therefore, if one could not pay their taxes for a given year, the rest of the village members had to make up the difference. If they felt overburdened, the villagers did not hesitate to bankrupt those who depended on aid and shame and punish them by forcing them to live in a hut or even expelling them from their communities (Kinoshita 2019a). For instance, in 1699, Higashi-ando village (Heguri county, Yamato province) deconstructed 19 houses, ranging from 6 to 13.75 *tsubo*, and sold the building materials, since their dwellers became a communal burden due to their unpaid taxes, and forced those nineteen families into bankruptcy and life in a *koya* (Andocho 1990: 293–97). Though people were suffering from the effects of famine in the latter half of the 1690s and already thirteen households in Higashi-ando village had become compelled to dwell in huts, the villagers gave priority to lessening their communal financial burden by deconstructing one-sixth of the total housing for sale of building materials (the total population in 1722 was 186 households, 872 people; Andocho 1991: 175–82) over the village's dependents' well-being and comfort of living in a decent house.

Furthermore, in 1880, the Ministry of Justice surveyed the social customs in the Tokugawa period and collected several cases that mentioned the relationship between bankruptcy and a hut dwelling. In Ano county of Ise province, villagers provided the bankrupted with earthen-floor huts that stood on the edge of their communities and did not associate with them until they revived their household economy; in Aichi county of Owari province, the kin or the community prepared a hut for the bankrupted, but they could not be elected as the village officials for three generations; in Shida and Mashizu counties of Suruga province, most bankrupted community members had to live in a hut built on riverside because they were ostracised and isolated from the village; in Atsumi, Kakami and Katagata counties of Mino province, bankrupted village members were not merely prohibited from living inside the village and forced to dwell in a peripheral hut but had to build them in an irregular way such as not using a cornerstone or thatching upside down to ostracise their housing visually (Shihosho 1880/1976: 473–92). For early modern and perhaps modern Japanese villagers, living in a hut was not just an unrespectable lifestyle in terms of the size of the dwelling but also because fellow members of the community ostracised them.

Housing Security and Policy in Modern and Post-war Japan

The Japanese decentralised lordship state system was abolished from 1869 to 1871, and a centralised modern state emerged thereafter. Following the implementation of the 1874 Poor Law (*Jukkyu kisoku*) and the 1880 Granary and Saving Act (*Bikochochikuho*),[6] nationwide relief systems based on the general account of central and local government budget were legislated for the first time in Japanese history, aiming to save the destitute and the victims of disasters. However, from the perspective of housing security, it seems that the traditional 'self-help and only a hut' attitude prevailed in modern times as well.

Figure 9.3 shows the expenditure from 1876 to 1917[7] for poor relief disbursed from central and local public finance and the expense for emergency relief backed by the

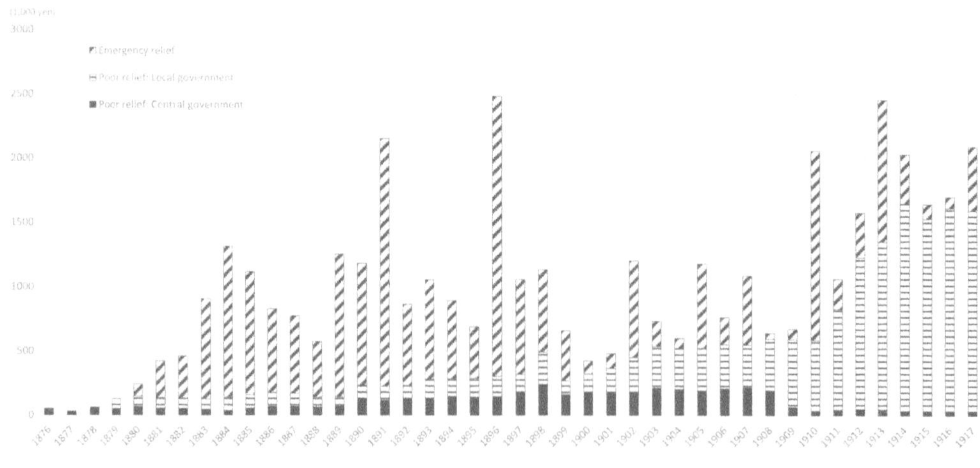

FIGURE 9.3 Expenditure for poor and emergency relief by public finance, 1876–1917.

Source: Nihon teikoku tokei nenkan (The statistical yearbook of the Japanese Empire).

Granary and Saving Act. While the benefit of governmental poor relief was based on staple food expenses (central government relief provided 1.8 *koku* of rice per recipient per year, equivalent to 5 *go* per day), the Granary and Saving Act arranged emergency food (up to thirty days), farming equipment and seeds (worth up to 20 yen per household), and shelter construction cost (worth up to 10 yen per household) called *koya-gakeryo* – that is, building an emergency hut – for the victims of natural disasters.

After the Granary and Saving Act was enacted in 1880, the annual amount of emergency relief far surpassed that of the central and local governmental poor relief almost every year until 1910. It shows that the centralised modern state tackled disaster relief management in a more systematic manner than the decentralised early modern lordship state, but, on the other hand, it demonstrates that, as in the Tokugawa period, modern Japan did not pay attention to supporting housing construction even if people lost their homes by as a result of the disasters.

When the Great Nobi Earthquake occurred in 1891, especially hitting Gifu and Aichi prefectures, in Gifu prefecture alone, 5,349 houses were burned down (3.0% of the total population of 181,322 houses), 42,945 houses were completely destroyed (23.7%) and 15,606 houses were partially destroyed (8.6%) (Kitahara 2006: 287–304). In particular, the number of houses that were burned down, completely destroyed, or partially destroyed in Gifu city was 2,225 (41.6% of the total prefectural burned down houses), 1,095 (2.5% of the completely destroyed) and 2,035 (13.0% of the partially destroyed), respectively (Gifuken 1998: 781). Fire damage was relatively concentrated in urban areas, but most of the damage occurred in rural parts of the prefecture.

As Table 9.2 shows, the central and Gifu prefecture government provided shelter construction relief for 83,917 households – that is, for more than 63,900 damaged houses – by using the Granary and Saving Act funds. The shelter expenditure reached 513,898 yen, and the total amount of 780,361 yen in Gifu prefecture accounted for 40% of the nationwide annual emergency relief in 1891 (1,928,948 yen). Considering that the nationwide annual amount of the central and local government poor relief in 1891 was 116,188 yen and 106,704 yen, respectively, the sum of the shelter aid granted in Gifu prefecture was immense. However, from the housing security's point of view, only building cost of a *koya* was provided, so a miserable one that appeared smaller than a standard 6-*tsubo* emergency hut (Figure 9.4), and even when more than a quarter of people lost their dwelling, and at least 63,900 houses had to be rebuilt, neither the central nor the prefectural government assisted them in reconstructing housing. As in the early modern

TABLE 9.2 Emergency relief for the 1891 victims in Gifu prefecture

Items	*Number of recipients*	*Expenditure*
Foods	383,726 people (41.9% of 916,338 people)	¥266,194.93
Farming equipment and seeds	566 households (0.3% of 181,322 households)	¥267.46
Shelter construction	83,917 households (46.3% of 181,322 households)	¥513,898.23
Total		¥780,360.62

Source: Kitahara (2006: table 8).

FIGURE 9.4 An emergency hut built after the 1891 Nobi earthquake.
Source: Kitahara (2006: figure 64).

days and the 1950s fire case in Tottori prefecture, the rural fire victims in the modern era could not rely on governmental or communal support to rebuild their houses and had to overcome disasters and misfortunes on their own. This again demonstrates that the self-help attitude dominated housing security initiatives in rural parts of Japan.

Housing policy finally came into effect in 1918 as part of social policy that was sparked by the chain of economic boom during World War I, the progress of urbanisation, and the worsening quality of living conditions in urban areas, especially that of low-income dwellers. In July 1918, the Ministry of Interior inaugurated the Research Commission on Relief Work (*Kyusai jigyo chosakai*) as an advisory body and consulted the Commission about the installation of retail markets, protective institutions for the unemployed and children and slum upgrading. Regarding the latter, the Commission submitted 'The Outline of Improving Small-Scale Housing' (*Shojutaku kairyo yoko*) in November 1918, which analysed the situation of not only low-income urban dwellers but also urban middle-class housing. This report informed what became the starting point of housing policy in pre-war Japan, and later, public housing constructions for low-income households, the establishment of cooperative housing associations for middle-class dwellers, and slum upgrading were executed from the 1920s to 1940s (Honma 1988). However, these days, housing policies and projects are concentrated on urban areas, paying little attention to rural dwellers. The birth of a housing system covering the entire nation had to wait until the post-war era arrived.

After Japan lost WWII in August 1945, the new constitution was established in November 1946. The turning point in the history of housing security was Article 25, which ensured the right to living for the first time in Japanese history, declaring '[a]ll people shall have the right to maintain the minimum standards of wholesome and cultured living.' Based on this article, four important acts relating to housing security were legislated in rapid succession in the 1950s. On 4 May 1950, the Public Assistance Act (*Seikatsuhogoho*) was enacted that guaranteed a minimum standard of living for all citizens who were living in poverty and stipulated the type of public assistance, such as livelihood, educational, medical, maternity, occupational, funeral and housing assistance; two days later, the Housing Finance Corporation Act (*Jutaku kinyu kokoho*) was legislated to lend low-interest mortgages to those who had difficulties in borrowing loans from commercial banks when they sought to build or buy a 'wholesome and cultured living' housing; aiming to provide low-rent housing to low-income families, the Public Housing Act (*Koei jutakuho*) was established in 1951; and the Japan Housing Corporation Act (*Nihon jutaku kodanho*) was enacted in 1955, providing multifamily housing for both rent and sale for middle-income households.

Furthermore, backed by the 1960 Housing Upgrading Act (*Jutakuchiku kairyoho*) that succeeded the 1927 Slum Upgrading Act (*Furyo jutakuchiku kairyoho*) and by the 1969 Special Act for Dowa Area Measures Project (*Dowa taisaku jigyo tokubetsu-sochiho*), upgrading underprivileged areas, especially of the *Dowa* areas (*hisbetsu-buraku*), where the historical outcasts called *eta* in the Tokugawa period had been living, started in full-scale from the 1960s onwards. While, in 1969, housing conditions of 92,525 houses (32.6% of 283,954 houses) in *Dowa* areas were assessed as very poor, 68,176 new houses were built from 1970 to 1979, covering 73.7% of those substandard dwellings (Umemoto 2014). These upgrading projects changed the living conditions and housing conditions of the *Dowa* area so drastically that the residents of the Kyowa community, a suburban *Dowa* area located near the old city of Sakai, remember that when they first moved into the new public housing in 1962, '[i]t was like a dream come true to have a restroom and running water in your own house' (Henomatsu Jinken Rekishikan 2018). Kyowa community was the first area in Japan to which the Housing Upgrading Act was applied in 1960. Before the upgrading project started there, 81% of households (5,099 people) were living in very low-standard housing conditions, including a lack of cornerstones, tilted pillars and overcrowding (Henomatsu Jinken Rekishikan 2018).

Conclusion

Viewing from a long-term perspective, what characteristics can be confirmed in the history of housing security and well-being in Japan?

First, the introduction of the Constitution of Japan in 1946, especially Article 25, must be considered the most important historical turning point. Supported and prompted by the article, the housing security system finally extended to cover not only urban areas, as pre-war housing policy had attempted to, but also rural dwellers. Whether living in a city, town or a village, low-income households could become eligible (if they passed the strict means test) to receive housing assistance, which itself appeared for the first time in Japanese history, or rent a (somewhat) decent public housing, instead of living in a hut that was a traditional way to relieve people in housing difficulties. Since 2010, the annual value of housing assistance has accounted for 15–16% of the total public assistance, after medical and livelihood assistance, which account for approximately 50% and 30%, respectively (Iwata 2021: figure IV-1).

Second, however, the market-based self-help attitude in housing security seems to persist socially and politically from the early modern period until now. Therefore, the strong market-based tendency in the post-war housing system that Yosuke Hirayama revealed could be connected to the long-term historical conditions from the eighteenth century or even the seventeenth century. Moreover, the 'only a hut' attitude did not seem to disappear as easily. Though the victims of the 2011 Great East Japan Earthquake were able to use private rented housing hired by local governments as an adequate temporary shelter, those of the 1995 Great Hanshin-Awaji Earthquake, during which 105,000 houses were completely destroyed, were only provided an emergency shelter, which historically meant living in an unrespectable hut (Hirayama 2020: 250–52). Well-being underpinned by adequate housing and the protection of one's dwelling right has been left to people's ability for self-reliance for centuries, and this long-term self-help attitude likely created the historical background contributing to the 'coldness' towards housing issues in twenty-first-century Japan.

Restricting severely who is eligible to use the post-war housing security system may relate to the self-help attitude as well. As shown in the case of the 1783 Great Eruption of Mount Asama and the 1891 Great Nobi Earthquake, even though, or because, emergency huts were not respectable dwellings, they were provided socially or politically on the basis of the so-called universalism. On the contrary, historically, Japanese people have not experienced at all a universal arrangement of decent housing. Both housing assistance and public housing have been so restrictive that most low-income households have been excluded from using those systems: the Public Assistance System is said to be capturing merely 20% of the people in need (Iwata 2021: 15–19); while the poverty rate in 2018 was 15.7% (OECD Data), the share of public housing in the same year was only 3.6% (Hirayama 2020: table 3.1), showing that the construction of public housing has been far from sufficient (Hirayama 2013; Hirayama 2020). In 2007, the Housing Safety Net Act was enacted, but its target was restricted to the low-income group, disaster victims, older adults, people with disabilities, and families with small children. Similar to the history of poor relief, the history of housing security in Japan has been dominated by strict 'targetism' (Kinoshita 2019a). Moreover, whereas the average housing cost overburden rate of low-income groups in the EU was under 40% in 2017, in Japan, it accounted for 73% (Otsu 2021: 93–95). It seems that the 'traditional' market-based self-help attitude towards housing problems has not been functioning well in securing people's well-being in contemporary Japan.

Long-term historical analysis brings about a suggestive viewpoint towards comparative study as well. For instance, Table 9.3 shows six European countries, the US and Japan's contributions (or lack thereof) in 2020 towards instituted public housing, social housing, a housing system that provides reduced-rent houses from the private sector such as non-profit organisations, and a universal rent subsidy system that covers not only low-income groups but also middle-income population. Here, we can recognise that the comparative characteristics of Japan lay in the absence of social housing and universal rent subsidies, suggesting a strong dependence, even more than the UK and US, on the market economy and citizen's self-help in housing security – the same historical trend revealed in this paper.

This also reminds us of Gøsta Esping-Andersen's well-known theory, 'the three worlds of welfare capitalism,' that categorised 18 welfare states in 1980 into clusters of

TABLE 9.3 Housing security types in Japan, Europe and the US, 2020

	Public housing	*Social housing*	*Rent subsidy*
Japan	○	×	×
UK	○	○	○
France	×	○	○
Germany	×	○	○
Netherlands	×	○	○
Denmark	○	○	○
Sweden	○	×	○
US	○	○	○

Source: Kokuritsu Shakai-hosho Jinko Mondai Kenkyujo (2021: 275–83).

'conservatism,' 'liberalism,' and 'socialism' by examining how private and public welfare provisions were blended with 'de-commodification' of people's living standards. In this theory, 1980 Japan was ranked as 'medium' conservatism, 'strong' liberalism and 'low' socialism (Esping-Andersen 1990: table 3.3). While housing issues did not receive in-depth attention in Esping-Andersen's discussion, housing security in contemporary Japan can be categorised as 'strong liberalism,' depending heavily on the market and people's self-help, and from the long-term perspective attempted in this paper, this 'housing liberalism' in Japan seems to start not in the modern era but from the eighteenth or even seventeenth century, far from the time when industrialisation, or capitalism, began in Japan at the turn of the twentieth century.

From a long-term historical and comparative perspective, we can discuss why Japan did not or could not accept a 'social housing and universal rent subsidy' doctrine for providing and securing decent housing. At the same time, we can question why European and American societies did or could shift to that value system while the historical path of Japan seems to be most 'traditional' in the sense of housing provision and security. These discussions do not imply one country's superiority or inferiority vis-à-vis another: even though the US possesses a social housing and rent subsidy system, it is not doing well to tackle homelessness in comparison to Japan (Goto et al. 2022) due to its own unique historical conditions. It is a matter of how the weight of the historical path affects each society's shape of well-being represented by the structure of housing security.

Manuscript and Digital Sources

The Archives of the Kataoka Family. Ouda-tawara, Uda city, Nara prefecture.

The Archives of the Makiura Family. Nara Prefectural Library and Information Center.

Minutes of the Committee on Land, Infrastructure, Transport and Tourism, House of Councillors. No. 20. May 30, 2006. Full-text Database System for the Minutes of the Diet. National Diet Library, Japan. https://kokkai.ndl.go.jp/#/detailPDF?minId=116414319X02020060530&page=1&spkNsp=0&current=1, accessed May 19, 2024.

Comprehensive Survey of Living Conditions [Kokumin Seikatsu Kiso Chosa] 2021. Portal Site of Official Statistics of Japan (e-Stat). https://www.e-stat.go.jp/dbview?sid=0001980333, accessed May 19, 2024.

OECD Data. Poverty Rate. https://data.oecd.org/inequality/poverty-rate.htm, accessed May 19, 2024.

Notes

1 Housing policy and system in pre-war urban Japan is well analysed by Honma (1988) and Ono (2014).
2 In early modern Japan, the Tokugawa shogunate served as the central government, reigning over the lords on one hand and as an individual lord on the other.
3 1 *tsubo* equals 3.24 square meters, 1.8 meters (1 *ken*) in length, 1.8 meters in width.
4 The volume of 1 *go* equals 180 milliliters and weighs approximately 150 gram in polished rice.
5 In 1700, as the central government, the Tokugawa shogunate ordered the market to exchange gold for silver at the rate of 1 *ryo* = 60 *monme* (Hoseishigakkai 1959: 113).
6 The Victim Relief Fund Act (*Risai kyujo kikinho*) succeeded the Granary and Saving Act in 1899.
7 Though the relief data after 1918 can be collected from *Nihon teikoku tokei nenkan* (The statistical yearbook of the Japanese Empire), we have to omit them from Figure 9.3 since the total annual amount of relief after 1918, when social services started functioning in urban areas, far surpasses that of until 1917 and makes the 1876–1917 data a 'ripple.' While the poor and emergency relief sum of 1917 amounted to 1,671,583 yen, in 1918, it was 13,106,447 yen.

References

Andocho. 1990. *Andochoshi* [The History of Ando Town]. Shiryohen Jokan. Andocho.

Andocho. 1991. *Andochoshi* [The History of Ando Town]. Shiryohen Gekan. Andocho.

Esping-Andersen, Gøsta. 1990. *The Three Worlds of Welfare Capitalism*. Cambridge: Polity Press.

Gifuken. 1998. *Gifukenshi* [The History of Gifu Prefecture]. Shiryohen Kindai 1. Gifuken.

Goto, Hiroshi, Dennis P. Culhane, and Matthew D. Marr. 2022. "Why Street Homelessness Has Decreased in Japan: A Comparison of Public Assistance in Japan and the US." *European Journal of Homelessness* 16, 1: 81–99.

Henomatsu Jinken Rekishikan. 2018. *Wa, kon-nan yume mitai! Sumai, shigoto ni miru Dowa taisaku jigyo* [Wao, It's like a Dream Come True! Housing, Occupation, and the Dowa Area Measures Projects in Post-War Kyowa Community of Sakai City]. Sakai: Henomatsu Jinken Rekishikan.

Hirano, Tetsuya. 2022. "Edo-jidai koki no mura no sainan to hyakusho no taio" [How Villagers Dealt with Disasters and Misfortunes in Late Early Modern Japan]. *Tochigikenritsu Monjokan Kenkyu Kiyo* 26: 17–39.

Hirayama, Yosuke. 2013. "Public Housing and Neoliberal Policy in Japan." In *The Future of Public Housing: Ongoing Trends in the East and the West*, edited by Jie Chen, Mark Stephens, and Yanyun Man, 143–61. Berlin: Springer.

Hirayama, Yosuke. 2020. *My-home no kanata ni: Jutaku seisaku no sengoshi wo do yomuka* [Beyond Home Ownership: Housing Policy in Post-war Japan]. Tokyo: Chikuma Shobo.

Honma, Yoshihito. 1988. *Naimusho jutaku seisaku no kyokun: Kokyo-jutakuron josetsu* [The Housing Policy of Ministry of Interior in Pre-war Japan: Historical Lessons for the Discussions of Public Housing]. Tokyo: Ochanomizu Shobo.

Honma, Yoshihito. 2004. *Sengo jutaku seisaku no kensho* [Verifying the Housing Policy in Post-war Japan]. Tokyo: Shinzansha.

Honma, Yoshihito. 2009. *Kyoju no hinkon* [Poorness of Housing in Contemporary Japan]. Tokyo: Iwanami Shoten.

Hoseishigakkai, ed. 1959. *Tokugawa kinreiko* [The Document Collection of the Tokugawa shogunate Acts]. Zenshu 6. Tokyo: Sobunsha.

Iida, Takashi. 2013. "The Practice of Timber Granting from Lords to Peasants: A Forest-Historical Perspective of the *Gutsherrschaft* in Brandenburg-Prussia from 1650 to 1850." *Agricultural History* 87, 4: 502–24.

Iida, Takashi. 2019. "Lords' Forestry for People's Basic Needs: Evidence from Prussia's Royal Domains and Forests during the Eighteenth and Nineteenth Centuries." In *Public Goods Provision in the Early Modern Economy: Comparative Perspectives from Japan, China, and Europe*, edited by Masayuki Tanimoto, and R. Bin Wong, 238–54. Oakland: University of California Press.

ISSP Research Group. 2018. *International Social Survey Programme: Role of Government V ISSP 2016*. GESIS Data Archive.

Iwata, Masami. 2021. *Seikatsuhogo kaitairon: Safety net wo aminaosu* [Dissolve the Public Assistance System: Rebuilding a New Safety Net]. Tokyo: Iwanami Shoten.
Kingendai Shiryo Kankokai, ed. 1996. *Nihon kindai toshi shakai-chosa shiryo shusei* [The Document Collection of Social Survey in Modern Urban Japan]. Tokyo: Kingendai Shiryo Kankokai.
Kinoshita, Mitsuo. 2017. *Hinkon to jiko-sekinin no kinsei Nihonshi* [Poverty and Poor Relief in Early Modern Rural Japan]. Kyoto: Jinbun Shoin.
Kinoshita, Mitsuo. 2019a. "Sanctions, Targetism, and Village Autonomy: Poor Relief in Early Modern Rural Japan." In *Public Goods Provision in the Early Modern Economy: Comparative Perspectives from Japan, China, and Europe*, edited by Masayuki Tanimoto, and R. Bin Wong, 78–99. Oakland: University of California Press.
Kinoshita, Mitsuo. 2019b. "Sonmin seikatsu no suchika: 1795–1836 nen no Yamatonokuni Yoshinogun Tawaramura" [Peasants' Livelihood in Tawara Village, Yoshino County, Yamato Province, 1795–1836]. *Saga Buraku Kaiho Kenkyujo Kiyo* 36: 44–73.
Kitahara, Itoko, ed. 2006. *Nihon saigaishi* [The History of Disasters in Japan]. Tokyo: Yoshikawakobunkan.
Kokuritsu Shakai-hosho Jinko Mondai Kenkyujo, ed. 2021. *Nihon no kyoju hosho: Teiryo bunseki to kokusai hikaku kara kangaeru* [Housing Security in Contemporary Japan: A Quantitative and Comparative Study]. Tokyo: Keiogijuku Daigaku Shuppankai.
Koryocho. 2001. *Koryochoshi* [The History of Koryo Town]. Shiryohen Gekan. Koryocho.
Kusano, Kuzuo. 1995. *Kinsei minka no seiritsu katei* [The Formation of Private Houses in Early Modern Japan]. Tokyo: Chuokoronbijutsu Shuppan.
Laslett, Peter, and Richard Wall, eds. 1972. *Household and Family in Past Time*. Cambridge: Cambridge University Press.
Naganoken. 1982. *Naganokenshi* [The History of Nagano Prefecture]. Kinsei Shiryohen 7, 3. Naganoken.
Naganoken. 1989. *Naganokenshi* [The History of Nagano Prefecture]. Tsushihen 6. Naganoken.
Nakamura, Takumi. 2015. *Kinsei minka fushin to shigen hozen* [The Building of Private Houses and Resources Conservation in Early Modern Japan]. Tokyo: Chuokoronbijutsu Shuppan.
Nishiyama, Uzo. 1968. *Nishiyama Uzo chosakushu* [Collected Works of Uzo Nishiyama] 2. Tokyo: Keiso Shobo.
Oishi, Shinzaburo. 1967. "Kinsei shoki Shinano ni okeru nomin kaoku ni tsuite" [Peasants' Houses in the First Half of Seventeenth Century Shinano Province]. In *Nihon shakai keizaishi kenkyu: Kinseihen*, edited by Hozuki Keigo Sensei Kanreki Kinenkai, 125–38. Tokyo: Yoshikawakobunkan.
Ono, Hiroshi. 2014. *Jukukan no keizaishi: Senkanki Tokyo no toshi keisei to shakuya shakuma shijo* [Economic History of Living Space: Urbanization and Rental Housing Market in Pre-war Tokyo]. Tokyo: Nihonkeizaihyoronsha.
Ono, Mizuo, ed. 2008. *Edo-bakufu zaisei shiryo shusei* [The Document Collection of the Tokugawa Shogunate Finance]. Jokan and Gekan. Tokyo: Yoshikawakobunkan.
Osakashi. 1989. *Shinshu Osakashishi* [The New Edition of the History of Osaka City] 3. Osakashi.
Osakashi. 1990. *Shinshu Osakashishi* [The New Edition of the History of Osaka City] 4. Osakashi.
Otsu, Yui. 2021. "Kokusai shihyo de mita Nihon no kyoju suijun: Teishotokusha he no kyoju hosho no zeijakusei" [Comparative Study of Housing Standard in Japan: The Weakness of Housing Security for Low-Income Group]. In *Nihon no kyoju hosho: Teiryo bunseki to kokusai hikaku kara kangaeru*, edited by Kokuritsu Shakai-hosho Jinko Mondai Kenkyujo, 87–102. Tokyo: Keiogijuku Daigaku Shuppankai.
Oyamacho. 1991. *Oyamachoshi* [The History of Oyama Town] 2. Oyamacho.
Saitamaken. 1984. *Shinpen Saitamakenshi* [The New Edition of the History of Saitama Prefecture]. Shiryohen 13. Saitamaken.
Saito, Osamu. 1998. "Two Kinds of Stem-Family System? Traditional Japan and Europe Compared." *Continuity and Change* 13, 1: 167–86.
Saito, Osamu and Masanori Takashima. 2016. "Estimating the Shares of Secondary- and Tertiary-Sector Outputs in the Age of Early Modern Growth: The Case of Japan, 1600–1874." *European Review of Economic History* 20: 368–86.
Shihosho, ed. 1880/1976. *Zenkoku minji kanrei ruishu* [The Survey of Social Customs in the Tokugawa Period]. Chiba: Seishisha.
Tachibanaki, Toshiaki. 2003. "Kakei" [Family Budget]. In *Sengo Nihon keizai wo kensho-suru*, edited by Toshiaki Tachibanaki, 537–93. Tokyo: Tokyo Daigaku Shuppankai.

Takao, Kazuhiko. 1958. "Edo shoki no noson kosei to sono hatten" [Village Structure and Its Development in the First Half of Seventeenth Century Japan]. *Kenkyu: Shigakuhen* 16: 99–135. Edited by Kobe Daigaku Bungakukai.

Takao, Kazuhiko. 1961. "Kaneiki Kawachi no watasaku noson ni tsuite" [Cotton growing villages in the first half of seventeenth century Kawachi province]. *Kenkyu: Shigakuhen* 25: 1–68. Edited by Kobe Daigaku Bungakukai.

Tani, Naoki. 1990. "Kinsei minka ni kansuru bunkenteki ichikosatsu" [Peasants' Houses in Early Modern Japan]. *Osakashiritsu daigaku seikatsukagakubu kiyo* 38: 129–38.

Tsuchiya, Takao, ed. 1982. *Taisho 10 nen fukenbetsu kosaku kanko chosa shusei* [The Document Collection of the Survey of Landowner System Customs in 1920s Japan]. Tokyo: Shozansha.

Umemoto, Tetsuya. 2014. "'Kodo-seicho' ki ni okeru jutaku seisaku to Dowa taisaku jigyo" [Housing policy and Dowa area measures project in the rapid economic growth period of Japan]. In *Buraku mondai kaiketsu katei no kenkyu* 3, edited by Buraku Mondai Kenkyujo, 123–52. Kyoto: Buraku Mondai Kenkyujo.

Watanabe, Takashi. 2003. *Asamayama daifunka* [The 1783 Great Eruption of Mount Asama]. Tokyo: Yoshikawakobunkan.

SECTION IV

Well-Being in the Twenty-First Century

10

WELL-ROUNDED WELL-BEING

The Low-Carbon Bioclimatic Architecture of the Balearic Housing Institute

Rafael Gómez-Moriana

Housing: Between Individual and Planetary Well-Being

Housing is the building type that most directly affects our well-being. We spend most of our lifetime at home, on average, and spend most of our wealth paying for it. Shelter, a basic necessity for human survival, is fundamental to both our physical and mental health, or 'well-being' as it is most widely understood. Yet housing also greatly affects *planetary* well-being. The construction and use of buildings emits around 37% of all anthropogenic greenhouse gases,[1] the lion's share of which is residential, the most common building use worldwide. Housing is therefore the building type that most contributes to climate change, the greatest current threat to planetary sustainability.

Paradoxically, then, the very collective well-being of the planet is compromised in no small part by the high degree of domestic comfort and well-being enjoyed by the average western household. Indeed, there is a growing consensus among scientists that if our planet is to remain habitable for future generations, advanced economies must degrow, entailing sacrifices by those enjoying the highest standards of living.[2] Does this mean that planetary and individual or familial well-being are intrinsically at odds? The slowness of political change in the face of an impending global climate breakdown reveals that we humans generally tend to prioritise our *private* well-being over that of larger collectives we form part of; especially when it comes to our planet. Our human competitive urge to be materially 'better-off' than others is precisely what has led to this climate crisis.

> We have been mortgaging the health of future generations to realize economic and development gains in the present. By unsustainably exploiting nature's resources, human civilization has flourished but now risks substantial health effects from the degradation of nature's life support systems in the future.[3]

Can housing better ensure *planetary* well-being while maintaining adequate levels of individual and familial well-being? Is it possible to strike a balance between these opposed notions of well-being? In Spain, a regional governmental social housing agency

DOI: 10.4324/9781003527930-15

has sought to answer this question through a series of experimental residential buildings that attempt to minimise greenhouse gas emissions while maintaining adequate levels of human comfort. The *Instituto Balear de la Vivienda* (Balearic Housing Institute), or IBAVI, an agency of the Ministry of Housing, Territory and Mobility of the Government of the Balearic Isles, is responsible for constructing and managing public social housing in this Mediterranean archipelago, one of Spain's 17 administrative regions. Over the last decade, IBAVI's policies have radically changed the way social housing is commissioned, designed, built and managed in its jurisdiction, mainly through the application of research findings on bioclimatic design and low-carbon construction materials. The result is a body of buildings that, through their natural materials, craftmanship, natural light and biophilia moreover provide an experience of comfort, soulfulness and delight that fosters personal and familial well-being.

The IBAVI Agenda

In 2009, at the height of a global economic crisis that struck Spain especially hard, and six years before the Paris Agreement on climate change, IBAVI decided to embark on a path towards sustainability by constructing low-carbon bioclimatic buildings.

> The starting point lay in the term 'sustainability'... tools that must be put in place so that our current well-being does not jeopardize the well-being of future generations.[4]

In 2012, with the support of the Balearic General Directorate of Energy and Climate Change, IBAVI applied to the European Union LIFE + 12 program for a climate change adaptation project grant, receiving 754,012 euros to 'demonstrate the feasibility of developing a multi-family residential building with a significantly reduced ecological footprint.'[5] In preparation for the design of this demonstration building, IBAVI, together with researchers from the University of the Balearic Isles, began to study and compare the carbon footprints of diverse local and imported building materials, developing what it has termed a 'resource map.'[6] This table, which charts both *transportation* as well as *embedded* carbon emissions, would enable IBAVI architects to compare locally sourced building materials with ones that are imported at specific building site locations, allowing the most eco-efficient materials to be selected for a given project at a given site. The dependency of this archipelago upon the transportation of goods by ferryboat from the Spanish mainland encouraged IBAVI to also research the carbon footprints of historical vernacular building materials and techniques that became outmoded under modernity. Examples of these include *Marés* sandstone vaulting, dried seagrass thermal insulation and rammed earth load-bearing walls; traditional building methods that were abandoned in the late 1960s in favour of steel and reinforced concrete, which enabled taller and larger building types demanded by a rapidly growing tourism industry.

To prepare the resource map, construction materials were analysed with respect to both their embodied production energy as well as all transportation energies involved from extraction through processing to on-site delivery. Even the type of fuel used by different brickyards was taken into consideration. The resource map also considered the local availability of industrial byproducts and building elements salvaged from the demolition of older buildings that could be re-used.

Embodied energy is a relatively new concept. Traditionally, the energy efficiency of buildings was mainly rated in terms of *operational* energy consumption, mainly heating and air conditioning. But it has recently been shown that the carbon 'embodied' in the very materials used in building construction is equally if not more important than the carbon emitted by buildings during use. 'Environmental policies have traditionally focused on improving energy efficiency and renewable energies in the use phase while neglecting material efficiency in construction.'[7]

The research into outmoded traditional building materials involved the laboratory analysis of material samples taken from centuries-old buildings, mainly to analyse how well they have held up over time. It was discovered, for example, that Posidonia seagrass,[8] a protected plant species that washes up on beaches throughout the Mediterranean and is therefore considered a nuisance by tourists, was long ago harvested and sun-dried for use as thermal insulation in houses, and that the very sea salt it contains helps preserve it as well as adjacent timbers from insects and rot.[9] Since it is a protected species that forms part of the ecosystem of the Balearic Isles' shores, Posidonia seagrass may only be harvested in limited quantities for local use.

IBAVI's resource map also identified certain newly developed construction materials whose outstanding eco-efficiency deems them worthwhile importing from mainland Europe. Despite their greater transportation carbon emissions, engineered wood products such as glue-laminated (glulam) beams and oriented strand board (OSB) panels manufactured in Austria and Italy, respectively, turned out to have a smaller carbon footprint than locally produced concrete when used for comparable tasks.[10] The reason: the forests from which wood products are produced *sequester* CO_2 from the atmosphere, whereas the manufacturing of Portland cement, which requires very high heat, *emits* vast quantities of carbon. Wood therefore has a *negative* carbon footprint, making it highly advantageous to use.[11] Furthermore, wood is a renewable material, whereas the ingredients required to manufacture steel and cement are finite. The use of concrete in the demonstration building was therefore restricted exclusively to basements and foundations.

The selection of the most eco-efficient materials for the demonstration building implied, furthermore, that the architectural design would have to employ these materials as efficiently as possible, minimising waste, while at the same time minimising eventual operational carbon emissions. The design process was therefore based on bioclimatic design principles in which architectural form is determined mainly by climatic factors and material efficiency. Rather than, as is often the case, 'form follows function'[12] (or 'form follows parking'[13]), here form follows eco-efficiency.[14]

In IBAVI's demonstration project, dwellings were therefore designed to capture passive solar energy for winter heating as well as prevailing winds for summer cross-ventilation and were equipped with features by which these natural energies could be stored as well as modulated by users (see Figure 10.1). Windows and doors thus feature operable exterior shutters, while high thermal inertia floor and wall materials such as lime concrete and natural stone, in conjunction with dried Posidonia seagrass thermal insulation, ensure that this energy is stored.

The specific objectives for IBAVI's demonstration building were to reduce the carbon embedded in building materials by at least 50%; to reduce construction waste by 50%; and to keep any increases in construction costs below 5% compared to a conventionally

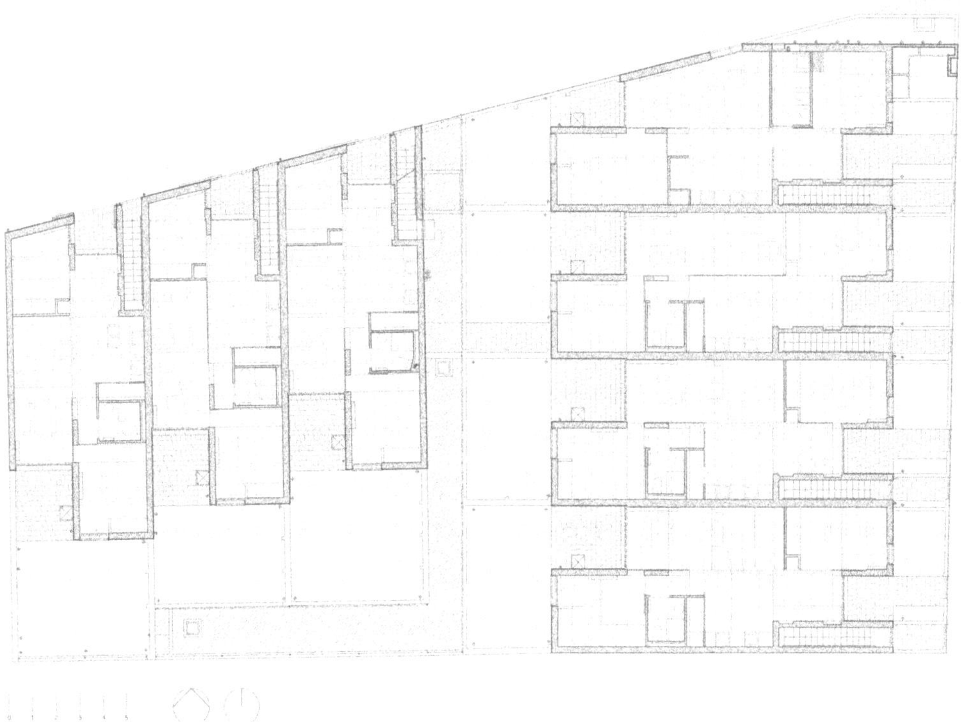

FIGURE 10.1 Ground floor plan, *Life Reusing Posidonia* social housing, Formentera, Balearic Isles, 2017. Plan ©IBAVI.

constructed equivalent building. Operational carbon emissions were aimed to be reduced by 75%, while water consumption was intended to be reduced by 60% through the implementation of a grey water recovery system.

The Demonstration Building 'Life Reusing Posidonia'

In 2017, after a lengthy period of research, design and construction, IBAVI finally completed the demonstration building *Life Reusing Posidonia* on Formentera Island – the smallest of the four main Balearic Isles – at the edge of the rural village of Sant Ferran de ses Roques. Situated on a site at a street corner, the building consists of a discreet pair of two-story terraces containing 14 dwellings (see Figure 10.1). Each dwelling is accessed directly from the street and equipped with a private outdoor space of its own: a rear garden for every ground floor flat, and a roof terrace for every upper floor flat.

In addition to maximising cross ventilation and solar capture, the dwellings were also designed to maximise flexibility in the use of space, an important consideration in contemporary social housing that is normally highly restricted in size, and whose inhabitants are usually more socially and culturally diverse than those of free-market housing. Dwelling flexibility was achieved by designing non-hierarchical rooms that could be joined together or separated by means of large doors as need arises, enabling them to accommodate a wider range of uses. A precedent being emulated in the design of some Spanish

FIGURE 10.2 Exterior view, *Life Reusing Posidonia* social housing, Formentera, Balearic Isles, 2017. Photograph ©Marià Castelló.

social housing dwellings is the traditional Japanese house, in which generic rooms organised as enfilades and enclosed by means of *fusuma* or *shōji* screens allow adaptation to different uses at different times.[15]

Each dwelling contains two equally sized bedrooms situated at diagonally opposite corners that open onto a central, zig-zagging daytime space. Such a diagonal layout perceptually enlarges the daytime space and increases the penetration of natural light, thereby contributing to psychological well-being. The upper-floor dwellings, which are more subject to temperature extremes, feature thermal chimneys in living room ceilings in the form of a small one-meter roof outcrop with two openings: a south-facing fixed clerestory window for winter passive-solar heating that is shuttered in summer, and a north-facing operable clerestory window for natural cooling of the space in summer. Through these bioclimatic features, a dwelling's electric air-source heat pump only needs to be activated when temperatures are at their most extreme, greatly helping to reduce both carbon emissions as well as utility bills.

The above-ground structure of the demonstration building consists of load-bearing walls built of lightweight 'Ytong' blocks imported from France, while floor slabs consist of an assembly of glue-laminated wood joists and OSB panels finished with lime concrete and terra cotta tiles to provide adequate thermal inertia. The exposed wood of the ceilings confers warmth while contributing, in conjunction with the private gardens, to the presence of biophilia (see Figures 10.2–10.3). Wood is also present in the doors, which were salvaged from demolished buildings and so differ eclectically from one another in

FIGURE 10.3 Interior view, *Life Reusing Posidonia* social housing, Formentera, Balearic Isles, 2017. Photograph ©Marià Castelló.

style. These re-used doors provide each dwelling with delightful touches of uniqueness; a highly unusual feature in institutionally built housing. Equally unusual is the use of dried Posidonia seagrass as thermal insulation in the roofs, a technique revived here for the first time in over half a century.

The *Life Reusing Posidonia* demonstration building is holistic, synthesising findings from the scientific research of materials and bioclimatic design principles to arrive at an outcome that, in the end, doesn't appear very experimental or ecological at all. In fact, from a distance, the demonstration building resembles an ordinary local vernacular construction more than a work of award-winning architecture.[16] This is a virtue in the climate emergency we face: vernacular normality, an aesthetic that is generally preferred by the lay population, is a useful strategy for this 'new' bioclimatic low-carbon architecture to gain popular acceptance.

> The map of local resources [...] ended up linking us with our cultural heritage. Thus, a symbiosis was produced between the user's comfort needs and everything that makes up a cultural landscape.[17]

Upon inhabitation of the *Life Reusing Posidonia* demonstration building, analyses determined that the actual carbon embodied in construction materials was reduced by 63.45% compared to a conventional equivalent building,[18] significantly better than was aimed for. It is important to note that the particular low-carbon materials that were selected for this demonstration building, together with its bioclimatic design features, are highly specific to its site in Formentera. At sites located elsewhere, a different resource map would recommend different materials, and bioclimatic principles would have to be adapted to different site conditions. 'IBAVI have identified the benefits of locally sourced materials that might not be considered viable in other environments.'[19]

Clearly, there is no universal, one-size-fits-all approach: the diversity of planet Earth's terrain, climate, culture and locally available materials, which are precisely the factors that shaped vernacular building traditions before the onslaught of modernisation, will always condition low-carbon architecture. This is a far cry from the International Style architecture of the early and mid-twentieth century, which promoted an architecture irrespective of local differences. By reviving certain local building traditions while incorporating modern eco-efficient materials that merit importation from afar, *Life Reusing Posidonia* amalgamates tradition and modernity.

IBAVI's findings from this experiment, the post-occupancy performance of which was monitored for several years, served to establish a set of guidelines for commissioning future projects through public national architectural competitions. Since *Life Reusing Posidonia*, IBAVI has developed 46 social housing projects in the Balearic Isles, five of which were designed by in-house architects while the bulk were commissioned through competitions. A sizable body of built work has thus emerged that permits different bioclimatic design principles and different low-carbon construction materials from varying resource maps to be tested and compared. Each successive housing project built by IBAVI has led to improvements and optimisation, a highly empirical process of learning from experience. Indeed, the more recent housing projects contain no artificial heating or air conditioning systems whatsoever. 'What we have done is dispense with active heating and cooling systems and invest that part of the budget in passive systems.'[20]

The Historical Spanish Social Housing Context of IBAVI

> No public—nor private as far as I know—housing developer has ever tackled the need to transform the production of habitability in such a direct way. ...the [Balearic Housing] institute's actions are based on its conviction that today's habitability is rooted in the very causes of the crisis.[21]

The sustainability turn initiated by IBAVI in 2009 represents a significant departure from Spanish social housing models, not only for its experimentation with bioclimatic, low-carbon building construction and management but also for the scale and the building types it develops. IBAVI's residential buildings are generally low-rise structures developed on brownfield sites, including urban infill, and are built to be *rented* rather than purchased, which is unusual in Spain. This anomaly is perhaps explained by the high dependence of the Balearic Isles' economy upon international tourism and luxury real estate development; industries that have been shown to raise housing costs beyond the reach of local working populations throughout the world.[22]

As in the rest of Europe, Spanish social housing is very much a product of the industrial revolution of the nineteenth century, when an influx of rural migrants seeking jobs in factories caused rapid urban growth. Grave public health problems associated with shoddily built housing, over-crowding and air- and water-pollution emerged, prompting discussions on urban planning in relation to public health. The 1859 urban plan for the extension of Barcelona by the reformist civil engineer Ildefons Cerdà was unprecedented for its hygienist scientific approach, with the treatise[23] that accompanied his plan going largely unnoticed outside of the Spanish-speaking world at the time. Decades later, Ebenezer Howard's *Garden Cities of Tomorrow* of 1898 would become highly influential.[24]

In Spain, social housing was first promoted in the early twentieth century through a series of social reforms and fiscal benefits to private developers that led to the development of thousands of *casas baratas* (affordable houses) in the late 1920s.[25] The *casa barata* is a small, single-story rowhouse that was reproduced in large tracts, often on agricultural greenfield sites at the edges of cities. Built on a shoestring, these tiny rowhouses suffered from a lack of space, humidity and poor ventilation, but many nevertheless continue to be inhabited to this day.

During the short-lived Second Spanish Republic of 1931–1936, architecture took a markedly avant-garde turn, adopting the principles of the emerging Modern movement in architecture and urbanism, especially the ideas of Le Corbusier. Ambitious urban plans were drawn for some cities, most notably the *Macià Plan* for Barcelona, but the Spanish Civil War (1936–1939) and the ensuing military dictatorship of General Franco halted the implementation of many of these efforts.

Reconstruction after the Civil War was sparse due to the Franco regime's policy of autarky, producing very little social housing. It was not until the abandonment of autarky in the 1950s, when Spain's tourism industry was launched amid an opening up to foreign trade and influences, that social housing – for ownership more than rental – began to be built on a significant scale. As before, social housing took the urban form of large developments on greenfield sites at the peripheries of cities, though this time in the form of mid- to high-rise buildings that proved more difficult for rural migrants to adapt to, eventually leading to social problems in what was popularly termed 'vertical shantytowns.'[26]

The return of democracy to Spain in the late 1970s provoked major shifts and turns in urban planning and social housing construction, with large-scale modernist estates beginning to be eschewed in favour of more traditionally planned neighbourhoods, now including novel community facilities such as public libraries and secular schools. The last decades have consolidated this shift; however, government-developed social housing remains to this day a tiny percentage of overall housing construction, especially when compared to Scandinavian countries, Austria, or the Netherlands. Spanish housing policies continue, for the most part, to prioritise ownership,[27] an inheritance from the Franco dictatorship.[28] This is even the case for *social* housing, with rental tenancy forming an exception, though in the last years, the tide has begun to turn.

While sustainability for new construction is now written into all European building codes, it is being implemented in Spain mostly through improved thermal insulation and more efficient heating and air conditioning systems, or operational as opposed to embodied carbon. IBAVI differs from most other Spanish regional government housing agencies for its focus on affordable *rental* rather than owned housing, its efforts towards minimising operational *and* embodied carbon emissions, and for the bioclimatic and biophilic design of the buildings it develops.

> The developments IBAVI is building in a region seriously affected by tourist pressure and which, in 2019, had the worst housing accessibility index anywhere in Spain, show that protected public housing can be done differently, and that quality social housing, in terms of space, materials and the environment, is possible.[29]

Neo-Traditional, Vernacular and Critical Regionalist Precedents of IBAVI

Efforts to create radically more ecological buildings have been around for over half a century. The earliest efforts, however, were initiated outside of officialdom in a 1960s countercultural context. A notable example is the utopian Arcosanti project initiated in 1970 in the Arizona desert by Paolo Soleri, which, like IBAVI, attempts to minimise resource consumption. The 1980s saw the rise of the neo-traditionalist New Urbanism movement throughout the US to counter the ills associated with the urban sprawl of post-Second World War suburban development. IBAVI is also comparable with the Critical Regionalist movement in architecture, which also begun in the early 1980s, though in this case in a more academic context. The latter two movements arose out of a criticism of instrumental modernism and a loss of regional identity brought on by modern urban development; however, their architectural responses are markedly different. New Urbanism seeks to revert to the architecture and urbanism of the pre-automobile age, abandoning modernism, while Critical Regionalism seeks a built environment that reconciles modern architecture with locality and site specificity.

The Charter of the New Urbanism begins as follows:

> We advocate the restructuring of public policy and development practices to support the following principles: neighbourhoods should be diverse in use and population; communities should be designed for the pedestrian and transit as well as the car; cities and towns should be shaped by physically defined and universally accessible public spaces and community institutions; urban places should be framed by architecture and landscape design that celebrate local history, climate, ecology, and building practice.[30]

New Urbanism is mainly concerned with seeking an alternative to the suburban sprawl that typifies much post-war and contemporary development in the US, promoting instead master-planned communities that are walkable, compact, mixed-use, and incrementally built. Its urban planning principles, such as 'traditional neighbourhood development' (TND) and 'transit-oriented development' (TOD), emulate historic small towns in urban morphology, building typology, and architectural style. The New Urbanist demonstration project par excellence is the new town of Seaside, Florida, established in 1981 and master planned by Miami architects Andrés Duany and Elizabeth Plater-Zyberk using traditional town planning principles similar to those promulgated by Camillo Sitte.[31] A pastiche of the wood-framed, pastel-coloured, white-picket-fenced vernacular architecture of small-town southeastern US, Seaside was famously used as the filming location of the 1998 dystopian science-fiction movie *The Truman Show*, where it is depicted as the stage set of an insidious reality show.[32]

New Urbanism's motives for promoting traditional urbanism and architecture are mainly cultural; some say nostalgic.[33] Although the high environmental and human health costs of sprawl are often cited in New Urbanist critiques, the design methods behind NU counterproposals can be seen as rather doctrinaire, leading to a conviction held by some that it is in fact a neo-classicist movement that only vilifies sprawl – as well as modern architecture – for having broken with tradition and historical continuity. 'New Urbanists have placed themselves at the opposite end of the spectrum of urban ideologies vis-à-vis Modernists.'[34]

IBAVI, by contrast, bases its architectural approach upon the scientific research it undertakes into low-carbon building construction and operation, an approach whose built results resemble traditional vernacular buildings by coincidence more than doctrine.

> Traditional architecture is, by definition, the local resource map. That is, by regarding traditional architecture, we can discover the natural resources available at the time of construction.[35]

Indeed, IBAVI started its *Life Reusing Posidonia* demonstration building project by selecting the lowest carbon-emitting materials, many of which coincide with those used for traditional vernacular buildings, but designing with these materials in a contemporary architectural language. They soon realised that such a language was not, in fact, the most suitable one to use.

> When we designed Formentera, we still retained a certain heritage from orthodox modern architecture. At that time, we understood that traditional architecture was simply the lens through which we could access resources that until now we hadn't considered using. We believed that we should learn only the concept of traditional architecture, discarding its form. Later, with practice, we began to realize that when working with the repertoire of traditional architectural materials and trying to optimize their use, one finds formal results similar to those of vernacular architecture, without having initially sought them.[36]

Unlike historicist architects such as the New Urbanism movement, whose work seeks to establish continuity with another historical era, IBAVI goes to some length to stress that its architecture is, in fact, highly *contemporary*: it is based on the latest scientific research, employs cutting-edge technology and is a response to the contemporary climate emergency.

> Sometimes we are asked whether the design and construction model we are working with at IBAVI does not have an element of anachronism, precisely because we are recovering the materials from the Balearic resource map that gives rise to the vernacular architecture of each island. But the truth is that we arrived at this model thanks to the current information available on the internet, the latest digital tools for modelling and simulating atmospheric conditions, and CO_2 databases.[37]

Curiously then, IBAVI's work is highly specific to both its time *and* its place, when usually it is one or the other. New Urbanism, much like the influential architect Christopher Alexander, sees its architecture as 'timeless'[38] but specific to place, while the Modernist movement of the early to mid-twentieth century saw its architecture as placeless ('the international style') but specific to its time (in tune with the 'zeitgeist'). This is precisely why the Nazi regime of Germany banished the Bauhaus: Hitler believed that art and architecture had to be highly specific to place but *not* to time.

> Until the moment when National-Socialism took power, there existed in Germany a so-called 'modern art,' that is, to be sure, almost every year another one, as the very meaning of this word indicates. National-Socialist Germany, however, wants again a 'German Art,' and this art shall and will be of eternal value, as are all truly creative values of a people.[39]

The fact that IBAVI-built housing responds, in a timely manner, to our contemporary climate emergency makes it very much of its time, yet the bioclimatic architecture and the resource maps recommending local materials also make it highly specific to its place. Moreover, IBAVI buildings have been designed and built to last long – to be 'sustainable' – precisely because of our climate emergency. When instead of being re-used old buildings need to be demolished and replaced out of obsolescence, their embodied carbon is released into the atmosphere, figuratively speaking. The emerging notion of embodied carbon[40] greatly problematises demolition, urging us to build durably once again. For buildings to endure and withstand cultural and technological change, their spaces must be sufficiently flexible and adaptable to future changes of use that cannot be foreseen. For this reason, the dwelling units of IBAVI housing are designed with indeterminate, non-hierarchical rooms that can be used relatively interchangeably.

> This long-term flexibility strategy [via indeterminate, non-hierarchical rooms] responds to one of the main issues of the circular economy: durability as an alternative to planned obsolescence. The thing is that, at IBAVI, as public developers who own buildings [sic], as well as providing for the future comprehensive recycling of the buildings now being built, we prioritize their capacity to be transformed and adapted during their lifetime. And, in this sense, the type of space we propose works better on several levels, not only in terms of flexibility, but also in terms of reducing CO2 emissions and waste derived from a lesser need for demolition in order to adapt it.[41]

Modern architecture, which as we know sought to be of its time, is often termed 'functionalist' for its high degree of exactitude regarding the use of space. Every room in this type of architecture has a designated use, and every use has a designated space. It is also true that many Modernist buildings are today obsolete, for reasons of both functional inadequacy as well as energy inefficiency. The materials of architectural Modernism – steel, glass, concrete – have not aged or weathered well, moreover, requiring much cleaning, maintenance and repair work. For these reasons, works of modernist architecture are being demolished in many countries, with struggles often arising to preserve them.[42] Of course, by its very definition, a modernist architecture that embodies the zeitgeist or spirit of the moment was never intended to last a long time. With energy being plentiful and cheap at the time, demolishing and replacing modernist buildings was not an issue. Today, this is no longer so; the Anthropocene has rendered modernism itself obsolete.

Another reason for building durably while incorporating flexibility is social pluralism. Today's society is much more diverse, with many different types of households, including families with single or same-sex parents, cohousing and work-at-home households. Today the traditional nuclear family is a minority in many parts of Europe, so dwellings with rooms that are generic lend themselves to more diverse inhabitation scenarios.

Spatial flexibility is, then, an important aspect of housing that improves both individual and planetary well-being. A lack of flexibility demands adaptation on the part of the dweller, which is the case with most private-sector housing. Here, aspirational marketing and advertising are used to encourage adaptation with glee, creating a false sense of well-being. As Mirko Zardini has observed: 'the happiness industry asks us to relinquish our claim to transform the world around us, insisting instead that we transform ourselves, adapting to new moral and behavioural imperatives.'[43]

Another movement that emerged at approximately the same time as New Urbanism in the early 1980s is that of 'Critical Regionalism.' Unlike New Urbanism, and indeed post-modernist architecture in general, proponents of Critical Regionalism seek a reconciliation between Modernist architecture and the notion of place, rejecting historicist architecture as the way to redress the shortcomings of Modernism. Jürgen Habermas's notion of modernity as an 'incomplete project'[44] is influential here, but so is Martin Heidegger's notion of 'boundary' – a demarcation of place – as an essential component of Being.[45] The term Critical Regionalism was first coined by the architectural theorists Liane Lefaivre and Alexander Tzonis in 1981.

> Although this regionalism, which we may call critical regionalism, still derives from ideals of the singular and the local, of liberty and anti-authoritarianism, it fits into different social, economic, political, and cultural contexts. Its opponents are not the repressive absolutist regimes and their restrictive academic pseudo-universal theories, but the despotic aspects of the Welfare State and the custodial effects of modernism.[46]

As Kenneth Frampton puts it, 'The fundamental strategy of Critical Regionalism is to mediate the impact of universal civilization with elements derived indirectly from the peculiarities of place.'[47] More recently, by contrast, the emergence of Critical Regionalism has also been described as having 'supported socially engaged practices that addressed the crisis of modern architecture without rejecting its progressive sociopolitical agenda.'[48]

Both the Critical Regionalism school and IBAVI seek to root their work firmly in the climactic, topographic and cultural specificity of place while at the same time acknowledging contemporaneity. Nevertheless, some important differences remain. Whereas Critical Regionalist architects tend to use principally *modern* materials to build site-specifically, IBAVI uses both modern and local vernacular materials and methods in its constructions. Moreover, while IBAVI's architecture is ostensibly shaped by criteria of economy, service and sustainable building performance, Critical Regionalism constructs architecture as a more autonomous and poetic aesthetic expression. IBAVI thereby comes across as highly practical and vernacular in comparison to the more polemical ideological stance of Critical Regionalism. Indeed, in his essay on the work of IBAVI, Stephen Bates critically writes:

> while the research documented in published [IBAVI] projects focuses on materials and how to use them, these choices have consequences in terms of architectural form and language. [...] That is why, although explanations portray projects as determined by use and function or by the optimizing of cost constraints, it is also evident that these buildings are the result of formal decisions made on their own terms, at all scales.[49]

Indeed, Bates goes on to note that 'the poetic dimension of architecture, the artistic instinct, inspired by fundamental ideas of architecture, beyond mere function or problem solving, is not so explicitly acknowledged [by IBAVI].'[50]

It would seem that IBAVI is not very interested in participating in intellectual debates over architectural styles, attempting instead to create a contemporary vernacular building culture for the Balearic Isles. It must be remembered here that before the massive industrialisation and urban growth of the nineteenth century, architecture and housing were two very distinct categories. The only residential buildings designed by pre-industrial era architects were mansions for the land-owning class; the common dwelling was considered to belong to the lower, uneducated category of (vernacular) building.[51] Yet IBAVI, with its basis in scientific research and its use of digital climactic simulation, building information modelling (BIM), and building performance monitoring is clearly not in the category of vernacular building either, at least not in the traditional sense.

IBAVI's Learning Experience

After the pilot project *Life Reusing Posidonia*, IBAVI designed three experimental social housing projects in and around the Balearic capital city of Palma de Mallorca: one in a central neighbourhood, another in its urban periphery, and a third in a rural village outside the city. At each of these sites, local *Marés* sandstone was recommended by the local resource map as the most eco-efficient structural material. Accordingly, load-bearing stone piers and cavity walls were implemented in the design of each of these projects, which are moreover thermally insulated with cotton upcycled from locally discarded clothing. At the two peripheral locations, ground floor dwellings were structurally spanned by means of impressive stone vaulted ceilings, very probably unprecedented in the history of publicly built social housing (see Figures 10.4–10.6). Such an extensive structural use of stone forges a cultural bond with the history of the island of Mallorca, where local sandstone was used until the late 1960s for building everything from the Mediaeval stock exchange and the Cathedral of Palma to the most utilitarian barns, windmills and sheds.

> Justified on environmental grounds by its reduced carbon emissions, on economic grounds by its longevity, on social grounds for the promotion of local labour and on cultural grounds by being embedded in local vernacular buildings and its profound familiarity, [Marés stone] has literally become the 'bedrock' of many of IBAVI's recent projects.[52]

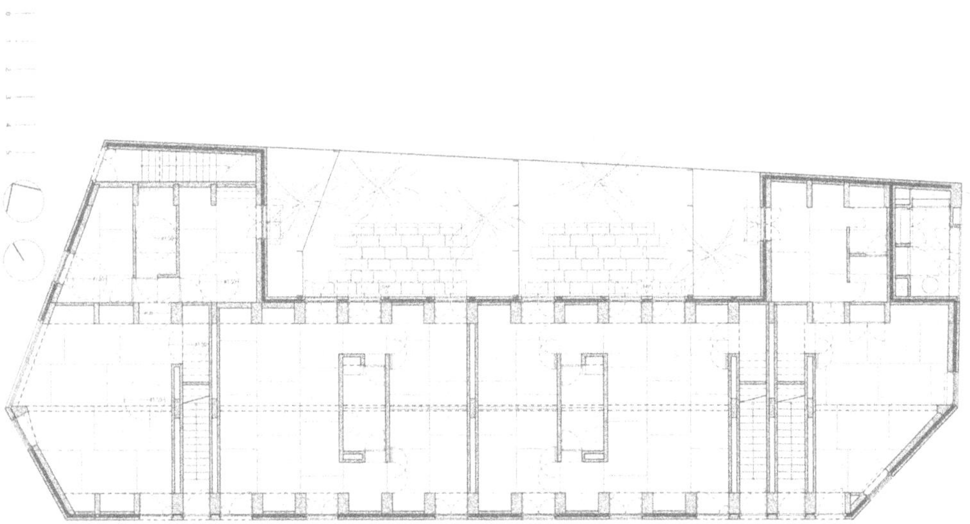

FIGURE 10.4 Ground floor plan, Salvador Espriu social housing, Palma de Mallorca, Balearic Isles, 2021. Plan ©IBAVI.

FIGURE 10.5 Exterior view, Salvador Espriu social housing, Palma de Mallorca, Balearic Isles, 2021. Photograph ©Milena Villalba.

FIGURE 10.6 Interior view, Salvador Espriu social housing, Palma de Mallorca, Balearic Isles, 2021. Photograph by author.

Subsequent projects initiated by IBAVI have progressed towards greater vernacularity in architectural form, and greater use of traditional natural materials; the result of a learning experience in which every completed project provides lessons to apply in subsequent projects. This increased presence of natural materials inside buildings also represents a transition towards biophilic design, which has been shown to provoke a psychological well-being in humans comparable to that of being in the presence of plants and animals.

> [Biophilic design] might involve incorporating natural materials like wood or stone into a building's design, or creating spaces that offer views of natural landscapes or access to natural light and fresh air. Biophilic design is based on the idea that humans have an innate connection to the natural world, and that this connection can have a positive impact on our health and well-being.[53]

Architectural forms that are biomimetic have a similar effect (see Figures 10.7–10.9): 'arches, vaults, and domes in the built environment resemble or copy forms found in nature, including beehives, nest-like structures, shell forms, and cliffs.'[54]

Yet IBAVI's use of natural materials is the result of research and experience gained from building low-carbon architecture, not from simply using what was close at hand. It is from an agenda of *sustainability* that the architectural quality emerges, doing so in a way that is moreover highly organic and natural as opposed to wilful and contrived.

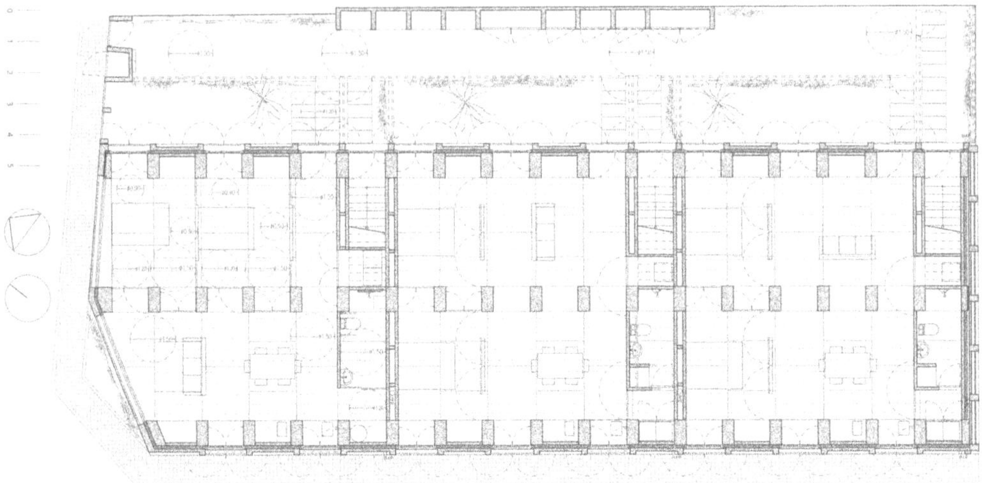

FIGURE 10.7 Ground floor plan, Ses Monges social housing, Santa Eugènia, Mallorca, Balearic Isles, 2022. Plan ©IBAVI.

FIGURE 10.8 Exterior view, Ses Monges social housing, Santa Eugènia, Mallorca, Balearic Isles, 2022. Photograph ©Milena Villalba.

FIGURE 10.9 Interior view, Ses Monges social housing, Santa Eugènia, Mallorca, Balearic Isleses, 2022. Photograph ©Milena Villalba.

Conclusion

The work of IBAVI shows that it is possible to build a truly vernacular architecture in a techno-scientific era. Theirs is not a pseudo-vernacular architecture built with modern – often toxic – materials in which nostalgic imagery is used merely as a superficial commercial marketing ploy. On the contrary, it is an architecture that has organically emerged from actual needs and an appropriateness of materials; an architecture coherent with both the time and the place in which it exists.

The design and construction methodologies perfected gradually by IBAVI through experimentation and empirical analysis, as well as the involvement of the many competition-winning architects IBAVI has commissioned, have yielded, in the end, a series of contemporary 'ordinary' residential buildings that are surprisingly comfortable, soulful and delightful; buildings that circumvent architectural dogma and whose natural materials and craftmanship uplift the human spirit while reinforcing local cultural identities. An intrinsic link between *planetary* well-being as well as *individual* or familial well-being can thus be clearly traced, showing that these different scales of well-being need not be considered mutually exclusive. Could it be that individual or familial well-being is in fact *improved* by taking better care of our planet? Is it possible that IBAVI's bioclimatic low-carbon architecture provides better individual and familial well-being precisely because it is *not* luxurious and ostentatious?

> A home serves as a shelter against a world that is shaped by the struggle to pay for that shelter. The bigger our home the more stressed we are to hang onto it—too exhausted

to really use it: bigger beds go with less sex and sleep; bigger kitchens with less cooking; bigger living rooms with less socialising; bigger windows with less looking outside; bigger terraces with less being outside.[55]

Perhaps planetary and individual or familiar well-being are in fact intrinsically and interdependently linked, rather than oppositional. Perhaps our contemporary western malaise comes precisely from our economy of plenty and an overabundance of 'luxury' that we all know to be planetarily unsustainable yet expect *others* to relinquish. Perhaps, not unlike IBAVI social housing, individual well-being is best achieved by being moderate, sensible and well-rounded with respect to our planet.

Notes

1 United Nations Environment Program (2022: 42).
2 Sekulova, Kallis, Rodríguez-Labajos, and Schneider (2013: 1–6).
3 Whitmee, Haines, Beyrer et al. (2015: 386).
4 Ballester Parets (2023: 9).
5 European Commission LIFE Public Database.
6 LIFE Reusing Posidonia Catàleg de materials sostenibles de les Illes Balears 2018.
7 Zhong, Hu, Deetman et al. (2021: 2).
8 *Posidonia oceanica* is also known as Neptune grass or Mediterranean tapeweed.
9 Oliver, Martín, and Moyá (2018: 80).
10 Oliver, Martín, and Moyá (2018: 101.)
11 The long-term durability of glue-laminated timber remains the subject of testing. See Uwizeyimana, Perrin, Laügt, and Eyma (2022).
12 Louis H. Sullivan's exact words were "form ever follows function." Source: Sullivan (1896: 403–9).
13 Pobiner (2014: 243).
14 This is perhaps somewhat more in line with Louis Kahn's famous statement: "You say to brick, 'What do you want, brick?' Brick says to you, 'I like an arch.'" See Lesser (2017).
15 Marta Peris has analyzed the flexible architecture of the traditional Japanese house through the films of Yasujiro Ozu. See Peris (2015).
16 International, national, and regional prizes won by the demonstration building *Life Reusing Posidonia* include: 2018 Iberian FAD Prize for Architecture, 2018 XIV Spanish Biennial for Architecture and Urbanism (BEAU) Award, 2019 Spanish Architecture Prize, 2019 EU Mies Prize shortlist, 2021 EU LIFE Environmental Award, 2022 Ibiza and Formentera Architecture Award.
17 Oliver (2023: 35).
18 Oliver, Martín, and Moyá (2018: 116).
19 Bates (2023: 353).
20 Oliver (2023: 25).
21 Cuchí (2023: 361).
22 Cró and Martins (2023).
23 Cerdà (1867).
24 Tizot (2018: 87).
25 Tatjer (2005: 194).
26 See Expósito Jiménez (2016).
27 World Population Review, Home Ownership by Country (2023).
28 The Franco regime's housing minister from 1957 to 1960, José Luis Arrense, famously stated in 1959: "We don't want a country of proletarians, but of property owners." Prime Minister Margaret Thatcher would echo this sentiment decades later.
29 Obal (2023: 7).
30 Charter of the New Urbanism.
31 Sitte (1945).

32 *The Truman Show* is possibly the only dystopic science-fiction film to have been shot at a real location designed with the best of intentions.
33 See, for example, Jarvis and Bonnett (2013: 2349–70).
34 Vanderbeek and Irazábal (2007: 43).
35 Oliver, Martín, and Moyá (2018: 41).
36 Oliver (2023: 29).
37 Oliver (2023: 27).
38 Alexander (1979).
39 Hitler (1937) as cited in Harrison and Wood 1992: 424.
40 Hammond and Jones (2008: 87–98).
41 Oliver (2023: 21).
42 See, for example, the conservation campaigns of the International Committee for Documentation and Conservation of Buildings, Sites and Neighborhoods of the Modern Movement (Docomomo).
43 Zardini (2019: 249).
44 Habermas (1983: 3–15).
45 Heidegger (1971: 154).
46 Lefaivre and Tzonis (2016: 125).
47 Frampton (1983: 21).
48 Giamarelos (2022: 1).
49 Bates (2023: 355).
50 Bates (2023: 357).
51 Adolf Loos famously stated: "an architect is a bricklayer who has learned Latin." See Loos (1924: 187).
52 Bates (2023: 353).
53 Sanglier Contreras, González Lezcano, López Fernández, and Pérez Gutiérrez (2023: 58).
54 Kellert (2008: 8).
55 Niermann (2019: 285).

References

Alexander, Christopher. 1979. *The Timeless Way of Building*. New York: Oxford University Press.
Ballester Parets, Cris. 2023. Interview by Obal, Liliana. *El Croquis* 219.
Bates, Stephen. 2023. "Man-Made Measure: IBAVI and the Quest for Identity." *El Croquis* 219.
Cerdà, Ildefons. 1867. *Teoría general de la urbanización, y aplicación de sus principios y doctrinas a la reforma y ensanche de Barcelona*. Madrid: Imprenta Española.
Charter of the New Urbanism. https://www.cnu.org/who-we-are/charter-new-urbanism, Accessed 12 May 2024.
Cró, Susana, and Antonio Miguel Martins. 2023. "Tourism Activity Affects House Price Dynamics? Evidence for Countries Dependent on Tourism." *Current Issues in Tourism*. https://doi.org/10.1080/13683500.2023.2204398, Accessed 12 May 2024.
Cuchí, Albert. 2023. "A Necessary Experience." *El Croquis* 219.
European Commission LIFE Public Database. https://webgate.ec.europa.eu/life/publicWebsite/project/details/3827, Accessed 12 May 2024.
Expósito Jiménez, David. 2016. "Memory of a nightmare." *Barcelona Metropolis* 101.
Frampton, Kenneth. 1983. "Towards a Critical Regionalism." In *The Anti-Aesthetic*, edited by Hal Foster. Port Townsend, WA: Bay Press.
Giamarelos, Stylianos. 2022. *Resisting Postmodern Architecture: Critical Regionalism Before Globalization*. London: UCL Press.
Habermas, Jürgen. 1983. "Modernity – An Incomplete Project." In *The Anti-Aesthetic*, edited by Hal. Foster Translated by Ben-Habib, Seyla. Port Townsend, WA: Bay Press.
Hammond, G. P., and C. I. Jones. 2008. "Embodied Energy and Carbon in Construction Materials." *Proceedings of the Institution of Civil Engineers - Energy* 161 (2). https://doi.org/10.1680/ener.2008.161.2.87, Accessed 12 May 2024.
Heidegger, Martin. 1971. "Building, Dwelling, Thinking." In *Poetry, Language, Thought*. Translated by Hofstadter, Alfred, New York: Harper Colophon.

Hitler, Adolf. 1937. "Speech Inaugurating the 'Great Exhibition of German Art." In As cited in *Art in Theory*, edited by. 1992. Charles Harrison, and Paul Wood. Oxford and Cambridge, Mass: Blackwell.

Jarvis, Helen, and Alastair Bonnett. 2013. "Progressive Nostalgia in Novel Living Arrangements: A Counterpoint to Neo-Traditional New Urbanism?." *Urban Studies* 50 (11). http://www.jstor.org/stable/26145585, Accessed 12 May 2024.

Kellert, Stephen R. 2008. "Dimensions, Elements, and Attributes of Biophilic Design." In *Biophilic Design: The Theory, Science and Practice of Bringing Buildings to Life*, edited by Kellert, Stephen R., Judith Heerwagen, and Martin L. Mador. Hoboken: Wiley.

Lefaivre, Liane, and Alexander Tzonis. 2016. *Times of Creative Destruction: Shaping Buildings and Cities in the Late C20th*. London: Routledge. https://doi.org/10.4324/9781315550916, Accessed 12 May 2024.

Lesser, Wendy. 2017. *You Say to Brick: The Life of Louis Kahn*. New York: Farrar, Straus and Giroux.

LIFE Reusing Posidonia. Catàleg de materials sostenibles de les Illes Balears. 2018. http://eng.reusingposidonia.com/catalog-of-materials/, Accessed May 12, 2024.

Loos, Adolf. 1924. "Ornament and Education." In *Ornament and Crime: Selected Essays*. Riverside: Ariadne Press.

Niermann, Ingo. 2019. "This Home Will Make You Happy." In *Our Happy Life: Architecture and Well-Being in the Age of Emotional Calitalism*, edited by Francesco Garutti, MOntreal and Berlin: Canadian Centre for Architecture and Sternberg Press.

Obal, Liliana. 2023. "Protected Public Housing: An Alternative Model." In *El Croquis* 219.

Oliver, Carles. 2023. Interview by Obal, Liliana. *El Croquis* 219.

Oliver, Carles, Antonio Martín, and Joaquín Moyá. 2018. *Life Reusing Posidonia*. Palma: IBAVI.

Peris, Marta. 2015. "La casa japonesa a través del cine de Yasujiro Ozu." PhD dissertation. Barcelona: Universitat Politècnica de Catalunya. http://hdl.handle.net/10803/403498, Accessed 12 May 2024.

Pobiner, J.A. 2014. "The Impact of Population Increase and Urban Migration on Global Sustainability and Quality of Life." In *Sustainable City VIII*, edited by S.S. Zubir and C.A. Brebbia. *Southampton*: WIT Press.

Sanglier Contreras, Gastón, Roberto A. González Lezcano, Eduardo J. López Fernández, and María Concepción Pérez Gutiérrez. 2023. "*Architecture Learns from Nature. The Influence of Biomimicry and Biophilic Design in Building*." *Modern Applied Science* 17 (1). https://www.researchgate.net/publication/370345940_Architecture_Learns_from_Nature_The_Influence_of_Biomimicry_and_Biophilic_Design_in_Building, Accessed 12 May 2024.

Sekulova, Filka, Giorgos Kallis, Beatriz Rodríguez-Labajos, and Francois Schneider. 2013. "Degrowth: from Theory to Practice." *Journal of Cleaner Production* 38. https://doi.org/10.1016/j.jclepro.2012.06.022, Accessed 12 May 2024.

Sitte, Camillo. 1945. *The Art of Building Cities: City Building According to Its Artistic Fundamentals*. New York: Reinhold.

Sullivan, Louis H. March 1896. "The Tall Office Building Artistically Considered." *Lippincott's Magazine,* 403–9.

Tatjer, Mercedes. 2005. "La vivienda obrera en España de los siglos xix y xx." In *Scripta Nova* IX 194. https://www.ub.edu/geocrit/sn/sn-194-23.htm, Accessed 12 May 2024.

Tizot, Jean-Yves. 2018. "Ebenezer Howard's Garden City Idea and the Ideology of Industrialism." (La Cité-jardin d'Ebenezer Howard et l'idéologie de l'industrialisme). *Cahiers Victoriens et Edouardiens* 87. https://doi.org/10.4000/cve.3605, Accessed 12 May 2024.

United Nations Environment Program. 2022. *2022 Global Status Report for Buildings and Construction: Towards a Zero-emission, Efficient and Resilient Buildings and Construction Sector*. 42. Nairobi.

Uwizeyimana, Placide, Marianne Perrin, Emmanuel Laügt, and Florent Eyma. 2022. "Durability Study of Glulam Timber Under Cyclic Moisture Loading." In *Construction and Building Materials* 315. https://doi.org/10.1016/j.conbuildmat.2021.125715, Accessed 12 May 2024.

Vanderbeek, Michael, and Clara Irazábal. 2007. "New Urbanism as a New Modernist Movement: A Comparative Look at Modernism and New Urbanism." *Traditional Dwellings and Settlements Review* 19 (1). http://www.jstor.org/stable/41758514, Accessed 12 May 2024.

Whitmee, Sarah, Andy Haines, and Chris Beyrer et al. 2015. "Safeguarding Human Health in the Anthropocene Epoch: Report of The Rockefeller Foundation–Lancet Commission on Planetary Health." *The Lancet* 386. https://doi.org/10.1016/S0140-6736(15)60901-1, Accessed 12 May 2024.
World Population Review, Home Ownership by Country. 2023. https://worldpopulationreview.com/country-rankings/home-ownership-by-country, Accessed 12 May 2024.
Zardini, Mirko. 2019. "This Happiness Is Making Me Suffer." In *Our Happy Life: Architecture and Well-Being in the Age of Emotional Capitalism*, edited by Francesco Garutti. Montreal and Berlin: Canadian Centre for Architecture and Sternberg Press.
Zhong, X., M. Hu, and S. Deetman et al. 2021. "Global Greenhouse Gas Emissions from Residential and Commercial Building Materials and Mitigation Strategies to 2060." *Nature Communication* 12, 6126. https://doi.org/10.1038/s41467-021-26212-z, Accessed 12 May 2024.

11

LIVING TOGETHER WITH DEMENTIA

Domestic Rearrangements

Lilian Chee and Lim Kun Yi James

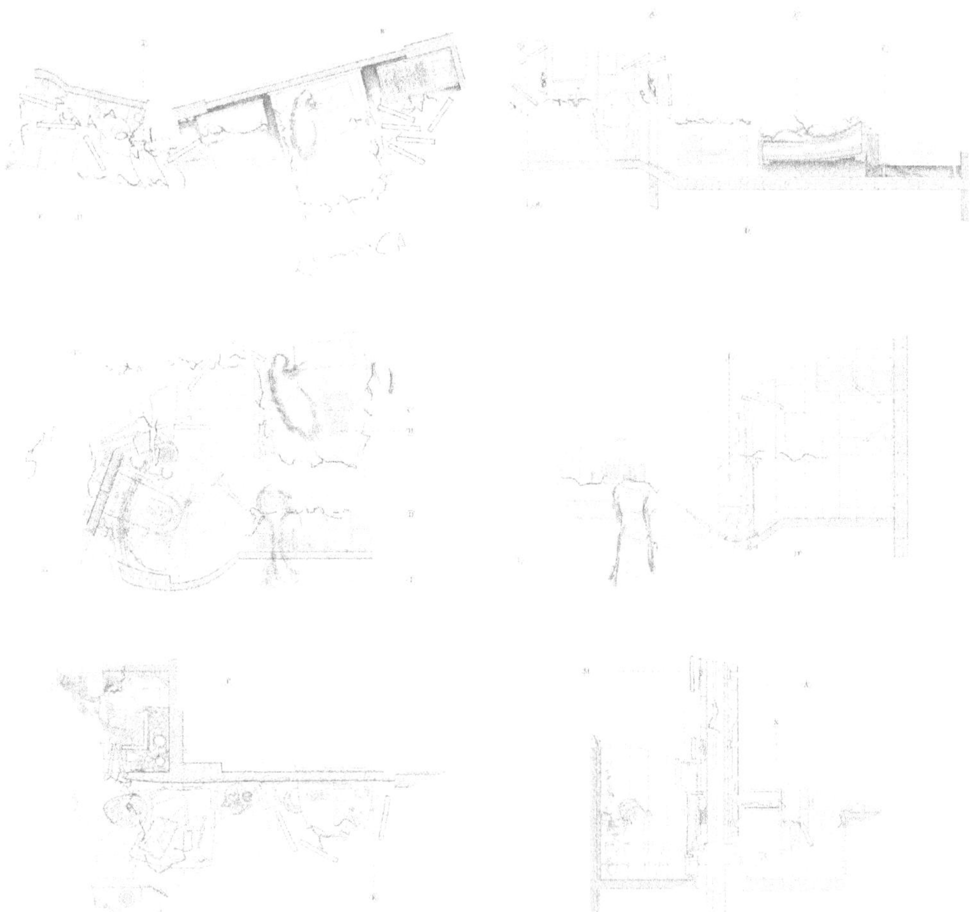

FIGURE 11.1a 'Hallucinatory Cartographies,' Lim Kun Yi James, *Please Give Gong Gong a Call*, 2023.

DOI: 10.4324/9781003527930-16

Visual Studies into Lewy Body Dementia

A Protraction of Thresholds; Parkinson's-like symptoms
cognitive; mobility
Shuffling walk, slowed movement or frozen stance; Tremor or shaking most commonly at rest; Stooped posture.

A' Protraction of Thresholds; Parkinson's-like symptoms
cognitive; mobility
A 30mm step down into the bathroom is perceived as a 300mm ledge, requring the LBD body to brace itself physically and mentally each time they cross this tiny sliver of threshold space.

B Task Repetition
cognitive
Difficulty planning or keeping track of sequences (poor multi-tasking)

C Visual hallucinations
cognitive
Visual hallucinations occur in up to 80 percent of people with LBD, often early on. Nonvisual hallucinations, such as hearing or smelling things that are not present, are less common than visual ones but may also occur.

C' Visual hallucinations
cognitive
5 people stay with Gong Gong - A burly man who sleeps beside him, a lady who sleeps on the floor by his bed, and 2 teens who reside in the living room.

"they are driving up my electricity bills and won't go back to their homes!"

D Surface Prosthesis
mobility
Balance problems and repeated falls: Using surfaces to approximate a series of islands/surface supports for movement within and between rooms.

D' Surface Prosthesis
cognitive; mobility
Grab bar placements are important in providing viable convenient routes within rooms. Yet the placement of a grab bar here before the bathroom folding door presents an obsolete source of support for Gong Gong.

E Spatial Cognition; Complex Tasks
cognitive
Difficulty with sense of direction or spatial relationships between objects; Trouble with problem solving or analytical thinking - in this case, the routines of grooming, bathing and evacuating the body.

F Object Orientation and Permanence
cognitive
Wayfinding takes reference from the body as opposed to space. A turn of a head/torso obscures a view and erases space, troubling the wayfinding process of the lewy body elderly.

G Incontinence
physiological
Loss of bladder and bowel muscle control particularly at night

H Plastic Sheet; Urine Pad
physiological; caregiving
Layering plastic sheets and urine pads in incontinence-prone areas alters the materiality and maintenance of the bed - crinkling sounds, regular washing and the detective work of scent detection the next morning.

I Object-Category Recognition
cognitive
Difficulty with sense of direction or spatial relationships between objects; The categories of objects between pull-out drawer, rubbish chute and laundry machine become flatenned into one.

I' Object-Category Recognition
cognitive
Water supplies become indiscriminate - brown water, tap water and water dispensed from the shower head. The tap then becomes a space dedicated for washing the hair and wiping down after the wet bath.

J Boundary Registration
cognitive
The corner of the room facing the window beside the bathroom door registers as a suitable space to relief oneself, the deteriorating body experiences a threshold just by encountering it.

K Stacking Under
cognitive; caregiver
Concealing soiled and dirty laundry under stacked pails underneath the table to prevent visual and literal contamination.

L Discretising Bathing Process
cognitive; caregiver
Breaking down complex tasks of dressing and drying from bathing; Personal affects kept nearby for sense of security; Spillover of bathroom rituals into kitchen/laundry surfaces

M Built-away Thresholds; Storage
cognitive; caregiver
Thresholds and slivers of tucked away spaces become prime real estate for the live-in helper to tuck away - a makeshift built-in for a packet of detergent, scrub, sponge, scrapper, mop, tongs.

N Surface Colonisation
cognitive; caregiver
Surfaces adjacent to thresholds of rooms and processes become integral to the process of discretising and simplifying cleansing rituals to prevent cognitive challenges and visual distractions.

FIGURE 11.1b

Three sets of corresponding distorted and fragmented plan and section drawings of domestic interiors depicting the decline in visual-spatial cognition and mobility of a Lewy Body Dementia elderly.

Through a spatial-somatic reading of Lim's grandfather's (Gong Gong) flat, a series of fragmentary visual studies into the elderly man's behavioural and psychosocial episodes were produced. Paired with care work annotations and categorised Lewy Body Dementia (LBD) symptoms, the drawing is dialogically positioned between medical literature and LBD's affective experiences. In embodying Gong Gong's particularised modes of visual-spatial cognition, the drawing adopted unconventional techniques to overlay the difficulties of care and Gong Gong's distressed bodily postures. These include using a non-dominant hand and atypical digits to draw; binding the arm to restrict joint articulation; and transcribing hallucinatory recounts of care episodes experienced between Lim, his grandfather, the family and their live-in helper.

Dementia-in-the-world: Dementia, Ageing and the Spilt Self

> A 50mm step is a 500mm cliff drop. Gong Gong takes a long pause each time he reaches the bathroom door. Just like when he gets up from the sofa, you see him tensing. Preparing to shift his body and launch it into a new posture in a room that to him seems familiar yet not quite so. That moment of entering the bathroom feels like an eternity, pronounced in time, distance, and anxiety.

Dementia is framed in biomedical terms as a chronic and progressive condition affecting memory, cognitive abilities, emotions, motivations and behaviour which may debilitate the affected person's daily life (WHO 2023). Persons suffering from dementia, ranging in type and severity including vascular dementia, Alzheimer's disease, Lewy Body dementia and frontotemporal lobe dementia, amongst others, often experience spatiotemporal disorientation. This, in turn, produces difficulties in verbal communication, contextual understanding and social relations. Age is known as the biggest risk factor but because dementia is not categorised as part of normal ageing and is incurable, it is often seen as an intractable problem faced by individuals, families, societies and policy makers. There remains considerable stigma surrounding the illness (Higgs and Gilleard 2017; Lee 2024, 22–61; Swinnen and Schweda 2015, 9–20).

Challenging biomedical perspectives, there is now research from the fields of critical gerontology, performance studies and critical dementia studies which reframe dementia as a sociocultural construct as much as an incurable disease (Ward and Sandberg 2023; Zeilig 2014). The sociocultural construction of dementia emphasises a movement to recover personhood, an aspect often denigrated by the illness. Social initiatives and critical research into dementia aim to return dignity and humanity by considering degrees of autonomy and agency possible in the life of affected persons. Dementia activism (Bartlett 2014) and awareness of ageing citizens' rights have accelerated across many countries making possible transformed policies and collaborative platforms which bring together diverse parties including affected individuals, their families, their immediate communities, volunteer agencies, and state bodies involved in housing, care and health as stakeholders (Kiyota 2018, 2019a). The last two decades' return to the agential capacity of persons living with dementia (PLWD) for self-determination of their own lives has gradually shifted the approach from one of dependent care to enabling life with dementia in the midst of others (Hydén and Antelius 2017).

Yet, a persistence on normality, even in the life course of ageing, poses barriers for embracing radical change in mindsets. The elderly find themselves cornered by institutional demands to enrol as active stakeholders in increasingly normalised calls for 'healthy ageing' where illness lands them in a doubly alienated position of being biologically old *and* regrettably disabled by disease. To this end, critical dementia studies have situated dementia in the realms of disability and disability rights to challenge a 'curative imaginary' which aligns futurity with curative possibilities (Shakespeare et al. 2019; Thomas and Milligan 2018). Adopting instead an inclusive 'crip futurity' (Kafer 2013; Rice et al. 2017) which adapts and reimagines environments and social structures for differently abled bodies and minds means that mainstream ideas of dependent elderly care and its isolating environments which disconnect and further disable, also need retooling.

In 'Dementia is Dead, Long Live Ageing,' psychologist Julian C. Hughes (2013, 1:835) outlines why it is problematic when 'dementia' seemingly refers to a singular 'discrete disease entity.' This tendency undermines dementia's range of conditions and symptoms. It oversimplifies dementia's complex suite of diseases. In doing so, clinical research and practice truncate the understanding of dementia's varied diagnoses and implications. Referring to the definition of 'dementia' as typically encompassing 'cognitive failure, chronic behavioural dislocation and psychosocial incompetence' (Berrios 1987). Hughes highlights how dementia research is often conducted through a 'hypercognitive' lens, erroneously eliding the psychosocial and behavioural impairment that accompany this condition. This argument outlines the pitfalls of isolating the experience of dementia as separate from 'ageing,' especially in the drawing of an artificial and often opaque threshold between diagnosis and pre-/un-/under-diagnosis: 'It is by no means simply a matter of scoring above or below a cutoff on a memory test. "Dementia" affects the whole person, and judgments about dementia must, accordingly, be whole-person judgments' (Hughes 2013, 1:838). Instead, Hughes (2013, 1:845) suggests a 'broadening concept' where the 'possibility of difference (of alternative ways to experience life)' is steeped within a 'host of biological, psychological, social and spiritual concerns.' Hughes' (2011) 'dementia-in-the-world' implies that old age is to be lived in the world, rather than sequestered away from the fullness and complexities of life.

Instead of pathologising old age, 'dementia-in-the-world' urges a consciousness towards the broad lens of ageing, countering social bias that consigns the elderly to debilitated modes of living (Bavidge 2005 quoted in Hughes 2013, 1:845). Hughes (2013, 1:846) notes that in engaging ageing 'as a proxy for living,' we can start to alter perceptions of the ageing body in 'ways that are creative and potentially therapeutic.' 'Dementia-in-the-world' necessitates a cultural and historical embodiment amidst other beings and requires comprehension of ageing persons through an understanding of their personal narratives and intimate life stories. Hughes also argues for the situated nature of human beings and that it is through relationships with others that our own subjectivity becomes realised: 'We need to see the person as a situated human being, who engages with the world in a mental and bodily way in agent-like activities, showing (amongst other things) desires, choices, drives, emotions, needs, and attachments' (Hughes et al. 2006).

The experience of care in the modelling of dementia-in-the-world asks for our 'whole sight' (Hughes et al. 2006) which means not dislocating the person from their various diminishing faculties. Such solicitude demands attentiveness and concern for the infirmed other as part of one's community. Instead of 'doing to' PLWD, the emphasis here shifts to 'being with' them (Hughes 2013, 1:847). Following this framework of being-in-the-world, 'our practical arrangements for and social attitudes toward our ageing lives' (Hughes 2013, 1:847) are altered. 'In-the-world' in this chapter refers specifically to the familiarity of domestic space as sites where relational identities are being co-constructed through modes of care, supported by new conceptions of spaces that allow for the elderly to being-in-the-world as they live out their lives.

To understand how an elderly person might possibly live freely amongst others first requires an understanding of how the elderly self realises/is realised and how s/he perceives/is perceived. Writing three volumes on ageing – *A Very Easy Death* (1964), *The Coming of Age* (1970) and *Old Age* (1977) – Simone de Beauvoir casts the ageing person as socially a marginalised and abject entity (Pickard 2023). Yet, the ageing self is not merely clarified biologically and socially but comes into being through a psychological process of personal discovery, the unravelling of a human condition which De Beauvoir focuses on. Philosopher Sara Heinämaa (2014) points out that de Beauvoir's thesis shows how ageing is a sudden transformation, and that ageing poses an unexpected existential crisis since there is a tension between how we know ourselves and how others perceive us. We *become* old as we relate to and encounter others, who see in us an *other*, a disparate self. For the child, this passage of becoming other signals towards a delimiting adolescence, while in old age, the horizon is foreshadowed by death:

> The crucial idea here is that our own bodies are always given to us in a double way: originally and immediately as systems of sensibility and motility, and secondarily and mediately – via our relations with others – as perceptual and movable objects. These are not two separate realities but are two sides or dimensions of one complex phenomenon.
>
> *(Heinämaa 2014, 173)*

In *Old Age*, de Beauvoir reiterates the psychosocial consequences of this bodily disparity. In the chasm between 'the other-in-me' which manifests through the gaze of the other, and the 'for ever present me' which exists as an unshifting sense of self, De Beauvoir conceives a 'double alienation' (Gilleard 2022, 286) experienced in ageing. She lodges the condition of ageing as 'still recognizably my body but alienated,' both in the onset of realising self-identity and later from 'which old age only alienates further' (Gilleard 2022, 288). Jean Paul Sartre, whose work De Beauvoir responds to, iterates such alienation by distinguishing the precedence of the 'body-for-others' as an externalised and socialised entity realised for presentation to others, over the 'body-for-itself' a subjective and often hidden entity aligned with one's perception of oneself (Sartre 2003 quoted in Gilleard 2022, 289). Thus, old age materialises the self as external from the body and the elderly person is frequently 'realised through the gaze of the other' (Gilleard 2022, 288). De Beauvoir argues that in old age 'our being-for-ourselves – is incrementally subsumed beneath our embodiment for others' (Gilleard 2022, 289). The 'I' that we perceive ourselves diminishes until it is gone.

The argument for ageing-in-place, at home, is meant to mitigate this existential loss. Surrounded by people and objects the ageing person holds dear, the spilt between how they are perceived externally versus who they believe they are, is held in abeyance. Yet, ageing-in-place presupposes that 'place' is more or less stable. In this situation, how the home is configured – in its placement of objects, by the familiarity of social relations, and through persistence of everyday routine – is key. Furthermore, while architecture is specifically signposted as catering to different and often marginal groups, including women, children, the elderly, the disabled, the refugee/migrant, amongst others, truly inclusive architecture, for example, housing, should embrace all groups of people without needing specialisation. This means that if something is designed to afford good light, ventilation and thermal comfort; enable connectivity and freedom without compromising safety (latterly enhanced through assistive technologies); and encourage sociality by preserving contexts for new companions and tangible opportunities for reviving shared experiences, then that architecture should be adjustable for all groups. Hence, designing for dementia and the elderly – important aspects of humanity's diversity – is in essence designing better spaces for everyone.

In the second section, we offer a historical overview of Singapore's public housing landscape as it prepares itself for an imminently ageing demographic. Originally constructed around a youthful citizenry, since the 1990s, housing policies and design have begun to address a population where more than 21% are expected to reach 64 years of age in 2026. There are several challenges to overcome. Firstly, care remains dependent on a unitary model of the family core, a structure coincident with Singapore's housing policies. Secondly, while public housing suggests shared amenities and spaces, affected

FIGURE 11.2 'Mealtime,' Lim Kun Yi James, *Please Give Gong Gong a Call*, 2023.

Plan drawing of lunch preparation itinerary, delineating a route through three adjacent housing units.

'Mealtime' depicts a travelling sous chef – Gong Gong – as he meanders across neighbouring flats amidst lunch preparations to oversee his neighbours' cooking techniques. The intricate repertoire of tasks to prepare a meal deters cognitive decline by engaging hand-eye-mouth coordination, olfactory and gustatory systems, and muscle and procedural memory (Lekker Architects and Lanzavecchia + Wai Design Studio 2020, 128). Echoing Julia and Paul Child's kitchen mapping diagrams, the drawing choreography co-creates mealtime through 'conscious enabling relationships to cooking techniques, ingredients, tools, and domestic spaces' (Penner and Rice 2024). By reconfiguring shared rituals to encircle Gong Gong's living and migratory body, concerted mealtime repertoires work to preserve his agency through decision-making exercises and interactions with loved ones in meaningful and involved ways.

persons and their carers are often contained within the insularity of their homes/flats as newer housing promotes more privatised and insular living with no common corridors, removal of ground-level open void decks and fewer neighbours living on each floor. Thirdly, centralised care facilities are separated from communal and domestic infrastructure, ultimately resisting opportunities for community-based models of care and mutual efficiencies within the extended networks of a lived housing block. In other words, housing models which prioritise privatised space, nuclear family living and centralised care amenities are at odds with the communality and familiarity desired by affected occupants and their families. Contrasting bureaucratic structures, we revisit the Ibasho principles for elderly care with its focus on relationality, tactility, continuity and agency.

In the third and final section, we demonstrate how doing architecture for dementia necessitates a constant movement between, and an attention to, different scales and objects – from the interior of the flat to the public spaces of the block; between the concerns of domesticity to matters of housing and planning. We will examine these shifts through a discussion of three creative practice outputs: *Objects for Thriving* (2022) by filmmaker Ian Mun and architectural and visual theorist and creative practitioner Lilian Chee, a short film on ageing, identity and reservoirs of memory, and *Losing Myself* (2015–ongoing) by academic Yeoryia Manolopoulou and architect Niall McLaughlin, a research on dementia and conceptions of space. We conclude with *Please Give Gong Gong a Call* (2023–2024) by designer Lim Kun Yi James, a design and drawing research on how to imagine public housing for dementia occupants and their carers. Additionally, Lim's annotated drawings feature in between the sections of this chapter offering a parallel narrative of architecture for dementia. In so doing, the ambition is to shift the conception of spaces for living with dementia from that of caring in isolation to an affective architecture of scenarios, bound by relationality and social compacts. The implication here is that architecture might recover its utopian purpose as a social condenser, serving a group where the fundamental question of what it means to be human is ultimately at stake.

Ageing in Place: Healthcare and Housing in Singapore, with a Rejoinder

> There have been many DIY modifications to Gong Gong's furniture. We reduced the height of his bed to prevent another accident. Then, he began to scratch his arm against the bed frame. An open wound formed. Mum said the elderly have "butterfly skin".

Dementia-in-the-world proposes that the world around those with dementia also change for the better. Indeed, designing for dementia is a test of architecture's ability to accommodate difference: the ageing population's changing neurodivergent identities and their transformed relationships with surrounding places and people. In this section, we discuss housing and healthcare infrastructure for an ageing population in recent Singaporean context, outside of the bounds of the institutional nursing facility. Ageing in the home for as long as possible is critical to maintain the older person's identity and body image. Given that autonomy is stripped from older persons through social bias, we ask what kind of care in the built environment might restore and rebuild this spilt self. Here, we situate architecture's role as mediating in-between biomedical and sociocultural perspectives. Beyond fulfilling urban restructuring plans and providing medical and care infrastructure for an ageing population, we look to architecture's proactive agency in imagining and configuring possible scenarios where the elderly might thrive.

Following United Nations' standards, a nation assumes 'super-aged' status when the proportion of its population aged 65 and above surpasses 21% (MCA 2024). In Singapore, national-level healthcare initiatives, policy-informing research and care frameworks preparing citizens for the inevitability of old age are fully operational. During the 2023 President's Address, Minister for Health and Minister-in-charge of Ageing Issues, Ong Ye Kung, unveiled *Healthier SG*, a national enrolment-basis healthcare initiative spearheaded by the Ministry of Health (MOH) in response to the country's oncoming status by 2026. Encouraging early disease detection, tiered financial assistance schemes for chronic conditions, and monetarily incentivised adoption of healthy lifestyle programmes (MOH 2022) the rollout mirrors social pressures and national priorities confronting Singapore's once-youthful population.

By 2030, Singapore will join the ranks of more mature nations like Japan, Germany, Italy, South Korea and the US (Visaria and Malhotra 2023), far more rapidly than her global counterparts with a quarter of its citizens constituting this metric. According to Singapore's Ministerial Committee on Ageing (MCA), an expected 83,000 elderly residents will live in isolation and roughly 100,000 elderlies will suffer mild disability, requiring assistance to conduct minimally one daily task by 2030 (MCA 2023, 8). Refreshed in 2023, the *Action Plan for Successful Ageing* led by the MCA expounds three core pillars: 'Care, Contribution, Connectedness' to galvanise government agencies, voluntary welfare organisations, academic research, corporate sectors and community leaders (MCA 2023, 7). A decade-long funding for a multi-ministry taskforce involving health, housing and transport sectors will reform transport networks and domestic infrastructure to enable active ageing and enhanced care services (MCA 2024). Since 2014, 36 Silver Zones in designated housing estates have pioneered safer elderly mobility (MOT, n.d.) in line with age-friendly neighbourhoods. Active Ageing Centres (AAC) foster community partnerships with religious organisations and interest groups to broaden the reach of care networks.

Dementia management assumes a key focus with 1 in 10 Singaporeans aged 60 afflicted (Subramaniam et al. 2015). Following the shift to early identification, assessment and management, 16 memory clinics, 61 Community Outreach Teams (CREST) with Post Diagnosis Support (PDS) service and 24 Community Intervention Teams (COMIT) island-wide form an on-ground social armature for at-risk seniors and caregivers (MCA 2023, 37). Enhanced research on dementia, particularly scalable and novel care models demonstrating capacities in delaying and managing dementia are nationally funded (MCA 2023, 38).

A longitudinal design ethnographic study (AIC, CLC, and SUTD 2019) found that PLWD and caregivers are more sensitive to urban risks and stimuli, noting that built environment changes should 'introduce choice and new purposes incrementally' and 'preserve spaces that hold positive familiarity and value for residents' (Chiu and Lim 2023, 103). Pilot community-based participatory action research (CTPCLC and Dementia Singapore 2020) also engaged PLWD and caregivers in grassroot community workshops to raise dementia-awareness and implement murals as wayfinding anchors (Nanda et al. 2022). Noting the rise in Young-Onset Dementia and the rippling impact of dementia on family caregivers, Dementia Singapore explores individualised care, bringing support services into the home and neighbourhood to defer admission into specialised care facilities that heighten delirium and accelerate cognitive decline in absence of familiar spatiotemporal routines (Nanda et al. 2022). More senior volunteers are participating in befriender programmes, acting as caregivers to peers through meal preparation and para-counselling services (Ng and Koh 2023).

In large part, these schemes exist as social compacts requiring not just top-down funding but also ground-up initiatives, anticipating that demand for eldercare over the next decade might overwhelm national healthcare capacities if not managed downstream. With most Singaporeans residing in public housing, the issues of ageing, care and connectedness have decidedly become key threads to the rejuvenation of ageing housing estates. In effect, the most relevant place to understand the needs of ageing residents is to study their needs at home.

Housing almost 80% of the population nationwide (DOS 2023), Singapore's leading public housing agency, Housing and Development Board (HDB hereafter), continues to be influential in its research and policies for growing together with the country's rapidly ageing population. HDB has been similarly pre-emptive in its policies on the changing resident demographic. Such policies transition from the preferred nuclear family popularised in the 1970s to an extended family structure in the 1990s. Several national initiatives since the 1990s address homeownership for an evolving workforce by shifting from housing provision for married couples with children to new singleton occupants and a burgeoning elderly demographic. These include priority balloting schemes and housing grants for homeowners who choose to stay near parents (HDB, n.d.-b). Across flat typologies, HDB has provided several senior housing options including new and resale multigenerational flats and purpose-designed community-care apartments launched in 2021 with pre-fitted senior-friendly fixtures (HDB, n.d.-c). Since 2009, the government purchases a portion of the lease for older flats through the Lease Buyback Scheme, allowing elderly homeowners to remain in their homes with lifelong fixed-sum monthly payouts until the residents themselves expire (HDB, n.d.-a).

Estate-scaled pilot schemes like integrated purpose-built high-rise housing village for the elderly were realised in Kampung Admiralty (2015) (Zhuang 2020) and planned for Yew Tee (2027) (Lin and Chan 2021). HDB's most recent health-focused age-friendly neighbourhood and precinct design, the Health District @ Queenstown, was announced in 2021. Situated within one of Singapore's oldest housing estates, the pilot scheme for research and policy on integrated health and living is a multidisciplinary and cross-sector effort (HDB, NUHS, and NUS 2021) to create an environment affording 'preventive health and care delivery programmes' reconfigurable to other housing estates (HDB 2021).

Singapore's coordinated national drive to prepare for ageing through healthcare initiatives and housing provisions is significant. At the same time, intensively choreographed age-friendly infrastructure could also be conceptualised to remain intentionally 'unfinished,' open to occupant input. Co-experiencing such infrastructure – a place for many bodies and minds, bringing together young adults and children together with the elderly – can begin to address issues of isolation and loneliness often exacerbated by exclusively age-focused design. Co-creation is key to ownership, since 'community is something that we make with others' (Kiyota 2018, S49). Today, the oldest public housing estates in Singapore have either been upgraded to cater to new demands of the multigenerational family or demolished to make way for ageing residents and shrinking young families. Collectively, these Estate Renewal Programmes – introduced in 1995 in alignment with HDB's 5-year building programmes – often involve a complete overhaul of older housing stocks, including demolishing landmarks crucial for memory and orientation. The wholesale renewal of neighbourhoods departs from current efforts to 'anchor ageing in the community' (MCA 2024). Environmental gerontologist Emi Kiyota (2018) emphasises that the challenge for architecture is to create an environment that does not sequester the elderly away but provides connectivity to the world at large so that elders can be supported without having to drastically change their lives or sever relationships.

In the Queenstown pilot, the Margaret Drive Active Ageing Centre could potentially distinguish itself. A ground-up initiative to engage seniors in varying degrees, from programme organisation to workshop facilitation, or simply participating (Li 2024), it is a collaboration between local social service agency FaithActs with global non-profit Ibasho, founded by Kiyota. *Ibasho* which translates to 'a place where you can feel like yourself,' is an elder-led community that engages the elderly population as 'change agents' (Kiyota 2019a, 172). Founded in 2011, the eldercare model was pioneered in the town of Ofunato following the devastation wrought by the Great East Japan Earthquake. Since then, Ibasho has culturally adapted and led elderly programmes in other post-disaster sites including Nepal and the Philippines (Aida et al. 2023). The elder leaders and community members planned, built and still lead operations and programming of the Ibasho Café, which has been instrumental in the physical and psychological recovery of the Ofunato community. In its first 6 years of operation, the Ibasho Café has served more than 70,000 people and hosted more than 5,250 events, at which elders shared knowledge on traditional cooking, organised a farmer's market, led afterschool care groups and showed young people how to manage daily life without electricity (Kiyota 2024).

Kiyota (2018) asks if there is a middle ground between well-intentioned institutional care on the one hand, and keeping the elderly living for a longer time in their own homes, on the other hand. Through Ibasho, the aim is to change elderly care mindset from that of 'total independence or near-total dependence' into one of interdependence and relationality. The organisation works with elderly leaders through formal and informal ways to 'co-create physical infrastructure that is then managed by the elders' (Aida et al. 2023, 1). Through the social and collaborative placemaking process, a robust social network can grow and social capital is strengthened between community members. The Ibasho method focuses on relationality, interdependence, continuity and tactility, privileging use of existing sites and systems which are recognisable, adaptable so as to grow together with their occupants.

In *Home Bodies,* literary critic James Krasner (2010) similarly advocates tactile and embodied domesticity as central to identity-construction. He argues that life-altering events such as grief, ageing and chronic illness demand a somatic reconfiguration of our relations with our homes, memories and identities. Reconceptualising domestic space through tactility instead of kinaesthesia, 'one we push and rub up against rather than moving through gracefully' (Krasner 2010, 16), the home is constituted primarily through relations of attachment and togetherness, as opposed to isolation. Tactile domesticity informs an occupant's 'body schema' as opposed to their 'body image.' The former 'describes the continual, sensorimotor mapping of the body in relation to its immediate surroundings,' while the latter constitutes the 'neural self-representation of one's body in relation to surrounding space, based in part on memory and habit' (Krasner 2010, 16). For the elderly whose cognitive abilities are in decline, a body schema's affective domestic space allows for new experiences and new memories to be made.

Advocating a middle ground, Krasner (2010, 28) asks how to mend the binary between 'the healthy and the impaired body,' especially given that other bodies – in grief, in pain, in confusion, under stress – are essentially fragmented rather than healthy and whole. He references feminist author and bioethicist Rosemarie Garland-Thompson's (1997) work on the figuration of the 'culturally normative body' where spaces built for the normative body inevitably polarise and debilitate non-normative bodies, 'The cripple before the stairs, [...] the amputee before the typewriter, and the dwarf before the counter' (Krasner 2010, 23). This universal body image is entrenched in Ernst Neufert's ubiquitous Architect's Data (Neufert and Neufert 2012), a handbook for architects (Boys 2017, 141). Instead, the body schema depends on rituals, relationships and interdependent interactions between ourselves and the people around us which that 'other bodies become incorporated into our body image' (Krasner 2010, 33). We are defined through our relationality with people and things around us. Such relationality is accentuated particularly for the elderly whose definition of selfhood becomes increasingly eroded through social bias and isolation. Hence, tactile domesticity is an affective and relational space made of objects and people, routines and practices, which grow and adapt into a domestic realm where we 'understand our bodies as companied, accompanied, beloved' (Krasner 2010, 33).

In this situation, where and how architecture might operate most effectively, and what forms it could take, if not on the scale of the building, need reconsideration. In *Architecture and Affect*, Lilian Chee (2023a) argues for architecture's potential to operate critically from the middle ground. Placing itself in connection to, and in the midst of things, rather than a standalone object, architecture is conceived as a situation-specific construct which leverages on relationality between sites, human and nonhuman subjects and objects, practices and relationships. Thinking through a situation means that architectural methods cannot proceed from *a priori* assumptions of what is best for the dementia elderly from architecture's perspective. Best practices of safety and security in design for example, often lead to isolation, alienation and anxiety amongst elderly and their caregivers (Kiyota 2019b; Manolopoulou 2022). To create architecture from within affective dementia relations and situations means to listen for, record and translate new patterns of becoming: fear towards shadows, forgetting and remembering via objects and arrangements, enjoying a day out in the sunshine, being around with others who care. In a situation where the ageing self requires a scaffolding of things, relationships and rituals to create affective contexts for new memories and experiences, the opportunity is not just to adjust architecture for an elderly population but as de Beauvoir has argued, the occasion opens itself to changing architecture so it accommodates all minority groups.

In other words, making and thinking architecture through relationality benefits everyone. The shift in perspective here will entail relooking at architecture in two ways: first, as spatial strategy for sociality, longevity and respite, and second, as creative modality for new expressions of ageing and dementia drawn from lived experiences. These shifts will influence how we see, make, draw, think about, and with, the ageing occupant, or imagine what PLWD, might appreciate. If the future horizon seems increasingly limited for the elderly, how can spaces and ways of living be imagined, moving away from an unlimited futurity towards a richly textured and eventful present time?

FIGURE 11.3 'April Showers,' Lim Kun Yi James, *Please Give Gong a Call*, 2023.

Plan drawing of two bathrooms connected by a meandering route that Gong negotiates when it is time for his shower. The plan shows a series interconnected passageways articulated by openings, vestibules, gaps, doors, windows, sliding panels, etc.

'April Showers' shadows Gong Gong's intimate bathing ritual. Here, the 'bathroom' is no longer confined to one area but spatially scattered throughout the flat. Gong Gong meanders, pauses, undresses, and cleanses between two wet rooms, pursuing his own unravelling spatial itinerary. Space and time scatter and stretch as 'bathing' happens across his flat and over an afternoon. Tracing Gong Gong's detour, a continuum of tactile supports (Lekker Architects and Lanzavecchia + Wai Design Studio 2020, 181) engender autonomy and resist an 'environmental centralisation' of infirmed bodies (Krasner 2010, 146). The design co-opts shelves, table tops, door frames, and a kitchen countertop as inconspicuous forms of support. It works through 'leaky' typologies – anterooms, courtyards, bathroom stack shafts, windows which are envisaged to connect eight neighbouring units – to create a network of caregiver stations. The neighbourhood monitors Gong Gong's roaming body through amplified shadows and sounds, enacting a neurodiverse landscape of co-presence and collective care.

As surgeon Atul Gawande (Gawande and Tippett 2017) emphasises, the most important question for doctors attending to elderly patients facing their later years of decline is neither better medications nor better medical procedures but simply asking, what a good day would look like to such persons. For architecture, as much as medicine, it would be to understand what the elderly would prioritise for happiness and fulfilment given their loss of control and independence. In short, tangible and achievable well-being is key. In the last section, we look at what architecture's creative practice research might reveal about enabling well-being in this limited but challenging situation.

Doing Architecture for Dementia: Objects, Rituals, Domesticities for Well-Being

> In Gong Gong's kitchen, red and white pails nest like Russian dolls under the marble table. Dirty clothes are tucked in between the pails to discourage further rummaging episodes. Clothes soaked in urine are separated from clothes soiled with sweat and flaking skin.

In the essay film *Objects for Thriving* (Mun and Chee 2022), three elderly homeowners are depicted in their own flats in the suburban public housing estate of Whampoa, located in southeastern Singapore. The estate has a high prevalence of older occupants, with more than 10% being over 65 years of age. Since 2015, a pilot project led by non-profit organisation Tsao Foundation has supported elderly residents here allowing them to age in their homes for as long as possible (Basu 2015). One of us went into the estate prompted by questions of legacy and heritage, but ultimately to articulate how cultural memory might resonate with citizens on the ground. Focusing on three domestic objects – a Butterfly brand sewing machine, a granite pestle and mortar, and talismans deemed to bring good fortune to the family home – the film observes how personal memory is acquired and preserved, asking the septuagenarians and octogenarians what is meaningful and how life might be lived to the fullest within their modest public housing flats.

The three women are in good health. In turn, they take good care of the objects which reciprocally serve them – the sewing machine and the pestle and mortar were, respectively, bought or handed down when the two women got married. In the third family flat, talismans of various shapes and materials are hung in significant corners of the large flat combining two separate units; one owned by the mother, and the other by her son and daughter-in-law. The talismans extend the aura of family altars, one placed in the front room and the other at the rear end of the flat. These objects are essential to scaffold memory, both old and new ones (Krasner 2010; Rubinstein and Parmelee 1992, 47). These objects allow the older occupants to thrive because they trigger memory, evoke lived experiences and events, become points of conversation, signal care and stewardship and mark a lineage between the elders' past and their families' future. The reciprocity of care between person and object extends to the domestic spaces where these objects are held. The flats also enable these elderly to thrive. They house the objects whose heft and bulk appear anachronistic and out of place for today's compressed daily rhythms.

These domestic objects reveal how psychical, social, material and cultural relations come together in their midst. Chee (2023b, 2022) has argued elsewhere that 'domesticity' can act as an analytical frame to delineate the fine-grained material-social configurations of belonging, which escape definition in the monolith concepts of 'home' or 'housing.' Such domestic configurations include a network of physical and imagined spaces; passive and active agents; mundane and ritualistic practices; housing policies and identity politics, class and gender norms, and the uneven distribution of power and resources including that of affective care labour. Drawing on Judith Butler's (2016) conception of bodily vulnerability being interwoven into our surrounding infrastructure, Chee (2023c) makes a case that to think public housing through the analytic of domesticity is to conceptualise an affective infrastructure of interdependency where architecture is equally fragile and granular, wedged in-between things human and nonhuman. Seeing a flat through objects enmeshed within their complex domestic settings enables an understanding of lived space, multi-perspectival experience and shared aspiration, often obscured by architecture's defined brief, its specialised modes of representation and its singular history. Within domesticity's ambit, what might an architectural process or project resemble?

Repositioning the architect's vision and control in the realm of lived experiences, the multimodal research project *Losing Myself* (Manolopoulou and McLaughlin 2022, 2016) begins by returning to a nursing home, the Alzheimer's Respite Centre in Dublin by Niall McLaughlin Architects, completed in 2009. Built within an eighteenth-century walled garden, the centre occupies the middle of three terraced levels. It was planned as a series of new garden rooms where occupants could freely wander while anchored to their surroundings by changing seasonal light and evolving garden colours and textures, much like one could do if one were at home. When management of the facility changed from volunteers to professional healthcare workers, the occupants' independence was traded for their safety, and the building's autonomous agency came into question (McLaughlin 2020, 56).

Referencing a tapestry of perspectives from disciplinary and user expertise housed in an inclusive website (Manolopoulou and McLaughlin 2016), architect/academic Yeoryia Manolopoulou (2022) describes their attempt at a dialogical approach to reconsider the Dublin facility after seven years of use, but particularly to get past architecture's own blind spots of 'best practices.' Constructed around a rich ethnographical archive of dialogue which involves careful listening, *Losing Myself* captures diverse voices from neurological, gerontological and anthropological research, caregiving stories, patient anecdotes, healthcare accounts and lessons from art, media and design.

Using dialogue as a creative method, the multimedia installation at the 15th International Architecture Exhibition at the Venice Biennale involved 16 draughtspersons attempting to redraw imagined experiences and movements of 16 occupants using the Dublin facility. The 16 partial and hybrid plan drawings enacted a series of open-ended negotiations within the facility's base plan drawing, where significantly, each drawing was recorded on film, 'as actions rather than as static artefacts' (Manolopoulou 2020, 305). It is the action, the experiment of ephemeral, collaborative, relational and partial drawing – drawing after or before another person; drawing in relation to one's immediate perception of specific objects and spaces; drawing with partial knowledge which is not drawing blindly but often drawing deeply detailed and textured manifestations – that comes closest to accounts from dementia patients and their carers about how the world comes into focus for the former. The act of being in another's position and sensing location and sequence, without the tools and cognition we have taken for granted, makes the social drawing radical and important to designing for dementia.

Contrasting the architect's all-seeing, sole-authored allocentric plan to the egocentric cognitive abilities of dementia individuals who comprehend relationships from self to other in simpler, circumstantial and scenario-specific instances (Manolopoulou 2020; Manolopoulou and McLaughlin 2022, 26), *Losing Myself* might be seen as the architects' own search for another kind of spatial sense that reconciles not just the dementia patient's loss but equally our myriad, fragmented, and perhaps confused experience of the world around us. The '16 lessons' (Manolopoulou and McLaughlin 2022) about care, autonomy, connections, the benefits of staying home and living with purpose,

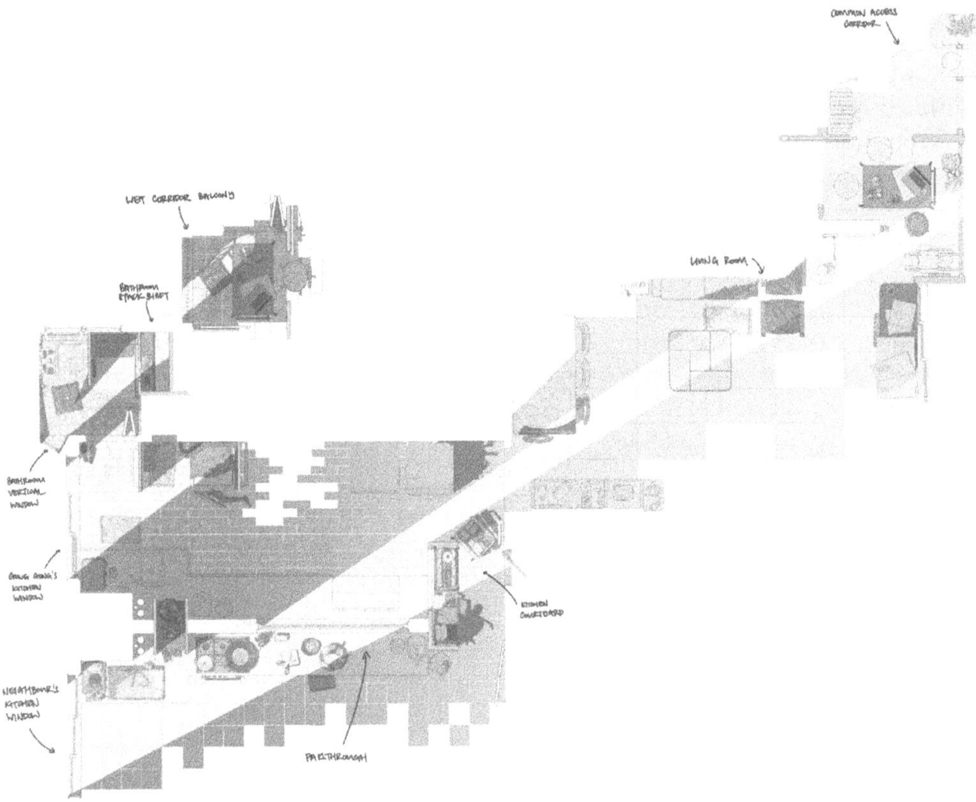

FIGURE 11.4 'Shall We Greet the Sun?,' Lim Kun Yi James, *Please Give Gong Gong a Call*, 2023.

Plan drawing showing sunlight streaming through a kitchen window connecting one adjacent unit to the next, and towards the common access corridor outside the individual units. Hallucinated figures are depicted amongst the shadows.

'Shall We Greet the Sun?' captures the liminal moment of twilight – before sunrise and after sunset – when long shadows turn into phantasmic figures. In the high-rise insular public housing block, the act of greeting the sun is enabled through a series of connected apertures: from a neighbouring unit's kitchen window, through another's drawn curtain, passing between a mesh frame housing fidget objects for Gong Gong, and out into the external common access corridor. Intensified visual and auditory hallucinations during 'sundowning' – a term describing a state of confusion that starts after sunset and lasts into the night – causes spectral anxieties in the LBD elderly (Khachiyants et al. 2011, 275). Olfactory, textural and aural prompts – morning coffee, bedtime moisturiser, birdsong – situated along this passage of light, act as sensory anchors. These anchors reinforce the occurrence of diurnal cycles, reminding Gong Gong there will be light soon.

amongst others, are concrete and specific scenarios drawn from external expertise and expert users. These are instructive of the kind of situational spatial sense that architecture needs to embrace and to be in-the-midst-of. Mclaughlin (2020, 53) writes that our 'spatial sense' determines how we understand the world, and as such is a 'cornerstone of the self,' which begins to erode as we lose our bearings together with 'who we are in our deepest identity.'

Conclusion: Another Dementia Story

> The window facing the corridor is Gong Gong's portal to the outside world. He cannot move too much but he likes to sit by the window. Here, he rocks his body back and forth, back and forth. It is at this window that we say hello to Gong Gong during our visits.

In place of a conclusion, we would like to tell another dementia story.

The drawings featured in this chapter are from *Please Give Gong Gong a Call* (2023–2024), a speculative design project by one of us that examines how shared boundaries configured around the domestic routines of an LBD elderly might reconceptualise alternative care networks. Lim's family's struggle with caregiving prompted his research. Through a constellation of 'leaky' typologies that connect eight neighbouring units, the design research is based on his own experience as a carer to his Gong Gong (grandfather) who suffers from dementia. The design for collective care literally begins from inside out, starting from objects, activities and relationships within the life of an LBD elderly, radiating out towards the architectural fabric of the public housing flat and the block.

In weekly research sessions with Chee, his then thesis tutor, Lim would skirt around the design thesis, spending a lot of time describing a meticulously drawn plan punctuated with verbal tales of his grandfather's domestic adventures. These include: how Gong Gong's bathtimes are adventurous romps between two bathrooms; Gong Gong's regular sightings of a Malay woman he recognised seemingly marooned on an island in his dark living room where the couch is located; Gong Gong asking if he had come to visit by boat; Gong Gong's flat having six rooms with another floor below (mixing up his three bedroom flat with his ancestral house in Hainan); how all kinds of visitors ended up sitting on Gong Gong's bed, watching TV into the night and driving the electricity bill up! These were probably longer-term memories from Gong Gong's past, lived on another faraway island but played out behaviourally and emotionally in his small Singapore flat. Yet, the colourful dementia stories remained frustratingly outside of Lim's architectural drawings.

Not unlike what Manolopoulou and McLaughlin have emphasised, Lim struggled with the autonomy of the allocentric plan drawing and his knowledge of the public housing flat. His personal lived experience with his grandfather's scrambled sequence of space and time, interfered with his own disciplinary training. The questions of how to draw and how to think otherwise of the given – a room, a door, a couch and a bed – which no longer held known meaning or hierarchies, forced a series of drawing experiments. Significantly, Lim also figured out ways of retelling these stories authentically, not short-changing their vibrancy and details. He wrote a brief that was cyclical, taking lessons from these stories, and one that regarded architecture as a tactile somatic frame, something existing amidst everything else, to support Gong Gong who needed to be cared for, and equally, to sustain Gong Gong's caregivers who would need to be there for him, for the long haul:

> For those who suffer from dementia or who can no longer communicate, the only story left may be the simplest kind: two lovers embrace; a mother holds a child. Such stories can only be told with the body, through the sense of touch. The caregiver creates a space in which that story can be told and offers a body to help tell it, even when doing so is perilous and terrifying.
>
> *(Krasner 2010, 136)*

As Krasner (2010, 190) notes, 'domesticity can be collapsed to the body's edge; we can feel at home irrespective of the architectural space that surrounds us through sharing body image or bodily engagements with others, or simply through certain somatosensory comforts.' This leaky domesticity – from an intimate bathroom shaft to a convivial common access corridor – disrupts the atomistic family model by involving many others in the performance of care 'in-the-world.' Lim's project approaches care for the neurodiverse elderly, situated in the public housing flat, as a shared, co-creative and enabling enterprise where new insights for what it means to be human, and what humanity can offer each other in all our differences, are supported by domestic architectural rearrangements percolating from a piece of furniture to the entire housing block. This is not to say that what dementia patients and their families face are negligible. Yet, in diversifying the scales of dementia care from flexible third spaces to affective intimate spaces, *Please Give Gong Gong a Call* argues that caregiving can be something we shoulder together. And the concept of ageing in place can develop into a vision of having lived, loved, and been loved by others, while remaining at home together. Enabled by architecture's renewed purpose as social condenser, the dementia elderly's legacy of dignity, humour and hope may be glimpsed against a kinder and caring future horizon.

Acknowledgements

This research is supported by the William Lim Siew Wai Fellowship towards the project 'Limited Study on Dementia, Care and Housing' (Grant Number: E-470-00-0088-01; Ethics Approval Code: NUS-IRB-2024-217) under the NUS Centre for Cultural Studies in Asia (CSA).

Bibliography

AIC, Agency for Integrated Care, Centre for Liveable Cities CLC, and Singapore University of Technology and Design SUTD. 2019. 'Dementia-Friendly Neighbourhood Study: Singapore's First Local Evidence-Based Dementia-Friendly Environment Design Project'. Singapore.

Aida, Takeshi, Emi Kiyota, Yasuhiro Tanaka, and Yasuyuki Sawada. 2023. "Building Social Capital with Elders' Leadership through a Community Hub "Ibasho" in the Philippines and Nepal." *Scientific Reports* 13 (3652): 1–7. https://doi.org/10.1038/s41598-023-30724-7.

Bartlett, Ruth. 2014. "The Emergent Modes of Dementia Activism." *Ageing and Society* 34 (4): 623–44. https://doi.org/10.1017/S0144686X12001158.

Basu, Radha. 2015. "Whampoa's Way: Residents Live out Their Golden Years in Their Own Homes." *The Straits Times*, 14 April 2015. https://www.straitstimes.com/singapore/housing/whampoas-way-residents-live-out-their-golden-years-in-their-own-homes.

Bavidge, Michael. 2005. "Ageing and Human Nature." In *Dementia: Mind, Meaning, and the Person*, edited by Julian C. Hughes, Stephen J. Louw, and Steven R Sabat, 41–53. Oxford: Oxford University Press.

Berrios, G. E. 1987. "Dementia during the Seventeenth and Eighteenth Centuries: A Conceptual History." *Psychological Medicine* 17 (4): 829–37. https://doi.org/10.1017/S0033291700000623.

Boys, Jos, ed. 2017. *Disability, Space, Architecture: A Reader*. London; New York: Routledge, Taylor & Francis Group.

Butler, Judith. 2016. "Rethinking Vulnerability and Resistance." In *Vulnerability in Resistance*, edited by Judith Butler, Zeynep Gambetti, and Leticia Sabsay, 12–27. Durham and London: Duke University Press.

Chee, Lilian. 2022. "Housing and Domesticity." *Architecture and Culture* 10 (3): 554–58. https://doi.org/10.1080/20507828.2022.2121898.

Chee, Lilian. 2023a. *Architecture and Affect: Precarious Spaces*. Routledge Research in Architecture. London: Routledge.

Chee, Lilian. 2023b. "Domesticity and the Architecture Film: Caring-With Architecture." In *Architectures of Care*, edited by Brittany Utting, 1st ed., 43–68. London: Routledge. https://www.taylorfrancis.com/books/9781003296553/chapters/10.4324/9781003296553-4.

Chee, Lilian. 2023c. "Domesticity, Gender, and Architecture." In *The Routledge Companion to Contemporary Architectural History*, edited by Duanfang Lu, 185–201. Routledge. https://doi.org/10.4324/9781315674469.

Chiu, Elly, and Ren Ai Lim. 2023. "Creating Dementia-Inclusive Neighbourhoods through Partnerships with the Community; Singapore | Inclusive Communities." In *Urban Solutions Issue 22: Building Partnerships*, edited by Shawn Tan, Geraldyne How, and Nicole Lum, 98–104. Singapore: Centre for Liveable Cities.

CTPCLC, NUS Chua Thian Poh Community Leadership Centre, and Dementia Singapore. 2020. "Building an Inclusive Dementia Friendly Community (iDFC) in Kebun Baru." Singapore.

DOS, Singapore Department of Statistics. 2023. "Households - Latest Data." Government Agency. SingStat. 2023. http://www.singstat.gov.sg/find-data/search-by-theme/households/households/latest-data.

Garland-Thomson, Rosemarie. 1997. *Extraordinary Bodies: Figuring Physical Disability in American Culture and Literature*. New York: Columbia University Press.

Gawande, Atul, and Krista Tippett. 2017. "Atul Gawande: On Mortality and Meaning." On Being with Krista Tippett. 26 October 2017. https://onbeing.org/programs/atul-gawande-on-mortality-and-meaning/.

Gilleard, Chris. 2022. "Aging as Otherness: Revisiting Simone de Beauvoir's Old Age." *The Gerontologist* 62 (2): 286–92. https://doi.org/10.1093/geront/gnab034.

HDB, Housing & Development Board. 2021. "HDB | Health District @ Queenstown." Government Agency. HDB InfoWEB. November 2021. https://www.hdb.gov.sg/about-us/news-and-publications/publications/dwellings/Health-District-Queenstown.

HDB, Housing & Development Board. n.d.-a. "HDB | Lease Buyback Scheme." Government Agency. HDB InfoWEB. Accessed 15 July 2024. https://www.hdb.gov.sg/residential/living-in-an-hdb-flat/for-our-seniors/monetising-your-flat-for-retirement/lease-buyback-scheme.

HDB, Housing & Development Board. n.d.-b. "HDB | Priority Schemes." Government Agency. HDB InfoWEB. Accessed 29 July 2024. https://www.hdb.gov.sg/residential/buying-a-flat/buying-procedure-for-new-flats/application/priority-schemes.

HDB, Housing & Development Board. n.d.-c. "HDB | Seniors." Government Agency. HDB InfoWEB. Accessed 29 July 2024. https://www.hdb.gov.sg/residential/buying-a-flat/understanding-your-eligibility-and-housing-loan-options/flat-and-grant-eligibility/seniors.

HDB, Housing & Development Board, National University Health System NUHS, and National University of Singapore NUS. 2021. "Pilot Health District in Queenstown to Focus on Residents' Holistic Well-Being." *NUS News*, 20 October 2021, sec. Press Release. https://news.nus.edu.sg/pilot-health-district-in-queenstown-to-focus-on-residents-holistic-well-being/.

Heinämaa, Sara. 2014. "Transformations of Old Age: Selfhood, Normativity, and Time." In *Simone de Beauvoir?S Philosophy of Age: Gender, Ethics*, edited by Silvia Stoller, 167–87. De Gruyter. https://philarchive.org/rec/HEITOO-2.

Higgs, Paul, and Chris Gilleard. 2017. "Ageing, Dementia and the Social Mind: Past, Present and Future Perspectives." *Sociology of Health & Illness* 39 (2): 175–81. https://doi.org/10.1111/1467-9566.12536.

Hughes, Julian C. 2013. *Dementia Is Dead, Long Live Ageing*, edited by K.W.M. Fulford, Martin Davies, Richard G.T. Gipps, George Graham, John Z. Sadler, Giovanni Stanghellini, and Tim Thornton. Vol. 1. Oxford University Press. https://doi.org/10.1093/oxfordhb/9780199579563.013.0049.

Hughes, Julian C., J. Stephen, Steven R. Louw, and Sabat, eds. 2006. *Dementia: Mind, Meaning, and the Person*. International Perspectives in Philosophy and Psychiatry. Oxford; New York: Oxford University Press.

Hydén, Lars-Christer, and Eleonor Antelius. 2017. *Living with Dementia: Relations, Responses and Agency in Everyday Life*. London: Palgrave Macmillan.

Kafer, Alison. 2013. *Feminist, Queer, Crip*. Bloomington: Indiana University Press. https://www.jstor.org/stable/j.ctt16gz79x.

Khachiyants, Nina, David Trinkle, Sang Joon Son, and Kye Y. Kim. 2011. "Sundown Syndrome in Persons with Dementia: An Update." *Psychiatry Investigation* 8 (4): 275. https://doi.org/10.4306/pi.2011.8.4.275.

Kiyota, Emi. 2018. "Co-Creating Environments: Empowering Elders and Strengthening Communities through Design." *Hastings Center Report* 48 (S3): S46–49. https://doi.org/10.1002/hast.913.

Kiyota, Emi. 2019a. "IBASHO CAFÉ Giving Elders a Role to Play in Making Communities More Resilient." In *The Global Age-Friendly Community Movement : A Critical Appraisal*, edited by Philip B. Stafford, 169–87. New York: Berghahn Books. https://doi.org/10.1515/9781785336683-013.

Kiyota, Emi. 2019b. "Living with Independence and Purpose." In *Ethos* Issue 20, edited by Alvin Pang. Singapore: Civil Service College Singapore. https://knowledge.csc.gov.sg/ethos-issue-20/living-with-independence-and-purpose/.

Kiyota, Emi. 2024. "Ibasho Model of Elder Empowerment." 24 April 2024. http://generations.asaging.org/ibasho-model-elder-empowerment.

Krasner, James. 2010. *Home Bodies: Tactile Experience in Domestic Space*. Ohio State University Press. http://www.jstor.org/stable/10.2307/j.ctv16qk3fb.

Lee, Heunjung. 2024. "Performing (Ab)Normal: Reframing Ageing, Dementia, and Temporality." https://era.library.ualberta.ca/items/a30cca24-427d-4e3b-8fa1-5b7c631eaa76.

Lekker, Architects, and Lanzavecchia + Wai Design Studio. 2020. *Hack Care: Tips and Tricks for a Dementia-Friendly Home*. https://hackcare.sg/.

Li, Thian Wen. 2024. "Pilot Project in Queenstown Aims to Get Seniors to Lead and Plan Activities, Contribute to the Community." *The Straits Times*, 30 March 2024. https://www.straitstimes.com/singapore/pilot-project-in-queenstown-aims-to-get-seniors-to-lead-and-plan-activities-contribute-to-the-community#:~:text=This%20is%20the%20first%20Ibasho,are%20aged%2065%20and%20above.

Lim, Kun Yi James. 2023–2024. *Please Give Gong Gong a Call*. M Arch Thesis, Singapore: National University of Singapore.

Lin, Cheryl, and Emil Chan. 2021. "HDB Unveils Key Features of Yew Tee 'Vertical Kampung' Project, with Housing for Seniors." *Channel News Asia*, 21 October 2021, sec. Singapore. https://www.channelnewsasia.com/singapore/yew-tee-development-kampung-hdb-senior-healthcare-2257792.

Manolopoulou, Yeoryia. 2020. "Performing the Architectural Plan: Egocentric and Allocentric Drawing." In *Arts & Dementia*, edited by Ruth Mateus-Berr and L. Vanessa Gruber, 294–309. De Gruyter. https://doi.org/10.1515/9783110720556-019.

Manolopoulou, Yeoryia 2022. "Dialogic Drawing." In *Developments in Neuroethics and Bioethics*, 5:173–97. Elsevier. https://doi.org/10.1016/bs.dnb.2022.08.005.

Manolopoulou, Yeoryia, and Niall McLaughlin. 2016. *Losing Myself*. http://www.losingmyself.ie/.

Manolopoulou, Yeoryia, and Niall McLaughlin. 2022. "Losing Myself: Architecture and Dementia." In *Design Research Folios*, edited by Manolopoulou, Yeoryia, Barbara Penner, and Phoebe Adler. London: Bartlett Design Research Folios.

MCA, Ministerial Committee on Ageing. 2023. *2023 Action Plan for Successful Ageing: Living Life to the Fullest*. Singapore: Ministry of Health.

MCA, Ministerial Committee on Ageing. 2024. "What Is Age Well SG?" Government Agency. Age Well SG. 2024. https://www.agewellsg.gov.sg/about/.

McLaughlin, Níall. 2020. "Losing Myself: Designing for People with Dementia." *Architectural Design* 90 (6): 50–59. https://doi.org/10.1002/ad.2631.

MOH, Ministry of Health Singapore. 2022. "White Paper On Healthier SG." Government Agency. Ministry of Health Singapore. 21 September 2022. https://www.moh.gov.sg/news-highlights/details/white-paper-on-healthier-sg.

MOT, Ministry of Transport. n.d. "MOT Singapore – Inclusive Transport Infrastructure." Government Agency. Ministry of Transport. http://www.mot.gov.sg/what-we-do/motoring-road-network-and-infrastructure/inclusive-transport-infrastructure.

Mun, Ian, and Lilian Chee, dirs. 2022. *Objects for Thriving*. Documentary. NUS and Roving Productions. https://www.youtube.com/watch?v=ZYtBmE4_Qrk.

Nanda, Akshita, Charlene Chua, and Rebecca Pazos. 2022. "Living Outside with Dementia: How Singapore Builds Its Dementia-Friendly Neighbourhoods." *The Straits Times*, 21 September 2022. https://www.straitstimes.com/multimedia/graphics/2022/09/dementia-neighbourhoods-singapore/index.html?shell.

Neufert, Ernst, and Peter Neufert. 2012. *Architects' Data*. 4th ed. Chichester, West Sussex, UK; Ames, Iowa: Wiley-Blackwell.

Ng, Sabrina, and Fabian Koh. 2023. "More Seniors Stepping Forward as Caregivers to Their Peers, as Singapore Approaches "Super-Aged" Status." CNA. 16 May 2023. https://www.channelnewsasia.com/singapore/more-seniors-stepping-forward-caregivers-their-peers-singapore-approaches-super-aged-status-volunteer-red-cross-3491906.

Penner, Barbara, and Charles Rice. 2024. "Julia Child's Kitchens." *Places Journal*, September. https://placesjournal.org/article/julia-childs-kitchens/.

Pickard, Susan. 2023. "The Red Dressing Gown." December. https://doi.org/10.1163/25897616-bja10069.

Rice, Carla, Eliza Chandler, Jen Rinaldi, Nadine Changfoot, Kirsty Liddiard, Roxanne Mykitiuk, and Ingrid Mündel. 2017. "Imagining Disability Futurities." *Hypatia* 32 (2): 213–29. https://doi.org/10.1111/hypa.12321.

Rubinstein, Robert I., and Patricia A. Parmelee. 1992. "Attachment to Place and the Representation of the Life Course by the Elderly." In *Place Attachment*, edited by Irwin Altman and Setha M. Low, 139–63. Boston, MA: Springer US. https://doi.org/10.1007/978-1-4684-8753-4_7.

Sartre, Jean-Paul. 2003. *Being and Nothingness: An Essay on Phenomenological Ontology*. London: Routledge.

Shakespeare, Tom, Hannah Zeilig, and Peter Mittler. 2019. "Rights in Mind: Thinking Differently About Dementia and Disability." *Dementia* 18 (3): 1075–88. https://doi.org/10.1177/1471301217701506.

Subramaniam, Mythily, Siow Ann Chong, Janhavi Ajit Vaingankar, Edimansyah Abdin, Boon Yiang Chua, Hong Choon Chua, and Goi Khia Eng, et al. 2015. "Prevalence of Dementia in People Aged 60 Years and Above: Results from the WiSE Study." *Journal of Alzheimer's Disease* 45 (4): 1127–38. https://doi.org/10.3233/JAD-142769.

Swinnen, Aagje, and Mark Schweda, eds. 2015. "Popularizing Dementia. Public Expressions and Representations of Forgetfulness." In *Popularizing Dementia. Public Expressions and Representations of Forgetfulness*. Bielefeld: transcript Verlag.

Thomas, Carol, and Christine Milligan. 2018. "Dementia, Disability Rights and Disablism: Understanding the Social Position of People Living With Dementia." *Disability & Society* 33 (1): 115–31. https://doi.org/10.1080/09687599.2017.1379952.

Visaria, Abhijit, and Rahul Malhotra. 2023. "Commentary: Live Long and Prosper? A Super-Aged Singapore Society Does Not Have to Be a Sad One." *The Straits Times*, 26 August 2023, sec. Commentary. https://www.duke-nus.edu.sg/newshub/super-aged-singapore-society.

Ward, Richard, and Linn J. Sandberg. 2023. "Thinking Back and Looking Ahead: Co-Ordinates for Critical Methodologies in Dementia Studies." In *Critical Dementia Studies*, 263–77. Routledge.

WHO, World Health Organization. 2023. "Dementia." World Health Organization. 15 March 2023. https://www.who.int/news-room/fact-sheets/detail/dementia.

Zeilig, Hannah. 2014. "Dementia as a Cultural Metaphor." *The Gerontologist* 54 (2): 258–67. https://doi.org/10.1093/geront/gns203.

Zhuang, Justin. 2020. "Ageing Well Together; Singapore | Kampung Admiralty." In *Urban Solutions Issue 16: Health and Well-Being*, edited by Joanna Tan, Pei En Tan, and Jiayun Zou, 86–91. Singapore: Centre for Liveable Cities.

INDEX

Note: Page numbers in *italics* and **bold** refer to figures and tables, respectively; and those followed by "n" refer to end notes.

For Product Safety Concerns and Information please contact our EU
representative GPSR@taylorandfrancis.com
Taylor & Francis Verlag GmbH, Kaufingerstraße 24, 80331 München, Germany

www.ingramcontent.com/pod-product-compliance
Ingram Content Group UK Ltd.
Pitfield, Milton Keynes, MK11 3LW, UK
UKHW050230200926
475702UK00020B/2948
* 9 7 8 1 0 3 2 8 6 5 2 9 4 *